CO-AXI-284

FOR ALL THESE RIGHTS

POLITICS AND SOCIETY IN TWENTIETH-CENTURY AMERICA

A list of titles in this series appears at the end of this book

Jennifer Klein

FOR ALL THESE RIGHTS

BUSINESS, LABOR, AND THE SHAPING OF AMERICA'S PUBLIC-PRIVATE WELFARE STATE

PRINCETON UNIVERSITY PRESS PRINCETON AND OXFORD

Published by Princeton University Press, 41 William Street,
Princeton, New Jersey 08540
In the United Kingdom: Princeton University Press, 3 Market Place,
Woodstock, Oxfordshire OX20 1SY

Library of Congress Cataloging-in-Publication Data

Klein, Jennifer, 1967–
For all these rights: business, labor, and the shaping of America's
public-private welfare state / Jennifer Klein.
p. cm. — (Politics and society in twentieth-century America)
Includes bibliographical references and index.
ISBN 0-691-07056-3 (alk. paper)
1. Pensions—United States. 2. Old age pensions—United
States. 3. Retirement income—United States. 4. United
States—Economic policy. I. Title. II. Series.

HD7125 .K584 2003
368.973—dc21 2002029279

British Library Cataloging-in-Publication Data is available

This book has been composed in Baskerville

Printed on acid-free paper. ∞

www.pupress.princeton.edu

Printed in the United States of America
JK
10 9 8 7 6 5 4 3 2 1

To the Suloways and Kleins, ______________________________

WHO CROSSED THE OCEAN AND BECAME AMERICANS

Contents

Acknowledgments

THIS PROJECT began as a dissertation at the University of Virginia. I left my job in New York City and moved to Charlottesville, without a car, at the urging of Nelson Lichtenstein. I received a wonderful education in this southern place where I had never been. I would like first to thank my dissertation committee: Nelson Lichtenstein, Brian Balogh, Margaret Weir, and Olivier Zunz. Brian Balogh and Olivier Zunz offered important advice as I conceptualized this project, suggesting research directions that helped me develop the project beyond the boundaries of labor history. Margaret Weir has always offered astute readings of my work and challenging insights about American politics.

Very fortunately, I received generous financial support from several institutions, which made possible the research and completion of this project. Fellowships from the Hagley Museum and Library, the State Historical Society of Wisconsin, and the Bankard Fund for Political Economy at the University of Virginia enabled me to travel to archives from Washington, D.C., to Madison, Wisconsin. The Rovensky Fellowship in Business and Economic History supported my research and writing in business history. Dissertation-year fellowships from the Brookings Institution and the American Association of University Women supported the final stages of the dissertation. As I worked to turn the dissertation into a book manuscript, Smith College generously supported research trips and research assistants. A fellowship from the National Endowment for the Humanities sustained me through the completion of my book. I also thank the National Academy of Social Insurance for awarding me the John Heinz Dissertation Prize.

There were many individuals at these institutions who helped me develop this project. At Rutgers University, James Quiggle generously let me view the papers of the International Union of Electrical, Radio, and Machine Workers even while he was knee-deep in the processing of the collection. Jonathan Coss, at the Equitable Life Assurance Society Archives, offered enthusiastic help as I waded through the Equitable papers. While doing research at Hagley, I benefited from the assistance, advice, and support of Roger Horowitz, Philip Scranton, and Marjorie McNinch. At the Brookings Institution, I gained from the insights and knowledge of scholars in disciplines outside my own, especially from Margaret Weir, Joseph White, and Kent Weaver.

It is hard to believe that I worked on this project for a decade. A number of people read individual chapters or sections and offered thought-provoking suggestions and engaging insights. I would like to thank Edward D. Berkowitz, Eileen Boris, Dorothy Sue Cobble, Alan Derickson, Daniel Ernst, Joshua B. Freeman, Gary Gerstle, Beatrix Hoffman, Daniel Horowitz, and Andrea Tone. Work presented at the Hagley Museum and Library and the Five College History Seminar at Amherst College always drew exciting comments that spurred me on to further thinking about my subject. I warmly thank the participants in these seminars, and I hope I will be able to return the favor some day. Colin Gordon and David Brody read the manuscript in full and provided me with the essential road map I needed to create the final book. Linda Gordon did a tremendous job editing the final manuscript, and I deeply appreciate the thoughtful work she put into making this a better book.

I would also like to thank several colleagues at Smith College who helped me negotiate the pressures of an intense teaching job, long-distance commuting, and writing history: Martha Acklesberg, Joan Afferica, Ravina Aggarwal, Ernest Benz, Rob Eskildsen, Dan and Helen Horowitz, Marilyn Schuster, Ruth Solie, Susan Van Dyne, and Suzanne Zhang-Gottschang. Smith College students Stacey Kerr and Amber Watt provided excellent research assistance, and Katrina O'Brien stepped in at the end to help me tie all the crucial loose ends. Kelly Driscoll of Performative Visuals and Patricia Shoemaker of Shoemaker Design did the graphics reproductions. Thank you to copy editor Joanne Allen for pushing through the manuscript with fortitude and good humor, through many summer days and nights. Thanks would not be complete without mentioning Herbert Sloan, my undergraduate adviser and mentor at Barnard, who always encouraged my striving toward being an historian. And likewise, let me thank Darryl Christie.

Nelson Lichtenstein has been the ideal dissertation director, colleague, and friend. He has read these chapters more times than one would believe is humanly possible. From the time I wrote my original seminar paper on this topic, he pushed me to think about the larger implications of the specific topic, to broaden the ideas and take every thing to its limit—to do more, more, more! While at first I was often confounded, I know his advice and brilliance made this book a much fuller and richer project. Nelson's support was invaluable in seeing me through this project, and I look forward to many more years as collaborators, colleagues, and political comrades.

The Kleins and the Bergers, of course, have lived with this project almost as long as I have. My parents, Leslie Klein and Theodore Klein, always offered me models of political courage, integrity, and humanism, as well as humor and creativity, that shaped and inspired me. As my brother, Andy Klein, worked on his own dissertation in psychology over the last few years, we have sought to encourage each other that we could see our respective projects through to the end. And I began to feel that my brother's focus on individual therapy and my focus on macro-level politics are complementary endeavors to confront the inequalities and the promises of American life. My father-in-law, Arthur Berger, an eager student of the New Deal, showed the most enthusiastic interest in this project, and I am glad he had an opportunity to make his own contribution to it, providing me with legal research.

My husband, James Berger, truly made it possible for me to complete this project. He read every hopeful chapter, every frustrating revision, and gently chided me for my insistence that *every* piece of documentary evidence was crucial. He sustained both of us through work and play and daily life. Through it all, he showed great love, patience, and enthusiasm. I know we will be partners in many projects to come—in work and life.

Abbreviations

AALL	American Association for Labor Legislation
AFL	American Federation of Labor
AHA	American Hospital Association
AMA	American Medical Association
CCMC	Committee on the Costs of Medical Care
CES	Committee on Economic Security
CIO	Congress of Industrial Organizations
EMIC	Emergency Maternity and Infant Care
FLSA	Fair Labor Standards Act
FSA	Farm Security Administration
GHA	Group Health Association, Washington, D.C.
HIP	Health Insurance Plan of New York
HMO	Health maintenance organization
ILGWU	International Ladies Garment Workers' Union
IUE	International Union of Electrical, Radio, and Machine Workers
NAM	National Association of Manufacturers
NICB	National Industrial Conference Board
NLRB	National Labor Relations Board
NWLB	National War Labor Board
OASI	Old-Age and Survivors' Insurance
PHS	United States Public Health Service
PSB	Policyholders' Service Bureau
SSA	Social Security Administration
SSB	Social Security Board
TUAHA	Trade Union Accident and Health Association of America
UAW	United Automobile Workers
UE	United Electrical, Radio, and Machine Workers of America
UMW	United Mine Workers
USWA	United Steelworkers of America

FOR ALL THESE RIGHTS

Introduction

EARLY in the twenty-first century some of America's best-known corporations went bankrupt or teetered close to the edge of economic viability. Among them were Bethlehem Steel, National Steel, Polaroid, Enron, Lucent Technologies, and WorldCom. As their financial solvency disintegrated, so too did the promise of social welfare support and long-term economic security these firms had offered workers and their families.

Old-line steel companies, once the keystone of twentieth-century American capitalism, now claimed they could no longer survive under the weight of company health insurance and pension benefits. For Bethlehem Steel, for example, with 75,000 retirees on its pension rolls—more than five times the number of current employees—the unfunded retirement liability of the company stood at $2 billion, and unfunded health care costs at another $3 billion. The LTV Corporation simply liquidated itself, leaving 70,000 employees and retirees without the health care and pension benefits the company had proffered workers.[1]

Some companies had failed to put sufficient funds in reserve to pay for future retiree benefits, yet the bill still came due. Other companies like Enron and Polaroid had used company stock to meet their retirement pledges—after all, there was always plenty of paper. Unfortunately, once their stock nosedived into worthlessness, paper was all the employees had left. The Houston-based energy company Enron Corporation had once been touted as the flagship of the "new economy," but in the fall of 2001 Enron's stock bubble burst, precipitating the nation's largest corporate bankruptcy. Just as the stock plunged, the company instituted a lockdown on employee 401(k) plans, blocking employees from shifting their retirement savings out of Enron stock. Thousands of employees were left with empty retirement nests. Kathleen Salerno, an Enron employee for seven years, found that her "personal [retirement] account amounted to $46. Another friend with almost twenty years service had $102. . . . Now friends and co-workers have lost everything."[2] Not only will former Enron workers receive no future supplemental retirement income from their years at Enron but many had to postpone immediate medical care for themselves and their family members. One laid-off worker cancelled his cancer surgery. Another stopped the therapy service for his three-year-old autistic son. Workers severed from the bankrupt Polaroid Corporation and the floundering Lucent Technologies told of similar personal tragedies.[3] It was clear that even in the newest, most dynamic sectors of the economy company welfare schemes could not provide security against the risks of sickness, old age, and unemployment. Indeed, the very attachment of benefits to firms heightened their insecurity.

The Big Steel companies were unionized, so their welfare pledges could not be so easily dissolved. The health and pension benefits were embodied in legally binding contracts, some of them a half-century old. The steel industry called these obligations "legacy costs," but the question is, what is the exact nature of that "legacy"? Is it the legacy of "overly generous" union contracts, as financial analysts suggested, or is it the legacy of a persistent corporate political strategy? Since the late nineteenth century, American employers have relied on a program of welfare capitalism to deflect incursions into the workplace from the regulatory state or organized workers. Welfare capitalism encompasses social welfare benefits and health, safety, or leisure programs offered through the workplace, programs established and directed by the employer. In periods of labor upheaval and social reform American firms have relied on workplace social welfare as a private, managerial response to political pressure from the state and workers, especially when workers sought to use the state to improve working conditions and guarantee economic security. Ironically, the steel industry's burdensome health and pension obligations arose as a cost of their deliberate corporate strategy, designed to tip the balance of state power away from workers and toward business. The employee benefits programs that came to full fruition in the 1950s and 1960s represent a political settlement forged amidst the social upheaval of the New Deal and the growth of union power. These "fringe benefits" emerged from a political battle that American business leaders believed they had won since corporate executives had managed to thwart a more expansive welfare state, industrywide collective bargaining, workers' ability to turn to other sources for needs unmet by work and wages, and union control of firm-based insurance. Out of this conflict emerged a public-private welfare regime that relied heavily on private sources and permitted the distortions and inadequacies that have become so manifest in recent years. Any narrative of the American welfare state, therefore, must be told within the context of the century-long story of welfare capitalism.[4]

The United States has a mixed welfare system in which social provision is dispensed through public and private institutions. Designated groups within the population—veterans, the elderly, the long-term disabled, the medically indigent, and poor children—receive benefits through the public sector. Most of the able-bodied working population, however, depend on private sources, primarily business firms, to assist them in meeting the costs of sickness, hospitalization, vacations, and old age. More than two-thirds of the American population under age 65 depend on employer-sponsored health plans; job-based health insurance has remained the primary door to health coverage for nonelderly Americans. In 2000, employers spent $874 billion on employee benefits, including $186 billion on employee retirement programs and $300 billion on health insurance.[5] Despite the overwhelming dependence of a majority of the population on employer-provided benefits, the development of this private system has been largely neglected. This book uncovers the historical emergence of a system of voluntary insurance and pensions based in employment and investigates its interaction with and effects on the public social insurance system.[6] In addition, I show how strategic decisions about insurance benefits and income support were embedded within contests to define the ideological meaning of security—job security, health security, economic security—as this concern gained legitimacy in the wake of the New Deal.

By analyzing the historical development of private-sector insurance and corporate social welfare programs, this book offers a study of the closely linked politics of social provision and industrial relations. Although the New Deal was a watershed in American political culture and political economy, employer-provided welfare also represents a strand of continuity from the pre–New Deal period. Hence, this book spans the 1910s through the 1950s, reconnecting the threads of American labor relations with the struggle over economic security. Rather than viewing the 1930s as a definitive break, a chasm separating welfare capitalism from the welfare state and from collective bargaining, I emphasize continuity in the provision of social benefits from the 1920s into the post–New Deal period.[7] Beginning with the origins of specific private social welfare plans within the welfare capitalist and scientific management movements of the 1910s and 1920s, I trace the development of group insurance through the Depression and the New Deal to the post–World War II period. Gauging business responses to industrial relations imperatives, both on the shop floor and in the wider polity, and to political developments in social policy, I show how these pressures affected the specific nature of the company social welfare plans themselves. In turn, I uncover the ways in which American labor relations and labor policy affected social policy.

The politics of the New Deal put *security* at the center of American political and economic life. The enactment of federal mortgage assistance, bank deposit insurance, minimum wages, Social Security, and laws bolstering labor's right to organize created social and economic entitlements that legitimized the modern state. Though initially excluding many women, Latinos, and African Americans, the entitlement to security was capable of being expanded upon, and indeed would be, as various groups of Americans mobilized to demand inclusion and full citizenship rights. Yet the New Deal did not simply create the welfare state; it launched a new economy of welfare in which the ideology of security proved a powerful construct. The New Deal's politics of security set in motion a rapid expansion of the insurance, health care, and income maintenance options offered by nonstate institutions. Insurance companies, seeking to preserve a commercial market in group insurance, aggressively marketed new lines, such as group retirement annuities, hospitalization insurance, and disability benefits, both to supplement and to compete with the incipient welfare state. This book traces the fate of the New Deal emphasis on social entitlement as the private sector competed with and emulated the values of the New Deal.

Life insurance companies would have to compete with a whole range of players who were stimulated by the politics of security. Labor unions, consumer cooperatives, hospitals, and new nonprofit agencies and alliances had begun experimenting with programs that would meet the demand for income support beyond the wage relation. Mobilized citizens and social movements had played a critical role in pushing security to the center of American politics in the 1930s. New Deal legislation, in turn, stimulated further citizen engagement, as workers and community residents took action to make these policies a living reality in their communities. After the passage of the National Labor Relations Act in 1935, incipient unions had to fight for recognition and power. With government housing funds available, labor groups organized to win federal funding for working-class housing.[8] And with the passage of Social Security, unions and community groups sought to organize local residents, both to demand expansions of government income support and to build institutions that could provide social services. These activists and community members hoped to construct nonprofit organizations distinct from both employer welfare plans and commercial insurance policies. In the 1930s and 1940s, trade unionists, leftists, African Americans, rural residents, women's auxiliaries, and physicians experimented with economic security programs aimed at generating security independent of employers. Even after World War II, organized labor promoted benefit programs that would have involved labor representatives and consumers as planners and would have broken the links between benefits and the individual firm, options they continued to push for well into the 1950s. Organized labor hoped to use the power of the federal government to bolster these efforts, thus firmly connecting citizens to an expansive welfare state.

American corporations fought aggressively to sever the links between the workers and the state. In the post–World War II period company health benefits, disability payments, and pensions were part of a major offensive by employers to regain the ideological high ground in American society. Employers recognized the social and political premium placed on security as vividly as did the Democratic Party, the labor movement, and the architects of federal Social Security. After World War II, the National Association of Manufacturers called on business leaders to enlist in "the competition for leadership in a welfare economy." As one business executive proclaimed in 1949, "Now . . . it is high time for business leaders of the United States to get back into the act and enter this competition in a big way for the greatest of all stakes."[9] As the public welfare state expanded together with the union movement, American business firms and commercial insurance companies became partners in creating and expanding nonstate alternatives to public social insurance. Using the public Social Security program as a foundation, large firms came to offer supplemental pensions, disability wages, and unemployment benefits. Employers also provided paid sick leave, hospital insurance, medical insurance, and, less often, retiree health benefits. At the apogee of this system, in the late 1970s, private pensions covered 49 percent of the private wage and salary workforce (40 million people), while private hospital and surgical coverage reached more than 80 percent of Americans.[10] When it comes to the United States' unique mix of private and public social welfare, business and government cannot be thought of as inversely proportional levers. Private welfare schemes have developed, expanded, and contracted in tandem with public ones.

The terms *public* and *private* are not mutually exclusive. Private economic arrangements are always sustained by an element of state support. Private nursing homes and hospitals, for example, receive public funding from various sources. Further, because of the economic and political power of big business in the United States, public social legislation could often be turned into public mandates for business-controlled programs. From Progressive Era workmen's compensation laws enacted in the 1910s to managed care companies' contracts with Medicare in the 1990s, public programs have been used to promote the commercial insurance trade. Thus, we have to consider two questions: In what historical moments did public legislation substantively challenge employers' prerogatives over the conditions, compensation, and security of employment? And how did the ensuing political struggles between business, labor, and the state turn this result around, enabling business to use government to facilitate its ability to insulate and control such ostensibly public matters?

The politics of security involved a political struggle between business and labor; commercial insurers and nonprofit, community- or labor-controlled means of social provision; the state; and private capital.

What differentiates the period after the New Deal from the previous era is that workers had an opportunity to transform employer gratuities into employee rights. The New Deal did create new working-class entitlements and did democratize the nation's political and economic life. What happened, then, to the social democratic possibilities unleashed by the New Deal, the Congress of Industrial Organizations movement, and World War II?[11] This book uses the story of struggles over health security and old-age security, social rights, and the welfare state to answer this question and thus to trace the fate of New Deal liberalism—as a set of ideas about the state, security, and labor rights—in the 1950s, the 1960s, and beyond.

We will see, for example, how commercial cash-indemnity health and disability insurance emerged dominant over nonmarket alternatives such as union-based health centers, community health cooperatives, and service-based health plans (the original Blue Cross model). Despite a presumptive "labor-management accord" in the postwar years, management often implemented welfare plans without consulting a union or labor representative. Management offered insurance coverages that met the imperatives of industrial relations more than the security needs of American individuals and families. Additionally, the emphasis on medical insurance eclipsed the orientation toward community public health and occupational health that had characterized earlier group health center approaches. These choices in favor of cash-indemnity insurance and private pensions not only affected the balance of power in post–World War II labor-management relations; they also influenced the direction of governmental social policy and the increasing fragmentation of the American welfare state.

Security occupied a central place in American cultural and political life from the 1930s through the 1960s, but varying players clashed over who would get to define it.[12] As chapter 4 shows, security was grounded not just in the liberal notion of rights but also in the communitarian norms of solidarity and shared social responsibility of grass-roots, Popular Front politics. For many of the trade union or activist women and men who worked on what they called "social security" issues—which went beyond social insurance to include health care clinics, housing, public health measures, minimum wage struggles—building security meant building community institutions, linking grass-roots activity with national social policies. In the political lexicon of the New Deal order, *security* embodied a class challenge and collective power. Public social programs, of course, encompass and represent a particular relationship between individual citizens and the state, as well as one between citizens. The ideology of security also defined a relation between the state and the economy. New Dealers identified economic security as a grand national project, "a great cooperative enterprise" among "the citizens, the economic system, and the government."[13] Therefore, in addition to the idea that there is a public claim to resources of the nation, security entailed an explicit element of public power. The state would compel that claim to be distributed sufficiently to ensure Americans a standard of living and social well-being above subsistence.

Private providers of benefits, while accepting security as an important value, waged a battle to influence its meaning as well. For employers, workers' security plans demonstrated that the firm was a generous employer, bestowing its beneficence on workers. Insurers and employers used the language of free enterprise, individual initiative, and voluntarism to characterize security. They endeavored to shift its emphasis away from the state and the political arena to private, individual economic relationships. Amid these political and economic struggles of the immediate postwar period, the labor-liberal conception of security narrowed until it meant security primarily as a right of the wage worker. Security would provide support for periods when the wage income was interrupted, for example, by old age or disability, or supplemental support for wage earners, such as health insurance. For those who received the fruits of welfare capitalism, the link between security and the state became increasingly attenuated. By the 1960s, middle-class and working-class Americans saw General Motors, IBM, AT&T, or local employers as a source of social security. Since then, such workers have proved increasingly unwilling to support expansions of public welfare programs beyond supplements to their employer-provided benefits. Insurers and employers thus redefined the meaning of security, creating a new private, firm-centered definition of security.

In the 1940s, when the federal government played an essential role in labor-management bargaining, employment issues became highly visible. Industrial relations were very much a public matter, their outcome seen as having general ramifications for the entire political economy. But after 1950 the federal government withdrew from this arena. Congress, the courts, and the White House deferred to employers and to purveyors of private insurance when it came to providing for working, nonindigent, nonelderly Americans. Neither the New Deal nor the Fair Deal created a sufficient basis in labor policy, law, or welfare policy to enable workers to prevent employers from unilaterally implementing management-chosen benefits or from determining which groups of workers received income support or insurance benefits. In the 1950s collective bargaining became merely a system of privatized mediation of economic security issues. Democrats, the New Dealers' heirs, came to see the expanding private social security system as increasingly necessary to supplement the stalled public welfare state. They accepted business leaders' contention that "the costs of these benefits are private business costs, have no relation to employee compensation, and are therefore of no concern to employees or others."[14]

A collective bargaining agreement is a reflection of the balance of power. Under the postwar industrial relations system, management maintained the balance of power at the level of the firm through control of production, finance, and discipline and ultimately through plant closure.[15] Management, not the unions, controlled social welfare. Historians celebrating postwar unionism have focused solely on labor's apparent success in winning important benefits at the bargaining table. They have rarely, however, considered the details of these plans.[16] If we take health coverage as an example, the specific nature of the chosen health plan had major political ramifications in the workplace and in the polity. Management's choice of commercial group health insurance over service plans such as Kaiser Permanente or Blue Cross often represented a significant political victory for management, for only the employer was a legal party to the group insurance contract. Employers excluded health benefits and pensions from grievance procedures. Thus, managers did resurrect welfare capitalism, even in an era of union power.

The privatization of this social agenda had manifold consequences. Besides creating uneven, unequal benefits across regions and sectors, it left many Americans outside the fold. Few unions could follow in the footsteps of a powerful union like the United Automobile Workers. Beyond the oligopolistic sectors where domestic competition was minimal, companies rarely replicated the benefit packages set in steel and auto, especially once the industrial union movement stalled in the late 1950s. As in the case of the public welfare state, the gender discrepancies grew more stark. In the early years of the CIO and community activism surrounding social security, women were critical players in trying to build a community, social-union movement. Yet the CIO organized largely male-dominated production industries, and collective bargaining contracts focused on benefits for the worker, rather than institutions for the community, reinforcing the patriarchal assumptions of the family wage in private as well as public benefits.[17] Industrial relations experts of the early postwar era thought that collective bargaining could itself substitute for the weakness of the U.S. welfare state, extending the benefits of social citizenship to ever greater sectors of the workforce. But collective bargaining could not and did not substitute for social policymaking at the national level. Instead, the new definition of social citizenship ascendant with the New Deal came under attack as private benefits boomed and public ones stagnated.[18] The parsimonious expansion of public benefits became evidence that worthy citizens were served best not by the state but by the private sector. Thus, after forty years of expanding the reaches of social citizenship, we are now reining it in, sharply curtailing our delineations of who is entitled to what from the state. The concept of economic security has regained an atomistic ideological cast.

In writing about the American welfare state I am fortunate to have a wealth of new scholarship on which to draw. The institutionalist approach of historical sociologists and political scientists has greatly enhanced our understanding of welfare state development over the last decade. By focusing on the organizational structures of American politics—bureaucracies, courts, parties, and Congress—these scholars have shown how U.S. federalism, the regional divisions of the polity, and the degree of bureaucratic development within the state have shaped social policy formation and implementation. Moreover, the competition among state agencies over programs and ideas had substantive consequences for public and private welfare systems, as chapters 4 and 5 in this book demonstrate. Nonetheless, an exclusive focus on autonomous state structures tends to obscure nonstate power relations.[19]

Departing from this institutional approach, this book explores the influence of social movements and mass politics and of the wider economy, especially economic relationships and economic power, in shaping public and private welfare policies. Mobilized groups of people created shifts in social and structural power relations, which in turn influenced state behavior. Grass-roots movements pushed economic security to the center of national politics in the 1930s, provoking major transformations in both private and public social welfare. While the state is capable of independent action, we still have to consider how the state is bound up within a network of relationships among economic institutions (business firms and financial intermediaries), labor unions, and service institutions. Thus, this book attempts to demonstrate how institutional relationships between business, labor, and the state determine social welfare regimes and labor's compensation, both wage and nonwage.[20] Moreover, these relationships shift over time, and as the balance of power tips toward different players, a new set of political options becomes possible. In order to explain the passage or defeat of social policies and the structure of particular public and private social welfare benefits in the United States, it is necessary to examine the balance of power in the political economy. This was just as true of health insurance politics in the 1990s as in the 1940s.

As a historiographical theme, *corporate liberalism* no longer explains the course of American reform. Business leaders may have tried to domineer social legislation, but they did not always get what they wanted.[21] Yet, when we widen our view beyond the state, it is clear that business firms have a tremendous ability to affect the nature of U.S. social provision. They do so not just by shaping a particular piece of legislation but by making strategic choices within their own firms and communities about the transfer of resources beyond wages and about the structure of employment within their firms. Labor unions too affected social welfare, by establishing wage structures, benefit standards, bargaining regimes, and expectations outside of the state. Social policies and income support provisions have a dynamic of their own: they raise expectations, possibilities, or frustrations, which are acted on in numerous venues.

The growing literature on the gendered and racialized welfare state has also had an essential impact on how we understand the historical development of American social policy and the welfare state. The historians in this school have shown how gender assumptions about family roles and family maintenance and gender-based power within the government forged a welfare state that, in turn, conferred different, and substantially unequal, levels of economic security on women and men, people of color and whites. By focusing on programs such as Social Security and Aid to Families with Dependent Children, they demonstrate that labor market discrimination, as well as gender and racial divisions in labor, were reproduced in the welfare state.[22] The private benefits system that wrapped itself around the public welfare state base could only replicate these inequities. Indeed, the employer-based benefits system widened wage and income disparities among workers rather than closing them. And insofar as the state has encouraged and shaped Americans' heavy dependence on firm-based benefits, it too was often an agent promoting or hardening the lines of social stratification in twentieth-century American society.[23]

Life insurance firms were essential to the creation and maintenance of the private welfare system. Chapter 1 uncovers the origins of the modern private benefits system: group insurance. In the 1910s and 1920s, life insurance companies created group insurance—life insurance, accident and sickness insurance (disability wages), and pensions—which could be sold to employers to cover thousands of workers under one policy. Insurers such as the Equitable Life Assurance Society and Metropolitan Life promoted group insurance as a social and economic innovation that would improve relations between capital and labor—and without social insurance legislation. These companies sold the idea that American employers could and should meet the social welfare needs of their workers. Although most workers received little, insurers had laid a foundation for the proliferation of private security programs during and after the New Deal.

But what would happen to welfare capitalism in the era of the welfare state? Chapters 2 and 3 examine the response of employers and insurers to the Great Depression and the Social Security Act. After examining the early history of industrial pensions, Chapter 2 investigates efforts to sustain welfare capitalism during the early years of the Depression and the challenges raised by popular social movements that demanded state action. Chapter 3, on the Social Security Act and the 1939 amendments, explores the relation between an ascendant politics of security and the coalescing welfare capitalist view that the welfare state should be a minimal base supplemented by private institutions. I do not intend to revisit the debate over whether the Social Security Act was a creature of business interests; I come down on the side that it was not.[24] Instead, this chapter looks first at the ways in which insurers and welfare capitalists sought exemptions from a public social insurance program and then at how they tried to adapt welfare capitalism to the newly expanded state. In response to the Social Security Act, many employers turned to private, managerial strategies, as well as to political, legislative ones. Insurance companies, who came around to supporting the Social Security Act by 1936, served as advisers and intermediaries for employers on both fronts. Insurers came to see Social Security as a great boon to the "security business." After 1935 the language and rationale for welfare capitalism shifted from scientific management and industrial efficiency to "security," as large insurers eagerly embraced the politics of security. Subsequently, New Deal liberals consciously and inadvertently encouraged the development of this "supplemental" social security system, first, through tax laws and amendments to the Social Security Act and, second, by accepting the ideological arguments for private supplementation of the public welfare state.

In chapter 4 the attention shifts to focus on how social welfare experts, health reformers, community activists, and labor unions were swept up in the search for security as well. As New Dealers enacted old-age pensions, unemployment insurance, and aid to poor children, they also began planning for a new round of benefits, inaugurating an era of social experimentation, particularly at the local level. Among various prototypes, I also contextualize the origins of Blue Cross, group-practice medical plans, community health plans, and health care cooperatives.[25] Organized labor and Popular Front activists developed a broad social democratic agenda that included government programs for unemployment, old age, disability, and health insurance linked to a nationalized social wage. From the mid-1930s, they pushed hard for both state-provided social security and "voluntary" social security linked to unions or community institutions.[26] Indeed, their ability to conceptualize a national health program depended on their experiments with voluntary health plans that were built at the community level and outside the employment relation.

World War II would affect private and public welfare benefits in contradictory fashion. On the one hand, as chapter 5 shows, the federal government became directly involved in running local health care programs and providing health insurance on a national basis. Many New Deal liberals hoped to build on these precedents after the war, drawing on experimental programs such as Emergency Maternity and Infant Care. On the other hand, strategies chosen by the Social Security Board and the National War Labor Board would channel public and private economic security projects into much narrower parameters in the postwar period.[27] The momentum for health security, as well as for other social welfare benefits, shifted to employers and channeled independent community initiatives into the mold of collective bargaining.

Chapter 6 demonstrates how employers circumvented union plans for employee benefits, implementing their own programs based on group insurance that enabled management to dominate—firm by firm, even plant by plant. In the 1930s and 1940s insurers created group hospital, surgical, and medical policies to build on the security foundations laid by the federal government. Employers, anxious to quell demand without further empowering the state or the unions, eagerly began signing up for basic group insurance policies. The commercial policies offered a perfect fit with management needs because of the way in which insurers defined risk. They insured something against loss, calculating premiums and benefits based on exposure to loss, or risk. Naturally, insurance companies sought to minimize their own risk exposure, and therefore they would only cover persons who were not exposed to too much risk. In designing group insurance these companies found that "employed individuals enrolled on a group basis . . . are undoubtedly the best risks"—thereby constructing what has since appeared to be a natural link between insurability and employment.[28] But social insurance and public welfare proponents claimed that those who needed protection were all the people who were regularly exposed to economic insecurity and ill health, that is, everyone, healthy or sick, employed or unemployed. They wanted risk to be pooled at the societal level. Such open-ended inclusion was precisely what commercial insurers sought to shield their companies against. In the case of health insurance, risk meant exposure to medical care or health services, and what was lost was the cash used to pay for them. By necessity, then, coverage had to be limited, and commercial cash-indemnity plans covered only a fraction of any given set of medical costs. Commercial insurance applied a variety of mechanisms to protect this principle, including highly varied premiums and deductibles for routine care. The more one used medical care, the higher the premium became, and the lower the net benefits. Those who had health problems and needed the services had to pay the most money. Insurers defined risk either as a characteristic of individuals or, in the case of group insurance, circumscribed groups of individuals. Risk, then, should be pooled only among the safest groups.[29] This orientation attenuated any connections between individual health and community health, individual security and social security.

Moreover, because insurers designed health insurance within the construct of the family wage—a single breadwinner and dependent family—they forged a health care system in which many people had no direct access or claim to medical care. Their only claim was through a wage earner; in turn, the wage earner became dependent on the employer for meeting all family needs. Insurers, then, not only made possible the resurrection of welfare capitalism; they perpetuated its patriarchal character.

Chapter 6 demonstrates how, despite the range of health care alternatives that existed in the 1940s, commercial cash-indemnity insurance emerged dominant. The commercial life insurance industry enabled business firms to contain the reach of the New Deal state. They underwrote private welfare benefits, fragmented demand for expanded public benefits, and helped insulate firms through their increasingly significant role as financial intermediaries. By revealing this nexus of welfare and investment, we can see how these institutional linkages fragmented and redirected the development of American social provision, privileging private, firm-based benefits. Insurers soon received the support of the medical community, which helped commercial insurers undermine the health programs that organized labor had advocated.

Collective bargaining drew a boundary around the well-paid, organized working class and left other workers out in the cold. But the problem with private group insurance was not simply its restrictive demography. The benefit policies themselves were inherently flawed. Commercial group health insurance was the most inflationary, limited form of health coverage available, even when it was incorporated into a collective bargaining contract. Yet because organized labor could not penetrate the links between insurance companies and employers, often longstanding associations dating back to the 1920s, they could not win the benefits they thought would best meet workers' security needs. Likewise, most unions did not have the power to control the administration of pensions and annuities. By the mid-1950s, neither organized labor nor Democratic liberals had the ideological commitment or the political weight to use the state to recast private welfare plans as matters of public security and public interest. Through tax policy, labor "reform" politics, and the Cold War embrace of "free" collective bargaining, Democratic policymakers allowed private insecurity to endure. Business interests were able to alter the role of the state in industrial relations politics and in fact use it to sustain an increasingly insular, private, firm-centered definition of security.

The reach of firm-based benefits would continue to grow into the 1970s, after which even this carefully circumscribed system began to shrink.[30] Yet the historical ideological legacy of the American public-private welfare state—the basic welfare state, contained and limited, with all other needs met by private sources—continues to dominate policy proposals and legislation up to the present day. Indeed, we are now witnessing the unraveling of the New Deal system of social entitlements. A Democratic president presided over the dismantling of Aid to Families with Dependent Children. A Republican president has launched an active campaign to privatize Social Security. The positive language of security has been replaced by the pejorative nomenclature of dependency. Solutions to social and economic security, many claim, lie in an "opportunity to invest."

In this context, this book demonstrates several key principles in the relationship between business, social welfare, and the state. First, proponents of social welfare privatization have argued that if we reduce or eliminate the role of the state in social welfare provision, business will fill in the gap. But this claim ignores our history. Business firms increased their commitment to corporate social welfare programs when government itself expanded its social welfare and labor intervention roles. The very language that has been attached to current welfare privatization proposals is the phrase *personal responsibility*—not *corporate responsibility*.

Second, for more than half a century critics of national health insurance and an expanded welfare state have tried to discredit national, public programs by claiming that such programs would be "political," inefficient, and inflationary; private programs, by contrast, would be intrinsically "apolitical" and efficient. This historical work demonstrates that private benefits were political, inefficient, inflationary, and unreliable from their inception. Indeed, the very logic of organizing benefits around employment is a flawed concept. By perpetually fragmenting risks (through experience rating or employer self-insurance), rather than pooling them, it utterly subverts the social purpose and the economic efficiency of insurance. The administrative and financial burden of such a system has only grown more immense over time, especially as ever-increasing numbers of Americans have gone to work in service-sector or small firms, shattering even the isolated actuarial islands of those who worked in mass-production industries.

Third, business enterprises are not stable foundations for long-term social security. Profitable firms prosper and decline as markets change; in the large scheme of things they are rather temporary institutions. No one knows this better than business managers themselves. In response to the collapse of Enron in 2001, Secretary of the Treasury Paul O'Neill (a former chief executive officer of ALCOA) remarked insouciantly, "Companies come and go . . . it's part of the genius of capitalism."[31] Consequently, the management view of social welfare has always been Janus-faced and politically contingent. Business and insurance executives have long recognized that firms cannot always bear the social benefits burden; that there are firms that cannot or will not pay for them at all; and that it is financially advantageous to avoid such benefits. Meanwhile, corporate executives assured their workers, their communities, and the public that there was no need to call in the state; they could meet all economic security needs, at least until the company merged, "down-sized," or relocated to meet other cost imperatives.

This inconsistency raises the issue of accountability in two senses. To what degree do firm-based benefits confuse an administrative convenience with an actual assumption of employer responsibility for social needs? Workers and voters once strove to make business more accountable to labor and to the public. A temporary change in the balance of power during the 1930s and 1940s, when unions and the federal government commanded significant public support, had pressured employers to expand these programs and offer more meaningful benefits than in previous years. But once the ambitions of the federal government shrank and the labor movement went into retreat, many business firms renounced the private welfare state as well.

This book is a work of political economy that links labor policy, social policy and social welfare, institutional economic relationships, and political culture. It shows that the private social security system is just as much a legacy of the New Deal and the Fair Deal as federal Social Security. This study moves beyond the traditional assumptions about post–New Deal labor policy and social provision by demonstrating the extent to which collective bargaining itself was part of an ongoing story of the development of private benefits. And this work restores to discussions of social provision, the welfare state, and welfare capitalism the centrality of economic power and economic relationships in a liberal capitalist political economy.

1

Mass Marketing Private Insurance

THE ORIGINS OF A PRIVATE EMPLOYEE BENEFITS SYSTEM, 1910–1933

THE AMERICAN system of firm-based social welfare has, until the recent proliferation of managed care, been anchored in group insurance. In its familiar, post–World War II form this system encompassed hospital and medical benefits, pensions, disability coverage, life insurance, and supplemental unemployment benefits. These postwar social welfare benefits grew out of the group life insurance plans first created by commercial life insurance companies in the 1910s. Insurers devised these policies so that employers could provide life insurance coverage for a large group of employees under one group risk factor; individual employees did not have to pass a medical examination to be included in the plan. Under a group life insurance policy, each enrolled worker received a certificate entitling a beneficiary to a burial benefit and one year's salary. Life insurers soon expanded group insurance to include group pensions and annuities. In the 1920s, companies like Equitable Life and Metropolitan Life also underwrote group accident and sickness insurance, which is what we refer to today as disability compensation: reimbursement for wages lost during sickness. By the end of the 1930s, life insurers used the same group insurance framework to develop hospital and surgical insurance. Medical insurance, benefits to pay for physicians' services other than surgery, appeared in the 1940s. Whatever the innovations in group policy benefits, the employer remained the only legal policyholder.

Large, eastern life insurance companies, led by the Equitable Life Assurance Society, created group insurance, first, in order to sell insurance on a mass scale and to rationalize a business that depended on the high administrative costs of selling individual policies door to door. But second, insurers wanted to prevent the growth of state-provided social welfare programs. These imperatives collided at an opportune moment with the interests of American corporate employers.

In the early twentieth century, business managers in large-scale corporate enterprises, wracked by two decades of labor strife, began preaching a new industrial relations doctrine. Rather than continually engaging in violent battles, business had to strive for a harmony of interests between capital and labor. The best way to achieve this new class accord, leading industrialists thought, was not through collective representation for workers but through each firm's assuming some obligation for its workers' well-being, either inside or outside the workplace. This "welfare work" program relied on employee benefits that ranged from company cafeterias and lunch plans to athletic activities, picnics, English language and home economics classes, company housing, and company doctors. Some employers offered pecuniary forms of welfare work—loans, savings plans, profit sharing, or accident relief funds. Companies offered different mixes and approached welfare work with a variety of motivations and expectations. Some executives believed welfare work improved productive efficiency: these programs would inspire the employee to become a better worker, whether more efficient, healthier, or more loyal. Others sought to avoid labor upheaval and discourage unionization; still others hoped to attract and keep skilled workers. In all cases, however, welfare work was a strategy to retain complete managerial control over the terms of employment.[1]

The need to shore up managerial control appeared especially acute by the 1910s, as the labor movement gained in numbers and political clout and social reformers pressed for regulatory labor legislation. Welfare capitalist firms intended to thwart the growing strength of unionism. Yet just as critical in this equation was the political reform context of the Progressive Era. While labor unions lobbied for employers' liability laws, social reformers worked for maximum hours for women workers, minimum wages, factory inspections, child labor laws, and antisweatshop laws. They sought to bring the state into the employment relation. Here insurers' interests and employers' interests met. Both sought mechanisms to check the fledgling regulatory welfare state, and each found the other a useful partner. Equitable developed group insurance specifically to deter social insurance legislation. To promote its new alternative to social insurance, Equitable could point to the new concern for peaceful relations between employers and workers stressed in the new welfare capitalism.

In doing so, Equitable and the life insurance companies that soon followed it into the group business directly linked social welfare to employment. Through group insurance, the alleged social function of life insurance and old-age annuities—to meet needs outside the employment relation—would be channeled through employers, subject to managerial discretion.

Equitable invented group insurance, but the Metropolitan Life Insurance Company wove it into a fully articulated, comprehensive program for industrial relations and nonstatist economic regulation. Metropolitan entered the group market shortly after World War I, and by 1924 it was the leading seller of group policies. Group insurance enabled Metropolitan to reach far more workers than its field force could ever contact traveling door to door. Yet group insurance was not simply industrial insurance sold in greater volume. For Metropolitan, marketing group insurance also meant venturing into all facets of employee relations. Metropolitan sought to construct an entire industrial relations system that would sustain its welfare services, a system in which American corporations would provide for the security needs of American citizens.

Metropolitan's prescription for bureaucratized, technocratic managerialism excluded workers from having a voice in these developments. Metropolitan participated in the search for industrial democracy prevalent in the 1920s, but with a distinctly corporate perspective. Industrial democracy never represented a single vision but rather a spectrum of ideas on how to solve "the labor question."[2] Companies like Metropolitan represented the more conservative end of the industrial democracy spectrum. They called for an end to coercive labor relations, hazardous working conditions, seasonal unemployment, and the absence of job security; they promoted the idea of a "system" of industrial peace. Yet whereas Taylor Society reformers such as Mary Van Kleeck envisioned an industrial democracy with "power rather than reward" as its primary principle,[3] Metropolitan preferred rewards to power. It offered insurance, promotions, vacations, cafeterias, and incentive raises to workers in order to achieve social and economic stability. This emphasis on managerial rewards and gratuities rather than employment rights became a permanent part of corporate employers' and commercial insurers' view of industrial relations and social welfare.

Insurance companies, by selling employers reliable pecuniary security polices that management could control, made possible the transformation and rejuvenation of welfare capitalism well beyond the 1910s and 1920s. Even as the New Deal, of the 1930s, brought the state more fully into economic management and industrial relations, the foundation of social science management, internal labor markets, and private social welfare benefits laid in the 1920s would subsequently work in conjunction with the New Deal state to assure private control of the employment relation.

Group Insurance

How the mighty Equitable had fallen. At the beginning of the twentieth century the Equitable Life Assurance Society was the most powerful life insurance company in America, with assets of more than $400 million. By 1906, in the wake of scandal and investigation, the Equitable had fallen to sixth place in the industry: new sales had dropped from $307 million to $88 million, half the agency sales force left. The company's troubles had begun in 1905, when an internal power struggle over stock control erupted into public view, laying bare lavish expenditures by company officers and sordid financial dealings between major shareholders, banks, and syndicates. The malfeasance was so flagrant that it resulted in the ouster of the entire board of directors, including the president, the first vice president, and the comptroller.

Public outrage over mismanagement at Equitable fueled demands for a public investigation of the insurance industry. Under the aegis of New York State, the Armstrong Committee investigations set out to assuage the fears stoked by muckrakers that malfeasance in the insurance industry might threaten middle-class savings. The Armstrong Committee, led by Charles Evans Hughes, uncovered numerous abuses at all of the major companies, from dubious political contributions to nepotism, excessive executive salaries, misuse of proxy votes, and risky investments. In particular, the committee conducted extensive scrutiny of Equitable. At the end of the year, the state insurance superintendent published a preliminary report specifically identifying financial, political, and contract irregularities at Equitable. The 1906 report led to new legislation that standardized policy forms and dividend payments, put a cap on the amount of new insurance a company could write, prohibited stock ownership in banks, industrials, and trusts, outlawed campaign contributions, and mandated new directorial elections—hence stripping the Big Three (New York Life, Mutual Life, and Equitable) of much of their political and financial clout. Equally as damaging for insurers, their reputations as protectors of the public's savings deteriorated. Equitable brought in a new president to restore order to the company, but new business continued to plummet, while old policies lapsed. Over the next three years several major stockholders sued the company. The financial recession of 1907 kept new business in the doldrums.[4]

Paul Morton, the company's new president, instigated internal reforms, but Equitable needed to do more than stop the bleeding; it needed new business.[5] The Armstrong investigations may have eliminated flagrant abuses of power and shady financial dealings, but fierce competition in the industry by no means subsided. Insurers still searched for a way to rationalize their business. Insurance remained a labor-intensive business because it depended on a sprawling, quasi-independent agency force to sell its product one policy at a time and to do the follow-up work required just to keep each policy in place. Paul

Morton wanted a new product line that would reach a large untapped market.

As it turned out, the muckrakers and investigative reformers exposed the worst vices of the private insurance industry just as the idea of public social insurance was gaining currency in America. Although Germany, Austria, Hungary, Denmark, and France had enacted various kinds of workers' insurance programs by the early twentieth century, American social reformers had generally ignored the issue, concentrating instead on casework designed to push nonworking individuals into work. In 1906, however, several prominent social scientists, including Richard Ely, John R. Commons, J. W. Jencks, and Isaac Rubinow, formed the American Association for Labor Legislation (AALL) to launch an effort to study and promote government social insurance in America. They began with the issue of industrial hygiene, exposed poisonous work conditions in some industries, and then moved on to the issue of workers' compensation for occupational injuries. New developments promised success. In 1908 the Workmen's Compensation Act, for federal employees, provided full wages for up to one year in the case of temporary disability and one year's wages for fatal injuries. Massachusetts established a state Commission on Old Age Pensions, Annuities, and Insurance. A 1909 conference on child welfare, called by President Theodore Roosevelt, set in motion the organized movement for widows' pensions. During that same year a trade unionist turned congressman actually introduced a proposal for a national pension in the U.S. Congress, and the American Federation of Labor (AFL) endorsed noncontributory pensions for the needy elderly.[6]

The growing U.S. interest in state social insurance heightened as dramatic changes took place in Britain between 1908 and 1911. William Beveridge began promoting a program for unemployment insurance and enlisted the support of key members of the Liberal Party, especially Winston Churchill. In 1908 the Liberal Party enacted old-age pensions for needy elderly persons who could pass a means (and worthy character) test. This was followed by the Trade Boards Act, under which public boards would set minimum wages in selected industries. The National Insurance Act of 1911 set up contributory unemployment insurance and workers' health insurance, including maternity benefits for the wives of covered workers.[7] With these reforms, Britain established the principle that the state would be responsible for ensuring some minimal level of social welfare, a crucial link between workers and the state.

Social reform in Britain piqued the interest of American social reformers, insurance companies, and employers. Life insurance executives perceived the rising interest in social insurance as a threat, especially at a time when the life insurance industry needed to rejuvenate its image as a socially responsible endeavor. Thus they too began studying European schemes in search of social welfare innovations. In 1908 Equitable sent Henry Rosenfeld to Europe to study how Britain had been handling economic security needs of workers through voluntary means. Rosenfeld examined the British railway companies, which used a system of payroll deduction to provide life insurance to their employees. The workers paid the entire premium. Rosenfeld also found that the British insurance companies offered Home Purchase insurance to workers through their employers to help them become homeowners. Upon returning home, he began working on new versions of these types of policies.

President Morton explained to Equitable's staff, agency force, and directors that the purpose of Rosenfeld's research was to find a private-sector alternative to workers' social insurance programs. "There is a much greater sphere of usefulness in which I hope to see Equitable do its full share. That sphere is to give protection to the people who cannot afford to carry a big line of insurance. I refer to the artisan, to the man behind the plow, to those engaged in the humbler walks of life. . . . Insurance by the state is neither desirable nor necessary in this land of the greatest life insurance corporations the world has ever known." Over the next two years Rosenfeld continued to study developments in Europe, returning in 1910 to examine the public social insurance programs in England and Germany. This time he made the trip in cooperation with the National Association of Manufacturers (NAM) Committee on Industrial Indemnity Insurance.[8]

Concerned about the potential spread of social legislation, the NAM had contacted insurers to enlist their help not only in preventing legislation but in offering a "voluntary" alternative. Concerned that "half a dozen states will adopt the English system," the NAM contacted Henry Rosenfeld, urging the "necessity for the manufacturers taking hold of the economic, legislative, and insurance phases of indemnity work." Inviting Rosenfeld to join them on their trip to England and Germany in 1910, the chairman of the NAM's Committee on Industrial Indemnity Insurance concluded that "some kind of insurance proposition must be launched almost immediately upon our return." Indeed, Rosenfeld proposed to Equitable's directors that the company offer old-age pensions, home purchase loans, employers' liability insurance, and disability and sickness insurance as a comprehensive package.[9]

The most immediate issue facing employers was the labor movement's campaign to reform accident liability laws. The AFL distrusted state-run workers' insurance programs as much as it distrusted employer welfare capitalist schemes; AFL President Samuel Gompers viewed both as paternalistic mechanisms that reduced labor's autonomy. Instead, the AFL supported employers' liability laws that would increase liability for workplace injuries at common law. The AFL wanted to keep the issue of injury compensation within the courts, where it had traditionally been handled, but wanted to eliminate employers' common-law defenses against liability. Workers could then act independently through the courts to win larger disability settlements from employers. Under the doctrine of assumed risk, employers' only responsibility to workers was to inform them of any unsafe conditions, while the fellow-servant rule held that if the foreman contributed to the accident, the employer could not be blamed. Finally, if the injured worker could not prove that the accident was solely and entirely the employer's fault, the employer did not have to pay any compensation. Overwhelmingly, then, court cases under these traditional rules favored the employers. The labor movement wanted to shift the balance of power toward workers and realize their economic security goals by removing these common-law defenses.[10]

Employers' liability reform posed a fundamental challenge to traditional master-servant employment relations because it made employers responsible for the welfare of workers in their employ. Under master-servant rules, an employee was always free to leave the job; therefore, he was responsible for his health and safety on the job. In framing the employers' liability issue the labor movement argued that employers were perpetrators of a wrong (the injury) and employees were victims. Therefore, justice demanded that employers should be blamed and punished and that workers should receive a decent pecuniary settlement. Labor also argued that workers rarely won compensation under the status quo, so the lack of employers' liability caused a larger social problem: poverty, public relief, and almshouses.[11]

Opposing employers' liability, business instead had to throw its support to workers' compensation, the alternative preferred by social scientists because it eliminated the notion of fault.[12] Industrial accidents were presumed to be an inherent aspect of production, and so workers would automatically be compensated; no class struggle would have to ensue. By setting up a defined compensation schedule for each type of injury (literally limb by limb), workers' compensation laws established a routinized, dependable, and ultimately very limited liability for employers.[13]

But beyond this contained social legislation, the NAM's Committee on Industrial Indemnity Insurance suggested that business had to offer its own social welfare remedies. Employers had to counter the charge that they were inhumane or unjust. Progressive employers affiliated with the National Civic Federation concurred. The NAM's Committee on Indemnity Insurance asked Equitable's executives to come up with an employer-based policy that would include "insurance of employers' liability, workmen's compensation, sickness, etc."[14] If insurance companies could devise a policy that employers could use to cover their own liability and offer compensation to their workers, insurers could provide employers with a vehicle to prove that they were socially responsible, but at their own discretion. Trade unionists may have lost the battle for their legislative program, but their ideological argument proved influential. Employers slowly accepted some social responsibility for workers' welfare while in their employ. A couple of years later, Equitable's president commented on this change when describing group insurance: "It marks . . . a departure on the part of the employer in recognizing an important necessity to the employee."[15]

Rosenfeld, Morton, and William Day eagerly agreed with the NAM that private business should offer its own social welfare alternative, preferably in the form of life insurance. He assured the NAM that some sort of employer scheme was under review. In a speech to the NAM's annual convention, Rosenfeld assured those present that the president of Equitable "has a keen desire . . . to place the services of his company at the disposal of manufacturers." Rosenfeld clearly saw profitable potential in this workers' security endeavor, noting that "upon a proper solution depends so much of social as well as financial gain."[16]

Just as Rosenfeld was working on policies that could be sold to workers, Equitable received a specific request from Montgomery Ward & Company to provide death benefits, disability benefits, and retirement annuities for 2,900 workers in Chicago and Kansas City.[17] Although these employees already had death and sickness benefits through their Clerks' Benefit Society, Montgomery Ward was looking for a social welfare plan that could displace the employee-run mutual benefit fund. Skeptical that such a comprehensive plan could be financed, Equitable at first declined. But Equitable was desperate to pick up new business and reach new clients, especially lower-middle-class and working-class patrons. So within a year the directors agreed on a group plan. A blanket life insurance policy would be sold to an employer to cover all his employees, without individual medical examinations. The company, however, would have to undergo a medical and safety inspection by Equitable representatives. To ensure a wide risk pool, Equitable would only cover groups of one hundred or more. Employers would have to pay the entire premium. And Equitable added a new feature to this group life insurance, so that it would resemble a pension plan. In addition to an immediate burial payment, benefits would be paid out to survivors over the course of three to four years (rather than in one lump sum), thereby preserving the wage income for a few years after death. Finally, group clients would receive mutual dividends on these policies. Equitable tested the policy with some local businesses and its own employees before agreeing to insure a large, high-profile group such as Montgomery Ward.[18]

Montgomery Ward's group insurance plan went into effect on 1 July 1912. The group plan included a one-hundred-dollar burial benefit and a weekly annuity of 25 percent of the deceased's salary for four years. Those who reached the age of 70 and retired received a service pension of 25 percent of their salary for the rest of their lives. Anyone who left employment with the company, however, immediately lost all benefits and contributions paid toward the plan. Each worker had to contribute 3 percent of weekly wages for the plan. From the very beginning, the plan stated that "all the provisions . . . shall apply to male and female employees alike." Dependent and disabled husbands would be considered surviving beneficiaries of deceased female employees, just as dependent wives were entitled to deceased husbands' benefits. Montgomery Ward also offered a separate disability insurance plan, although the company dropped it when it became clear that employees were unwilling to pay for it. With this plan management dislodged the employees' "union." In announcing the new plan to its employees the company explicitly told them that it would be superior to that of the Clerks' Benefit Society and should replace it. Whereas the Clerks' Benefits Society had been run entirely by employees, the group insurance plan would be run by Montgomery Ward managers.[19]

Group insurance was designed for rank-and-file workers, not top management. Equitable set a salary cap for eligible workers. After all, Equitable did not want to undermine its ordinary (individual) insurance business. It expected executives to purchase their own life insurance policies. Indeed, it hoped that these limited policies would encourage all employees to buy more insurance on their own. And where employees had to contribute to the policies, both the insurer and the state insurance commission required that at least 75 percent of the employees enroll in the plan. Therefore, the plan was meant to serve as a workers' income maintenance plan, more than as an executive perk. It functioned as a wholesale way of selling insurance. As Rosenfeld explained, group life insurance sold life insurance "more universally, more economically, and more effectively than previously possible through forms of individual insurance." As such, it helped both Equitable's cash flow and its public image, both of which were in need of resuscitation.[20]

Yet Equitable never ceased to emphasize its role as an antidote to state welfare. In referring to the "sociological" functions of group insurance, Equitable initially relied on the language of family and paternalism, long a part of insurance selling, over the more modern arguments for industrial efficiency. For individual firms group insurance was a "form of welfare work that life insurance has offered the employer for the collective necessities of his extensive business family." Group insurance manuals instructed agents that "we want to link the man's wife and family up more closely with his work so that the man's two chief interests in life will be working together." Equitable even referred to its group policyholders as "members of the Equitable group family." They described group insurance as "a great wall stretching around thousands of homes," keeping mothers and children out of poverty. Insurers had long promoted insurance as a measure to relieve poverty. Now Equitable insisted that group insurance showed that employers could handle problems that were increasingly being given over to the state in Europe. This language of saving mothers and children in particular could counter the movement to enact mothers' pensions. While advocates of mothers' pensions claimed that industrial work threatened domesticity, Equitable linked the protection and security of domestic sanctity to employers. "Let us help those who are seeking to solve economic problems of our day to appreciate that every conscientious employer of labor is to-day a benefactor of his community."[21]

And Equitable assured employers that it would be the company's policy. When Equitable's executives originally created group insurance, several of them thought the group policy could be sold to labor organizations, lodges, or beneficial societies. Within a few years, however, they had abandoned this idea, partly for legal reasons, partly for marketing reasons. On the one hand, the New York state insurance commissioner was wary about selling to self-selected groups because regulators feared that only sick people would join such pools. On the other hand, the company decided to market group policies as "The American Plan for Employers." An Equitable promotional piece assured potential clients that "the plan of insurance is within the control of the employer and can be devised to meet his particular needs."[22] The designation "American Plan" had a double meaning in this context: to emphasize that private insurance was the American alternative to European social insurance and also to preserve the open shop and expunge labor unions.[23] Thus, group insurance could displace two rival sources of workers' security: the state and the unions.

Nor did these nonemployer groups really want the product insurers had to offer. Far from seeing themselves as potential clients or policyholders, fraternal associations, the major providers of death and old-age benefits at that time, perceived group insurance as a threat. Fraternals were worker- or member-controlled social service organizations. Group insurance ceded control over workers' resources back to corporate interests. Hence, fraternals vigorously fought its approval by the state legislature and insurance commission. Labor unions too remained rather wary that employers planned to use group insurance to displace workers' organizations, even though labor's social welfare programs remained underdeveloped. Many Jewish union members, though, affiliated with the Workmen's Circle, a fraternal society that provided workers with both the social solidarity and the economic support of a community organization, offering social activities, educational and cultural programs, sickness benefits, and funeral benefits.[24]

Throughout the second decade of the twentieth century Equitable continued to respond to the political strategies of social reform groups such as the AALL. After 1915 the AALL focused its efforts on compulsory health insurance. The AALL's model bill consisted of sick pay (two-thirds of wages for up to twenty-six weeks); medical care, including physician visits, surgery, nurses, and maternity care; and a funeral benefit. California and New York both considered a compulsory health insurance bill in 1917. Equitable had initially tried to come up with a disability plan in 1911–12 but had quickly abandoned the idea as unworkable; nor did the demand or political need really seem to be there. Once the AALL began campaigning for public health insurance, however, Equitable soon got back to work on it. When the Department of Labor convened its major, national Conference on Social Insurance in 1916, Equitable's new president insisted that "the principles of social insurance find practical exposition in group insurance as it has been and is being woven into the fabric of our industrial and commercial life." In 1917 the company followed through on this promise, adding weekly indemnities for nonoccupational temporary disabilities as supplementary to life insurance. Aetna and Travelers had already moved into this business. A year later Equitable began issuing temporary and permanent disability policies as discrete policies. Companies with more than fifty employees could purchase group accident and sickness plans for their employees as of 1920. During that decade the most common disability policy paid benefits of ten dollars a week, about 35 percent of the average worker's wage. Coverage lasted for a maximum of two years. Few of Equitable's large group clients actually purchased this coverage, but it did serve a useful political function, helping to undermine legislative support for AALL's compulsory health insurance bill.[25]

Group insurance helped Equitable break into the working-class market. The company was content to accept the new business that came its way and then let the group insurance business coast. The Studebaker Company purchased a life policy to cover 10,000 employees, B. F.

Goodrich enrolled 18,000, and the Union Pacific Railroad's plan covered 35,000. The American Rolling Mill Company and the Palmolive Company signed on too. After World War I, Equitable added E. I. Du-Pont de Nemours & Company, U.S. Rubber, and some of the Standard Oil companies to their client list. Thus, group insurance initially attracted large, high-profile welfare capitalist firms. Equitable promoted group policies by stressing the dividends that policyholders, in this case the employer, could earn. But it did not aggressively promote the group line. Many of Equitable's general agents and representatives in the home office resisted selling group insurance because the commissions were lower and they did not want group insurance to interfere with the individual business. In 1919 Equitable had $325 million worth of group insurance in force, compared with almost $2 billion in individual insurance. By 1929 the amount of group insurance had reached only $1 billion in force, while individual insurance stood at $5.5 billion. Although it had pioneered the group business, Equitable had fallen to a distant third place behind Metropolitan and Travelers by 1925. Equitable was still a high-finance firm oriented primarily toward upper-middle-class and wealthy individual policyholders.[26]

For the Metropolitan Life Insurance Company the working class was the heart of the company's business. Until 1905 Metropolitan trailed behind the industry leaders, New York Life, Mutual Life, and Equitable. Whereas the Big Three primarily sold ordinary insurance—large insurance policies for well-to-do persons who generally possessed large estates or substantial assets—Metropolitan based its growth on the sale of industrial insurance to working-class families. Industrial insurance was insurance sold in relatively small amounts, usually enough to cover funeral expenses, to workers, who paid for the policy in weekly installments. In order to save workers the expense of remitting the premiums directly to the company, field agents collected premiums personally. Metropolitan relied on agents from the ethnic communities whom they served, tapping into the fraternal, ethnic, union, and charity networks there. As a consequence, Metropolitan always considered itself the "working-man's" firm, for only one other company, Prudential, had preceded it in offering industrial insurance.[27]

Metropolitan's competitive position began to change as a result of the Armstrong Committee investigations. The committee's report resulted in several restrictions on ordinary insurance, the type primarily sold by the Big Three, but the Armstrong Committee did not suggest any changes regarding industrial insurance. While the other three companies faced civil and criminal charges and company reorganization, Metropolitan emerged unscathed. Not only did Metropolitan not have to contend with new restrictions on industrial insurance but the limitations placed on ordinary insurance in 1906 were far fewer for industrial companies than for straight ordinary companies. After 1906, then, Metropolitan expanded its ordinary and industrial business until it had become the largest life insurance company in the world.[28] The Armstrong Committee's report had suggested, however, that it would consider the problems of industrial insurance at some point in the future.

Consequently, Metropolitan executives set out to prove that their firm was a socially responsible enterprise. Building on its claim to be a company for workers, Metropolitan announced in 1909 that "insurance, not merely as a business proposition, but as a social program, will be the future policy of the company."[29] Metropolitan President Haley Fiske recruited Dr. Lee Frankel, a progressive reformer with connections to the Charity Organization Society and the settlement house movement, to direct Metropolitan's Welfare Division. Frankel had also been active on behalf of workers' health through the AALL, which had focused heavily on the issue of occupational diseases. When Frankel and his partner, Louis Dublin, first arrived at Metropolitan, they launched programs designed to keep policyholders healthy. The company sponsored a visiting-nurse program, published pamphlets on health education and advice, held picnics, gave medical exams, and set up the Health and Happiness League for youths. Fiske established cooperative bridges to welfare agencies as well. In 1915 Metropolitan converted from a stock company to a mutual company, in which all policyholders received the dividends earned by the company. The directors believed that through mutualization Metropolitan would become a public-spirited company. Metropolitan represented an intersection of business and social service.[30]

Metropolitan began experimenting with group insurance before World War I, offering coverage to home office employees, but the company was not prepared to offer it to other firms until 1917.[31] Insurance was a state-regulated industry. Companies could only sell the precise amounts and types of coverage specified by state law. Since Metropolitan had already reached the limits set on ordinary and industrial insurance, the company had to find another way to launch the group insurance business. Yet large insurers generally had a cozy relationship with state regulators and commissioners, which often enabled life companies to channel regulations to their own competitive advantage. In the face of bitter opposition and attacks from small insurers and fraternal societies, the large life companies interested in the group business steadily pressed state regulators to circumvent the concerns and precedents raised by group insurance opponents. First, in 1913 the New York state legislature amended the insurance code, which prohibited the issuance of an insurance policy without the consent of the insured, to allow an employer to take out an insurance policy covering his employees collectively. In 1916 Metropolitan, along with representatives from Equitable, Prudential, Aetna, and Travelers, successfully convinced New York's superintendent of insurance to recommend to the state legislature that group insurance policies be excluded from the mandated ceilings on new business. The legislature soon complied, amending the insurance laws so that group insurance would not be included in the maximum amount of ordinary insurance that could be written by one company. Then, as state commissioners set out to establish standard requirements and policy provisions for group insurance to be used in all states, they relied on an advisory committee made up of actuaries from Equitable, Aetna, Metropolitan, Prudential, and Travelers. Following this consultation, the National Convention of Insurance Commissioners adopted a circumscribed definition of group life insurance that appeased both camps: "Group life insurance is that form of life insurance covering not less than fifty employees with or without medical examination, written under a policy *issued to the employer,* . . . and *insuring only all of his employees,* or all of any class or classes thereof determined by conditions pertaining to employment" (emphasis mine). This definition cornered the potential employee market for group life companies but protected the preserve of the fraternals and the individual market of the small companies. Finally, to ensure the continued viability and perpetual growth of the group business, the new group insurance code also included a provision that "the group or class thereof originally insured shall be deemed to include from time to time all new employees of the employers eligible to insurance in such group or class."[32] Companies like Metropolitan were now looking at a wide-open market.

In 1917 Metropolitan set up a separate Group Insurance Division, positioning itself to sell more insurance than any other firm. With group insurance, one or two agents could insure hundreds or even thousands of workers, while the premium was remitted only by a single employer. Thus it was a more efficient form of collection, as well as sales. "By the stroke of one pen," Haley Fiske exclaimed, "we took in over 80,000 employees of the Southern Pacific Railroad; in another case, the General Electric, we took in 50,000."[33]

Selling group policies to employers also gave Metropolitan a chance to market policies that they had great difficulty selling to individual workers, such as accident or disability coverage. Low-wage industrial workers, along with African Americans, Asians, and Mexicans, had been considered "uninsurable risks." Many workers could not afford wage-loss insurance, while others were deliberately shut out of the market by insurance carriers wary of insuring industrial workers. Once workmen's compensation laws had been passed, the number of individuals purchasing accident insurance declined further.[34] By selling a policy to an employer, Metropolitan could reach these workers and bring them under the coverage of accident and health insurance. Henry Bruere, an officer at Metropolitan in the 1920s, claimed that group insurance doubled or tripled the amount of insurance coverage the average worker could afford. By ushering in new categories of workers, namely white, urban workers, to "insurability," group insurance thus also slightly shifted the cleavages of class and race built into insurance underwriting.[35]

The experiment proved uncertain at first: most industrial workers did not have predictable or safe employment. For the first two years few companies purchased Metropolitan group policies. Among those who did, labor turnover, hazardous conditions, and the lack of employment records threatened actuarial calculations that were based on the predictability of a group profile. Controlling these aspects of employment placed extra demands on employers, which they were unwilling to meet. By 1919 Metropolitan executives had begun to consider ways to market group insurance more effectively. Vice President James Kavanaugh suggested that the Group Insurance Division establish an Industrial Service Bureau, modeled on the one in the Welfare Division, as a competitive promotional device. Metropolitan would distinguish itself from other life insurance companies by providing services as well as cash indemnification. To reduce what managers considered extra burdens of an insurance policy, Metropolitan would provide a package of insurance-related benefits. Visiting nurses and health literature would be made available to employees under the group policy. Moreover, Metropolitan offered to visit firms and obtain information they might need to solve glaring problems, particularly regarding safety and health measures. This exchange on health and safety needs could help firms in high-risk industries lower their premiums. "At once we have mutual interests which give rise on our part to aid in the solution of our policyholders' industrial problems," Metropolitan informed clients.[36]

Fiske stressed these common interests between insurers and employers. He had decided to move into the group insurance business for reasons beyond selling larger volumes of insurance. Group life insurance could improve relations between capital and labor, he asserted.[37] Underwritten by a model business firm, offered by employers directly to their workers, it would help pacify volatile class relations in a way that was apolitical, rational, and organized. Managers and actuaries could make the decisions on behalf of working people but without the interference of the masses. As Fiske wrote,

> Through the Policyholders' Service Bureau, the Metropolitan with its group policyholders is participating in an organized effort to build up in American industry sympathetic cooperation between employers and employed, and to place those cooperative relations on foundations of good health, security against disaster, confidence in the American industrial system, and a sincere conviction that by the right use of the power and opportunities of industry, the just aspirations of the American working people may be justly attained.[38]

After World War I these goals became imperative among reformers. Many of the liberals with whom Frankel and Fiske had been associated before the war emerged from their recent experiences disillusioned and shaken by what they perceived to be the uncontrollable passions of the masses at home: pro-war vigilantism, nationalism, and government-sponsored repression. The Russian Revolution and ensuing civil war produced the specter of violent revolution. Liberals in America, particularly in eastern and midwestern industrial and commercial centers, decided that they needed to focus on "developing a rational and controlled democratic politics" while taming capitalism at the same time. Following the lead of Herbert Hoover, Walter Lippmann, and Felix Frankfurter, they turned to hierarchical notions of expertise, engineering, and technocracy, believing that a cadre of highly trained experts could manage and reconstruct a liberal polity. Metropolitan offered its scientifically trained experts to this social enterprise.[39] Invoking the positive public relations value of welfare work lent social credibility to the insurance industry's new product and mass-marketing scheme.

As the postwar strikes swept through major industrial sectors, these goals took on added significance. Not only had union membership soared during World War I (AFL membership reached 3.2 million) but the strike rate had jumped 25 percent toward the end of the war. In 1919 one in every five workers participated in a strike against his or her employer. General strikes briefly closed Seattle, Portland, and Butte. Neither government nor organized labor appeared to have a rational solution to these upheavals. Congress dismantled the War Labor Board in 1919, but sheer force failed to prevent strikes or curb radicalism.[40] As a business firm, a major investor, and a source of social welfare, Metropolitan was well positioned to correlate the interests of capital and labor.

The big breakthrough in group insurance came at the end of 1919, when Metropolitan closed a deal with General Electric (GE) for a $50 million group life contract. Soon afterwards, the company signed another major contract with Westinghouse Electric and Manufacturing Company. Once Metropolitan landed these contracts, other employers began signing up, especially railroad companies. Within one year Metropolitan underwrote $125,450,000 in new group life policies. Initially, employers paid the total premium for all employees covered by the group insurance. Within a few years, however, contributory policies became the norm, in particular among railroads. Metropolitan continued to charge an extra premium for particularly hazardous industries, which may in fact explain why railroads chose contributory plans. In general, group carriers relied on experience rating for groups rather than a test of individual risk potential, such as a physical medical exam, used for industrial insurance.[41]

Not only did these policies launch the group insurance business but they brought Metropolitan into close contact with firms that shared similar goals concerning the political economy. Through group insurance, Metropolitan extended its contacts within an industrial reform network specifically focused on the workplace rather than on the state or voluntary social institutions. Now, in addition to links with social welfare agencies and philanthropic foundations, Metropolitan established direct relationships with a group of liberal, innovative business firms that experimented with the latest developments in business management and industrial relations. Just as Metropolitan's Welfare Division became involved in the lives of industrial policyholders by offering advice on health and hygiene, so the Policyholders' Service Bureau (PSB), the Group Insurance Division's service arm, would participate in some of the internal operations of corporate policyholders. As Haley Fiske, president of Metropolitan during the 1920s, noted, "Those who sell Group Life insurance are constantly finding occasion to discuss various phases of employee relations at work."[42]

That the first major contracts were with GE and Westinghouse is significant. Electrical manufacturing companies were among the leaders in corporate scientific research, welfare capitalism, and the promotion of antistatist industrial reform. On the level of plant management, GE and Westinghouse pioneered in the use of personnel management as a program for solving labor problems. They hired employment managers to develop hiring, promotion, and layoff systems. Between World War I and the mid-1920s they implemented employee testing, job classification and wage ladders, seniority systems, employee representation councils, and apprentice training schools. Railroads too had well-developed seniority systems and job ladders for blue-collar and white-collar employees. Among Metropolitan's smaller group clients were companies such as Curtis Publishing Company and Plimpton Press, two of the earliest companies to set up employment departments and to combine scientific management with welfare work. In addition to shop-floor innovations, executives at companies such as GE and Eastman Kodak, another group insurance client, formulated new ideas on postwar reconstruction and industrial democracy. GE's Gerard Swope and Owen Young and Kodak's Marion Folsom promoted a comprehensive, distinctive social philosophy that held that corporate management could rectify the problems that neither the political system nor the free market could solve. Through countercyclical planning, mass production and distribution, high wages, and firm-based welfare policies, employers would provide workers with what they needed most: economic security and a rising standard of living.[43] Henry Bruere, who regularly remarked on this new industrial reform alliance, noted that "these companies, as purchasers of this insurance, . . . are concerned, as is the life insurance company, with establishing and keeping the right basis for successful relations with their employes."[44]

Metropolitan would learn much about industrial relations and management from these clients; in turn, the affiliation of these companies with New York's premier life insurance company, also a welfare work employer, set in motion a dynamic that improved the firms' ability to realize their own welfare capitalist goals. Because of this newly created group market, Metropolitan began developing a wider range of policies for employers to provide for their workers. After 1919 Metropolitan offered disability clauses in group life policies, group accident and sickness insurance (coverage for lost wages during illness), and annuities. In response to requests by railroad clients, in 1922 Metropolitan developed a group policy to insure loss of life, limb, or sight by accidental means. Metropolitan first underwrote a group pension plan in 1921, although group pensions remained in the experimental phase throughout the first half of the 1920s. In 1923 Metropolitan began a series of conferences to which it invited executives of major corporations to discuss the new pension idea, so that "the [Metropolitan] Company has been able to outline in general the pension requirements of different industries."[45] Thus, Metropolitan, in conjunction with its employer clients, began to develop the private system of social security that would later prove so pervasive.

And from the very beginning Metropolitan aggressively defended its privatized domain. Metropolitan waged a vigorous, sustained campaign against the AALL's proposals for public health insurance. Although Frankel had been a member of AALL, he broke with the organization over this issue and publicly denounced AALL's compulsory health insurance plan. The plan included a funeral benefit, which would directly compete with industrial insurance. In fact, Metropolitan and Prudential were the most militant opponents in this campaign. Prudential and others worked with the Insurance Economics Society of America (IES), founded by the Casualty Company of Detroit, which propagandized against compulsory insurance. In an effort to "educate" the medical profession, IES presented distorted accounts of European conditions under public health insurance programs and succeeded in provoking hostility on the part of the medical profession.[46]

Metropolitan faced a more formidable opponent in women social welfare activists who sought to involve the federal government in the provision of social welfare services. Through the Sheppard-Towner Maternity and Infancy Act of 1921, the U.S. Children's Bureau and women reformers began using the resources and power of the federal government to build up social services at all levels of government. They established local health stations, well-baby clinics, and visiting-nurse programs with the goal of establishing permanent, public clinics. Inspired by their success in the administration of the Sheppard-Towner Act, these women became the primary activists on behalf of an American welfare state in the 1920s. Likewise, they lobbied for protective labor legislation at the state level, seeking the positive use of the state to regulate employer-employee relations.[47] Coming on the heels of the fight over AALL's attempt to enact compulsory health insurance—which in New York had also included maternity benefits—this federal children's welfare program raised fears that public agencies might replace private insurance carriers as social welfare providers. After all, workers purchased industrial insurance to protect their families. Metropolitan had to find a way to ensure that private insurance carriers would not be squeezed out of the industrial security business.

During the 1920s, innovative strategies emerging in unionized sectors convinced Metropolitan that it was as crucial to sell the *idea* of the social welfare partnership between the insurance company and the employer as it was to sell insurance policies. The nonunion environment in which Metropolitan and its group insurance clients had unilaterally executed employment policies was being challenged to some degree. In the early 1920s the Progressive coalition, or what was left of it after the war, had begun to turn its attention toward the activities of labor leaders like Sidney Hillman, who were pioneering a new unionism. Labor leaders in unstable industries such as clothing and textiles allied with social scientists, Taylor Society industrial engineers, and desperate clothing manufactures to offer unions as the best means to enforce "standards of production" and reverse the declining fortunes of their industries. Amid the chronic instability of the firms and the absence of state-sponsored social insurance, unions such as Hillman's Amalgamated Clothing Workers moved away from workers' control and socialist goals toward a new, regulatory, social welfare unionism. According to Steven Fraser, "In the cross-pollinated fields of security and property, the new unionism pioneered a set of innovations—unemployment insurance, an employment stabilization exchange, labor banking, cooperative housing."[48] Union leaders intended these programs to enable labor to pool its own financial resources and use them independently to promote both labor enterprises and socioeconomic security for workers. In the mid-1920s several unions, led by the AFL's William Green, formed the Union Labor Life Insurance Company, owned and operated by trade unions. The officers of the new company tried to eliminate many of the special charges imposed by commercial insurance carriers and thereby lure workers away from employer-sponsored insurance programs.[49] The policies of the new unionism and the Union Labor Life Insurance Company conceivably posed a direct threat to the sale of group insurance.

Indeed, Metropolitan competed directly with the new unionism in sectors such as southern textiles. Like the labor movement, Metropolitan wanted to combine production planning and welfare work to stabilize the industry. PSB argued that this strategy would enable conscientious businessmen and their firms to provide for the general welfare of a community or region, not just the welfare of a few employees. In its 1923 annual report, PSB declared: "Because the South has recently shown a very active interest in Metropolitan Group Insurance, the Bureau is equipping itself to give special service to Southern Groups. . . . The Metropolitan should during the coming year take an important part in the promotion of Southern welfare."[50] In a brewing contest over the structure of the political economy, Metropolitan saw where the stakes lay and prepared to make its services widely available and indispensable. Metropolitan did not so much want to suppress the new unionism as to absorb it. Through a service arm like PSB, Metropolitan planned to show that the new unionism's goals could be achieved by giving managers the tools to make enlightened decisions. Or if unable to absorb and displace the new unionism, Metropolitan at least wanted to get the unions to rely on Metropolitan to provide their social welfare services.

Metropolitan in fact initiated a communitywide project of social welfare and industrial stabilization in Kingsport, Tennessee. Kingsport had undergone a burst of industrial development during World War I and consequently had experienced a massive in-migration of rural and mountain folk in an extremely short period of time. Many of the new workers set up tent towns and rows of shacks both within Kingsport and on the fringes. The town's developers and planners, initially assisted by New York's Bureau of Municipal Research (Henry Bruere's former agency) and Columbia University, were disturbed by these developments. As postwar production slowed, they were at a loss as to how to handle the rising unemployment and worsening living conditions. In 1919 one of Kingsport's new industrialists invited an executive from

Metropolitan's Group Insurance Division to survey the situation. Metropolitan coordinated a multipronged approach in what became an early effort at regional industrial stabilization. Its "community insurance plan" included a life insurance policy for each worker, based on length of service, and accident and sickness protection, coverage of 50 percent of lost wages during illness. After collecting the premiums, the Metropolitan's Welfare Division then sent in visiting nurses and established community health stations, as Metropolitan had done in other demonstration towns, such as Framingham, Massachusetts, or Thetford, Quebec. Metropolitan also invested in new housing for workers. Metropolitan hoped that "it is an experiment in insurance and welfare work which will most assuredly be watched very carefully by many other towns and cities."[51]

What differentiated the Kingsport project from Metropolitan's previous local projects was the involvement of the Group Insurance Division and its service arm, the Industrial Service Bureau (ISB, later renamed Policyholders' Service Bureau). In the fall of 1919 ISB worked in conjunction with various industries to install standardized employment policies and thereby "jointly attack the labor turnover problem."[52] The bureau also presented employers with a system of introducing employees and their families to the benefits of their Metropolitan insurance policies, another essential mechanism for controlling turnover. Metropolitan's goals in Kingsport clearly extended beyond its usual interest in health stations; the goals specifically involved combining personnel research, personnel management, and economic security to ensure the health, stability, and longevity of firms and thus workers. ISB's project deliberately linked health and welfare to corporate responsibility, or to use Sanford Jacoby's phrase, it "emphasized the links between corporate and social efficiency."[53] The bureau attempted to advance the interests of the employers and the workers by standardizing labor costs throughout the local economy, thereby eliminating labor costs as a source of cut-throat competition. ISB's strategy for accomplishing this goal was to encourage internal bureaucratization of the individual firm and to ensure that all employers shared the burden of workers' welfare through a citywide group insurance plan. In turn, this coordinated effort would create a regionally stable, more predictably healthy (and hence "insurable") workforce.

The Kingsport project was an exercise in regional stabilization and planning, an antecedent to experiments conducted later in the decade by firms in Rochester, Seattle, and Wisconsin. The consultants at ISB had witnessed government's efforts at planning during World War I. Now they attempted to demonstrate that private-sector planning, centered around the private provision of welfare, could take its place. Unfortunately for Metropolitan, they never turned this particular project into a successful business venture. By the end of the 1920s Metropolitan still spent far more money in Kingsport than it collected in premiums.

To keep employers sold on these ideas, insurers told employers what they wanted to hear, providing a spectrum of reasons why employers might choose to implement welfare programs. For the large firms, Metropolitan told them, "group insurance enables the employer to reestablish that personal contact with [its] employees and that sympathetic interest in the welfare of the employees' home folks, which tends to become lost in this age of machinery." For companies facing excessive public scrutiny, "group insurance gives the employer excellent publicity of the right sort." This was a partnership that would enable firms to reach a key social political goal: "The certificate of insurance and the Metropolitan Service go into the worker's home and create there appreciation of the employer's generosity and thoughtfulness, thus winning over to him many a fireside ally back in the home."[54]

To follow through on this promise, Metropolitan expended great effort to communicate with workers directly about the benefits of the employer's group life insurance policy. Workers had to learn to view the corporation as their caretaker, or as Metropolitan liked to refer to itself, their "family rather than their enemy." An early group promotional piece claimed that Metropolitan group insurance also came with "a sales service whose primary objective is to 'sell' the Group idea thoroughly to your employees after you have provided the protection."[55] Workers often resented employer insurance policies. Since workers faced frequent layoffs, they preferred to invest for their family's welfare in what they perceived as a more reliable organization than the firm: the local ethnic society or mutual benefit fund.[56] PSB designed pay envelope leaflets, or "payroll-o-grams," and posters on the protection offered by their group plan. It prepared letters to be sent to new employees and their families explaining the benefits allotted by the group plan. It even published employee magazines for other companies. By the mid-1930s PSB annually distributed approximately 1.3 million payroll-o-grams on employer-provided insurance benefits. PSB stated its goal clearly: "to keep employees sold and continuously aware of the benefits of their Group protection."[57] Payroll leaflets carrying messages of corporate beneficence became especially useful to management as more group insurance policies became contributory during the 1920s. Employees might see deductions in their paycheck, but management was providing something more valuable in their stead: future compensation for the family.

Insurers used gendered sales pitches when they seemed expedient.

Both Metropolitan and Equitable tips to sales agents often stressed idealized family gender roles. In Equitable's *Suggestions for Selling Group Insurance*, sales pitch number 7 advised the agent to draw a diagram showing the personal relationships and roles of manhood established, or restored, by group insurance:

> Here is the situation. (Salesman here draws diagram showing the man as the connecting link in the chain of industrial life between his work and his home.)
>
> 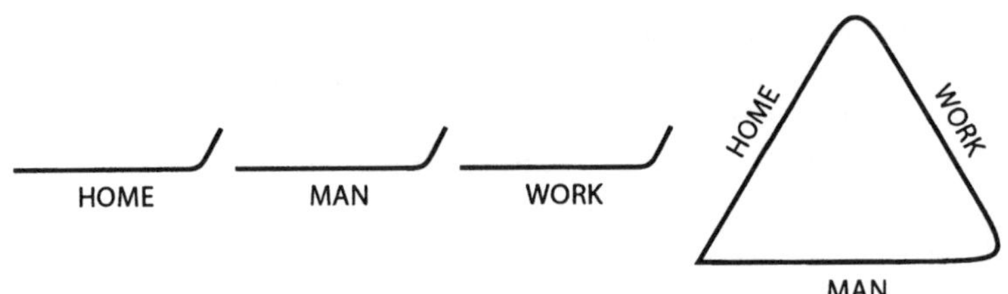
>
>
> Group insurance can bring them together.

Thus, insurers were willing to market patriarchal family relationships if it hooked the client. Yet, when it came to the literature on the policies themselves, insurers usually strove for gender-neutral language. In public statements and policy literature they used the terms *employee* and *dependents*. Equitable stated explicitly that "all employees actively at work at the time the contract goes into effect are eligible for coverage, regardless of age, sex, or color" and that there would be "no restrictions as to suicide, age, sex."[58]

Certainly, advocates of private group insurance contended that it protected men's breadwinning role and by extension the family—the family wage ideal. Insurers used the same language as proponents of social insurance: the policy would continue the paycheck, "protect the pay envelope." Yet, the family wage was a distant ideal for most workers, and group insurance did not necessarily make it a reality. In the face of organized labor's attempts to win higher wages by calling for a family wage (for men), employers could use group insurance to avoid paying an actual family wage. They could continue to pay the same individual wage but claim to provide enough for the worker's family as well; a life insurance policy would give the family one more year of wages if the worker died while in the company's employ. Subsidized by dividends, the life insurance policy did not cost the company as much as higher wages would.

While group insurance could be used as a surrogate for an actual family wage, this was not necessarily the intention of the insurance companies. Insurers did not want to be responsible for suppressed wages, and promotional literature made sure to state that a group insurance policy should not serve as a substitute for good wages or raises. Employers, however, could ultimately decide how to structure wages and benefits.

Interestingly, in response to claims by both public social insurance advocates and group insurers, Mary Van Kleeck, director of industrial research at the Russell Sage Foundation, argued that the insurance model ignored the reality and needs of working-class women. First, both were founded upon the principle of replacing a lost male wage, erroneously assuming that the loss of women's wages did not have a serious impact on the family's economic security. Second, neither of these insurance models took into account the conditions of women's work, which could militate against the effectiveness of insurance. "To name but four of their handicaps," Van Kleeck explained, "in most industries they are paid low wages, in manufacturing they are concentrated in seasonal occupations, in many occupations they are working long hours, and they are employed largely in unskilled, monotonous, fatiguing tasks or in casual, unorganized industries . . . ; and the mother who works for wages and bears children at the same time is believed by many to need special protection in the form of maternity insurance." Thus, she advised those working on the problems of poverty and industrial employment to put aside ideal prescriptions of family gender roles and focus on real conditions of the family economy. She doubted that payroll-based or contributory insurance, public or private, could fully sustain families in their struggle for economic independence.[59]

The Policyholders' Service Bureau and Economic Management

The elaboration of this employment-based private welfare system required stabilizing the employment relationship and the business cycle. Insurance, after all, depended on predictability. Consequently, PSB also offered clients advice on personnel management, industrial and personnel research, budgeting, regional planning, and the construction of internal labor markets. The bureau became a management consulting agency operating from within the Metropolitan, helping to create the conditions necessary for the institutionalization of group insurance. According to PSB, if managers were to realize the advantages of group insurance, they must first create a controlled, standardized workplace. Businessmen had to learn to control circumstances around them—markets, costs, business cycles, and workers; they needed, in short, to exchange drift for mastery. PSB offered a mélange of concepts and strategies that I will term *social science management.* Social science management combined the ideas of industrial psychologists, social workers, economists, medical scientists, labor consultants, industrial sociologists, and the more orthodox disciples of Frederick Taylor. Through service companies such as Metropolitan, this cluster of ideas on employment policies would be consciously spread by leading American firms in a slow but steady fashion. PSB and group insurance service divisions enabled insurance companies to exercise great influence over the personnel practices of large employers.

Charged with the responsibility of marketing mass-based industrial security, PSB had an extraordinary mission to fulfill. Haley Fiske recruited research-oriented experts to create a service bureau that could accomplish these goals and participate fully in experiments to reconfigure industrial relations. In 1923 the Welfare Division's ISB and PSB merged into one organization, under the name Policyholders' Service Bureau. Fiske, now president of Metropolitan, brought in Henry Bruere to run the new PSB. Bruere's impressive résumé of reform activities and prestigious positions made him an excellent candidate for combining welfare concerns and research to create pragmatic solutions to managerial problems. Educated at the University of Chicago—where he studied with Thorstein Veblen, George Vincent, and Wesley Mitchell—and Harvard Law School, Bruere began his career as a settlement house worker in Boston. He then moved into corporate welfare work when Gwendolyn Beeks, affiliated with the settlement house movement in Chicago, hired him to work with her at International Harvester. Bruere administered the cultural and educational institute at the McCormick Works. It was the great age of corporate mergers, and several manufacturers of agricultural implements had merged to form International Harvester. Bruere's circle of reformist acquaintances had been debating the merits and consequences of the new trusts. Bruere accepted the job at International Harvester in order to work on "the social problems growing out of the expansion of industry." Rather than subscribing to the trust-busting view, Bruere thought that social problems resulting from the imbalance of economic power could be solved from within the corporation. "The good that can be accomplished through government action is relatively unimportant as compared with the service opportunities of commerce and industry," he later wrote.[60] After working at International Harvester, Bruere went to New York, where he became a leading figure in the municipal reform movement. He gained experience in administering major research projects and surveys while serving as director of the Bureau of Municipal Research from 1907 to 1914. In addition, he conducted investigations for the Association for the Improvement of the Condition of the Poor and the New York City Committee on Unemployment. He left the

Bureau of Municipal Research in 1916 to serve as president of the Board of Child Welfare of New York City and chairman of Mayor John Purroy Mitchel's Pension Committee of New York.[61]

Bruere developed expertise in several areas of municipal reform in addition to his work on welfare issues. He played a central role in the movement for fiscal reforms in city government and more efficient city management. Many of the proposals he advanced came from the corporate world, particularly railroads. In fact, even while thoroughly immersed in the world of municipal reform, Bruere maintained his contacts with the business sector. He served as a management consultant for the American Metal Company and the Rock Island Railroad Company, both of which later became Metropolitan group policyholders. In 1916 Bruere became a director of the railroad, and in his capacity as consultant he initiated a detailed study of the organization and policies of the company. Also in 1916 Bruere, along with Louis Brandeis, George Kirschwey, and Judge Noyes, served on a committee appointed to arbitrate an International Ladies Garment Workers' Union (ILGWU) strike. Thus, Bruere was an excellent choice for Metropolitan: he endeavored to link the corporate world and the reform movement, to balance fiscal control and social responsibility.[62]

Bruere chose to go outside of Metropolitan to staff PSB. Although life insurance clerks joined the unit, Bruere built a specialized research unit by recruiting social scientists and industrial engineers from academia, bringing in industrial engineers from the Wharton Graduate School of Business Administration and the Massachusetts Institute of Technology; specialists in the new field of industrial medicine from the Harvard Medical School; librarians; and social workers. During the years that Bruere ran the unit, he also relied on full-time or part-time consulting of several personnel experts, often affiliated with groups such as the Taylor Society, the Personnel Research Federation, and the vocational guidance movement. There were "trained investigators of industrial relations questions; . . . specialists in questions affecting the employment of women."[63] Clearly, group insurance was an ambitious project.

During its first decade PSB created four primary mechanisms for the dissemination among businessmen of current information on new management techniques. PSB's primary method consisted in amassing data on particular economic sectors and assembling reports to be sent out to group policyholders. Over the next two decades requests for these reports multiplied year by year. PSB research kept pace with the latest developments in personnel management, employee welfare programs, and workplace health and safety issues. In addition to these reports on specific aspects of management or specific industries, PSB developed three other programs in the 1920s: management consulting, a managers' journal, and a roundtable conference program. Metropolitan offered these services as soon as a potential client considered purchasing a group policy. Metropolitan used these services as both a marketing device and a means for preventing policy lapses.[64]

Initially, PSB reports drew as much on the internal management practices of Metropolitan as they did on policies of other companies. According to Henry Bruere, Metropolitan "sought to be a model in personnel relations."[65] During the years 1910–20 psychologists such as E. L. Thorndike, Walter Dill Scott, and Walter Bingham were just beginning to design methods that they believed could make psychology an applied discipline of use to corporate administrators. As early as 1915 Metropolitan commissioned Columbia's Thorndike to design psychological tests for the purpose of selecting and hiring clerical employees who did not have high school or commercial school degree.[66] The "scientific selection" of employees would increase productivity, Metropolitan believed, by choosing the person best suited for each task, thereby reducing a whole range of employment problems—accidents and injuries, dissatisfaction, small on-the-job acts of sabotage, absenteeism, and turnover.

Metropolitan had other incentives for developing standardized personnel policies. The high percentage of female employees in the home office also contributed to Metropolitan's early development of a variegated and hierarchical personnel system. Out of 7,000 home office employees 5,000 were women. Because of concerns about social improprieties raised by the presence of women in offices, white-collar firms, especially life insurance companies, focused on personnel issues much earlier than did most manufacturing firms. Office managers attempted to separate men and women physically by means of gender-designated lunchrooms, rest areas, elevators, hallways, and work areas. Managers arranged furniture and office space to emphasize the status differences between male and female employees. Not only did they design this differentiation into the physical space of the office but job specialization and job categories began to carry gender identities as well. In order to ensure that the male clerk's job was not degraded in terms of salary or status by the increasing presence of women in the office, office managers segmented the workplace along gender lines by using different job classification systems, psychological tests, and job ladders for women and men. Women would not move along the same track as men. Job ladders achieved this separation at Metropolitan Life, where men and women might start out in similar clerical positions but the men ultimately moved on to positions not open to women.[67] Thus, PSB could offer firsthand knowledge of welfare benefits, employee testing and selection, and internal bureaucracies.

Further, under the leadership of Bruere PSB flourished as a unique, research-based agency within Metropolitan. As Metropolitan's roster of group policies expanded, it took in more clients from a wider array of industrial and commercial sectors. At the beginning of 1925, with more than 1,900 group contracts, valued at $860 million, Metropolitan had more group life insurance in force than any other company in the world. Two years later Metropolitan had more than 2,500 group clients. Nor were these group policyholders solely high-profile, typical welfare capitalist firms. By the mid-1920s Metropolitan's client list would include large and small enterprises in chemicals, coal, transportation, textiles, banking, hospitals, food products, retail distribution, construction, electrical, leather and furs, paper and printing, lumber, and metals. These companies were located in southern, northern, and midwestern states.[68] Consequently, Metropolitan had an exceptionally diverse base of information and experience to draw on and translate into a collection of vast knowledge on American industry. With this breadth of access to American business, Metropolitan used PSB to sell its particular vision of social well-being and bring it into companies, large and small, in almost every sector of the economy and almost every region of the country.

Drawing on this information base, PSB distributed to all clients reports on the "labor relations" programs of these firms: profit sharing, Americanization, the eight-hour day, bonus systems, gradated wage incentives, lunchrooms, employee handbooks describing benefit packages (especially Metropolitan group life insurance), and employee magazines. In 1920 the bureau decided to initiate a service to provide policyholders with information about new processes and developments in their industries. Case studies included everything from printing to hosiery to banking. Publications such as *Promoting Laundry Employees* provided a case study on establishing a promotion plan consisting of "a fully worked out line of promotion."[69] Soon policyholder requests for industry-specific reports and for employee programs began to accumulate.

In the 1920s, PSB reports began to emphasize the pecuniary welfare work benefits that had become more prevalent after World War I. PSB distributed booklets such as *Industrial Thrift and Savings Plans, Employee Stock Ownership Plans,* and *Mutual Benefit Associations,* addressing both white-collar and blue-collar workplaces.[70] Their reports discussed the standards of Taylorist scientific management, such as bonus and incentive systems, instructing managers on how they could integrate a bonus system into a balanced budget. PSB viewed all these programs as compatible and complimentary, meshing scientific management's ideas on efficiency with psychology's ideas on individual happiness and human engineering and welfare capitalists' strategies for obtaining a loyal workforce.

PSB proposed the same programs for white-collar workers and blue-collar workers. Vacations, for example, were one of the key distinguishing features between white-collar and blue-collar workers. By the end of World War I most white-collar workers had shorter work weeks than blue-collar workers, longer pay periods, seniority, greater job security, and one or two weeks of paid vacation. Vacations, paid sick days, and disability insurance did not become general policy among manufacturing firms until after the Depression.[71] Nonetheless, PSB avidly promoted these policies for industrial workers based on the belief that rested, healthier workers produce more. Also, of course, Metropolitan sought ways to increase health and life expectancy among workers, the majority of their policyholders. In *The "Why" of a Vacation* PSB declared that "employers of manual labor are recognizing what employers of office workers learned many years ago—that an annual rest period gives a decided impetus to production . . . workers at machines, as well as those at desks, need periodic rests."[72] According to Metropolitan executives, vacation pay and sick pay were just as important as incentive schemes and productivity counting in accomplishing the goals of scientific management; safety and health measures on the job were necessary correlatives to supervisory monitoring and efficiency campaigns; health insurance, life insurance, and pensions should accompany basic wage compensation. Metropolitan, a white-collar firm, offered all of these programs, often before many other American companies. Metropolitan used PSB to promote among manufacturing firms policies that had already become well established in white-collar firms.

PSB promised businessmen that an engineering approach to the "human problem in industry" provided managers with "new and keener edged tools of control than were required in times gone by."[73] The orientation of PSB represented the characteristic view being spread in technocratic circles during the second and third decades of the century. On one level, working out the "human problem" entailed measuring and evaluating humans according to terms and methods used for machinery and resources. Just as the machines could be retooled to increase productivity, so could humans. PSB recommended "an extensive and admirable piece of personnel research" conducted by the Human Engineering Department of GE's West Lynn, Massachusetts, plant. According to PSB's study of West Lynn, the department aimed at "constant upward revision of the production possibilities for each individual through unremitting research which discloses improved processes and methods, through work sample tests which indicate the type of work for which the worker is best fitted, through selective transfer, promotion, and pensioning."[74] These mechanisms of bureaucratic control became ever more important as GE machinists, molders, core makers, and other workers walked out between 1920 and 1922, challenging and disrupting the flow of production.[75] The idiom of human engineering perpetuated the legitimacy of managerial determination of work rules, discipline, pace of work, and production in this new era of industrial democracy.

The model companies promoted by PSB viewed welfare as an integral part of the human engineering project. When describing their scientific management systems, the companies referred to their pension programs, unemployment compensation, mutual benefit funds, sickness funds, stock options, or employee credit unions. In particular, pensioning was a key strategy in human engineering. At Kodak, for example, executives were perturbed by the large number of older workers with high pay who did not want to retire, complaining that they were "deadweight" and "privileged senility." Kodak initiated a pension plan to clear out the older, less productive employees. Pennsylvania Railroad, which initiated a pension plan in 1901, acted similarly. Since the railroad brotherhoods had won seniority rights before the turn of the century, there were lots of older, longtime railroad employees; creating "youthful 'ports of entry' " figured heavily in the decision to install pension plans.[76]

The technical expertise of industrial engineering combined with welfare benefits offered employers an antidote to the growing workers' health and industrial hygiene movement that gathered strength through the early 1920s. Labor reform groups and unions wanted workers or their representatives to be the ones to define the problems of industrial disease and health hazards. Organizations such as the Workers' Health Bureau (WHB) and the National Consumers' League forced a public debate about how industrial health and safety problems should be handled, what groups or agencies should evaluate dangerous processes, and who had the ability and prerogative to determine acceptable levels of risk and tolerance on the job. The WHB, founded by two women who had come out of the consumer and labor movements, Grace Burnham and Harriet Silverman, contended that industrial safety and health issues were class issues that should be controlled by unions and workers rather than by managers and medical experts alone. Beginning in 1921 the WHB investigated shops and factories, collected data, and produced reports to help workers and unions in their negotiations with management. And following the earlier model of the National Consumers' League, they armed unions with the "sociological data" needed to lobby city councils and state legislatures for occupational safety laws. Defining itself as "the research adjunct to the union movement for health and safety," the WHB set out to make sure that unions had precise and technical information about workplace conditions, health hazards, safety violations, and the causes and consequences of industrial diseases and injuries. The WHB and the National Consumers' League sought to make industrial health controversies matters of public concern and political intervention.

Management consultants insisted that this was strictly a business management problem, involving technical issues to be solved internally by technical experts. As Claudia Clark has shown in her case study of radium workers, employers often hired scientific consultants and medical experts to verify safe production procedures, to avoid or control the cost of compensation to injured employees, or to stem further government regulation. Harvard Medical School's Department of Industrial Hygiene was funded entirely by business corporations between 1918 and 1922, with large contributions coming from companies such as GE and U.S. Steel. Insurance companies, and particularly Metropolitan's PSB, could help employers limit their own liability for industrial disease and inhibit worker or state interference in shop-floor conditions.[77]

PSB itself maintained an Industrial Hygiene Division "to correct unhealthful working conditions and eliminate unnecessary hazards in employment" among group insurance clients. By the 1920s PSB was assuring clients that by drawing on developments in the human sciences, social sciences, and social welfare milieu, as well as the mechanical sciences used by Taylor, managers could create "a sense of loyalty and interdependence between the company and the employee and between employee and employee."[78] The mental revolution of which Taylor spoke could be achieved if firms concerned themselves with health and security.

PSB's prescriptions for economic organization reflected the new technocratic diagnosis that economic and social instability resulted from a mismanagement of material and labor processes rather than from any intractable, fundamental conflict between social classes or between workers and managers. Therefore, unemployment, destitution, ill health, and social discontent could be solved, just like the problems of production and distribution, through better organization and management. This technocratic faith in rational bureaucratic management was embraced as much by labor leaders like Sidney Hillman as it was by liberals like Herbert Croly, Felix Frankfurter, and Louis Brandeis or by businessmen such as Henry Dennison and Edward Filene.[79] Although these were macroeconomic problems, Metropolitan's PSB contended that they could be resolved at the microeconomic level, the level of the individual business firm. Responsible business firms with the proper managerial tools could engineer economic and social security for their employees, firm by firm. Thus Metropolitan insisted that group insurance, bureaucratic personnel policies, and production stabilization had to be sold and implemented together.

Another road leading Metropolitan into consulting was investment. PSB effectively established the credibility of its consulting services through a large-scale project in the railroad industry. Even after World War I, railroads continued to be a particularly dangerous and turbulent sector. Riddled with accidents, deaths, labor upheavals, and regulatory conflicts, railroads also faced general organizational chaos and declining profits in the industry as a whole. Nonetheless, by 1923 Metropolitan had insured employees in eighteen railroad companies—about 110,000 policyholders. Moreover, Metropolitan maintained substantial investments in railroad bonds and had financed much of the railroad maintenance and expansion of recent years. Well over $300 million in steam railroad and equipment bonds amounted to more than 20 percent of Metropolitan's total investments.[80] Metropolitan, then, held a particular interest in stabilizing the railroad sector: to protect the future return on its investments.

Yet the operation of the railways was also a major political issue; in fact, it was one of the most high profile political issues of the early 1920s. Class conflict and struggle for power and control continued unabated along the railways well after the end of the war. Following a political struggle to nationalize the railroads, Congress instead created the Railroad Labor Board in 1920. This did not end the controversy, and labor and management continued to battle each other, as well as the Railroad Labor Board, culminating in a massive, national railroad strike in 1922. The federal government's attempts to resolve the crisis were inept. The Railroad Labor Board itself had become an object of acrimony from all sides. Nor could presidential intervention quiet things down. The future stability of the industry appeared as uncertain in 1923 as it had been in 1919.[81]

At this point the Interstate Commerce Commission reached out to Metropolitan, as a major financier of the railroads, to conduct a survey of railroad employee relations policies. PSB also received an invitation from executives at the Rock Island Railroad (former associates of Henry Bruere) to collaborate with them on developing a personnel program. After surveying conditions at Rock Island Railroad, PSB prepared a personnel program that the railroad adopted and successfully implemented. The ICC then encouraged the bureau to study the industrial relations policies and employee welfare programs of eight railroad companies. Although Bruere himself participated in the data collecting and interviews, PSB also brought in Otto Beyer, a Taylor Society industrial engineer and labor consultant to the Baltimore & Ohio Railroad.

These commissions offered PSB the perfect opportunity to combine investment concerns with their interest in employee welfare and innovative labor relations techniques. PSB's work culminated in 1925 with the publication of a 213-page book, *Personnel Management in the Railroads.* By offering personnel management as a solution to one of the fiercest labor contests of the postwar years, PSB sought to depoliticize the operation of the railways—to urge the adoption of a "method of settling wages which will not always result in controversy and dispute and threatened strike."[82] The bureau's personnel management suggestions offered a purportedly noncoercive and nonpolitical means of resolving disputes, diffusing potential problems by eliminating them, and providing workers with security through group insurance and pensions.

And PSB offered them "scientific" implementation of employee welfare programs. Railroads had long offered pensions, but by the 1920s many of these pension programs had run into financial trouble. Railroad executives had never calculated the long-term costs of such programs according to actuarial principles nor established the proper reserve funds to cover future retirees.[83] Insurance companies, however, were required by law to maintain sufficient reserves and pay out policies. PSB insisted that railroad seniority and job ladders could be soundly combined with welfare benefits and put on actuarial bases so that they would not become a source of labor strife in the future. This regularity and standardization, in turn, would encourage investment and thus assist the rejuvenation of the railroad sector.

Once PSB had established a reputation as a management expert through these projects, individual firms began inviting Metropolitan in to survey their practices and design programs for them. PSB's projects included an analysis of the New England Power Engineering and Service Corporation's experience of workmen's compensation loss; a booklet of safety rules and regulations for Mathieson Alkali Works; and a review of chemical handling procedures for Republic Steel Corporation. Again, Metropolitan provided business-friendly, private experts to resolve issues raised by the workers' health movement. PSB also serviced white-collar businesses such as banks, telephone exchanges, and financial services companies. Typically, large companies became welfare capitalist leaders because they had the resources to innovate and set up various programs. Yet by using Metropolitan's management consulting service, large and small companies could install new managerial practices.[84] This service offered benefits to both sides. Firms that could reduce safety problems and turnover improved their experience rating and so lowered their group insurance premiums. Metropolitan, in turn, benefited from these services because it could sell and maintain more group insurance.

Even companies that pioneered in modern management techniques sought the services of PSB. General Motors Corporation (GM) had implemented numerous managerial innovations since the duPont family assumed control of the company in 1920. Like GE, Kodak, and other welfare capitalist firms, GM carefully designed internal bureaucracies, industrial research programs, standardized recordkeeping and accounting procedures, and shop-floor managerial innovations.[85] As a member of the Special Conference Committee, GM also focused attention on employment management and newer, less overtly paternalistic forms of welfare work. GM became a Metropolitan group policyholder in 1926, when it purchased the largest group life insurance policy ever written. The policy covered 100,000 workers. After becoming a group client, GM regularly used the management consulting services of PSB, calling on PSB consultants to analyze a variety of internal employment issues. As GM moved toward more systematic labor policies, Metropolitan helped the company augment its employee welfare benefits. In 1928 Metropolitan expanded the group life policy to cover almost 200,000 workers, or $400 million in coverage. In addition, it drew up the largest group disability contract implemented up to that point.[86] Together, Metropolitan and GM tried to show workers and political reformers that business corporations could manage the hazards of industrial life in an unprecedented fashion.

The partnership between the Metropolitan Life Insurance Company and General Motors also reveals the integral link between the fledgling regulatory state and the welfare state. During this period GM was the subject of scrutiny by the industrial health movement over the issue of lead poisoning. GM had introduced tetraethyl lead into gasoline in 1922, and since then a number of workers had acquired lead-related illnesses. Despite rubber-stamp approval of the lead additive by the U.S. Bureau of Mines, public controversy grew in the mid-1920s. Under pressure from the National Consumers' League, the U.S. Public Health Service (PHS) sponsored a national conference to discuss the health hazards of tetraethyl lead.[87] By using the consulting services of Metropolitan's PSB, especially on workplace health and safety issues, GM could employ private, corporate-based expertise to solve issues that could potentially bring in the state. These issues could be treated privately as matters of scientific expertise, not those of social policy or labor. In turn, Metropolitan used GM as an advertisement for private welfare. Metropolitan distributed a public relations booklet made up solely of newspaper and journal editorials praising GM's group insurance policies. An article in the *Chicago Tribune* clearly staked the political terms: "[With this policy] we are getting some of the benefits which collectivists say can come only from the state. Experience in this country would suggest that, in liberality of wage scales and regard for the welfare of employees, private employers for the most part are more enlightened than government."[88]

In the name of peace between capital and labor, PSB, like other industrial reformers of the 1920s, recommended the use of specially trained managers, who could quickly detect workers' needs and grievances and generate bureaucratic solutions—bonuses, job titles, merit ratings, standardized job definitions and expectations—that met individuals' psychological needs.[89] Such a management order would create a more lasting employment relationship. With less turnover, executives could take full advantage of group insurance and thereby meet workers' needs for economic security as well.

PSB management consultants intended scientific intervention in the workplace to benefit workers, but they defined workers' needs in management's terms. As sellers of group insurance, Metropolitan needed firms to generate a well-functioning workplace in order to sustain these group insurance policies. Yet PSB's test of such a work regime was merely uninterrupted production and risk prevention. From PSB's point of view, the problem with labor turnover was that it "carries the germs which produce anemic conditions and sometimes precipitate a complete breakdown in production routine." Consequently, PSB's labor relations experts allowed workers' needs to be cast in terms that were defined by employers, namely, shop-floor stability, efficiency, and continuous production. They promoted the notion that workers' social and economic security, as well as industrial harmony, were automatically reflected in increased productivity; in turn, an uninterrupted production routine would ensure economic security. By linking group insurance with bureaucratic rationality, nonworkplace social welfare needs with workplace hierarchies and production imperatives, Metropolitan and other insurance companies reinforced the insulated managerial authority of the New Era factory regime.[90]

Did group insurance provide economic security for workers in the 1920s? It indeed brought life insurance and funeral benefits to many. More than 40 percent of wage earners had no life policies of their own, and many industrial workers could not obtain their own individual policies because industrial diseases, occupational injuries, and poor health prevented them from passing the necessary medical exams. Life insurance companies categorically denied individual policies to workers in designated hazardous industries. For those workers who did carry their own policies, the average industrial policy amounted to $500 or less. But group insurance did not require individual medical exams, and these life policies ranged from $1,100 to $1,600. Group insurance benefited white workers, who were more likely than nonwhites to work in companies that made some effort to regularize employment and stabilize production, laying down a cleavage that would persist for the rest of the century. Moreover, group insurance was more reliable than the ethnic mutual benefits societies, which often collapsed or overdrew in hard times. Thus, group life certainly added some measure of security to a family's economic difficulties.

But that was about all they got out of it. The comprehensive Montgomery Ward plan was rather exceptional in its breadth. A 1927 survey by the National Industrial Conference Board (NICB) found that only 10 percent of those covered by group life were also covered by group accident and health (disability) insurance. Employers could choose different benefits, as well as different durations of benefits, anywhere between thirteen and twenty-six weeks. While group life was paid for entirely by the employer in most cases, disability, which usually required higher premiums, was most often contributory (jointly paid for by employees and employers) or entirely paid for by employees. Companies had to put heavy pressure on their employees to "sign up" for these policies. Most workers refused, especially when employers continued to deduct premium payments even when working hours or wages declined. Consequently, at the time of the Depression group life insurance covered 4.5 million workers, while group disability covered only 1.2 million. The numbers dropped even lower for pensions. In each of NICB's surveys of firms from 1927 to 1933, the percentage of firms that provided group pensions was 2 percent for firms with more than 250 employees and 0.2 percent for firms with fewer than 250 employees. In 1933 fewer than 200,000 persons had group pension or annuity coverage. For all three types of coverage, workers in larger establishments received higher benefits. Group insurance offered the most to those who worked in establishments with 10,000 or more employees.[91]

The industrial self-regulation movement of the 1920s could not remedy the structural problems in American capitalism. As each of Herbert Hoover's remedies failed to reverse the course of the Great Depression, new political remedies were pushed to the foreground. While the antiunion versions of microregulation and firm-centered employment stabilization were discredited during the early 1930s, the tenets of personnel management formulated by PSB became well established. In the long run, PSB and Metropolitan had helped to lay the foundations of the industrial order that would enable group insurance to flourish after the Depression had passed. Although Metropolitan and Equitable would adjust their ideas and proposals to accommodate the new presence of the federal government in employment issues and social welfare, they maintained their belief that American business enterprises could provide for the welfare needs of the nation's citizens. The New Deal would usher in a new industrial relations system based on collective bargaining. It would not, however, significantly alter the development of private-sector benefits.

In fact, the existence of this burgeoning private alternative and its incorporation into the New Deal industrial relations system of firm-based collective bargaining fundamentally shaped the course of development of New Deal policies during and after the 1930s. The struggle against social insurance and government intervention in the employment relation, the original impetus for group insurance, continued unabated. With the help of insurance companies like Metropolitan and Equitable, welfare capitalism would survive the New Deal. Ultimately, Metropolitan found itself promoting a contradictory prescription that would continue to haunt economic and social planners even in the post–World War II era. Metropolitan espoused minimum standards for conditions of employment and employee compensation regardless of sector or region. But by insisting that these standards could be met on a firm-by-firm basis, Metropolitan in fact undermined these goals. Although the New Deal would usher in nationwide wage and hours standards, old-age pensions, and unemployment insurance, the elaboration of private-sector social benefits through a combination of welfarism and social science–based managerial control enabled employers to limit the terms of public and private social provision.

2

Industrial Pensions

EFFICIENCY AND SECURITY

WHILE group insurance laid the foundation for the modern system of private, employment-based social welfare, industrial pensions did not immediately develop from group insurance. Insurance companies were not the only source of old-age and disability benefits in the early decades of the twentieth century; in fact, they were a relatively insignificant source, covering only 2 percent of the employees under industrial plans. Instead, American workers enrolled in pension plans provided by fraternal societies, labor unions, and self-insured employers. While each offered something unique in administration and employee choice, these schemes all shared an overriding characteristic: unsound, unplanned financing. It was not until the economy turned down at the end of the 1920s that employers began to consult actuaries, set aside pension reserves, or purchase insured pensions. Surprisingly, the Great Depression finally allowed private insurers to have a serious impact on industrial pensions—as consultants, underwriters, and public relations promoters.

By the time Franklin D. Roosevelt took office as president, one-quarter of the American working population was unemployed. Many of those who remained employed did so through work-sharing programs or part-time jobs, but employers eliminated older or slower workers in order to sustain earnings through higher efficiency and output. As the consumerist prosperity of the 1920s collapsed, economic and social instability deepened. Neither municipal governments, private charities, nor employers appeared to handle sufficiently the economic distress. After three years of despair and passivity, broken sporadically by communist-orchestrated demonstrations, unemployed workers and families without income began actively to demand some governmental support when there was no opportunity to work.[1] In this climate of political upheaval, grass-roots political movements—especially movements of the aged unemployed—and the Roosevelt administration pushed economic security to the center of national politics in the mid-1930s. Unorganized pressure far removed from any polity structures or state institutions provoked major transformations in both private and public social welfare.

Throughout the second and third decades of the century, debates over economic support programs such as old-age pensions or unemployment compensation focused on the goal of labor market regulation and incentives to businesses to rationalize production processes. Labor reformers such as John R. Commons and John Andrews of the AALL, as well as progressive businessmen, emphasized the goals of efficiency and prevention (of accidents and layoffs) over social welfare support for workers; insurance companies offering industrial welfare programs likewise stressed industrial efficiency. But with the Great Depression, efficiency gave way to workers' security as the objective of social insurance for wage earners.[2]

Far from disappearing, welfare capitalism persisted as a strategy business used to adapt to pressure from workers and the state during the Great Depression and the New Deal era. In order to gauge how welfare capitalists adapted to the economic and political upheavals of the 1930s, it is necessary to look closely at what was actually occurring within firms and within the realm of industrial welfare, particularly with industrial pensions. Yet, in addition, these developments must be placed within the larger context of the political struggle between managers and workers that occurred over the balance of social and political power within the broader polity. During the Depression, employers would have to respond to the political agitation of popular movements in California and other states and to elites in Washington, D.C., for social reform, as well as to their own internal fiscal problems and competitive anxieties. Insurers began to convince employers that while discontinuing welfare programs might seem an effective economic response, the most effective political response was to follow through on the promises of welfare capitalism.

Old-Age Security, 1910–1928

In the early part of the century, workers sought a measure of economic security through fraternal societies, ethnic lodges, or trade unions. Until the early 1920s, fraternal societies underwrote one-third of all life insurance plans. Modeled on the friendly societies in England, fraternal insurance associations offered insurance at a much lower cost than regular life companies did. They could do so largely because they were not required to carry large reserves to meet benefit claims. By the time of World War I, when membership peaked at more than 5 million persons, the fraternals had also added disability and old-age benefits. Within a few years, however, it became clear that the fraternals were not charging rates adequate to pay claims, especially old-age benefits.

In the 1920s, fraternals began reining in their policies, reducing membership and benefit amounts. When a series of financial scandals undermined public faith in the fraternals, they began to spend more money on publicity and advertising. They began merging with ethnic lodges, thus attenuating the links between mutual benefit societies and particular ethnic communities. These expenses, combined with the greater costs of actuarially calculated contributions, led to the swift deterioration of fraternals as a source of worker security. After the mid-1920s, fraternals represented only 15 percent of the life insurance business.[3]

African Americans were particularly likely to build fraternal organizations that provided insurance-type benefits. While black fraternals offered predominantly burial benefits, there were some, such as the New York City Benevolent Society, that offered funds to members who "by reason of sickness or infirmity, or either, [would] be incapable of attending to their usual vocation or employment." In the 1890s, industrial insurance companies such as Prudential adopted scientific racism, claiming that African Americans were an unfit race, unable to survive in the long run, and hence began dropping black policyholders or charging extraordinarily high premiums. So African Americans began to turn more toward their own organizations. Yet, black fraternals suffered from many of the same problems as their white counterparts. Because they were subject only to loose control by state authorities, there were often frauds, mismanagement, and insolvencies. Many of the major black fraternals collapsed in the early 1920s. Black life insurance companies stepped in to fill the vacuum, but their clients—working-class and poor African Americans—mainly bought industrial insurance to provide for funeral and burial costs. Throughout the 1920s and 1930s, policy lapsation rates were extremely high, as African Americans struggled to meet the costs of subsistence.[4]

Workers could also enroll in pension plans through unions. With the exception of railroad brotherhoods, union pension programs tended to be in different industries from those in which company plans existed; skilled craft unions, such as building trades unions, granite cutters, and printers—unions that generally excluded African Americans or nonwhites—had pension plans. Union plans offered a unique advantage that other options did not, namely, a voice for the workers, but they suffered from the same financial weaknesses as did other fraternal plans. Labor union plans were democratically run: members could vote on age and service requirements, financing, contributions, and benefit amounts. Unlike company pensions, union plans usually included survivor benefits for widows. Individuals could choose whether to participate. Of course, democratic decision making had its drawbacks. Often, a union executive board would approve a pension plan, but the membership would vote against it. Younger workers refused to be assessed to pay for benefits for older workers. Pensions approved by the boards of the International Jewelry Workers Union, the International Association of Machinists, the Pattern Makers League, the Order of Railroad Telegraphers, and the Plumbers and Steamfitters never went into operation because votes were overturned or reversed. In general, union plans underwent numerous, perpetual changes and even complete abolitions, much more so than employer pension plans.

The frequent modifications reflected the financial instability of trade union pensions. Oriented more toward disability and dismemberment compensation rather than old age, they did not plan or build an old-age reserve that could pay out benefits over an extended period of time. When the union confronted a large group of aged members ready to retire, the leadership voted to provide funds for the immediate needs of that particular group of needy aged but not to implement a permanent system of levying assessments to build a reserve fund. The bricklayers faced a deficit of $60,000 in 1916. Thus, old-age benefits functioned more like charity than pensions. Even unions that had worked out a steady system of assessments worried that they could not sustain it. The International Typographical Union established an old-age pension in 1908, assessing each member 0.5 percent of his individual earnings. By 1916 there were more than fourteen hundred pensioners on the rolls. Assessments just about equaled expenditures. The union's president, while clearly proud of the fund, also lamented that "these benefit features are not themselves insured. Their stability and future existence depend entirely upon laws and regulations which may from time to time be changed by the members." He predicted that in the long run workers alone would not be able to finance the weight of old-age social support.[5]

Indeed, in the 1920s, declining new membership and stagnating wages made it impossible to provide a solid financial base for trade union pensions. Lower-paid, younger workers often decided not to enroll in such plans. While 20 percent of all trade unionists (1.6 million persons) belonged to a union that had a pension plan in 1928, only about 12 percent were actually covered by the pension plan. At the same time, the number of retirees and benefits increased dramatically. By the end of the 1920s all trade union pensions faced acute financial problems owing to "unanticipated increases in expenditures." In 1928–29 Murray Latimer, a consultant for the Industrial Relations Counselors, conducted a study of union pensions in conjunction with the American Federation of Labor Research Department. He concluded that "the experiments are far from having reached a sound basis and that unless drastic financial reorganization is made, they are almost certain to end in failure in the relatively near future."[6]

Some workers had a third alternative: employer plans. Until the 1930s, firms with industrial pension programs almost always provided their own in-house plans. Industrial pensions initially spread through the railway industry, a sector in which companies needed to coordinate large, far-flung workforces and regulate independent field supervisors. Having implemented seniority and promotion systems early on, railroads found themselves with long-service workers who earned increasingly higher wages by the turn of the century. Pensioning offered a seemingly benign mechanism for discharging older, slower, more highly paid workers and hiring younger ones, and the practice spread rapidly among railroads, as did the purchase of group life and accident insurance. By the early 1920s, pension plans covered 84 percent of all railroad employees; coverage reached 1.5 million railroad workers by 1927. Banks and public utilities, including street railways, telephone, and telegraph companies, soon followed, setting up their own plans in the first decade of the twentieth century. Manufacturing firms implemented pensions in the World War I era and the 1920s. But many sectors remained virtually untouched by pensions. Coverage was negligible or nonexistent among sales enterprises, hotels and restaurants, and mining, auto, construction, and motion picture firms. Likewise, hardly any workers in the South, except for railroad workers, came under company pensions. A worker was more likely to have pension coverage if she or he was white and worked in an atypically large firm, generally very large companies with more than 8,000 workers. Eighty-seven of the largest corporations claimed some sort of pension plan (GM being one of the exceptions). By 1929 most of the pension plans clustered in railroads, utilities, iron and steel, oil, and electrical machinery and supplies.[7]

During the early decades of the twentieth century the typical pension plan was noncontributory: the employer carried the entire cost. Management preferred noncontributory plans because they seemed to offer full control of every element—contributions, benefit amounts, retirement qualifications, actual granting of benefits upon retirement, duration or suspension of pension payments. Self-insured noncontributory plans rarely adhered to any planned schedule of contributions, however, so employers did not have to follow any anticipated program of benefits. A survey of more than four hundred firms conducted by the Industrial Relations Counselors in 1928 found 115 different formulas for calculating benefits. Benefits generally had no relation to contributions. Management could decide at the time of retirement what to pay, if anything at all. Since the noncontributory plan was based entirely on company contributions, the employer had no moral obligation to pay up.

Nor did companies have any legal obligation to do so. No statutory law existed regarding the contractual status of pensions, and so workers and employers had to rely on court decisions. The body of case law built up in the first three decades of the twentieth century held that no contractual relation existed between employees and the company regarding retirement benefits. When workers sued over unpaid pension benefits, the courts ruled that the amount due did not constitute compensation for services. Instead, from the first case in 1898, *McNevin v. Solvay Process Company*, to cases involving Morris and Company meatpackers, Consolidated Edison in New York, and others in the 1920s, the courts saw monies put aside for employee pensions as "gifts" from the employer, "a mere benefaction." Even when an employee had fulfilled all the stated requirements for earning the pension, concluded a federal judge in *Eiszner v. Wilson and Company Inc.* (1929), "it is impossible to sustain the claimant's contention that the establishment of a pension fund created an obligation on the part of that company to pay." Courts insisted that employees had no legal right to the pension money.[8]

Consequently, employers treated pensions as trivial costs. One Metropolitan Life Insurance Company representative lamented that executives "give no more attention to it than they do to the purchase of lead pencils."[9] Whether small or large, the majority of companies failed to make any systematic effort to put monies aside for the purpose of paying benefits. Rather than accumulating funds that could earn interest and hence pay for benefits alone, most employers chose to pay pension benefits out of current operating expenditures. When someone came up for retirement, the company took money out of that year's budget to begin paying the pension. In other instances firms might put aside money in flush years and then use the funds for something else in dry years. Not only did they not set aside a trust fund for benefits but companies rarely budgeted for funding the administrative activities of a pension system, thus adding more unexpected costs. In the 1920s, 60 percent of firms claiming to have pension programs had made no provision to meet accruing liabilities. Another 24 percent had provided for reserve funds on their balance sheets but had not actually put any money aside. Only 16.2 percent of firms surveyed had set up a separate trust fund or had an insurance company underwrite the plan. Even fewer were considered to be actually sound enough to pay benefits over time. Accrued liabilities essentially remained unfunded.[10]

Employers avoided insurance company plans because they involved certain standards and procedures to which management was not ready to commit. First, in order to spread the risk sufficiently—a basic actuarial principle—group insurance retirement annuities necessitated that a large percentage of the workforce participate. This made it more difficult for employers to privilege some classes of employees over others, such as offering coverage only to executives or skilled craftsmen. Second, the policies cost more money up front. Insurance companies front-loaded premiums with "extra" costs in order to account for all potential risks in the long run. Higher premium rates up front assured that sufficient funds would exist to pay the pension but required employers to make the commitment early on to the pension. As for retirements owing to incapacitation, insurance company disability policies did not begin payments until six months after disability, and they placed a tight cap on disability benefits, which were often limited to just 25 percent of aggregate pay. Contrary to employer preference, insurers encouraged contributory plans. Such plans, however, required a more complex system of accounting and recordkeeping. Workers also had some vested equity in the plan. If an employee left employment before retirement, insurance companies would return the employee's contributions, sometimes even with interest. Thus, theoretically, if the policy had been paid up and the worker met the requirements for tenure of service, she or he would actually receive a pension, regardless of management's opinion. Group annuities conferred at least the pretense of contractualism. And as the National Industrial Conference Board found, "The large majority [of employers] expressly reject the contractual theory and with it the principle of legal liability for pensions in any form."[11]

Insured pensions or formal pensions with separate trusts were rare. Most companies offered so-called informal, or discretionary, plans. Under a discretionary plan the employee filed his or her request for retirement and pension benefits at the designated age (65–70 for men, 60 for women), and a management pension board reviewed his or her record. The board decided what to pay based on behavioral factors, such as work performance, cooperation with the foreman, the absentee and tardiness record, participation in labor disturbances, or even conduct outside the workplace.[12] If management decided that the employee met its criteria as they happened to stand on that day, the petitioner won a pension. Salary roll employees, especially well-paid executives, had a much better chance than payroll employees of receiving a pension. At U.S. Steel, semiskilled and unskilled workers made up 75 percent of the workforce, but they accounted for only 20 percent of those receiving pensions. In the oil industry, pensions all fell in the range of twelve hundred dollars and over, while at American Telephone and

Telegraph (AT&T) nine former executives received almost half the pension payments made by the company.[13] Moreover, that management granted the pension was no guarantee that the retiree would receive it in perpetuity. Employers often reserved the right to revoke benefits. AT&T maintained a discretionary pension plan beginning in 1913. Besides reserving the right to discontinue or change the plan, AT&T declared that benefits could be stopped at any time "for acts prejudicial to the interests of the company." Even companies that had an actual trust fund maintained the "right" to cancel benefits for those already on the pension rolls. They could also require pensioners to return to work or break a strike.[14] In other situations, pension benefits only extended for a limited duration, such as five years. Company plans rarely included any widow's benefits. A pension was a discretionary gift from the employer.

Management consultants and professional business organizations, like the courts, accepted the discretionary plan as a perfectly legitimate option—one solution among equally valued choices. In 1925 NICB offered support for discretionary, informal plans. "This large arbitrary element in the situation is viewed by many employers as a distinct advantage over a more formal scheme in that, on the one hand, it allows greater flexibility and adjustment to the individual case and, on the other, enables the employer to keep his pension expense at a minimum." NICB cited the "moral superiority" of paternalistic discretion "over any more impersonal procedure." Indeed, NICB suggested that the discretionary plan might be quite effective in realizing the goals of the American Plan, from preventing strikes and unionization to speeding up work, attracting skilled and loyal workers, and reducing turnover. "It is a significant fact," the study noted, "that most pension plans, as at present conducted, make the award in every case dependent on the discretion of the employer. . . . Indeed, the efficacy of the promise for stimulating continuity or quality of service depends in large measure on the employee's realization that the pension may be withheld in the event of his service falling short of expectation on either score."[15] A sense of insecurity on the part of the employees, then, gave the program its incentive or deterrent qualities. Although the study suggested that formal plans were probably a safer bet, for financial and industrial relations reasons, installing a plan that had neither money nor rules behind it was considered an employer prerogative.

Not only was it legally acceptable for employers "to frame a pension plan which will constitute no legal liability and which may be completely abolished at any time;"[16] it was politically possible to allow such lapses. On the one hand, the labor movement's attitude toward employer pensions ranged from ambivalent to hostile. On the other hand, reformers who had been crowing about old-age dependency and old-age insecurity for almost two decades had made little headway. Prior to World War I, progressives, distrustful of the workings of patronage politics, had usually blocked pension legislation or efforts to expand Civil War pensions into a more general, working-class old-age retirement system.[17] After the war, the new political ideology of progressives such as Herbert Hoover stressed the potential of business institutions to regulate and control the causes of economic insecurity. In the 1920s, when mainstream political economic ideology seemed to exchange laissez-faire precepts for those of economic management, proponents of New Era planning believed business managers and firms could regulate and stabilize business and employment cycles themselves.[18]

Welfare capitalist spokesmen like Henry Dennison told employers that welfare work "paid." In the 1910s and 1920s, organizations such as the National Civic Federation, the Taylor Society, the Special Conference Committee, the Industrial Relations Counselors, and Metropolitan's PSB promoted pecuniary welfare programs as tools of effective bureaucratic administration. Employers lost real dollars and cents because of labor discontent, and intensifying the pressure from line foremen could not make up the costs. Instead, "scientifically" engineered welfare benefits could achieve targeted economic results: stabilization of employment, reduction of strikes, and higher productivity.[19] Whether or not welfare capitalism achieved any of the so-called economic goals, and employers rarely had evidence that it did, this argument remained salient among large, highly bureaucratized firms.

Industrial pensions meshed well with the functionalism of scientific management and the increasingly mechanized workplace. Pension consultants and welfare capitalist proponents claimed not only the usual repertoire of results—lower turnover, higher morale and productivity—but also the elimination of superannuated, less fit employees who could not run the machinery as fast as others. In the early twentieth century, social scientists and physicians discovered the "problems" of old age as a matter of social and economic concern. Beginning in the 1910s they produced studies of work and fatigue, nervous strain, and tension in which they described older workers as "burned out," "used up," "exhausted." Drawing on a new body of health literature, group insurance safety consultants and personnel managers blamed older workers for higher accident rates and advised keeping them out of a long list of jobs. As scientific management proponents, economists, and physicians focused attention on the efficiency and productivity of workers, they sought means not only to heighten the productivity of workers but also to eliminate the drag caused by older workers who could not keep up with enforced speedups. At the same time, employers wanted to hold on to middle-aged workers, whom they believed to be more stable. Retirement programs and pensions met both these exigencies.[20]

Pensions, then, were an instrumental solution to the problems of workforce management. "The older worker . . . is a subject in human engineering which calls for intelligence of the first order," Roderic Olzendam, director of industrial relations at Metropolitan's PSB, told a conference of business managers. The problem of the older worker had to be dealt with in the same way that managers handled "mechanical, hydraulic, and electrical engineering."[21] Pension advocates referred to older employees in terms of "liabilities" and "assets." A NAM representative recommended pensioning older workers because "as human machinery they have depreciated to a point where their continued employment is unprofitable if not actually hazardous." While pension advocates acknowledged employers' humanitarian motive to care for their loyal, long-service workers, this concern usually followed other goals—increased production efficiency, reduced accident rates, reduced extra payroll costs, opening of promotion possibilities for younger workers, and fewer strikes and labor disturbances—in discussions of retirement systems. Employers installed pension systems for the purpose of selecting the right labor force and removing inefficient workers, and increasingly pensions carried mandatory retirement clauses.[22] The ethos of scientific management and microregulation encouraged experimentation with group insurance and other employee programs, but the ideology focused on these tools as a means to reach production goals; it was not sufficient to encourage a commitment to security.

Insurance companies likewise relied on the language of human engineering when promoting group life insurance and annuities in the period before the Depression. Although they also referred to old-age security, since after all it was their business to assure people continuing income, they followed the dominant discourse in discussions of old-age pensioning and superannuation of aging workers. A Metropolitan executive summed the issue as follows: "Each year a number—and probably a steadily growing number—of employees, with longer and longer terms of service, will reach the age of diminishing returns or incapacity. The employer is faced with the problem of human disposal." Yet he also acknowledged that a pension plan should constitute "a pledge of security to him for life." Metropolitan group insurance representatives instructed their agents to tell employers that "the problem of human obsolescence is similar to that of equipment depreciation and the same sound practice of building up reserves should be applicable to both." Insurers did consider workers' needs, among a long list of other motives.[23]

Under such a system few workers ever received a pension. The service requirements often were particularly prohibitive. Only 4–5 percent of men worked at the same firm for more than twenty years. Female employees were even less likely to meet the long-service requirements: at most 3 percent of women worked for the same firm for more than twenty years. In general, industrial pensions did not explicitly exclude women. The majority of company plans studied by the *Monthly Labor Review* in 1926 specifically included women, usually designating a younger retirement age than for male employees; out of 133 companies surveyed, only one specifically limited the pension plan to male employees. But any break in employment—say, for maternity or child care reasons—set the service clock back to day one. Both male and female employees lost any claim to benefits if they left the company before retirement age. Smaller companies tended to have contributory pensions, which theoretically gave the worker some equity in the plan. But these workers, too, rarely saw the pension money in the end. Smaller companies tended to discontinue pension plans at a high rate. (In fact, contrary to accepted wisdom about welfare capitalism, large companies with noncontributory plans rarely discontinued them.) In other situations, employers never actually made their contributions and let employees carry the entire plan. Ultimately, workers' contributions were simply not sufficient to pay benefits. While the industrial pensions movement claimed coverage for about 4 million persons in 1930, fewer than 2 percent of all retired workers received an industrial pension. Contemporary observers were well aware of this reality. Pension consultants such as Murray Latimer, many insurance actuaries, and even welfare capitalists themselves concluded that the likelihood of an employee's actually getting any benefits from a self-administered plan was exceedingly slim.[24]

Welfare Capitalism and the Politics of the Depression

The Great Depression represented a profound challenge to industrial pension endeavors. Unemployed workers, especially older workers, who faced slim prospects for reemployment, began expressing their frustration and desperation through public demonstrations, insisting that they had a right to economic support, a right that the state should enforce. Insurers and management consultants urged employers to respond by taking corporate welfare programs more seriously. They attempted to mobilize a serious defense of the private programs, to nudge employers toward reforming from within.

The downturn in the economy coincided with a demographic predicament. By the end of the 1920s the first generation of long-service workers under pensions began to retire. While the number of pensioners in the total workforce was minuscule, those companies that actually paid out pensions found that both the number of pensioners and the amount of pension payments increased rapidly after 1927. In general, older workers (45–64 years) were making up a larger proportion of the workforce. In 1920 they constituted 21.8 percent of nonfarm workers; by 1930, 24 percent. The iron and steel industry saw the proportion of workers aged 45–54 rise 61 percent, and the proportion of workers aged 55–64, rise 142 percent. Oil refining, meatpacking, agricultural implements, and coal mining also experienced aging of the workforce. In particular, firms that had established maximum hiring ages along with pensions faced aging workforces. Business organizations such as the American Management Association, the NAM, the Industrial Relations Counselors, and NICB and professional research organizations such as the Social Science Research Council, the AALL, the American Statistical Association, and even Metropolitan's PSB began writing voluminously on "this newcomer on our industrial stage," "The Older Man in Industry."[25] At one conference on the subject, an Equitable executive advised employers to take note "that there are more men over 45 numerically and relatively in industry to-day than at any other peacetime period."[26] This trend became especially pronounced during the Depression. With fewer new people being hired and fewer established workers voluntarily quitting, the age profile of the workforce increased.[27]

A traditional means of dealing with elderly employees had been to transfer them to slower, less demanding jobs and to pay them less. But this method of informal pensioning or partial retirement became untenable as the economy declined. It still added up to significant costs in wages, what many referred to as "hidden pension" costs. As it became more difficult to maintain employment levels in general, employers found that they could not just keep these older workers around anymore; they faced tremendous pressure to open up jobs for young workers. The Depression proved the last gasp for this method of informal pensioning.[28]

Formal pensions encountered greater stress. In 1930 NICB finally concluded that funding through current company income "has been proved to be financially unsound and in the long run unsafe." The Pennsylvania Railroad (PRR) ran up against this reality. The company had established a pension in 1900 in order to develop a long-service, loyal workforce; however, it never put aside any reserves to pay the pensions. Meanwhile, as Brian Gratton's study shows, "seniority rights (now rigidly enforced by the Brotherhoods), the tendency of older workers to remain with the firm, and most of all, a sharp drop in new hires ensured the aging of the PRR workforce." Those on the payroll in 1900 had reached retirement age and fulfilled the service requirements by the 1920s, and far more people applied for retirement than expected. In the mid-1920s PRR managers clearly recognized that pension rolls and costs drastically exceeded expectations and a financial crisis loomed. Yet they still did not set aside reserves. By 1930 this system of funding pensions simply could not be sustained. PRR unilaterally cut benefits.[29]

Railroads, of course, were already a declining sector in the 1920s and would eventually require a government bailout, but firms in other industries experienced similar problems. For all nonrailroad companies the number of pensioners increased by more than 50 percent, pushing expenditures up significantly. Public utilities, telephone, telegraph, and oil companies experienced similar problems. Among companies with long established pension programs, liabilities really came home to roost. For companies whose pensions had been in existence for more than twenty years, pensioners on the payroll increased by 488 percent, while pension costs increased by more than 500 percent; companies with pensions in existence for ten to fifteen years faced a 242 percent increase in the number of pensioners. The real problem lay not only in demographics but even more acutely in the failure to provide in advance for benefit payments. It would have been expensive to pay these pensions at any time, but the burden became particularly acute in times of financial stress. As Latimer found, "Hampered by uncovered accrued liabilities, the financial condition of an appreciable number of schemes at the end of 1932 was precarious in the extreme."[30]

The demographic bulge likewise threatened trade union pension plans. During the Depression, labor unions certainly continued to pay out old-age benefits to pensioners, but the number of pensioners grew dramatically every year. As the number of unionists applying for pensions mounted, the overall membership of unions and the number of members participating in pension plans declined. As wages stagnated, trade union plans paid a meager pension, averaging about $375 per year and in many cases falling to as low as $300 by 1931. With expenditures exceeding incoming receipts, the average benefit in 1931 was lower than that of 1928. The Brotherhood of Locomotive Engineers, which experienced a 30 percent decrease in members participating in the fund and a 17 percent increase in pensioners, began paying benefits in some cases below the minimum specified amount of $25 per month. Often, when faced with imminent financial crisis, unions chose first to terminate funds for members' widows and dependents. By 1932 almost half the net decline in the Bricklayers, Masons, and Plasterers Union pension rolls could be attributed to the termination of widow's benefits. Eventually, though, some unions had to terminate all old-age support. At the start of the Depression, twenty-five international unions had pension plans; five unions had abandoned them or were about to do so in 1932. Just as he had done in the case of company pension plans, Murray Latimer warned labor that trade union pension plans could not survive long.[31]

The demographic surge among older Americans and economic crisis alone might have caused the abandonment of employer welfare programs, but political pressures from workers compelled action rather than default by employers. The older workers who found themselves laid off with no pension emerged as a disgruntled and militant political force. Their demands focused on public assistance for the unemployed elderly and public pensions.

State pensions had become a public issue in the 1920s, mainly at the level of state government. The Fraternal Order of Eagles, made up of small business owners and working-class craftsmen, took up the issue in the early 1920s as a strategy for confronting declining membership and internal financial shortages. They launched campaigns for public pensions in states from California to Pennsylvania and were soon joined by other organizations. While the AFL had a long history of opposing social insurance legislation, state federations of labor, city central labor bodies, and local unions actively lobbied for old-age pensions at the state level. In several states labor federations formally aligned with the Eagles to work for pension legislation, succeeding in Montana, Pennsylvania, Nevada, and Wisconsin. Reform associations whose members were economists and social workers, such as the American Association for Old Age Security (founded by Abraham Epstein) and the AALL, prepared the pension bills. By 1933 twenty-five states had passed old-age pension laws, the number having increased most rapidly in the years 1929 to 1933.

For the most part, campaigns for state pensions were orchestrated by established institutions and professional reformers. On the one hand, organizations such as the Eagles or the AFL existed to serve many other functions, not just social welfare, and they had membership imperatives that superseded old-age assistance. On other the hand, men such as Abraham Epstein, Isaac Max Rubinow, Edwin Witte, the AALL's John Andrews, and economist Paul Douglas—the social insurance networks were almost exclusively male—were highly educated professionals, many with formal academic positions, who had long been involved in social service activities. Their organizations were not attached to any mass base. Paid staffers and reform experts carried out the work of the organization.

Once enacted, state pensions actually turned out to be a lot like industrial pensions: few people ever actually received one, and when they did, it did not amount to much. Courts struck them down in some states. In others, means tests, morality tests, or residency requirements kept the pension rolls low. Most pension laws included county-option provisions: counties could choose whether or not to offer pensions. In 1929 only six states, with 264 counties, had pension plans. Only 53 counties had opted to participate. The South remained virtually untouched by the movement. Only two southern states enacted pension programs, Kentucky and West Virginia. Replicating the pattern of welfare capitalism, black and white Southerners remained outside the reach of old-age income support.

Still, the pressure was on. These organizations had been campaigning for pensions quite steadily since the end of World War I, and their rate of success improved dramatically after 1929. Many of the post-1929 laws included compulsory rather than county-option provisions. Numerous state politicians in the Northeast, the Midwest, and the West began to embrace the cause of old-age security.[32]

In the early 1930s a mass movement for old-age support finally emerged. Old-age unemployment had become ubiquitous. For workers over 45 who lost their jobs during the Depression, finding another job proved increasingly difficult. This was especially true for women; employers and job ads insisted on "young girls." From 1930 to 1940 employment among persons over age 65 dropped by 22 percent. In California, for example, the number of persons in this age group increased by 25 percent, but the number employed decreased by 38 percent. During the Depression, the elderly in particular tended to lose their homes, unable to make mortgage payments. Widespread unemployment among all ages meant that families were no longer able to support aging parents. The elderly swelled the ranks of the poorhouses. Entering an almshouse and demanding state aid often meant leaving one's dignity and social status at the door. A person who owned any property had to accept a state lien or other encumbrance on it if she or he applied for public old-age assistance or state pensions. Frustration over such uncharitable options finally turned into political activism.[33]

Spontaneous social movements erupted and cohered specifically around welfare and relief issues—what Linda Gordon has called "welfare populisms."[34] Over the next several years older unemployed persons built and joined organizations such as the Railroad Employees National Pension Association, the National Annuity League, the Townsend movement, the American Pension Union, and the McLain Movement. Besides getting previously unorganized or depoliticized workers involved politically, these movements brought together blue-collar and white-collar older Americans, who were demanding the same goal for public income support. In the process, the old-age pension movement shifted the attention of welfare politics to the elderly as a quintessentially deserving group. Previously welfare politics had focused on widows, mothers with dependent children, and veterans. Now the masses of unemployed elderly asserted a claim of social and political rights as (former) workers and providers, thereby using old-age poverty and dependency to spark a national debate on the broad and universal issue of economic security.[35]

The popular old-age pension movements first demonstrated their electoral clout during Upton Sinclair's End Poverty in California (EPIC) campaign. EPIC called for land reform and "production for use," a program to pay poor people on relief to produce their own food on unused farmland and make their own clothes in idle factories, and progressive tax reform. EPIC also included an old-age pension of fifty dollars a month (more than double the typical California state pension) for needy persons over 60. EPIC became more than just a platform; through an alliance with the End Poverty League and grassroots support from thousands of EPIC clubs, it erupted as a movement that took control of the California Democratic Party. EPIC clubs and supporters succeeded in inserting EPIC into the party platform and winning Sinclair the nomination for governor in 1934. Sinclair lost the general election (after a massive mobilization and smear campaign on the right), but the GOP candidate who won had endorsed just about every pension proposal going. Twenty-two EPIC candidates were elected to the state assembly, and one to the state senate.[36]

While movements like EPIC shook up state politics, the Townsend movement began to jolt the national scene. Dr. Francis Townsend sought a national system of old-age pensions that would simultaneously reduce old-age poverty, jump-start the economy through higher levels of consumption, and open jobs for younger workers. Townsend mobilized supporters for his program through mass meetings in the Los Angeles area. Soon, hundreds of Townsend clubs sponsored meetings and rallies, handed out literature, and secured petition signatures. Townsendites wrote thousands of letters to Congress. By the end of 1934 the movement claimed about twelve hundred local clubs, and in 1935 Townsend launched his national newspaper, the *Townsend National Weekly*. Estimates of membership ranged from 1 million to 3.5 million, with several million more petition signers. Similarly, Huey Long's Share Our Wealth Movement, which advocated pensions for everyone over 60, claimed a following of 3 million through local clubs in 1934.[37]

The Lundeen Workers' Bill of 1931, which proposed a general system of social welfare including unemployment insurance, sickness and accident insurance, maternity support, and old-age pensions, generated mass grass-roots support as well. The bill itself had been heavily influenced by Communist unemployed councils. During the early 1930s it won broad grass-roots support from the labor movement. While the AFL remained ambivalent about public welfare programs, several thousand local unions, numerous central labor councils, and several state federations and internationals became active supporters of the Lundeen Bill. They referred to it as the workers' bill or the workers' program. African American organizations such as the National Urban League and the National Association for the Advancement of Colored People (NAACP) actively supported the bill, viewing it as a racially inclusive national program. Seventy counties and cities endorsed it. Civic organizations and ethnic mutual aid societies joined the cause and promoted the Lundeen program.[38] Advocates of industrial pensions now faced a challenge not just from social reformers, who had always been around during the heady days of welfare capitalism, but from a serious mass movement.

The tumult of the old-age movement finally jogged organized labor out of its slumbering ambivalence about public old-age pensions and social insurance. At its annual convention in 1930, the AFL Executive Council acknowledged that "agitation for the enactment of old age pension legislation has spread throughout the nation," providing compelling evidence that the state should offer support to the elderly. Still, the AFL held back from endorsing any public pension proposals or laws. A year later it was ready to commit itself to working for "old age security," and during 1932 the AFL actively promoted its own model old-age security bill. "The efforts to obtain enactment of old age security laws in all states should be pressed vigorously," it announced. The AFL made a deliberate point of using the term *old age security* rather than *pensions,* suggesting that *security* would have a broader appeal and perhaps would be less politically controversial than *pensions.* Yet, the AFL did not intend old-age benefits to be applied universally. Whereas Townsend's plan called for a pension for all persons over age 60, the AFL clearly intended pensions to go to particular male wage earners "so that every producing worker may be assured, after his productive years, of an adequate income." From the AFL's perspective, security was a reward for continuous, long-term service in the waged labor market.[39]

A third shift in the political and social context involved the tax code. The Internal Revenue Code first offered pensions a unique tax status as early as 1916. At first corporations could deduct actual payments to retirees as "ordinary and necessary expenses." A few years later the Department of the Treasury ruled that company donations to an employee pension trust that was entirely separate and distinct from the corporation could be deducted as "charitable" donations. This ruling did not include contributions to pensions that were run from within the company. In 1928, however, Congress passed legislation that allowed corporations to take tax deductions over a period of years for monies transferred from pension reserves to a formal trust fund or for contributions to a newly created trust fund.[40] Most employers had not maintained a pension trust fund, but that would now begin to change. The tax breaks may not have been significant enough to encourage a multitude of firms to suddenly start pension programs, but they provided an incentive for welfare capitalists who already maintained pension plans to move toward more formalized, soundly financed pension programs, with monies actually put aside for the purpose of paying benefits.[41]

The Middle Way: A New Foundation for Industrial Pensions, 1929–1935

The consequences of these pressures were not quite as simple as historians of welfare capitalism have made them seem. Certainly, some firms found themselves overwhelmed by the financial stress of the Depression and hence abandoned their welfare programs. Other firms, such as large retailers, were willing to support a legislated floor under wages and welfare. Insurers, however, embarked on a major effort to offer corporate employers an option that could enable firms to sustain welfare capitalism without resorting to statist solutions. They helped aggregate class interests, and their ideological message had an appeal across sectoral lines. In response to the social politics of the Depression era, many corporate employers, insurers, and other business-oriented institutions launched a determined effort to preserve private welfare efforts by shoring up their financial foundation.

Private pensions did not disappear during the Great Depression. The period 1929–32 reflected "an almost unprecedented activity in the establishment of industrial pension systems." A record 69 new plans were adopted, exceeding the annual rate of increase of the previous decade, and 434 pensions continued to operate normally in 1932. Yet the rate of discontinuance—10 percent—was surprisingly low considering the official mythology of welfare capitalism and the rise of the welfare state. Discontinued plans represented fewer than 3 percent of the employees with pension coverage.[42]

Latimer's studies reveal no structural or sectoral pattern among firms that abandoned pensions. Generally, these firms tended to be relatively small (fewer than 5,000 employees), but they could be found in a variety of sectors—iron and steel, banking, oil, street railways, printing, agricultural implements. Firms cited quite a variety of reasons for discontinuing, with mergers and reorganizations appearing most often but by no means predominant. Similarly, firms that were willing to "federalize" their labor costs, assenting to federal intervention in wages and welfare, cannot easily be categorized as belonging to competitive or noncompetitive sectors. GM, a price-setting oligopoly, and Kodak, basically a monopoly, took different positions toward public welfare and labor policy. GM opposed government social policy, while Kodak was willing to support public pensions and unemployment insurance. Fiercely competitive southern textile firms, which certainly could have benefited from state intervention, for the most part remained fearful of state control and hostile to social and labor policy. The ideological faith in management's prerogative to determine wages and income typically overrode structural factors.

While an iconoclastic group of corporate executives called for national social insurance programs, plenty of voices from within the business community believed that government solutions could be avoided if business made private options more dependable and realistic. In 1929 DuPont, an Equitable group life insurance client for more than ten years, expanded its policy to reach new branches or subsidiaries of the company and in 1930 implemented a contributory group "accident and sickness plan," disability payments. The company maintained its "pension" plan, which was basically a disability pension for long-service employees who had become incapacitated. DuPont executives even proposed new programs such as "a Termination Allowance, for the payment of Unemployment Insurance and for any other similar social benefits made compulsory by state or federal action." As one manager claimed, "By having such benefits paid out of the Employees' Investment Fund prior to the employee having equity in that Fund, we believe employes would more fully realize the questionable nature of such social legislation."[43]

Whereas in 1925 NICB had treated informal, discretionary pensions as an employer prerogative, it now insisted that the only workable pension plan was a funded one. Its 1931 report urged companies to convert existing pensions to actuarially based or insurance-underwritten plans, declaring that the practice of paying pensions out of current income "has been proved to be financially unsound and in the long run unsafe." A plan had to have "a definite assurance of the payment of pensions and obligatory retirement," and thus "full provision must be made each year to meet all future liabilities." The pension primer insisted that pensions had to be definite, uniform, automatic, and certain if they were to achieve any of the desired effects on the employees.

Along with the U.S. Chamber of Commerce, NICB urged sound financing to prevent the disillusionment of both workers (if pensions were not paid) and employers (if employers faced out-of-control costs owing to lack of planning).[44]

NICB and groups such as the Industrial Relations Counselors advocated switching from noncontributory plans, fully financed by the employer, to contributory ones, based partially on employee contributions. Although organized labor believed that contributory pensions suppressed wages, the pension advocates' motivations were not quite so miserly. First, personnel and industrial welfare experts believed that contributory pensions increased the likelihood that pensions would actually be paid out. Acknowledging that employees had a negligible chance of ever receiving a discretionary pension and thus very little reason to trust their employers, they argued that employers could not welch on their promise of a pension if employees' monies were involved. Indeed, more funds would be available to pay the benefits in the long run. Second, pension advocates thought employee contributions enabled the firm to pay higher benefits. (From the employers' point of view, contributory pensions appeared attractive because they reduced management's costs.) Third, responding to workers' distrust, industrial pension advocates contended that contributory pensions put employer and workers on a basis of "equal participation." NICB stated that "such an arrangement makes the pension plan a cooperative venture free from any taint of paternalism."[45]

The politics of the Depression had forced this shift in business sentiment. The NICB report remarked that "today the subject is a live issue in business management. . . . The agitation for old age pension legislation is a principal cause." In these times of potential political upheaval, it was essential for businesses to earn community favor, as well as the loyalty of employees, "to counteract agitation for legislative proposals to provide universal pensions for the aged."[46] A representative of the National Civic Federation told a convention of business men, "We have got to go ahead and improve things. . . . Unless we get things better, we may be driven to the European system of social insurance. . . . I say that unless we want to go to that extreme, we must . . . strive to the limit to bring it about that American industry shall take care of its own."[47]

Insurance companies had promoted the value of "actuarially sound" and fully funded pensions, but few had heeded their message—until the Depression. Large eastern life companies, such as Metropolitan, Prudential, John Hancock, Aetna, and Equitable, had all expanded their business in group life, accident, and temporary and permanent disability insurance. Still, they had not really pushed pensions. Sold as annuities that had to be paid up annually, pensions were of little interest to employers in the 1920s, and insurers kept them on the side for the rare employer that, like Kodak, chose to go with a funded pension. With the political agitation for government pensions and the unfolding demographic crisis, insurers intensified their efforts to sell group annuities and a more reliable welfare capitalism. Executives from life insurance companies promoted industrial pensions at business conferences, roundtables, and trade association meetings across the country. At once such event a Metropolitan executive presented a morality tale about the employer who meant well but did not plan right and ended up saddling himself with unnecessarily heavy pension costs. Unable to pay off the accrued liability, he deserted the workers. "There are few greater tragedies than busted Pension Plans," Metropolitan's representative admonished. Then the group insurance folks came along and rescued this unfortunate employer. They told him how to pay off his accrued liabilities through a schedule of annual installments and reinsured his plan with an insurance company, which would invest the money and make a return to cover the pensions. Welfare work clearly had not solved the problems of labor or economic management of the 1920s—high turnover, disgruntled workers, unemployment, business cycles—but it had not lost its relevance. Metropolitan now presented the insured pension plan as an essential product that offered employers a means to solve their Depression era financial and political problems.[48]

Metropolitan fared quite well during the Depression and hence continued to promote itself as a model for other business firms to emulate. Although the sale of life insurance policies declined, dividends remained at satisfying levels, cash equities continued to increase, and the firm maintained its ability to meet claims fully. What is most significant, Metropolitan did not have to cut wages or lay off its sales agents. Metropolitan owed its continued profitability to laws prohibiting the investment of reserves in common stocks. Instead, the company had invested in bonds and preferred and guaranteed stocks, which did not decline in value as much as common stocks did after 1929. Thus Metropolitan made a substantial profit when it sold its matured securities in 1931. The diversity of investments lent stability to the firm during troubled times.[49] Not only did Metropolitan's stability during the Depression validate the wisdom of its investment choices; it also affirmed the company's personnel management philosophy. As Metropolitan executives insisted, company welfare policies, "scientific selection" of employees, and an internal labor market had given each employee a stable, definitive position in the firm and promise of future advancement. These business practices offered security to American workers.[50]

After 1932 Metropolitan became an adviser to corporations on adjusting to New Deal policies. PSB advised firms on how to adapt to National Recovery Administration codes. Since the early 1920s major corporations such as DuPont had used employee representation committees, or company unions, to suppress independent labor organization. Metropolitan now taught other firms how they too could use this technique, especially to meet the threat from section 7a of the National Industrial Recovery Act (NIRA).[51] PSB clearly intended their reports to serve as advice on avoiding unionization, characterizing the employee representation council as "a procedure for collective negotiations (unhampered by external influences or irrelevant issues making for fruitless controversy.)"[52]

PSB also advised firms that sought to maintain welfare capitalist schemes, even as they scaled them back. Westinghouse and the General Foods Corporation called on PSB to help them reduce but preserve company pensions, to adjust stock options, profit-sharing plans, and sick pay, and to advise them on employee relations. GM sought advice from Metropolitan on the five-day week. PSB provided consulting for numerous clients on how to deal with unemployment.[53] Metropolitan sustained its confidence in the private sector's ability to weather the Depression on its own. In 1932 the company trumpeted, "Whenever a Metropolitan Field man is instrumental in setting up a scientific Group Retirement Program in his community, he establishes for local employees a practical demonstration of the opportunity American business has to solve its own old age problem with the cooperation of the life insurance companies and without recourse to the expedient of state insurance."[54]

Insurers now advised employers to set up pension reserves at once, whether or not they intended to buy an insured group annuity policy. The group insurance pioneer William Graham became a regular at business conferences on industrial pensions and employee welfare issues. Always the salesman for Equitable policies, he nonetheless had a political vision that centered on the integrity of corporate welfare efforts and management's responsibility to workers. He firmly chastised companies for using discretionary plans. "This situation has in it obvious elements of business hazard in direct ill will to the concern and in indirect menace to industry as constituted today and brings in its trail the subject of State and Federal doles for employables." In meetings from Princeton to California he argued for fully funded pensions. Ideally, plans should be run by a trustee, which would invest the funds, keep them separate from other business expenses, guard their safety, and ensure that employees received a pension. Rather than a mirage employees could envisage in the distance but never approach, a pension plan should be a program that functioned "at or near one hundred per cent use."[55]

Insurance companies hitched their product to a political imperative. Equitable Director of Pensions and Annuities G. Powell Hamilton issued a short advice manual for group insurance clients. Deploring the unfunded, noncontractual, arbitrary status of company pension programs, Hamilton advised, "The modern pension plan should be contributory. . . . It should be contractual. It should be sound at its inception. . . . It should be kept sound. . . . It should be funded and out of reach of the vicissitudes of the business." He then placed this goal within the political context of the Depression: "If this ideal condition could ever be attained, the need of State Old Age Pensions for the drifters could never obtain." In this climate of advice emanating from other institutions within the business community and armies of unemployed and poor marching outside of factories, city halls, and state capitols, businessmen began to make some changes.[56]

Insurance companies won big. The administration of industrial pension plans underwent a significant transformation on the eve of the New Deal. With one exception, all pension plans started after 1929 were underwritten by insurance companies. Firms with preexisting self-insured plans refinanced them with insurance companies. Insurance companies also reinsured four of five giant manufacturing company plans that converted from contributory to noncontributory. And employers liberalized some of the terms of pensions: 90 percent of new plans provided that all employees were eligible. Not all of these plans survived the Depression, but since contributions were now held in legal reserve, employees no longer lost all of their money that had been diverted into the plan. One insurance industry source estimated that 204 new group annuity plans had been issued in the years 1932–34, while only 15 such plans had been discontinued. Among the companies establishing these plans were the Pillsbury Flour Mills Company, the Standard Oil Company of New York (Socony), and the Quaker State Oil Refining Company. When Equitable experienced a surge in income from group insurance premiums, William Graham stressed that this gain over its previous high record of 1931 was due to the growth in the group pension business.[57] Even where companies did not reinsure with an insurance company, many of them called in actuaries to advise them on setting up a planned, minimally funded program. Metropolitan's PSB met with companies like Concordia Publishing House and W. H. Markham and Company and spoke to them "on the subject of unemployment, old age, accident, illness, and insurance."[58]

At the same time that employers strove to demonstrate the reliability of company beneficence, workers were increasingly required to help prop it up. While more employees could participate, the employees under these new and improved plans now also had to bear a larger burden of the corporate pension program. In 1928 the employer had carried the entire cost of the pension. After that there was a marked trend toward requiring employee financial support as contributory pension plans increased in number from 86 in 1929 to 281 in 1932.[59] Employees typically paid 2 percent or 3 percent of their wages into the fund. The increase in contributory pensions did not necessarily translate into greater old-age security, since the overwhelming majority of workers still did not work for the same firm long enough to meet service requirements. But with insured plans, employees did get their contributions back upon leaving, although not necessarily with interest.

The increase in contributory company pensions also raised a paradox. Social insurance advocates argued that, in contrast to the "paternalism" of company welfare, social insurance brought citizens together in a shared project that promoted both social rights and liberal ideals such as individual contract and self-reliance.[60] Welfare capitalism, on the other hand, rested on the premise of employer discretion, the employer's prerogative to reward employees for whatever management deemed "faithful" service; it was discretionary, not contractual, by design. With contributory plans, and their incumbent withdrawal rights, insurers turned this formulation on its head. As Equitable's William Graham explained, "An underlying distinction between the modern contractual movement and the term 'pensioner' . . . can be drawn from the dictionary, where the pensioner is defined as 'one who is dependent upon the bounty of another,' and the annuitant who is defined as 'one who receives or is entitled to receive an annuity.'"[61] Insurers tried to hold intact the "freedom of contract" doctrine that had propped up male workers' "independence" from the state since the Progressive Era and link it to welfare capitalism's pecuniary benefits.

Workers and unions remained skeptical. Organized labor did not abandon its suspicion that employer-provided pensions undermined workers' agency and autonomy. Since many company pensions had long maintained clauses denying pensions to "employees who leave the service under strike orders" or who have been "engaged in demonstrations detrimental to the company's best interests," many labor activists continued to view industrial pensions as subverting labor solidarity, discouraging workers from protesting poor working conditions, and preventing them from fighting for wage increases. Even if fewer pensions contained such clauses in the 1930s than earlier, these suspicions that company pensions endangered citizenship and independence ran deep. Indeed, these fears, along with the declining fortunes of union plans, finally outweighed the threat of state "compulsion." In 1933 the

AFL announced its intention to use "every serious effort possible to find ways and means to force the next session of the Congress of the United States to enact a compulsory old age pension as Federal and State laws."[62]

At the nadir of the Depression the Vermont Marble Company once again offered the promises of welfare capitalism to its employees. Although Vermont Marble lost money, it chose not to abandon its pension plan. Instead, in the middle of the Depression the company converted it to a contributory plan reinsured by an insurance company. In May 1932 Vermont Marble issued the following statement to its employees:

> For nineteen years, we have maintained a purely voluntary pension system . . . without costs to you. . . . The Plan expressly stated that it constituted no contract, conferred no legal rights upon any employe In order to put your pensions on a more stable basis, with fixed rights, we have arranged, after considerable investigation, to put into force July 1, 1932, a new Retirement Plan. . . . You are assured a Retirement Income at your normal retirement age provided by your and the Company's contributions. . . . Your contributions and those of the Company will be paid to The Equitable Life Assurance Society which will issue to each of you a certificate showing your rights under the new Plan. Thus instead of a voluntary system which the Company might become unable to continue, you will have your rights and privileges guaranteed by an independent Insurance Company under public supervision.[63]

In general, new pension arrangements and industrial relations were not quite as sanguine as Vermont Marble's declaration would suggest; indeed, courts had already ruled in the past that entries in a passbook did not constitute a right to benefits. Yet, the company's statement indicates a recognition among employers that in order to meet the political challenges from older workers, they would have to begin rethinking industrial pensions. In 1935 welfare capitalists would face an even more profound challenge as the federal government itself, through the Social Security Act and the National Labor Relations Act, intervened directly into the employment relation, challenging what employers perceived as their most basic prerogatives over work and compensation.

3

The New Deal Struggle

INSURERS, EMPLOYERS, AND THE POLITICS OF SOCIAL SECURITY, 1933–1940

THE MOMENTUM propelling the passage of a national social insurance program came from mass movements like the Townsend movement, while the design of the program came from social insurance experts.[1] With the passage of the Social Security Act, the grass-roots movements and New Dealers generated an *ideology of security*, as well as a new policy of government intervention in the wage relation, of which business had to take note. As the insurance industry journal the *Spectator* observed in 1936, "In the present time 'security' is the word that is being bandied about on every tongue. A pension must be provided against age and its debility."[2] Security became an essential goal in the task of national reconstruction. The emergence of an ideology of security in the 1930s would have major ramifications for public policy, industrial relations, and corporate decisions.

Insurers first reacted to the proposed economic security bill by seeking exemptions for employers with insured employee pensions. They would confront the welfare state by trying to opt out. Insurers, however, soon transformed their response to the welfare state from a strategy of exemption to a strategy of supplementation. After the act's passage, insurers decided that the new old-age program was a tremendous boon to the security business. As sales of group insurance and pensions rose, commercial purveyors of "social security" saw that they could thrive within the welfare state. Consequently, insurers began to adjust their thinking; they began to conceptualize the government's social insurance program as a foundation upon which they could build, as a minimum base for security.[3]

The idea of private-sector supplementation influenced not only decisions made by employers. It also affected the subsequent development of the welfare state, both influencing and gaining further reinforcement from the 1939 amendments to the Social Security Act and the 1938 and 1942 tax laws. In an effort to defend the old-age insurance program, Social Security policymakers also began to make the case for supplementation of the welfare state by private or commercial means.

This convergence with private providers of security signaled the acceptance of welfare capitalism in the era of the welfare state and limited the ideological space in which the welfare state could expand. In the future, the U.S. welfare state, pegged to wage work and market differentiation, would accommodate only incremental reform that did not challenge a market-conforming economic security system. Public social insurance and private supplementation would together reinforce patterns of inequality in labor markets.

The Rise of the Politics of Security, 1934–1936

Despite the attempts to shore up welfare capitalism and defend its efficacy, the federal government eventually prepared to enter the field of income support. The ideological and moral stature of business had fallen so low that business leaders could not successfully mobilize themselves or public sentiment on behalf of what they wanted, which left a vacuum for the state and popular social politics. A year after the New Deal's first hundred days President Franklin D. Roosevelt reviewed the accomplishments of his administration over the last year, pronounced efforts at relief and recovery well under way, and declared that the government now had to tackle economic reconstruction. As part of this reconstruction the American polity had to develop measures for permanent economic security for individuals and their families. On 8 June 1934 Roosevelt announced that his administration would soon offer proposals to provide for "security against the hazards and vicissitudes of life." In his message to Congress, Roosevelt explained that "our Federal Government was established among other things 'to promote the general welfare,' [thus] it is our plain duty to provide for that security upon which welfare depends. Next winter we may well undertake the great task of furthering the security of the citizen and his family through social insurance." Later that month Roosevelt signed an executive order establishing the Committee on Economic Security (CES) to prepare recommendations for "A Program of National Social and Economic Security." With these public pronouncements, Roosevelt catapulted the politics of security to the center of American political and economic life.[4]

Franklin Roosevelt and Secretary of Labor Frances Perkins had been interested in social insurance legislation for unemployment and old age since their days in New York. As governor of New York Roosevelt had begun the work of designing an unemployment compensation program, although he was unable to enact it. But he did sign into law an old-age pension act in 1930. When they moved to the nation's capital, Frances Perkins accepted her new position on the condition that Roosevelt would enact unemployment and old-age insurance legislation at the national level. Still, they were not compelled to proceed on this agenda right away. It was not until 1934 that political factors seemed to provide the opportunity to proceed with federal omnibus social legislation. The design of a bill for unemployment compensation and old-age security had been brewing for a while, especially a pension act relying on worker contributions. Yet Roosevelt's choice of language, the rhetoric of security, represented a response to left-wing social insurance experts, in particular Abraham Epstein, Isaac Max Rubinow, and Mary Van Kleeck.

The economist Abraham Epstein popularized the term *social security*. A Russian Jewish immigrant, Epstein had been a leading activist for state pensions since World War I. After directing the Pennsylvania Commission on Old Age Pensions from 1917 to 1927, Epstein founded the American Association for Old Age Security (AAOAS). Epstein had his first contact with Roosevelt when Rabbi Stephen J. Wise, an AAOAS board member, and he visited Roosevelt shortly before his inauguration as governor of New York. Governor Roosevelt worked closely with Paul Douglas, another AAOAS board member, on social insurance and emergency welfare legislation. In 1933, as the New Deal moved into action, Epstein renamed the group the American Association for Social Security to promote a national, comprehensive social insurance system.[5]

Through books such as Epstein's *Insecurity: A Challenge to America* (1933) and Isaac Max Rubinow's *The Quest for Security* (1934), left-wing social insurance experts emphasized that insecurity and lack of income were inevitable features of working-class life, at all stages of the life cycle.[6] They proposed a total system of social insurance to meet needs brought on by illness, unemployment, disability, birth of a child and heavy burdens of supporting a large family, and old age. Rubinow cast the issue of security in apocalyptic terms, organizing his book around the "Four Horsemen": accident, illness, old age, and unemployment. These were all risks that should be pooled across society. State laws presently in place, such as widows' pensions, mothers' aid, and old-age pensions "have not provided the full measure of security which is necessary." They did not pool risk. The New Dealers had to press forward and create "a complete structure of security."[7]

The language of security permeated the articles of national liberal political journals. The *New Republic* ran a series of articles in the fall of 1934 and the winter of 1935 entitled "Security for Americans." The seven-part series included articles on the Ohio and Wisconsin plans for unemployment insurance, the Lundeen bill, public relief, and old-age pensions, written by prominent figures such as Mary Van Kleeck, Paul Douglas, Elizabeth Brandeis, Rubinow, Epstein, and George Soule.

Most of these articles criticized Roosevelt and the CES from the left, arguing that the administration's program, as it was taking shape, would not do enough to provide security, especially since it appeared that health insurance would be left out. Mary Van Kleeck, leader of the social work movement, endorsed the Lundeen Bill because it was the only plan that set up a different concept of social insurance: "Mass provision by government and industry to provide for mass insecurity is the new definition of social insurance."[8] Moreover, she discussed these issues in terms of rights rather than charity. National policy should compensate all workers and farmers, as citizens in the American polity, for the risks inherent in a mass market economy. Van Kleeck specifically included compensation for loss of wages for part-time work, sickness, and maternity, thus enabling more women to be covered than under the traditional social insurance model. At a national conference on governmental objectives for social work, the American Association of Social Workers decided for the first time to recognize the federal government's "obligation to meet the needs of people" through a national economic security program. Over the next year the pages of *The Survey* included articles by a range of social workers, economists, and welfare experts debating both specific proposals and broader principles "for welfare and security."[9]

Left-leaning critics feared that Roosevelt would settle for half a loaf. *The Nation*, commenting on the role of the CES, acknowledged the pivotal project being undertaken. "The President," one columnist wrote, "gave it a hard task. It would have been enough to formulate a policy on social insurances. To this he has added the almost limitless word 'security.'" The writer doubted that the administration could achieve such a grandiose goal as security for all Americans in a single, sixty-day legislative session.[10] Once the House passed the Economic Security Bill, however, *The Nation* forcefully declared that this bill had fallen short of providing comprehensive security. *The Nation* suggested holding out for a better program rather than passing what essentially amounted to "a scheme of compulsory self-saving which neither protects the workers nor guarantees a steady flow of purchasing power."[11] Whether or not they supported the CES proposals, liberal journalists, welfare administrators, social workers, economists, and social insurance theorists had begun to link the concept of security integrally with the federal government and the *political* right of citizens to be free from economic insecurity.

By late 1934 New Dealers had claimed the language of security. While the CES was at work assembling a bill, Roosevelt repeatedly spoke about security in his radio addresses, even when the topic was banking legislation, industrial relations, or the gold standard.[12] In November 1934 Secretary of Labor Frances Perkins convened a National

Conference on Economic Security in Washington, attended by activists representing almost every state in the nation. Roosevelt himself addressed the gathering, equating "greater general security" with economic recovery. "Everything we do with intent to increase the security of the individual will, I am confident, be a stimulus to recovery." During this speech the president suggested that the initial bill might not include old-age pensions or health insurance. His remarks provoked so much protest from Townsendites and other supporters of pensions that within two days Roosevelt announced that old-age security would certainly be included in his economic security program, reinforcing the notion of different social welfare benefits brought together under one security, or social security, umbrella. CES members such as Edwin Witte and Barbara Armstrong and consultants such as the insurance men W. R. Williamson and M. Albert Linton gave talks and wrote articles for business, insurance, and reform organizations not only to explain the technical aspects of their social insurance proposals but also to stress the federal government's commitment to "security" for all workers. Edwin Witte, chairman of the CES, emphasized to his staff and the public that their project had transcendent importance, for "Economic Security is a much broader concept than social insurance."[13] The bill itself, originally the Economic Security Bill, finally passed the House in April 1935 and made its way to the Senate.

Business Confronts Social Security

In their attempts to stave off state action insurers and business advisers adjusted their arguments and language to the new discourse of security. In 1934 and 1935 businessmen and personnel consultants moved away from the idiom of human engineering and social science management that had dominated the previous decade and began to adopt the language of security. Security became the dominant language of insurers. William Graham, Equitable's chief group insurance spokesman, gave lectures to business groups around the country. Gone were the references to efficiency, human engineering, elimination of the superannuated. Equitable's vice president now agreed with the general political tenor of the times that "the individual by himself is usually unable to obtain full security through his own precautions." But Graham argued that the European model of government social insurance had been a disastrous experiment. Nor did America have to follow that model, he argued, because the United States had its own "general security program" just waiting to be implemented fully and properly. American business had only to draw on what it already had—profit-sharing plans, building and loan associations, credit unions, company un-

1. "Join the March to Old Age Security" (1936). The Social Security Board encouraged Americans to sign up for the new social insurance program by linking it with the popular movements and grass-roots mobilization of the mid-1930s. Courtesy of the Social Security Administration Archives.

employment loan plans, industrial pensions—but with greater commitment and rigor, and it would have the answer to insecurity, said Graham.[14]

Defending his company's business interests, Graham offered up the entire gamut of pecuniary welfare capitalist programs, especially group life, accident and sickness, and old-age insurance (and company-guaranteed employment plans, essential to making workers stay enrolled in group insurance) as all the elements of a "general security program." Graham insisted that because of the vitality of the American insurance industry and the fact that private insurance companies serviced the main public insurance program, workmen's compensation, "surely it can be maintained that the American working people today are the best-insured people on the globe." In fact, he promised managers insurers' help in developing new mechanisms for workers' security.

Security, of course, had also became a politically useful term now that economic times had changed. It was one thing for insurance companies to market a product using the language of engineering and efficiency during the prosperity of the 1920s, but amidst the mass unemployment and suffering of the Depression, talk of "scrapping human machines" would appear embarrassingly callous. And yet by giving further legitimacy to the notion that all Americans were entitled to economic security, security that had yet to be fulfilled, Graham's rhetoric added to the momentum fueling enactment of a government social security plan.[15] Acknowledging the ideological impact of New Dealers' economic security initiative, this insurance company executive presciently perceived the way in which the public sector was establishing values and modes of behavior that business soon would emulate.[16]

Roosevelt's Economic Security Bill generated a variety of insurance industry responses. The smaller life and casualty insurance companies, represented by the American Life Convention, tended to be openly hostile to all proposals for government social insurance. Unemployment insurance, in many ways the primary concern of the New Dealers, did not disturb insurers too much since they believed unemployment was simply an uninsurable risk. Yet the smaller companies feared a government program that provided retirement annuities, disability retirement benefits, and survivors' insurance. As sellers of individual policies, the smaller companies continued to view issues of economic security in terms of individual thrift and morality. They responded to proposed "absurd schemes for economic security" by maintaining that "individual risk since it involves a matter of duty is really a moral problem." The government could not compel individual "moral" behavior.

The industry journal, *Spectator*, representing the more conservative views of the smaller midwestern, southern, and western companies, repeatedly denounced proposals for national social insurance programs. By the time the Economic Security Bill passed in the House, the *Spectator's* editor acknowledged the change in political culture taking hold, but he assured readers that Americans could still find what they needed in the commercial annuity, which alone "will solve, to a large extent, a great number of social problems." For these insurance industry representatives, public and private insurance represented competing and mutually exclusive options.[17]

The large eastern life insurance companies, however, gauged the direction of the political currents and seemed willing to ride along. A key indiscretion that had brought down so much opprobrium on the insurance industry in 1905 was their extensive and corrupt political influence, wielded through flows of money, lobbying, and unseemly courting of legislators and regulators. This legacy may partially explain the lack of outright opposition to the proposed social security bill. Yet many insurers remembered with profitable pleasure two previous encounters with government social policy. First, although initially wary of workmen's compensation laws, insurance companies soon found these state programs to be good for business. State laws usually allowed employers to contract out and buy their own insurance from private companies; when insurance compensation cases were adjudicated in courts, insurance agents retained considerable power over benefit awards. Second, insurers even benefited from the federal government's World War I issuance of discounted life insurance policies to all soldiers. This proved to be a great boon to their business, first when soldiers bought supplemental life insurance policies and then after the war, when former soldiers, who had "learned the value of life insurance," purchased their own policies. Large insurers repeatedly cited this episode as an example of how public policies could boost private business. The *National Underwriter*, another major industry publication, wrote that many life insurance men were "in sympathy with the broad objectives of the bill and hopeful that it will rival war risk insurance as a stimulus to the life insurance business."[18] Public policies could promote the business of private insurance policies.

Executives of the major life companies were thus optimistic in 1934 and early 1935. Along with executives from companies like John Hancock Mutual and Metropolitan, Thomas Parkinson, president of Equitable, assured colleagues, "I believe that social insurance agitation forwarded by President Roosevelt and his official associates will result in renewed appreciation and great stimulation of life insurance activities, both individual and group." Grasping the ideological impact a national social security program could have, Parkinson concluded that "the efforts to provide through social insurance measures . . . will do much to arouse public interest in the whole subject of security." In turn, he argued, New Dealers' emphasis on security would lend cachet to the insurance business, for the public would see "the tremendous national and community service rendered by life insurance" as providers of economic security.[19] These executives believed that as long as the proposed social security bill offered a more conservative alternative to the Lundeen and Townsend programs, it would not compete with private business. As one insurance man expressed confidently, "The government is not in business to pour out the profits but to lay the foundation from which years hence prosperity and security may be harvested. . . . In this new arrangement, there must also be a new place for life insurance."[20] Commercial insurers had to come to terms with the New Deal.

While the large insurers could imagine a compatibility between public and private insurance, it was a compatibility that involved circumscribed realms. Public insurance and private insurance would serve different "markets." Insurance executives emphasized that any kind of government benefits, whether public assistance or social insurance, should be strictly for the unemployables and the losers of the world. They viewed social insurance as an optimal remedy for the "improvident, the incompetent, and most distressingly, the unfortunates," those who were not their market anyway. "This group . . . is not the group served by insurance."[21] The director of the National Association of Life Underwriters concurred that public pensions were appropriate for "the old, the defective, and the incompetent." Addressing agents who would sell private policies, he reassured them that "your field of activity is rather among the 15,000,000 American owners of corporate securities, the 45,000,000 savings banks depositors, and the 10,000,000 of building and loan associations."[22] Those insurers who were willing to accept a government social security program still intended to protect what had been traditionally known as the "class business."

Insurance companies began offering new types of policies targeted to their alleged niche within the market for old-age social insurance. Northwestern Mutual, Penn Mutual Life, and Mutual Life of New York were typical of several companies that launched new Retirement Income or Family Income Plans. "To a public yearning for greater 'social security'" these individually purchased plans offered a family income rider attached to a regular life policy. With the rider, the life policy would mature when the breadwinner reached age 60. This would provide a "simple but comprehensive 'social insurance' plan for the average family head," advertised Mutual Life of New York. The *Spectator* ran a large feature piece explaining the newly developed Salary Continuance Plan, attributing its editorial decision to "the current interest in Washington's Economic Security Program."[23] The increasing pressure of the New Deal impelled life insurers to develop more options for economic security. Insurers, though, designed these social insurance alternatives for individual middle-class consumers, those who could afford to pay premiums in addition to those of ordinary life insurance; they were meant to reach the class business.

As Roosevelt's Economic Security Bill wound its way into the Senate, it became clear that this program would do more than just supplement relief for the needy, and so insurers latched onto a new approach, state approved exemptions. A handful of influential insurance brokers and life company executives advanced a proposal that employers with group pension plans should be exempt from the payroll taxes for old-age pensions. They argued that such a provision would be necessary to protect private pensions "superior in benefits" to those of the government plan. Employers could afford to make contributions to one system or the other—private or public—but not to both, contended H. Walter Forster, an insurance broker for Towers, Perrin, Forster and Crosby Life Insurance and Pensions. Forster wrote and submitted an amendment for the Economic Security Bill that would enable a social insurance board to review and approve private pension plans for exemption. He additionally claimed that it would be impossible for insurers and employers to wrap a private industrial plan around a government plan. Forster had tried to get the House Ways and Means Committee to include the measure, but the House voted it down. In the Senate, however, he found an aggressive sponsor in Senator Bennett "Champ" Clark, from Missouri.[24] Thereafter known as the Clark Amendment, the exemption measure soon picked up support from most of the pension-writing insurance companies.[25]

Once the amendment reached the Senate floor, an apparent safeguard for workers was added: in order for a private plan to be certified for exemption, it would have to be approved by the Social Security Board (SSB), and benefits would have to match those of the public system. In addition, the amendment now expressly stated that to qualify for exemption, employers had to secure their pension plan and sufficient reserves with a private insurance company or an outside trustee responsible for investment of funds under the supervision of the SSB. The insurance companies seem to have gotten what they wanted. The Senate passed the amendment by a vote of 51 to 35.[26]

The issue would now have to be worked out in the conference committee. Employer exemptions became the most contentious issue of the joint session, causing a deadlock between the House and Senate that took weeks to resolve. Ultimately, the amendment failed. Not only did President Roosevelt and his close supporters oppose it but so did the actuarial consultants on the CES, who argued that contracting out by major employers would seriously undermine the government program.[27] Echoing the sentiments of the more progressive New Dealers, Murray Latimer, previously of the Industrial Relations Counselors and now the head of the Railroad Retirement Board, emphatically opposed exemption for employers with private pensions. He warned that such an exemption would encourage employers "to maintain low hiring ages, and to induce high turnover at the upper ages." More importantly, he reminded lawmakers, industrial plans could not substitute for a universal national pension. As he informed Arthur Altmeyer, "none are satisfactory as social insurance measures." The real problem was not so much whether the monthly pension payments were more generous than those proposed under Social Security, as Clark supporters claimed and Latimer denied; rather, it was that so few workers ever actually received a company pension.[28] Neither the pooling of risk nor the granting of benefits was broadly socially shared. Actuaries and business representatives working with the CES agreed.[29]

Although Clark Amendment defenders would try to keep the controversy alive, within a year their strongest backers, insurance companies, defected to the other side. The rhetoric of the Clark Amendment debate, especially the relentless lobbying of Forster and Hamilton, convinced some senators and congressmen that there was a substantive and substantial problem regarding the destruction of private pensions. It also gave Republican opponents of the welfare state an excuse to revisit the issue of social security when Congress returned for the next session. Consequently, a joint congressional committee convened closed hearings on private pensions and the Social Security Act in January 1936. In May the committee produced a new draft of the exemption bill. Although it was defeated again and relegated to obscurity, the Clark Amendment's fate illustrates a crucial shift in business firms' perception of their relation to the welfare state. By the time the Clark Amendment was reintroduced in the spring of 1936, insurers and large employers no longer supported it. Seeing that they could benefit and profit from within the new Social Security system, they transformed their response to the welfare state from a strategy of exemption to a strategy of supplementation. The controversy stoked by Clark Amendment supporters, though, stirred enough fear about maintaining the boundaries between public and private old-age security that even after its final demise in Congress, many workers and business managers continued to write to the SSB, charging that the Social Security Act had destroyed their company pension plans. In an effort to defend the program from these attacks, the architects of Social Security eventually adopted private insurers' argument about the supplemental relationship between public and private as well.

When Congress established a joint committee in January 1936 to draft a new exemption bill, both Democratic and Republican members saw their mission as literally "preserving private pension plans," especially since, in their view, "the private pension plans can do a better job." One congressman even went so far as to raise the question, seemingly solved in the previous session of Congress, "So why have the government in it at all . . . ?" The joint committee expressed concern about claims that the Social Security Act abrogated all employer pension plans. Several committee members boldly asserted that companies were discontinuing pensions at an alarming rate. Senator Clark, the exemption's original sponsor, admonished every witnesses that "it would be almost criminal to wipe out of existence the rights of some 4,000,000 employees now under private pension plans." Clark constantly invoked the specter of 4 million ruined pensions even though contemporary studies showed that only a small fraction of that number came under soundly financed pensions, while an even smaller number of workers ever actually received a pension. The members of the joint committee also expressed doubt that the Supreme Court would uphold the Social Security Act, given the Court's track record of striking down New Deal legislation. If the Social Security Act annulled private pensions (which it did not) and were then declared unconstitutional, workers would have nothing left. "They are left high and dry," one congressman lamented.[30]

ne of the witnesses appearing before the joint committee could confirm this gloomy view of the Social Security Act. In fact, they had a completely opposite one to report. Representing a variety of interests, they all made the case that far from withering, employer-provided pensions had proliferated since the act's passage. No one associated with the SSB, of course, would support Clark's case for employer exemptions. Although the joint committee repeatedly asked the SSB to devise an exemption plan, the board refused to submit any proposals or to review those of anyone else. Instead, it suggested that while the amendment was "likely to be dangerous to the accomplishment of the aims of Social Security legislation in general," the same could not be said for the impact of Social Security on private pensions. Arthur Altmeyer, acting chairman of the SSB, observed that companies had been adopting private annuities at an unusually rapid rate.[31] The SSB's opposition is no surprise. As Martha Derthick and others have shown, members of the SSB had a "strong sense of proprietorship in the program" from the very beginning. They strove relentlessly to stake out and defend their turf, especially that of old-age pensions, the one Social Security program directly under federal control. The SSB was acutely sensitive to pressure from Congress,[32] but it was not about to let its program or its jurisdiction over "security" get chipped away by Republican congressmen, insurance brokers, and brooding employers intent on reversing the enactment of Social Security.

Insurers and other pensions experts, however, also presented a case that contradicted that of the committee and in general showed few signs of hostility toward Social Security. Rainard B. Robbins, a pension consultant whose essays often appeared in insurance industry trade journals, disputed the claims of wiped-out private pensions, and like Altmeyer, he noted a surprising effect the government's new program seemed to be having on the private annuity business. Robbins surveyed fifty employers, representing about 1.2 million employees, beginning in December 1935. He found that "only three of these employers have discontinued their pension plans or admit any likelihood of such discontinuance because of the Social Security Act." Nine employers in his survey had decided to modify their pension plans so that they would supplement federal pensions in some way. The majority of the companies were simply waiting to see what would happen to the act if the Supreme Court ruled on it; their pensions therefore remained the same. Yet he also found that more group annuity contracts had been issued in 1935 than in any previous year. During the early months of 1936 the annuity business surged dramatically. Robbins did not argue that private pensions could in any way substitute for the new public old-age pension program. Social Security had to function as the nation's primary old-age security system, he suggested, and then if employers wished to do so, they could supplement the federal benefits. And employers in his survey were coming around to this belief.[33]

Upon realizing the excessive federal oversight, administrative costs, and increases in benefit payments involved in contracting out, as well as the fact that they would be giving up federal subsidization of existing plans, large employers who had previously favored the Clark Amendment dropped their support. Armour and Company, which had maintained an employee pension plan since 1911, informed the Senate Finance Committee that while it believed that its employees "will find themselves worse off by reason of the Federal Social Security Bill," "we believe that the restrictions and limitations imposed by any such measure as the Clark Amendment would be of no value in relieving this situation." The amendment "imposes burdens," stated Armour firmly, "with which it would be impossible to comply." While many small companies continued their support for the amendment, firms such as General Foods, Procter & Gamble, Standard Oil, Kodak, and GE agreed with Armour. Executives at Standard Oil and Kodak indicated that rather than compete directly with public social insurance, they preferred to modify their company pensions as supplements to the Social Security Act.[34] By 1936 these companies, all of which had their own pension plans, viewed the exemption amendment as not only unnecessary but potentially interfering with their previously independent industrial relations programs.

Insurers shared their opinion. The proposed exemption policy would require direct supervision of private plans by the SSB. The board would monitor the choice of insurance carrier, employer contributions, benefits, and the investment of pension funds. The exemption policy would also impose on insurance companies the burden of keeping track of employees' movement between jobs. The new bill stipulated that the insurance companies (not the employer) would have to notify the SSB upon the termination of every employee and either issue a deferred annuity to that employee at age 65, equal to Social Security benefits, or pay that amount to the U.S. Treasury. Moreover, if the employer decided to cancel the entire policy, the insurance company would have to pay the entire amount owed to employees over to the Treasury Department.[35] Originally a plan to avoid federal encroachment on their business, the Clark Amendment now seemed to ensure it. The terms of the already enacted Social Security seemed rather benign in comparison.

This time insurers informed Congress that such an amendment was clearly unworkable, impractical, and unnecessary. Owing to "the degree of supervision," Prudential remonstrated, approved exemptions were no longer of interest to the company. The Connecticut General Life Insurance Company, Travelers, Provident Mutual, Metropolitan, and Aetna all took the same position. They further advised their group insurance employers that the proposed amendment would not be advantageous to them.[36] As was the case with state-level regulation, public intervention or legislation was acceptable, even valuable, to insurers only insofar as it legitimated commercial private insurance; but they objected if it threatened to take any control out of their hands.

It was not merely the specter of federal regulation but the incipient boom in the "security" business that changed insurers' views on this matter. An actuary at Aetna proclaimed shortly after the act's passage that "the social security act in itself is a gigantic advertisement for the pension."[37] First, insurers noticed "a flood of business in annuities and single premium life insurance," bought primarily by well-off individuals. The *National Underwriter* displayed bold headlines declaring, "Emphasis on Social Security Is Changing Buying Attitudes. Income Plans Are Leading." The trade journal reported that "the trend of life insurance selling for the present is undoubtedly towards old age income and savings rather than protection [in the event of death]." Confirming this trend, the president of Philadelphia Life told a convention of agents that clients had been shifting to retirement income policies, "thinking largely in terms of social security for themselves." Retirement income plans accounted for almost a third of his company's new business in 1935.[38] Annuity premiums increased as a percentage of total premium income at all of the large eastern life companies, including Metropolitan, Mutual Life of New York, Penn Mutual, John Hancock, Travelers, and Massachusetts Mutual, and many experienced increases in the proportion of annuity reserves to total company reserves.[39]

Second, the sale of new group annuities, or group pension contracts, rose from 211 in 1933 to 480 in 1936. This meant that fully insured plans now exceeded the number of unfunded, in-house pensions before the New Deal. Companies such as International Harvester, the Ohio Oil Company, American Steel Foundries, Thomas Edison, Inc., and the Pennsylvania Water and Power Company initiated group annuity pension plans in 1935 and 1936. Social security consciousness extended beyond old-age security. Equitable announced that sales of group accident and health (disability) insurance reached record highs, as did group life and pensions. Employers also began purchasing insurers' new accidental death and dismemberment coverage for employees. And for the first time, companies began selling hospitalization coverage, the forerunner of modern health insurance.[40] Commercial purveyors of "social security" thus saw that they could thrive within the welfare state.

Consequently, they began to adjust their thinking, to conceptualize the government's national pension program as a foundation upon which they could build. The *National Underwriter* found that insurance sellers who specialized in pensions "are predominantly in favor of the new government pension plan," and "the majority feel that it is advisable to permit the government to carry out the new pension plan and be contented to service the extensive supplemental market which offers a fertile field." Aetna and Equitable quickly designed supplemental policies. In early 1936 Metropolitan announced that it would modify its own employees' insurance and retirement programs when Social Security payroll taxes went into effect the following year, and they advised their group clients to do the same.[41] The director of Equitable's Group Pension and Annuity Division advised all sales representatives that "a supplemental retirement plan is needed to complete the protection afforded under the Social Security Act." As an Equitable executive explained to a business association meeting, "The appeal of such a plan to an employer lies primarily in the fact that an employer, even in a highly competitive industry or business, may have a complete retirement program at not too great a sacrifice."[42]

Many employers with company pension plans soon recognized the hidden subsidy involved in supplementation. A survey conducted by NICB in 1936 found that "the Social Security Act is regarded as particularly attractive (1) to companies which find the cost of a private informal plan with pensions paid from current revenue becoming a serious problem . . . and (2) companies that have wished to make provision for superannuated employees but have been deterred by fear of the effect of the cost of such a plan on their competitive position." Overall, Robbins's study of the six major pension-writing insurance companies and fifty employers concluded that "the life insurance companies recommend, and a number of employers have accepted the recommendation, that group annuity plans be inaugurated or adjusted to supplement the annuities to be furnished by the federal government."[43] Supplementation could be used to sustain the promises of welfare capitalism.

Insurance companies became behind-the-scenes promoters of the government program, believing that each would legitimize and affirm the other. They strove to prove that they were in accord with New Deal values. Equitable's Graham expressed congruence with New Deal values by exclaiming, "What we want in the way of social security is more security! Let the seekers of security in America not forget the group insurance system!"[44] Advertisements for insurance companies and their policies highlighted Social Security. "Democrats and Republicans . . . They All Vote Yes for General Mutual's Social Security Contract," trumpeted once such ad. "The Life Underwriter Creates Social Security," Northwestern Mutual's full-page ad declared. As the *National Underwriter* advised all general agents, "The company or the agent who is overlooking the present opportunity to push for business hard by using the social security workout is passing by a golden day."[45]

At the same time, in order to sell the idea of supplementation, they had to argue that government pensions were inadequate. While conservative opposition to the Social Security Act had often stressed the demoralizing generosity of government pensions, insurers now emphasized their meagerness. Life insurance company presidents and agents from large and small companies all stressed the utter insufficiency of Social Security pensions without supplementary provisions, whether through individual insurance policies or employee benefits. Metropolitan Vice President James Kavanaugh told Chamber of Commerce members that employers ought to try to coordinate private and public pensions because "the federal plan provides only a meager basic pension which in many cases is inadequate without supplementary benefits." The *Spectator*, which acknowledged the significant role of the federal government in stimulating "a thoroughgoing discussion all over the Nation" on "the necessity for old age security," assured its readers that they could encourage insurance sales as long as Americans came "to appreciate the fact that they were going to need quite a lot of income to keep going through the twilight of their lives; quite a lot more than the Government was talking about giving them."[46] William Graham told audiences that "the Social Security Act is, therefore, not the immediate answer to any company's pension problem and certainly, from the employee's viewpoint, the security in old age provided under the Act is far from adequate. . . . The need for a supplementary retirement program to augment benefits provided under the Social Security Act can be readily understood."[47] This marketing strategy would have a major influence not only on the sales of private social welfare benefits but on the future development of the welfare state. It helped disseminate the concept, to use Sanford Jacoby's term, of the "basic welfare state," wherein the state provided a minimal, basic level of protection, which would not cover all needs, and left the rest to private institutions.[48]

A few corporate employers that had long maintained pensions chose a more retaliatory response. Some companies, such as DuPont, founder of the anti–New Deal Liberty League, disseminated propaganda to employees to discredit the Social Security Act. DuPont distributed a three-part series entitled "The Federal Social Security Act: A Summary of Information for Employes," which was in fact a screed against Social Security. The costs, the company explained, would certainly outweigh the benefits, and "neither prosperity nor economic security is likely to be attained through such a program."[49] Smaller employers who maintained pensions continued to write to Congress in support of the Clark Amendment, followed up by nervous letters from their employees. Two large employers, Western Union and AT&T, threatened workers with the termination of the company's pension plan if the Social Security Act went into effect. In a concerted letter-writing campaign dozens of Western Union and AT&T company unions or employee representation councils mailed letters (with scores of signatures attached) to members of Congress asking them to exempt their employers from the provisions of the Social Security Act applying to payroll tax and pensions.

These letters expressed fears that Social Security entailed the termination of their company pensions. A letter from the Association of Employees, Long Lines Department, AT&T, in Chicago, stated, "We fear that this destruction [of the company pension] would result, if our

Democrats and Republicans
. . . They All Vote

For General Mutual's

SOCIAL SECURITY CONTRACT

A life contract with a universal appeal . . . a sales story that attracts wage earners and white collar workers alike . . . a policy that every worker can afford . . . that describes the General Mutual Social Security Contract. It will help you increase your production. Unusually liberal commissions for recognized agents.

...Write today for full details!

THE GENERAL MUTUAL LIFE INSURANCE CO.
VAN WERT, OHIO • C.M.Purmort, Pres.

2. Insurance companies quickly strove to show that they were in accord with New Deal values and that private insurance was compatible with the new Social Security program. While Aetna had previously used the circular logo, it was not until the passage of the Social Security Act in June 1935 that the word *security* was incorporated directly into the logo. AETNA logo reproduced with permission from AETNA, 1908–1964, and the *National Underwriter.* Artistic Reproduction.

employer and ourselves are subject to the Federal Tax. We favor an amendment to the law, such as the Clark Amendment." Letters arrived from employee groups such as Northwestern Bell Telephone workers in Omaha, Nebraska, and the Association of Western Union Employees, claiming that they would "lose all benefits from private pension funds which will be disbanded on account of this act."[50] The identical phrasing of letters from various AT&T employees' associations in different regions of the country suggests that employees encountered an organized campaign of misinformation concerning the provisions of the Social Security Act and previously accumulated private pension credits.[51]

The responses of Western Union and AT&T represented defensive efforts to preserve an increasingly anachronistic system of in-house, unfunded pensions from a suddenly bygone era. Both companies had maintained pension plans for all employees since 1913. By the 1930s, long-service workers covered by these plans were finally retiring, while an even greater number waited just around the corner. Both companies had in-house, unfunded pensions and faced a dire challenge to meet their pension promises, regardless of the Social Security Act. The Social Security scare offered a convenient way to explain why a company would be unable to meet its outstanding pension obligations.[52] Indeed, AT&T had never been a reliable source for workers' social security. In the period 1913–34 only 6,005 employees received an AT&T pension—this at a company that employed more than 450,000 people until 1929 and about 300,000 after that. There were just under 5,000 former workers on the pension rolls in 1934.[53]

One Western Union employee in Chicago sought to expose his company's behind-the-scenes machinations. "I know of specific cases in which this company like many of the others, makes things so hot for the employee approaching the retirement age that the employee almost just has to quit," wrote John Dietrich. "Or they commence to lower his salary on grounds he can't work as much as the others, so that when he does get a pension, he is lucky to get thirty dollars monthly [the estimated amount of Social Security pensions]." Dietrich explained that in his own case the company stripped him of his seniority, first during a period of job-related disability and again when it reduced weekly hours during the Depression. "Where will I be when my pension is due?" he asked. He signed his letter, "Well dear sir yours for Social Security, John Dietrich."[54]

Thus AT&T's and Western Union's claims proved unpersuasive to the Senate Finance Committee and the House Ways and Means Committee. In June 1936 Congress dropped the Clark Amendment. There were objections to all aspects of the bill. The committees opposed it on constitutional grounds because it allowed some groups but not others to be excused from a national tax; on administrative grounds because of the vast bureaucratic undertaking that coordination and exemption involved; and on financial grounds because of concern that the actuarial solvency of Social Security would be seriously disturbed. The case for government-backed security had been established.

Hence, coercive resistance was not characteristic of the majority of companies with pension plans. Of 218 companies with pension plans in 1936, only 18 declared an intention to discontinue the company plan. Many employers engaged in various acts of passive resistance to the Social Security Act. They neither adapted their existing pensions to the act nor initiated new pension plans. They did not register their employees with SSB or begin paying taxes on 1 January 1937, as the law required.[55] Other employers, still trying to resist the national welfare state, decided simply to wait for a Supreme Court decision. A suit brought by employers in Alabama over the unemployment compensation part of the Social Security Act had already begun to work its way through the courts. Republican presidential candidate Alfred M. Landon called for the repeal of old-age insurance while out on the campaign trail in the fall of 1936. In April 1937 the Supreme Court agreed to hear the case and upheld the act. So by May 1937 it was clear that Social Security was here to stay.

Yet the establishment and ratification of Social Security's contributory pensions by no means quelled the grass-roots activism; instead, Social Security stimulated intensified popular agitation for more radical welfare measures, new "welfare populisms." Townsendites continued to flood Congress with letters, telegrams, and petitions demanding a universal flat pension for all elderly persons regardless of their work history. The SSB received all kinds of demands for pensions not based on wage differentials. New popular groups emerged. Factions of the Townsend movement broke off in 1937 and formed the General Welfare Federation, the National Annuity League, and the American Recovery Pension clubs. In 1937 another California eccentric launched the Ham and Eggs Movement, with the slogan "Thirty Dollars Every Thursday." It rested on a complicated and unrealistic plan to provide every unemployed person over age 50 with a weekly income. Nonetheless, it too gained support in every county in California, claiming 270,000 members by the end of 1938, and held innumerable local rallies. In general, Americans expressed widespread support for the notion that government should support the needy, find jobs for everyone who wanted to work, provide free medical and dental care for those who could not afford it, and collect enough taxes for public works jobs.[56]

And finally, of course, by 1937 organized labor was on the march. Workers demanded new rights to security at work and at home.

Business organizations took note of the ascendant ideology of security. Whether or not the Social Security Act passed the Supreme Court's test of constitutionality, "the country is committed to the policy of making adequate provision for aged workers," discerned the Personnel Research Federation. ". . . it is therefore the part of wisdom for employers to cooperate with the federal government."[57] Standard Oil's president, Walter Teagle, certainly an iconoclast in his early support for welfare capitalism and social security, preached the ideology of security to his colleagues in urging them to adapt their existing pensions to the government program. "We subscribe to the ideals of worker security," Teagle proclaimed in an essay in *Factory Management and Maintenance* entitled "Security—This Is More Like It." The president of the Packard Motor Company assured readers that "We Work Toward Worker Security." Both preached the message that business could engage the politics of security.[58]

Social Security and Private Pensions

The New Life of Private Pensions, 1936–1940

The rest of the decade saw growth and adaptation of private pensions and welfare capitalism to the New Deal welfare state. Sales of group annuity plans increased by 85 percent in the years 1935–39 as the total number of insured company pensions rose to more than seven hundred. Companies that purchased group pensions explicitly referred to the themes of supplementation, public pension inadequacy, and employer-provided security promoted by the underwriters of their pension plans. When the Pennsylvania Water and Power Company and the Safe Harbor Water and Power Corporation began an employee pension plan, underwritten by the Prudential Insurance Company of America, they explained: "Analysis of the [Social Security] Act discloses that it is an inadequate provision for the Employees of the Companies. . . . The Plan of Retirement now being inaugurated by the Companies therefore is intended to supplement the Old Age Benefits to be provided by the Government under the Social Security Act." The Allied Kid Company of Boston declared that it had "approved a plan supplementary to the Federal Social Security Act which is designed to furnish to eligible employees the assurance of more adequate aggregate retirement allowances than are provided solely under the terms of such Act." Companies from Bristol-Myers, which launched a pension plan in 1939, to the Pacific Gas and Electric Company sought the new credibility associated with the imprint of "security," featuring workers' security as the primary motivation of company welfare work. Business firms openly acknowledged that they were following in the footsteps of government social policy.[59]

It was not sufficient merely to invoke the language of security; employers contended that they were putting real money behind it. The Philadelphia Company, one of Equitable's longstanding group life insurance clients, emphasized the new values of soundly financed welfare capitalism. Initiating an insured employee pension in 1936, the company's management proclaimed, "An analysis of the Social Security Act shows that it does not fully meet the needs of our employees. . . . In view of the facts outlined above, your companies feel that the benefits to be provided under the Social Security Act should be supplemented, that the supplementary plan should be on a sound reserve basis."[60]

The government's new welfare policy influenced sectors left uncovered by the old-age pension titles. Many employers whose employees were excluded from the Social Security Act set up pensions: the Evangelical Press of Harrisburg, Pennsylvania, the American Education Press, the Associated Seed Growers, the Boy Scouts of America, and numerous banks.[61] The politics of security had a dialectical effect: bank and nonprofit employees now obtained new pensions, but in turn they demanded that the act be expanded to cover them, so they could join the national risk pooling project.

Insurers built on their network of group life insurance clients in selling their new old-age security policies. Life companies became advisers on Social Security policy. Equitable and Metropolitan sent their group pension clients booklets summarizing major bills and amendments to the Social Security Act and relevant tax policies.[62] In 1939 J. Douglas Brown, a Princeton economist and director of the SSB's Advisory Council, demonstrated how various companies had adapted their employee pension plans to the Social Security Act.[63] Even in the late 1930s employers with these types of plans continued to react to government security initiatives through group insurance. The SSB began drafting bills for disability insurance amendments in 1937. Wilbur Cohen and Arthur Altmeyer intended to include it in the 1939 amendments. Senator Robert Wagner drafted more comprehensive health insurance legislation. As New Dealers stirred up controversy over these expansions of the national social insurance program, companies began to adopt group disability or health insurance plans. The case of the American Meter Company illustrates how group insurance expanded into an incipient private welfare program. A group life insurance client since 1917, American Meter created a program covering employees and their families for any loss resulting from the employee's accidental or natural death and disability caused by sickness or a nonoccupational accident. And it planned to expand its group insurance program once again to include old-age security. American Meter not only acknowledged that the changes in public policy had contributed to this decision but adopted the specific language of the minimal welfare state and private supplementation that insurance companies had been promoting.[64] The life insurance industry's plan for the mass sale of life insurance to workers—group insurance—had now become the foundation for a burgeoning system of privately provided social welfare benefits.

What did employers mean when they said that they had "modified" their pension plan to dovetail, conform to, or supplement the Social Security Act? First, they switched from a noncontributory, in-house pension to a contributory, insured plan. Thomas Edison, Inc., Westinghouse Air Brake, Connecticut Light and Power, the Otis Elevator Company, Pacific Gas and Electric, the Kuhn Loeb & Company, and the McCray Refrigerator Company, for example, either closed out their existing pension plans, immediately succeeding them with a new insured annuity, or had the earlier plan reinsured by an insurance company. Of 220 active pension plans surveyed by NICB in 1939, 169, or 77 percent, were insured group annuity plans, a dramatic change from before the Depression and the New Deal. By 1939 three-quarters of these annuity plans had been "adjusted" to the Social Security Act.[65] Second, when insurers spoke of dovetailing, what they meant was that the annuity would be set up so that when it was added to the new payroll tax, the employer would not be spending much more than before the act. Equitable assured group pension clients that under the dovetailed plan, the company could pay into both the public pension plan and a private plan without an increase in expense. For example, explained William Graham, if the employer had contributed 3 percent of payroll to a private, insured pension prior to the act, under the supplementary arrangement the employer would pay 1 percent to the federal government and 2 percent to an insurance company. But as an NICB study concluded, "The most important revisions made in the company plans are the reductions in retirement allowance and corresponding decreases in contributions." Under the typical annuity plan, the company provided a pension of 1.5 to 2 percent of income for each year of participation. To avoid overlap, NICB determined, "the [modified] company plan provides a full 1% or 2% annuity only on income in excess of $3,000 on which no federal pension is paid, while the annuity on earnings up to $3,000 is approximately 1% less."[66] The supplementary pension in a sense mirrored the Social Security Act. Under Old-Age Insurance (OAI), benefits would be graduated relative to contributions so that individuals who had low incomes or who entered the system late in life would receive higher proportionate benefits.[67] However imperfectly, the Social Security Act was designed to benefit the low-wage worker; the supplementary pension seemed to work in reverse.

U.S. Steel's "dovetailed" pension plan reveals the dubious claims to security inherent in the new company plans. U.S. Steel immediately took advantage of the dovetailing idea. As both an SSB study and J. Douglas Brown's report discovered, U.S. Steel "modified" its pension plan so that "the total retirement annuity including Social Security benefits shall be the same as under the former plan." The company announced in 1935 that if the amount of a public pension should equal or exceed the amount owed by the company, "no [U.S.] Steel pension shall be granted to such employee." If the public pension were less than the amount of the Steel pension, the company would subtract the amount of Social Security benefits and pay only the remainder. Thus, contemporary observers concluded, "it would appear that the cost to the company for pensions will be decreased since the employee bears part of the cost of the Social Security payments."[68] Shell Union Oil's pension announcement stated that "in determining the pension payable in any month to a retired employee, there will be deducted an amount equal to the payment due him for that month under the Social Security Act of the United States."[69] These companies directly reduced benefits by the amount being paid by Social Security. If, for example, a worker had earned a monthly pension of $40 from the company and now earned a federal old-age pension of $30, the company would pay her or him $10. In the early 1940s DuPont found itself awarding company pensions that amounted to less than $10 per month. The Department of Labor's *Monthly Labor Report* concluded that most companies reduced their contributions and pension benefit amounts when they dovetailed the company plan with Social Security. "The appeal of such a plan to an employer lies primarily in the fact that an employer, in even a highly competitive industry or business, may have a complete retirement program at not too great a sacrifice," touted Equitable's chief group insurance marketer.[70]

Dovetailing benefited upper-income employees most, a fact insurers emphasized as a selling point. Graham told business groups that employers could modify the parameters of the pension policy for any group of employees they chose. If an employer wanted to insure only younger employees or older employees or highly paid executives, Equitable could arrange it. Employers immediately latched onto this idea and began offering supplemental pensions solely for their most well paid employees. Social Security's social insurance tax would apply to the first $3,000 of income earned by the employee. GE, which had implemented its first pension plan in 1912, reinsured it in 1928 as a contributory plan. With the passage of the Social Security Act, GE determined that "for new employes . . . pensions for all employees on the first $3,000 of wages and salaries will be solely under the Federal Pension Plan." Employees who made more than $3,000 salary per year would be eligible for GE's contributory plan.[71] In 1936 the Inland Steel Company inaugurated a pension plan for supervisors, managerial employees, and officials along the same lines as GE's. The Campbell Soup Company, which did not have a pension prior to the Social Security Act, established one solely for the employees earning more than $3,000 to supplement Social Security payments. Since the average income of manufacturing workers at the end of the 1930s hovered between $1,300 and $1,800 a year, companies clearly intended these pensions to serve salaried managerial employees.[72]

GM followed suit a few years later, creating an Employees Contributory Retirement Plan in 1940 for executives and managers earning more than $250 a month. GM assured its stockholders that "current practice among other representative American companies is in the direction of supplementing the Old Age Benefits under the Federal Social Security Act by providing additional benefits . . . for such employes." Kodak raised the stakes even higher, stating that anyone earning less than $5,000 would be excluded from the company pension plan, thus clearly establishing company pensions for the highest ranks of management.[73] In this way, business could use the welfare state as a class subsidy for the well-paid, salaried middle class.

Companies' motivations to implement and expand pensions for salaried personnel came from two political forces: the new welfare state and the rising industrial union movement. On the one hand, as Teresa Ghilarducci has argued, the Social Security Act, as corporations saw it, had taken care of the problem of older workers in low-paid groups. Supplemental pensions could be fully dedicated to the higher income groups. On the other hand, the industrial union movement not only stimulated rank-and-file workers in the late 1930s; it also began to stir foremen and lower level managers. Executives were not prepared to see this latter group of employees defecting. New welfare pension schemes could hold the line on front-line management. A Special Conference Committee report of 1937 registered a "growing realization that the efficiency, loyalty, and morale of salaried workers are of vital importance to the present success and future leadership of industrial organizations."[74] Finally, for top corporate executives, pension trusts became a useful tool for avoiding taxes since individual taxes on pension income were deferred.

New Dealers in the Treasury Department noticed this trend with some distress. Following Roosevelt's attack on the "economic royalists," Secretary of the Treasury Henry Morgenthau and Randolph Paul, the Treasury Department's leading expert on taxation, tried to close up loopholes in the tax system that favored large corporations and wealthy individuals. Morgenthau particularly singled out tax policies that encouraged "high-salaried officers [to] seek to provide themselves with generous retiring allowances, while at the same time the corporation claims a deduction therefore, in the hope that the fund may accumulate income free from tax."[75] Morgenthau and Paul tried to get a measure included in the Revenue Act of 1938 stipulating that companies could only qualify for tax exemptions on pension contributions if the plan applied to at least 70 percent of the firm's workforce. Conservative Democrats and Republicans in Congress, however, blocked most of the Roosevelt administration's tax proposals, and this one went down to defeat. As Christopher Howard has argued, Morgenthau's proposal represented an attempt to introduce nondiscrimination into the tax code—to defend the rights of "the forgotten man" in a passive way, one that would not actually require the spending of government funds. Yet there was a second motivation as well. Henry Morgenthau feared that Social Security's old-age pension program would grow out of control, offering "excessively generous annuities" and threatening the financial integrity of the U.S. government. Following the economic collapse of 1937 and 1938, he insisted that fiscal responsibility and a balanced budget take first priority.[76] Morgenthau lost the debate over deficit spending in 1938, but he won on the pension and taxation issue. The tax code would be used to encourage the development of a broad-based private pension system that would supplement Social Security pensions and thereby keep benefit levels in check.

Discussions among SSB representatives over the Revenue Act reveal a conscious strategy to use tax policy to encourage the growth of a supplemental private pension system. Eleanor Davis, an SSB official, advised removing phrases that allowed employers to offer pensions to "a class of his employees." Davis wrote: "It seems to me unwise to leave the door open for plans which apply to limited and chosen groups. If the Social Security Act is to be amended so as to encourage the development of industrial relations plans, there should be an attempt to encourage the more desirable types."[77] The New Dealers did manage to get a provision included in the Revenue Act that required employers to place pension contributions in an irrevocable trust fund in order to qualify for tax exemptions. This provision closed some of the loopholes that enabled employers to set aside pension funds during years of high earnings and then recapture them in poor years by revoking the trust. A nondiscrimination clause for pensions, however, would have to wait until World War II.[78]

Whose Security? Social Stratification and Old-Age Security

The Social Security Act dramatically expanded the federal government's welfare role. Social support for the elderly, however, was divided into two different programs—old-age contributory social insurance, or Old-Age Benefits (OAB), and old-age public assistance, or Old-Age Assistance (OAA)—thus fragmenting the elderly population along class and gender lines. New Deal policymakers, as well as legislators, insisted that the legitimacy of a permanent economic security program (OAB) depended on its connection to work. Yet only certain categories of work were included in its coverage. By excluding agricultural and domestic workers from the social insurance programs, Congress removed about 5 million workers from coverage. Half the African American workers in the United States would automatically be ineligible. Not only did the contributory feature, which rested on continuous earnings, disadvantage blacks and women but with the exclusion of religious and nonprofit workers, even more women, women who worked as teachers or nurses, for example, would be left out. Poor women and African Americans would have to apply for public assistance, eventually structured as means-tested programs for dependents rather than entitlements for citizens.[79]

The U.S. Women's Bureau soon realized that the pension program would do little to boost women's economic security. Mary Anderson, director of the Women's Bureau, tried to call attention to the regressive tax and benefit features of OAB that particularly disadvantaged women. For women who worked in covered industries, the flat payroll tax dug deeper into their smaller paychecks. Benefits were awarded for consistent wage work over the long term. Since most women's work histories did not fit this model, women paid the taxes but in the end were unlikely to receive the pensions. For those who did eventually qualify, benefits based on individual earnings would always bring a smaller pension to women. Such remuneration, of course, ignored women's many years of work raising or taking care of families and maintaining households. Finally, Mary Anderson lamented, few women were covered by old age social insurance at all, either because they did unpaid work at home or because they worked in excluded industries. Anderson acutely understood the paradox of the new Social Security Act. Women often interrupted paid work to take care of domestic responsibilities. This intermittent participation in the paid workforce meant that women lacked the "equal opportunity to save for their own futures." Thus, women in particular needed public support to obtain economic security in old age, and yet this same fact excluded them from the program.[80]

While the Social Security Act structured its benefits for a male breadwinner and a dependent wife, private pensions covered the employee who worked for the company, whoever that may be. Thus, many of the pension plans, especially group insurance annuity contracts, included women. From its inception, group life insurance had included male and female workers. Insurers wanted to spread the risk pool as widely as possible; limiting the group to either women or men could cause problems of adverse selection, not to mention reduced premium income. Therefore, insurers very much wanted women to be covered by group insurance, hoping also that they would go home and convince their husbands to buy more insurance to protect the family. If employers requested, insurers would draw up contracts for designated classes of employees, but the policy typically covered men and women within that group. Only three companies included in my study specified that the pension covered only "men"—Inland Steel, Brown and Williamson Tobacco, and AT&T—but they appear to have been in the minority. Some set up different tables for men's and women's requirements, contributions, and benefits. Apparently the main difference was in the retirement age: employer pensions set a lower retirement age for women, usually 55 or 60 years of age.

Yet since employers required long, unbroken service records, fewer women than men would actually qualify for these pensions. The Barnsdall Corporation provides an interesting case. Although the introduction to the employee pension booklet clearly indicated that women and men were eligible for coverage, every hypothetical example used to explain the pension was based on a man's work history, wage, retirement age, and the benefits "his wife" would receive, suggesting that the company certainly expected the pensioner to be male.[81] And since company pensions were based on a percentage of the employee's wage, and women tended to be concentrated in lower-paying jobs, a woman's pension ultimately would not amount to much. Most women made less than $1,000 a year if they were lucky enough to work year-round. In a brief study of women and private pensions, SSB's actuarial consultant concluded that "particularly at the older ages the proportion of women is almost always much lower than the proportion of men among those who are to be retired. Therefore, with a limited number of individuals to deal with, generous treatment to women does not run into very high outlay."[82] In one case, a female employee at DuPont applied for the company pension after seventeen years of service. DuPont had initiated a policy of deducting Social Security benefits from the final amount to be paid by the company. After deducting for Social Security payments, the woman's monthly pension from the company amounted to two cents. Recognizing this absurdity, DuPont's Board of Pensions voted simply not to award her the pension. Finally, in a supplemental private pension system one had to work in an industry that was covered by the Social Security Act; many women did not. Industries that employed many women, such as laundries or southern textiles, usually provided nonpecuniary programs—hot lunches, women's changing rooms, suggestion boxes, or Thanksgiving turkeys.[83] Private security for women workers foundered on structural obstacles, labor market inequalities that the public welfare state did not attempt to offset. Moreover, supplementation was not a compensatory system for those who did not receive welfare state social insurance benefits in the first place.

Nor were African Americans likely to retire on a private pension. African Americans typically worked in sectors with casual or intermittent work, and this was true in all regions of the country. In the South, the two-fifths of the African American population that did not work in agriculture or domestic service were concentrated most heavily in lumber, furniture, and construction. Even in other regions African Americans worked disproportionately in agriculture or extractive industries. Since employment in these industries was seasonal and mobile, they certainly could not sustain a long-term, consistent workforce, the kind of workforce that would make pensions possible. This meant, first, that African Americans worked for employers who did not have an interest in maintaining long-term employees or stable employment levels and thus had little use for welfare capitalist programs and, second, that they could not build up the long service record needed to qualify for a pension. Employers discharged African Americans more often than they did whites. Not only were African Americans more likely to be unemployed but they experienced longer spells of unemployment than did whites—whether the business cycle was up or down. Group insurance or pensions would not reach African American workers. Large group insurance companies did not write group insurance or annuity policies for small firms or casual employers. African American insurance companies did not even issue annuities (or offer company pensions to their employees) until well after World War II. For African Americans, the gaps in private and public welfare reinforced each other.[84]

Thus, while company pension plans grew steadily in the late 1930s, they did not significantly increase ordinary workers' financial security. Rather, the revived industrial pension movement helped preserve the notion of the paternalistic employer who cared for his employees' needs beyond the workplace as it continued to serve the earlier functions of welfare capitalism. Although more likely to be insured and funded than before the Depression, new pensions still retained the unilateral characteristics of their predecessors. Management chose to implement them, chose what the amounts would be, chose the carrier, and retained the right to discontinue them. Most employee pension handbooks contained a clause such as the one in the Ohio Oil Company's, Inland Steel's, or American Meter's pension booklet, the latter stating that "the company reserves the right to modify the plan or withdraw from the plan and to discontinue making payments in the future after 30 days' written notice to the members," or the one in Socony-Vacuum's booklet, stating that the company "reserves the right to change or discontinue at any time."[85] Nor did the legal context for employee pensions improve. In 1939 a New York University Law School professor contended that it was still "the unquestioned rule" that a pension was not a contractual obligation "but a gratuitous allowance in which the pensioner has no vested right." Even when the employee had made compulsory contributions to the plan but was ultimately denied a pension, few judges held that the pensioner had an enforceable right. Later, when the courts abandoned gratuity theory in pension cases and replaced it with contract theory, in practice employer prerogatives remained in place. Invoking contract theory, courts consistently upheld clauses in unilateral pension "contracts" stipulating that the employer could modify or terminate at any time. Neither gratuity theory, which excluded any employer obligation, nor contract theory, which permitted unilateral change in terms if that right was reserved by the employer, conferred any rights on employees. As Merck & Company informed employees about its new pension plan, "Employees should understand that such supplemental benefits are not guaranteed"[86]

The radicalized political climate of the 1930s had legitimized the principle of security to such an extent that it compelled business firms in core sectors to offer a degree of economic security they had previously ignored. But employers intended to do so on their own terms, without making old-age or illness support an employee right. Pressure from workers in the next decade would chip away at managerial control of private social security.

Establishing the Boundaries of the Welfare State

Two final developments illustrate the way in which the persistence and rejuvenation of welfare capitalism influenced the development of the

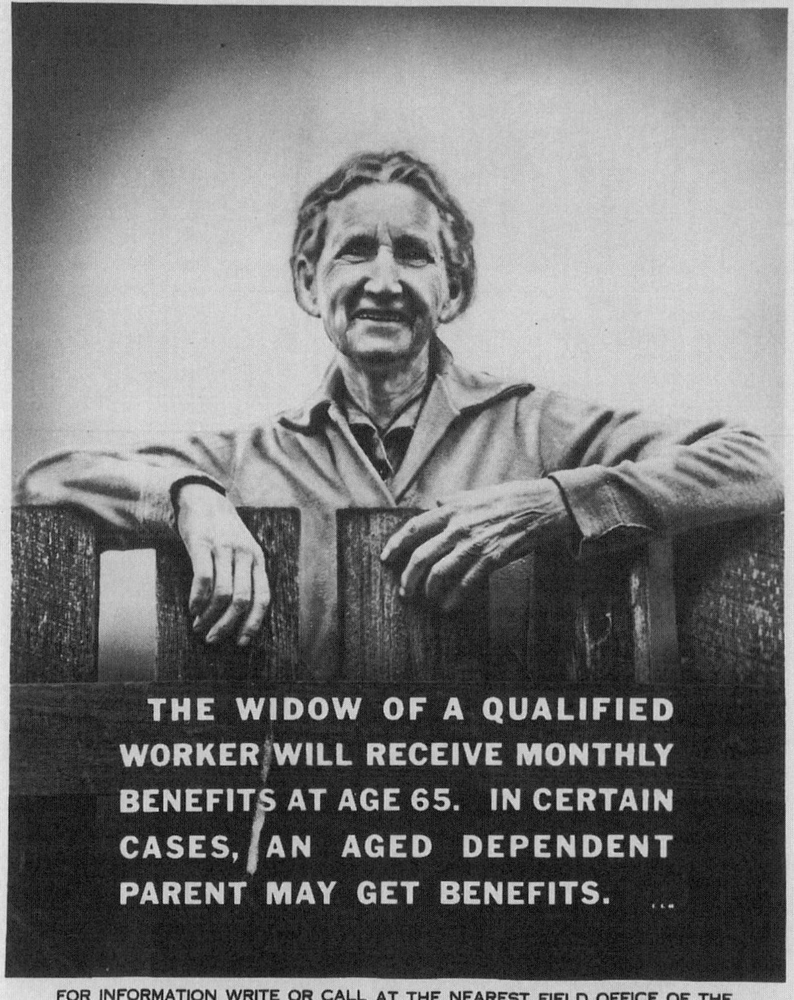

3. "More Security for the American Family." To promote the 1939 amendments to the Social Security Act, the Social Security Board issued a series of posters with this main headline stressing security. Courtesy of Franklin D. Roosevelt Library.

federal welfare state: the 1939 Social Security Act amendments and the SSB's adoption of the ideology of supplementation. The advocates of private social security took a tack different from that of 1935 when it came to amending the Social Security Act in the late 1930s. Their strategy this time reveals the acceptance of a minimal welfare state as a necessary or at least inevitable foundation for industrial relations peace. But they intended to channel the surplus political clamor for security into private benefits in order to cultivate workers' loyalty to the company and check the further growth of the welfare state. Insurers and some welfare capitalist employers supported SSB's plans to extend benefits to survivors or some other uncovered groups. Reinhard A. Hohaus, an assistant actuary at Metropolitan Life, called for extending social insurance benefits to provide "a minimum allowance for as large a proportion of the population as possible." He supported extending Social Security not only to widows or survivors but to "most of the classes of persons now excluded." Such an expansion would broaden the public security foundation upon which private entrepreneurs could build. At the same time, Hohaus vehemently recommended against raising the amount of benefits or taxes.[87] In fact, within months of the original act's passage, insurance organizations of all sorts began calling for a modification or elimination of the reserve fund in order to prevent public demands for benefit increases. Rainard Robbins argued in great detail in the *Spectator* against collecting a surplus of revenue. Albert Linton's address to the American Life Convention in October 1935 immediately stressed insurers' disapproval of amassing large reserves. The annual Report of the American Life Convention in 1938 called for a pay-as-you-go system instead of a surplus reserve fund and opposed any tax increases.[88]

Like Kodak's Marion Folsom, neither insurers nor other welfare capitalist employers wanted Social Security to develop a reserve fund. They believed that the presence of a large reserve would inevitably lead to regular increases in benefits. Insurers and large employers with pensions had philosophical and practical reasons for preventing the public pension program from developing in this direction. As J. Douglas Brown remarked in retrospect, after the final defeat of the Clark Amendment, "with the clarification of the issue of substitution of *forms* [public or private pensions], that of proper determination of appropriate levels of protection became the continuing issue." In superimposing private pension programs upon a universal social insurance program, the level of benefits of the public program became a critical concern for group pension employers. Brown explained that as long as the ceiling of wages covered under the social insurance tax rate held at a modest level, employers could easily make adjustments in a company annuity plan by tinkering with contributions or benefits. "A *drastic* rise in the social insurance tax ceiling, however, forces the employer to meet a much higher tax cost for higher-income employees who are near or above the new ceiling without a comparable sharing of the cost of the higher level benefits which he must provide under his own annuity program. An increased segment of his tax cost will have been used to assure favorable benefits for lower-income workers under the social insurance program."[89]

Linton, Hohaus, Folsom, and other businessmen argued to the SSB that employers (and employees) would have to spend $200 million extra if the program continued on its original terms. Linton and Hohaus, both insurance men, had gained significant influence among SSB Advisory Council members and Social Security policymakers.[90] Together with Folsom, they urged pay-as-you-go financing and lower tax rates. There was no need to have public benefits that cost more, when there could be a basic public program supplemented by a private one. As Hohaus told the American Association for Social Security, "Private and social insurance are complementary rather than conflicting . . . each having its part in providing old age security for the country as a whole and neither being able to do the job alone." In his testimony before the House Ways and Means Committee, Folsom argued specifically for keeping Social Security benefits at a minimum level of basic protection so that the individual could supplement it with earnings or a company pension. Again, welfare state policies would be designed around the labor market experience of white men. A subsistence-level, pay-as-you-go system would ensure that Americans still needed to rely on other sources of support during periods of absence from the labor market.[91]

The SSB and Congress heeded their advice. SSB refused to support including those who were already too old to make the necessary payroll contributions. They fought increases in state public assistance plans, even though research indicated that only 6 percent of the elderly would be eligible for Old-Age and Survivors' Insurance (OASI). Congress liberalized the program, adding survivors' benefits for widows and children, increasing benefits for married workers, changing the lump-sum death payment to a monthly income benefit, and bringing in two new groups, bank and public-sector employees. The amendments also required employers to provide workers with a receipt showing their contributions to OASI, something employers had fought against. The modifications made possible the vision of the limited, basic welfare state and private supplementation. While not fully ruling out the use of general revenues, the elimination of a large reserve fund meant that benefits would be strictly tied to payroll taxes. The decision against storing up surpluses built a rigidity into the pension program over the long term. The 1939 amendments strengthened the family wage biases of the program. Women were incorporated into the national social insurance program only as dependents of men. To qualify for their new entitlement, women had to be married, living with their husband at the time of his application or death, and not divorced. Thus, the national social insurance program would not compensate for the economic insecurity of single, divorced, or unmarried women. In addition, the amendments included a cap on survivors' benefits so that benefit checks would never amount to more than 80 percent of the wage earners' former average earnings, thus ensuring that without other sources of income, working-class women and their families remained at subsistence levels.[92]

Finally, and most directly supportive of the incipient system of private social welfare, the 1939 amendments exempted from the definition of wages, and hence from payroll taxes, employer payments made to or on behalf of employees for a retirement, unemployment, or disability benefits plan.[93] The potential effect of such a rule would be that employers diverted worker compensation into nontaxable, private pension trust funds (which an employee might or might not ever actually qualify for) rather than into increased wages and Social Security contributions.

Insurers, unsurprisingly, expressed satisfaction with the results. Albert Linton, president of the Provident Mutual Life Insurance Company, wrote to Arthur Altmeyer, "I feel that the old-age security program is on a much more satisfactory basis than it originally was."[94] Whether or not Congress had been aware of their concerns, the insurance industry press felt that Congress had vindicated its arguments about the future of Social Security. The *National Underwriter* concluded that Social Security benefits, with the new revisions, "are necessarily and properly limited to fulfilling minimum needs [which] leaves the way open for supplementary protection for those who want and can afford more than the minimum." Once again, the insurance trade press reported a general optimism among insurance companies that the Social Security Act, with its new amendments, would promote the sale of group insurance. "The impression prevails that after all this opens the way to a larger service for private insurance companies," based on, in the words of one editorial headline, "What the Social Security Act Doesn't Do."[95] The 1939 amendments effectively reinforced the idea of private-sector supplementation.

The second development was a rhetorical shift that allowed SSB members themselves to encourage this tendency. By the end of the decade SSB members and consultants had begun to make the same case for private pensions as necessary supplements to governmental ones. Although SSB won the battle over employers' compulsory participation in the old-age pension program, it remained on the defensive for the rest of the decade. Between 1936 and 1939 the SSB continued to receive letters both from employees worried about losing their company pensions and from Townsendites and other supporters of more radical, flat pension plans. Perceiving itself to be under attack, the SSB chose rather conservative strategies to defend its program.

Ironically, while the insurance industry strove to identify itself with Social Security, Social Security administrators began using the language of commercial insurance to legitimize their prized centerpiece of government security, old-age pensions. Initially, the phrase *social security* had embodied both social insurance and public assistance. After the Court upheld the act, SSB insiders proclaimed contributory social insurance the ultimate aim of government economic security efforts. They believed that to actually make it so, they had to deny redistributional goals. Arthur Altmeyer and his staff explained the program by using the terms *premiums* and *contributions*, terms that did not appear in the original Social Security Act. They stressed the principle of individual equity in the plan. Altmeyer claimed that Social Security benefits were just like those from an insurance company because individuals received them without having to pass a means test; they paid for them. Those fortunate enough to be included under the act's jurisdiction had opened an individual insurance account with the government. The insurance model socialized people in the belief that not only did one have to pay up to earn benefits but benefits could not exceed individual contributions or former wages. As many historians have noted, this strategy elevated contributory social insurance (old-age pensions) above all other forms of government social welfare, thereby narrowing the potential and reach of the New Deal's economic security project, confining it to a model that primarily suited white male wage earners in core sectors of the economy.[96]

Insurers' adoption of Social Security rhetoric and the SSB's use of insurance lingo soon became an ideological convergence that had a powerful effect—stimulating the simultaneous development of public and private welfare systems. In addition to adopting the language of commercial insurance, Social Security policymakers also began to make the case for supplementation by private or commercial means. In a defensive letter to Senator Morris Sheppard, who had received complaints from AT&T employees, Arthur Altmeyer insisted that social insurance would stimulate the growth of private plans. Altmeyer argued further that the board had supported the Social Security Act amendment excluding from the wage-based payroll tax employer payments into plans providing for retirement benefits, dismissal wages, disability benefits, and hospital expenses. The SSB actuary Robert J. Myers enthusiastically endorsed Westinghouse Air Brake's plans to integrate its group life insurance and a new group pension with Social Security benefits.

SSB members emphasized their support for company social welfare benefits to the public. Responding to a General Mills employee who apparently had sent him some material about the company's pension plan, Altmeyer assured the employee that "it can safely be said in general that, from the standpoint of the employee, virtually every private industrial pension plan is beneficial." The SSB chairman even brushed aside the potential pitfalls of company plans, saying that the possibility of an employee's losing his or her contributions was negligible at this point. W. R. Williamson, an actuarial consultant to the SSB, sent messages to concerned employees insisting that supplemental retirement plans dovetailed with Social Security offered a secure means of increasing the value of the Social Security plan. "Since the benefits under Title II are somewhat limited in extent," he argued, "retirements in the next few years can very wisely be dealt with by employers through additional benefits."[97]

By 1940 Williamson had articulated the idea of a dual system of social support in a memo to SSB associates, including Wilbur Cohen, I. S. Falk, and John J. Corson, head of the Bureau of Old-Age and Survivors' Insurance. Williamson reported on an essay by Nathaniel Horelick, director of Equitable's Group Annuities Division, explaining how the Social Security Act, group insurance, and individual insurance worked together to fill the gaps in social security. Williamson praised the essay as "an excellent representation" of "the three basic elements which are available to the industrial employee who has OASI and a package protection plan."[98] The ideology of corporate welfare capitalism and supplementation eventually became so accepted that in 1972 J. Douglas Brown, reflecting back on those years, concluded that "with the elimination of the possibility of parallel alternative coverage, the advantages of a three-level system of assistance, social insurance, and private mechanisms, as visualized by the planners of old age insurance" had been realized.[99] But this was not part of the original vision. It reflects instead the ideological move to the right that occurred during the late 1930s and the convergence with private providers of security—the acceptance of welfare capitalism in the era of the welfare state.

Inside "The Garden of Security"

By the end of the decade the idea of supplementation was firmly in place. It is reflected in the debates over the 1939 amendments, the SSB's defense of old-age social insurance, and employers' decisions to

4. "The Equitable Garden of Security," the Equitable Life Assurance Society's exhibit at the 1939 World's Fair in New York City. The Equitable statue *Protection* overlooked a garden and reflecting pool where Equitable policyholders could visit, relax, and find security. Courtesy of AXA Financial, Inc., and its subsidiary, the Equitable Life Assurance Society of the United States.

buy group insurance as supplemental Social Security. But the idea of security—guaranteed economic security for workers—remained the most compelling idea to emerge from the 1930s. The New Deal had established the principle that the government would provide economic support beyond the wage relation, and the ideology of security would gain even more legitimacy in the next decade. Roosevelt's "Four Freedoms" speech, with its Economic Bill of Rights, rested entirely on the premise of a pledge to ensure and protect economic security. Business executives had neither wanted nor created the Social Security Act, but now they had to devise a way to live with it. And that is what welfare capitalism always represented—a strategy for negotiating pressures from the state and workers, a means of deflecting political pressure from other sources.

Employers and insurers accepted the new political imperative of security, but over the next two decades, they waged a battle to influence the very meaning of security: to shift its emphasis away from the state and the political arena to private, individual economic relationships. At the 1939 World's Fair in New York City, quite the celebration of American industry, the Equitable Life Assurance Society offered an appropriate tribute to the times with its exhibit, "The Equitable Garden of Security." At the opening ceremony for the exhibit, Equitable's president, Thomas Parkinson, proclaimed, "Security! The modern world is in constant search of security." Although clearly invoking the language of the New Deal, reflecting the political upheaval of the decade, Parkinson sought to take this ideal and once again link it with the realm of industry and free enterprise. Looking out over all the "World of Tomorrow" exhibits of American corporations, many of them his clients, Parkinson maintained, "The Equitable Garden of Security stands at the Fair side by side with those great American institutions which have added so much to the comfort, stability, and therefore, security of the lives of American citizens."[100]

American workers and voters, however, knew that thus far business had not provided security, while President Roosevelt and the government had boldly stepped in to offer them relief in the present and support in the future. It would take quite a contest to transform the public's view of security.

4

Organizing for Health Security

COMMUNITY, LABOR, AND NEW DEAL VISIONS FOR HEALTH CARE AND HEALTH POLICY, 1930S–1940S

> My people are asking that our Government take health from the list of luxuries to be bought only by money and add it to the list containing the "inalienable rights" of every citizen.
>
> —FLORENCE GREENBERG, Women's Auxiliary, Steel Workers Organizing Committee

THE FEDERAL government's new role in economic security matters had a ripple effect among community and economic institutions. New Dealers, progressives, and labor activists expected the Social Security Act to mark a breaking point with the past, to inaugurate a new era in which individual concerns would be social concerns, and social concerns new rights enforceable by the state. After 1935 labor liberals and social welfare New Dealers eagerly laid plans for expanding the realm of security. In the late 1930s different ideas about family security—advanced by social workers, child welfare advocates, consumers' unions, women's groups, labor and farmers—converged on the issue of health security. The late 1930s and early 1940s would be a period of innovation and creative experimentation in voluntarist health care projects, perhaps more so than in policy formulation. After World War II, however, such localist experimentation came to an end. Unions' pursuit of social welfare became channeled almost exclusively into collective bargaining for insurance benefits, and employer-provided insurance policies became the primary source of health support in the United States. Subsequent historiography, by picking up the story in 1945, has missed the vitality of this earlier period. Yet it was the New Deal's promotion of security, not the War Labor Board and not wartime tax breaks, that impelled labor to seek new health benefits for its members.

In locations ranging from midwestern cities and southern towns to West Coast industrial and construction sites, doctors, unions, employers, and consumers began developing health care programs that would enable patients to pool the risks and costs of sickness and injury, thus bringing medical care within the reach of more people. Labor activists, as new supporters and constituents of the welfare state, actively participated in the movement for health security. During the era of the Popular Front this movement ranged from broad coalitions of community activists calling for health cooperatives to serve working-class families to business unions asking employers to deduct private insurance payments from wages. Initially, health security was not linked to collective bargaining; unions enrolled in early health programs on their own and even sought to develop community-based group health programs. Many of the programs that labor activists hoped to build stressed provision of services for all who needed them over cash indemnification for costs incurred by the worker. Labor and New Deal reformers viewed security against sickness as a matter of class justice, equality, and a citizen's right to social security. Because national health insurance was never enacted, and because the state, employers, and insurers ultimately advanced the most limited forms of health insurance, the breadth of these experiments and ideas for providing health care has been lost. Moreover, the existence of possibilities for financing medical care on other than an occupational basis has been obscured. Thus, we have not understood the extent to which the health insurance system that emerged after 1945 represented but one trajectory among many.[1]

Labor activists were increasingly influenced by a rising generation of professional health reformers who emphasized a medical model over a public health model. Prior to the 1930s, health activism ranged from issues of sanitation and control of infectious diseases to well-baby clinics for new mothers to factory inspection. In this chapter I refer to the activists who were concerned with these issues, whose ideas were formed by an older generation of public health reformers, as Progressive Era reformers. Although they would still be included in early New Deal policymaking, a new generation of health reformers, who emphasized narrower clinical aspects of health care, eclipsed the Progressive Era public health activists in the late 1930s. These New Deal health insurance reformers emphasized mechanisms that would help pay for individually dispensed medical care. The formative intellectual moment for this generation came during the national study by the Committee on the Costs of Medical Care (CCMC) in the late 1920s and early 1930s, a project that brought together intellectuals from universities and foundations, physicians, and public health officials. This new generation of health reformers would not really achieve political visibility until the late 1930s, when they could rally around the Social Security Act, which had legitimized the principle of contributory social insurance, and the new SSB, which provided an institutional base within the federal government.

Within the health security movement of the 1930s and early 1940s, the clinical services approach was integrated with a belief that "health is a social as well as an individual concern."[2] Thus, often these experiments in financing and organizing the delivery of medical care had a community benefit orientation.[3] In addition to group prepayment, they generally shared the characteristic of community rating: all subscribers paid the same rate, regardless of the amount of medical care services she or he might need or consume. Therefore, the healthier members of the community helped subsidize the less healthy members. Other group plans relied on progressive, graduated membership fees, with dues based on a percentage of family income. Beyond acute care, various activist coalitions intended community health plans to offer health education, preventive medicine, occupational health, and rehabilitation services. Where leftists and African Americans had a voice, they tried to insist on nondiscrimination policies. At their most ambitious, community-based group health programs sought to bring the resources of medical institutions under the control of community groups. Consequently, these voluntary group health plans were not seen as "private alternatives" to the welfare state. Rather, insofar as they could make health care services responsive to community needs, they represented a strategy of building democratic institutions that would remove health care from the realm of corporations, insular elite professional control, and private markets. Yet as Social Security policymakers and advisers focused more exclusively on contributory social insurance and individual medical care, the emphasis on public health, industrial and occupational health, local community control, and antipoverty measures would be marginalized after 1938.

Remaking Health Reform

The Emergence of the New Deal Health Reformers, 1920–1933

During the Progressive Era, health reformers and activists concentrated on issues of public health, occupational safety, and poverty. Public health activists promoted communitywide health activities—sanitation, water purification, registration of births, deaths, and vital statistics, reporting of communicable diseases, prevention and control of tuberculosis, and health education. Their approach to the control of infectious diseases concentrated on wide-scale urban cleanups, pollution control, tenement house regulations, and social welfare programs, such as child hygiene bureaus. The World War I–era campaigns for public health insurance legislation led by the AALL primarily emphasized wage loss protection; that is, health insurance would pay a percentage of the worker's wages while he or she missed work because of disability or illness.

Changes in medical knowledge (germ theory and bacteriology) and treatment in the early twentieth century boosted the validity of clinical medical diagnosis and therapeutic remedies in preventing the spread of disease. Medical care became a more important factor in how people thought about individual, household, and community health. The spread of health examinations, further spurred on by World War I draft procedures and findings, encouraged Americans to seek professional medical care. After the war, the medical care patients now sought was also more effective. With standardized scientific and clinical training of medical students, advances in scientific medicine and technology, and developments in pharmaceuticals, medical care by the 1920s had far more potential to help patients recover from illness. Hospitals focused on curing illness in its acute phase, particularly through surgery. A younger generation of health activists and social reformers came to see doctors and hospitals as providers of effective acute services.[4]

Yet the costs of such care were increasing dramatically. The tighter self-regulation and growing clout of the AMA restricted the number of doctors entering the profession. Doctors' fees began to rise in part because of the greater expenses they incurred—longer, more formal education; new state licensing fees; use of laboratories at hospitals. Diagnostic techniques and instruments fed fee increases. As therapeutic procedures became more complex and specialization proliferated, an individual patient required the services of a number of physicians, support staff, and technicians. Physicians, hospitals, and laboratories each had their own fees. As hospitals invested more in equipment, diagnostic laboratories, and specialized labor, they expected patients to pay. In an effort to attract middle-class (paying) patients, hospitals set up semiprivate accommodations, as opposed to open wards, and then charged extra for these accommodations. Thus while lost income had been the heaviest economic burden before World War I, sociological studies conducted in the 1920s estimated that medical costs were 20 percent higher than lost wages for families with incomes under $1,200 and 85 percent higher for families with incomes between $1,200 and $2,500. The expense of medical care was even getting out of the range of upper-working-class and middle-class persons. Families with incomes between $2,200 and $5,000—a middle-class income—voiced growing complaints about medical bills.[5]

Concerned that a large proportion of the American population might not be gaining access to modern medical care, health activists and medical professionals formed the CCMC in 1927 to investigate these concerns. A few leading Progressive Era public health experts, as well as a new generation of health reformers (their students), believed that different problems and solutions were at stake than those they had been trained to study.[6] Leaving behind their traditional emphasis on the links between sickness and environmental factors, they focused exclusively on questions concerning the costs and distribution of professional medical service. With funding from several private foundations, the CCMC brought together academic health professionals, public agency administrators, social workers, and physicians to conduct a massive national study of the health needs of the nation. Physicians made up a majority of the committee, and notably absent were occupational safety and industrial health activists such as Alice Hamilton, Paul Kellogg, and John R. Commons, who had long emphasized that workers' health depended on improvements in work and home environments. Dr. Alice Hamilton, in particular, had been a high-profile critic of corporate negligence and workers' health and safety conditions.[7]

Major foundations had been involved in health activities since World War I. They had focused primarily on supporting either public health initiatives or medical school training. Rockefeller and Carnegie foundations provided millions of dollars in grants and matching funds to American medical schools, in particular to ensure the dissemination of scientific research and applied science in medical education.[8] The Julius Rosenwald Fund, which established a Medical Services Division in 1928, supported projects on African American health. Intrigued by the ideas of the new generation focusing on individual access to medical therapeutics, several foundations agreed to underwrite the CCMC's work.

The personnel who dominated the CCMC's final recommendations formed a network that linked universities, foundations, and government; their movement among these institutions remained fluid, especially after the New Deal began. They generally held Ph.D.'s in public health, medical sociology, or economics. They linked foundation-sponsored research to state institutions such as the PHS, the New Deal's CES, and the subsequent SSB. They staffed the SSB's Bureau of Research and Statistics later in the decade. Isidore S. Falk, for example, left his position as a public health professor at the University of Chicago to participate in the CCMC field studies. Afterwards he went to the Milbank Memorial Fund, and he eventually ended up at the SSB. Several other researchers, such as Margaret Klem, Louis Reed, and Nathan Sinai, followed a similar trajectory during the 1930s. Others became key figures in the founding of Blue Cross. These reformers shared a heroic view of scientific progress and medical treatment. Yet they also shared the view that medical care was as much an economic activity as a scientific, professional one.

The CCMC agreed with the medical profession's contention that health could be fostered by encouraging more Americans to seek out modern, scientific medical care performed by "certified" scientific practitioners. Yet whereas the medical profession intended to advance this goal through asserting occupational control, eliminating any countervailing power, and establishing inviolable spheres of professional authority, the CCMC reformers believed that economic and scientific-professional issues could and should be separated. The CCMC researchers gathered statistics on income, the incidence of sickness, and the geographical distribution of hospitals, clinics, drugstores, laboratory stations, and physicians. They identified regional inequalities and differences between urban and rural health services. To the lay reformers, these issues were questions of economics; they had to think about the economic organization of medical practice in order to devise an appropriate policy. The issues of access, cost, and distribution did not have to be controlled by doctors; they were social questions of public interest and public policy. The reformers criticized the high fees and overhead expenses of "the predominant economic institution in medical practice today—individual practice" as creating "a barrier—in large part economic" between practitioners and patients. They came to believe that the individual practitioner acting alone, charging his patients according to his own sliding schedule, could not adequately manage the rising cost or the social allocation of medical care.[9]

Embracing a technocratic ethos, reformers sought to devise new means of organizing medical services. The CCMC emphasized that the solution to the health problems and economic security problems of workers could be resolved through health insurance that would help families pay for individual medical services. This latter emphasis would distinguish these reformers from the older, Progressive Era generation, whose emphasis lay on broad-based interventions through public or charitable institutions. In formulating the health needs of the nation specifically in terms of the need for more medical care, they interpreted health insurance as a means to budget larger expenditures for medical service. In particular, research increasingly highlighted "group organization for group practice for provision of care" and comparisons of "organized with non-organized services from the standpoint of adequacy and economy."[10]

In its study of the medical needs of "all the people," the CCMC excluded African Americans from its purview, noting that African Americans suffered from "health problems that are, on the whole, considerably more serious than those of whites." But the researchers decided not to investigate the specific barriers African Americans encountered in obtaining treatment for medical problems or preventive health care. The committee thus missed a critical opportunity to study issues not only of poverty and environment but also of sociopolitical power; whites, a group that had such power, could withhold medical care in numerous ways, from denying blacks hospital admission, to failing to provide public health nurses, to refusing to train black doctors. On the other hand, the CCMC staff viewed the economics of medical care in terms of class: people with low incomes could not afford medical care and thus could not sustain good health. "The Negro is America's principal marginal worker, and he suffers in the North as well as the South from the many disabilities this entails . . . ," the committee wrote. "Because of the extreme poverty of large areas [of the South], neither Negroes nor whites receive anything but the most deplorably inadequate medical service."[11]

The CCMC investigation proved to be a formative experience for a rising generation of health reformers, among them I. S. Falk, Michael M. Davis, Margaret Klem, Louis Reed, and Rufus Rorem. The activists learned about the delivery and organization of medical services at the community level. The investigation helped forge a consensus among the nonphysician members that fee-for-service individual practice should be replaced by group practice and group prepayment plans.[12] They began to formulate systematically the tenets of a group practice health plan. Through a series of more than twenty smaller research reports on community medical programs, the CCMC located and publicized fledgling and innovative prepay health insurance programs in obscure small towns, programs about which the broader public may have been unaware. Having brought these ideas out into the open, they set the idea of group medicine percolating in all kinds of places, sparking discussions of group prepayment and group medicine not only in specialized progressive journals like *Survey Graphic* but in popular magazines as well, from *World's Work* to *American Magazine* to *Collier's*.[13]

One of these studies examined a medical service program in the southern mill town of Roanoke Rapids, North Carolina. Roanoke Rapids township had a steady population of about 10,000, half of whom worked for three textile mills and a paper mill in surrounding Halifax County. The town had one hospital, built and financed by the mill companies. The hospital was connected to the physicians' practice, which was on the first floor of the same building. The hospital and the mills equipped and maintained the physicians' offices and paid for their supplies. They also employed registered nurses, visiting nurses, private-duty nurses, and several nursing students. Roanoke Rapids provided the CCMC with an excellent case study. First, the population was quite stable, with few people moving in or out; there were almost no foreign-born residents. African Americans made up 16.5 percent of the population of the township, but they outnumbered whites in the surrounding rural county. Second, all residents of the town used the same medical facilities and personnel. Those who worked at the mills received and paid for their medical services via a group purchase plan. All others went to see a doctor and paid for each visit or procedure on a traditional fee-for-service basis. Nonmill families paid all of their medical costs themselves. Thus, Falk and his research team had found a stable population sample that used the same medical resources but two completely different payment-remuneration systems.

Under the group prepayment plan each employee contributed 25¢ a week through weekly payroll deductions. In return, employees and their dependents could obtain all the hospital care they might need. They also received physician's care in the office, services such as laboratory tests and X rays, and home calls by physicians and nurses. One of the physicians held a well-baby clinic every Thursday afternoon in one of the mill villages. Physicians were employed on a salary basis, each one earning an annual salary of about $5,600 from the companies (not including what doctors made in additional fee-for-service charges to nonmill patients). Mill employees in the group plan could decide which physician they wanted to see.

The CCMC's study found first that mill workers used the outpatient services, the physicians' offices, and the hospital to a much greater extent than nonmill persons, even though the average income status of the two groups was roughly the same. (In fact, the average weekly income for mill families, $24.50, was slightly below that of nonmill families, $27.16.) In one sample, 1,000 persons from mill families received three to six times as many services as did 1,000 nonmill persons. Eighty percent of the hospital admissions and doctors' visits were for members of the mill group, while 75 percent of physicians' home calls were made to mill patients. When the research staff compared these statistics with the general findings of the CCMC, they found that the mill workers in Roanoke Rapids received a volume of services obtained only by persons in the highest income bracket ($10,000 or over per year) in the rest of the country. Moreover, because the cost borne by a mill family was fixed and evenly distributed, the proportion of the mill population receiving care far exceeded the proportion of the nonmill population receiving care. Many of the latter received no care at all.[14]

The CCMC research staff also determined that the group plan provided an "economy of organized services." The nonmill patients paid higher fees for less care. The researchers argued that the group plan achieved economies for four basic reasons: (1) physicians' offices were simple, small rooms in the hospital building; (2) physicians' assistants also served in the hospital; (3) lab and X-ray equipment was not duplicated; and (4) group practice and group purchase schemes guaranteed the use of facilities to a regular capacity. "By all tokens," the report determined, "medical care is relatively more expensive at local prevailing fees for the non-mill persons; each dollar contributed by the mill group provides more care for the mill population than each dollar spent by private patients was able to purchase."[15] According to the medical consultant the CCMC brought in from the University of Pennsylvania medical school, quality of care was high. In examining the doctors at work, Dr. David Reisman concluded that "the service rendered to the community is in quality above that receive by the middle and poorer classes in our cities and by the people in rural communities generally."[16]

African Americans did not have equal access to these medical services, a fact the researchers treated as rather irrelevant. African Americans in the county did go to the hospital, but they had to enter through a separate entrance and sit in a segregated waiting room. They would receive service from the physicians only after white patients had been treated. Of the total hospital admissions during 1930, 88 percent were for white patients, while 12 percent were for blacks, who accounted for only 6 percent of the outpatient hospital visits, a fact the report simply characterized as "not surprising." Generally lumping African Americans in with the nonmill population, the researchers made no attempt to tease out the factors of class and race that led to this wide disparity in medical care even within the nonmill group. For the CCMC researchers, segregation and racial discrimination were not part of the health security debate.[17]

What they did see as critical to this debate was the fact that physicians benefited from the plan. Not only were these doctors assured a steady, regular income; the salaried doctors at Roanoke Rapids also earned more money than the average general practitioner in the United States overall. In addition, the plan's physicians pocketed more of their income as take-home pay because significantly less money had to be put into professional expenses and maintenance of facilities.

In their final conclusions, the research group acknowledged that the Roanoke plan had weaknesses. There were gaps in coverage, such as dental care, prescription drugs, and prevention. The physical facilities needed augmentation, and the health center needed more specialists. Nonetheless, while subscribers may not have received "luxury care," as Falk put it, "they receive good care." Therefore, the general lesson drawn from the study was that "group practice by the professional personnel can effect important economies in the costs of providing medical care. This can be done without the sacrifice of essential quality in the service. . . . By eliminating the customary fee-for-service arrangement, more people who need care become enabled to obtain it."[18]

The Roanoke Rapids plan, as well as others studied by the CCMC staff, was a welfare capitalist program, designed, implemented, and run unilaterally by employers. The CCMC report did not comment on the industrial relations aspects of the company's maintaining such a program—whether it gave the companies greater leverage over employees or suppressed wages. The CCMC researchers seem not to have appreciated the power dynamics involved in what they called "industrial" programs.[19] Nor did they recognize the ways in which industry-organized medical plans replicated the racial inequalities of the labor market. Yet Falk and his staff did recognize the inherent instability in the long run of relying on a business firm to fund this kind of social welfare program. As Dr. Reisman stated in his consultant's report, "From an economic point of view, the Roanoke Rapids system lacks financial security. It arose as the paternalistic scheme of a local mill owner. . . . [W]ith declining profits the funds allotted to welfare work represented by the hospital organization may be curtailed." The continuance of the program depended on steady employment and good economic times, as did individual payment of medical bills.[20]

As it turned out, when the Great Depression deepened, the companies did retrench. Reisman suggested that the solution lay in general taxation. If all resident adults of the community paid taxes that went to support the community hospital and medical program, all residents could participate, the costs would be more equally distributed, and the overall cost of quality care would decrease. Tax support would make the Roanoke Rapids Medical Service a public project that could remain stable over the long term. This proposal, though, did not recognize the fact that the township residents were a poor population with limited means, so that the taxation would have to be spread over a much wider area. In addition, under a Jim Crow system would African Americans—more than half the residents of the surrounding county—shoulder the tax burden but be denied services? Although Falk's main report did not endorse tax funding, it did conclude that the Roanoke Rapids Medical Service, and other group plans like it, should function as a community program rather than just an industrial program.

The CCMC studies had a lasting influence on those who would become the primary authors of all the major health bills introduced by Senator Robert F. Wagner between 1939 and 1946, as well as all of President Truman's bills. The CCMC majority report recommended "encouraging" the development of voluntary health insurance, and in particular group practice plans. In a minority report the physicians dissented from everything in the majority report, including recommendations for any form of voluntary health insurance.[21] The CCMC staff spent the next several years promoting the study's recommendations in favor of prepaid health insurance through research and writing. Some, like Rufus Rorem, went on to become administrators of plans based on these models. The report stimulated foundations to pour money into health plan experiments throughout the 1930s, and its findings influenced a generation of labor activists. The CCMC health reformers returned to their private foundations or academic positions. Subsequently, these foundations—the Milbank Memorial Fund, the Julius Rosenwald Fund, the Rockefeller Foundation—now staffed by researchers or directors such as Michael Davis, I. S. Falk, Mary Ross, Rufus Rorem, and Edgar Sydenstricker, focused much more heavily on the delivery of medical therapeutics and organized means to pay for family care. They established new divisions to focus exclusively on promoting health insurance and provided a financial and institutional base for this rising generation of New Deal health reformers.

This emphasis seemed further justified by the impact of the Depression on medical practitioners themselves. Far fewer patients could afford to pay physicians' fees. Life insurers terminated life policy disability clauses, which people had been cashing in to pay medical bills. Consequently, incomes for those in private practice dropped by almost half between 1929 and 1933. As fewer people could pay, most doctors refused to provide free, charity care to the poor. They now insisted that government pay the fees incurred by patients on public relief. Municipal and state governments and the federal government soon stepped in, paying for emergency medical relief for recipients of public assistance and hence rescuing many distressed physicians' practices. Hospitals, whose paying patients declined precipitously, were having difficulty paying for even the most basic items. Hospital occupancy rates hovered below two-thirds full. Among those who did check into hospitals the number of charity patients quadrupled. Thus, medical insurance appeared to be a compelling imperative for both sides. It would both enable patients to obtain medical care and buttress the incomes of doctors and hospitals.[22]

Getting Started: Translating Research into Prepaid Health Services

Instead of returning to his academic position as a professor of public health, I. S. Falk, who would become one of the key New Deal health reformers, joined the staff of the Milbank Fund. Milbank's director of research, Edgar Sydenstricker, had also worked on the CCMC project. In Falk's assessment, the cost barrier rested on two traditions: individual arrangements for the purchase of medical service and fee-for-service payment by the patient. The working class, as well as some of the middle class, needed more dependable, systematic access to medical care; they needed health security. Falk contended that "medical charity and the sliding scale of fees have ceased to be altogether instruments of social justice. Their persistence is irksome to the profession and irritating to the public, especially in a complex, urban society where continuing personal relationships between doctor and patient are proportionately much less frequent than they once were."[23]

Likewise, Michael Davis, director of medical services at the Rosenwald Fund, concentrated on the issues of medical bills and prepayment. Looking for alternatives to fee-for-service care, Julius Rosenwald and Davis were at first attracted to the private clinic model because it seemed to offer a way for working persons to obtain medical treatment that was neither charity nor luxury care.[24] The private group clinic, although modeled on Minnesota's long-established Mayo Clinic, represented a new form of medical practice that spread after World War I. Under this arrangement, physicians engaged in the cooperative practice of medicine and used many facilities in common, particularly office space, laboratories, and medical equipment. The clinic brought together full-time physicians in several specialties. Patients were the responsibility of the entire group. The income was pooled; thus, physicians did not receive individual fees from each patient they treated. A business manager handled the collection of fees. The group clinic provided treatment and diagnostic services and hence represented direct competition with private practitioners. The Rosenwald Fund gave grants to the University of Chicago Clinics, the Institute for Mental Hygiene in Pennsylvania, and the ILGWU Health Center in New York City. Although the ILGWU had established its general pay clinic earlier, the Rosenwald Fund stepped in with necessary funding to help carry it through the Depression.[25]

Yet pay clinics did not relieve the financial burden of unexpected illness in any way. Patients still paid for each medical problem as it arose. The clinic did not put medical care on an insurance basis or a group payment basis, did not distribute risk or socialize costs for the patients. The incidence of medical costs still fell where it always had: on individual families with small means and high risks.

So the Rosenwald Fund began looking around for alternatives. During the early 1930s it provided financial support for selected experiments in prepayment of medical bills. It provided grants to experimental prepayment plans in places such as Keokuk, Iowa, and Boston, at the Massachusetts General Hospital.[26] Its staff also continued the local studies they had done under the CCMC, examining group payment programs in small midwestern cities and in places like Baton Rouge, Louisiana, where employees of the Stancola Oil Company organized an insurance plan.[27] By 1936 the Rosenwald Fund had collected information on more than 350 plans and projects for voluntary health insurance and group practice. In turn, it distributed more than 160,000 pamphlets and articles in response to inquiries from hospitals, industrial groups, government officials, physicians, and medical organizations about group payment arrangements for medical care.[28] These were models to which organized labor would later turn and for which the new generation of health reformers would try to get New Deal social policy support.

In 1936 the Rosenwald Fund donated half its Medical Services Division staff and its financial resources to the American Hospital Association (AHA) to help devise a hospital prepayment plan. The fund's staff and the AHA sought a prepayment plan that would solve hospital cash flow problems as much as patients' issues of access.[29] Rufus Rorem assumed the post of executive officer of the AHA's new Commission on Hospital Service. In 1938 the commission began issuing approval certificates for nonprofit hospital service plans that met designated standards. These were the hospital plans that would be given the official, and exclusive, AHA designation. The commission eventually became the Blue Cross Commission after World War II.

In the late 1930s the Commission on Hospital Service created a centralized definition of a nonprofit hospitalization plan—a hospital service plan (soon known as a Blue Cross plan). The basic principles laid out by the commission emphasized the clear establishment of the responsibility of member hospitals for *services* to subscribers. The Standards stated that the hospital service benefits of a nonprofit hospital plan should be guaranteed by the member hospitals during the life of the subscriber contract. The plan's administrative body should include adequate representation of hospitals, the medical profession, and the general public, although the commission advised that it would be desirable for a majority of the policymaking body to represent hospitals. The Commission barred private investors from advancing money in the capacity of stockholders or owners and mandated that the hospital service plan should be independent of any other corporate body or professional or lay group. A hospital that met these standards would be granted the right to use the AHA insignia superimposed over a blue cross.[30]

Under the hospital service plans of the AHA—Blue Cross plans—a group of local hospitals formed a nonprofit corporation. The corporation, acting as an agent of the hospitals, would supervise and direct the plans. Subscribers paid their fee to the hospital service corporation, which then contracted with the hospitals to provide the specified benefits. (In some cases, the arrangement allowed subscribers to remit their fee to the hospital.) The service plan paid a fixed amount of money per day for hospital services rendered to subscribers of the plan; in return, of course, the hospital agreed to render such services to subscribers and to abide by the terms of the subscriber's contract. The type and scope of benefits, as well as the rate charged, were determined at the local level. Unlike an actual insurance policy, the nonprofit hospital plan provided a service contract essentially without reimbursement features. The participating hospitals were paid directly by the hospital corporation, which meant that the patient did not have to pay at the time of treatment and then await reimbursement. As the Commission on Hospital Service described it, "The contract specifies a provision of service and not a cash indemnity."[31]

The Blue Cross plan provided hospital care only; it did not cover surgical expenses or outpatient or ambulatory care. A patient had to arrange for his or her own doctor. The rates charged by the hospital plan averaged $1.50 per month for a husband-and-wife contract or $2.00 a month for family coverage. Because of this common practice of establishing family rates, Rufus Rorem claimed that Blue Cross plans "recognize the family rather than the individual as the economic unit for the purchase of health service."[32] The subscribers, however, still had to pay doctors' bills separately. Consequently, hospitalization plans claimed not to interfere with medical practice or doctor-patient relations.

The hospital service plan was unique. It differed from earlier middle-rate plans in that it could reach working-class patrons as well middle-class persons. It differed from health insurance in Europe in that it did not provide routine medical care. And it elevated the role of the hospital in health maintenance. The first nonprofit hospital service plan of this type organized in 1933. By the end of the decade, the Commission on Hospital Service reported sixty Blue Cross plans. Enrollment increased from around 100,000 subscribers in 1935 to 4 million in 1939. The largest plans, with more than 100,000 subscribers, were in major industrial cities: Pittsburgh, Cleveland, New York, Chicago, Rochester, Newark. But smaller manufacturing towns, such as Youngstown, Buffalo, St. Louis, Toledo, Birmingham, and Minneapolis/St. Paul/Duluth had burgeoning Blue Cross plans as well. According to Rorem, these plans concentrated primarily on group enrollments—persons united either by a common employer or a previously existing economic group.

Most of the plans had already established a payroll deduction method of collecting fees from large groups.[33] Still, this model only covered the costs of hospital stays.

The health insurance reformers soon found the ideal model for prepaid health care that offered full medical services: the Ross-Loos Medical Group in Los Angeles. Two doctors, Donald Ross and Clifford Loos, originally opened their clinic to serve the employees of the Los Angeles Department of Water and Power. By the late 1930s the program served 60,000 patients, from industrial workers to white-collar professionals, family members included. Subscribers paid from $2 to $2.50 per month for complete medical care. There was no extra charge for eye care or hospitalization. Dependents, however, did have to pay for hospitalization and obstetrics. Physicians worked full time, either at the main clinic in Los Angeles or, by the late 1930s, at one of ten clinics in outlying suburbs. The Ross-Loos Group was set up as a partnership. Every doctor drew a salary, regardless of the number of patients under his care. At the end of the year, the partnership distributed any surplus as bonuses to the doctors. Throughout the 1930s the Ross-Loos Group showed an annual surplus, which greatly encouraged the reformers. As the *Survey Graphic* boasted, "Doctors of this medical group enjoy something almost unknown in private practice—a 44 hour working week, except for emergencies and for those doing night duty." In terms of income, "they are in the upper half of the California medical profession, probably well up in it."[34]

The public responded enthusiastically to the program, besieging the medical group with requests from all over the state to open clinics in their communities. The AMA responded differently. Alleging that the group "solicited" patients, the California Medical Association accused the Ross-Loos group of "unethical practices." The Los Angeles County Medical Society expelled Ross and Loos, and the state medical society upheld the action. (The AMA Judicial Council eventually reinstated them on procedural grounds.) Yet the program was so popular among its supporters, *Survey Graphic* reported, that "the Group has had difficulty in keeping their subscribers from flooding the newspapers with protests, organizing mass meetings, or sending angry statements to the county [medical] association."[35] Ross-Loos became one of the programs that the health insurance advocates, social scientists, and laborite intellectuals admired and to which they referred most often when speaking of health security.

In calling for group health plans like Ross-Loos the New Deal health insurance reformers envisioned a new institutional role for the health center. Prior to this period, Progressive Era reformers viewed the health center as an institutional mechanism that could coordinate the activities of municipal health programs and voluntary societies. The Progressive Era health center brought together such social services as infant care and well-baby stations, settlement houses, hospital outpatient departments, tuberculosis clinics, and venereal disease treatment. Reformers saw the health center as "an auxiliary rather than an alternative to the private practitioner." Even the early health centers that labor unions established for their members offered mainly diagnostic testing and examinations; patients then went to see private-practice doctors. During the 1930s health insurance reformers embraced a new concept: the health center as a general medical treatment center. In this conception, patients could obtain diagnostic, therapeutic, and preventive medical care; they could see general physicians, technicians, and specialists in one place. The medical societies had never been too happy about the first concept of the health centers on the grounds that it dispersed too much medical work to the laity. Now, the health center as the basis for group medical plans offered an explicit alternative to private practice. AMA opposition would be visceral and punitive.[36]

The corollary to the new health center was that the hospital was the most appropriate setting in which to treat acute illnesses. Health reformers cast the hospital as "an indispensable agency in the field of medical care and pubic health," the site of "vital and essential services," and the central institution for "scientific equipment, devices, and methods for performing the practices required by scientific medicine." Soon, however, partially because of the medical establishment's opposition to medical centers and partially owing to the large startup costs involved, the emphasis on hospital care would overshadow and outstrip the emphasis on the health centers. A generation and a half later this overemphasis on heavily capitalized, technological hospital care would come to haunt health care reformers.[37]

Health Security and the New Deal

Building the U.S. Welfare State, 1933–1939

The New Deal brought social welfare policymaking back to Washington. Of course, the older generation of Progressive Era health reform activists still had political clout and political connections. During the first phase of the New Deal, they managed to get their concerns incorporated into public policies. The foundational cornerstone of the American welfare state, the Social Security Act, would reflect their prescriptions for health more than those of the newer generation of health insurance activists. Yet as the social insurance component of

Social Security became the most prominent, the health insurance activists displaced public health advocates. The National Health Conference of 1938 reflected this transition. Contrary to the insurance companies' and welfare capitalists' ideas about the "basic welfare state," social insurance proponents conceived of the Social Security Act as a foundation that would inevitably have to be built upon if it was to provide real economic security. The passage of the act immediately generated calls to pass additional security measures and expand its scope. These proposals would fail to pass as public policies, but they would influence activists working on health care programs at the community level.

Emergency cash relief programs and work relief programs of the New Deal offered some health care. The first federal aid program, the Federal Emergency Relief Administration (FERA), which channeled $500 million to state and local agencies for direct cash relief, required state and local agencies receiving FERA funds to pay for emergency nursing, dental, and nonhospital care for relief recipients. FERA ordered that each state and local relief agency establish a uniform administrative plan that included a basic set of services for indigents and a means of enforcing their delivery. Although it is unclear how many states fully complied, by April 1934 forty-six states were receiving federal funds for medical care relief. Some states used the funds to provide broad general and special medical care, while others provided emergency care only. State and local relief agencies, under agreements with medical societies and individual physicians, paid physicians on a reduced-fee basis. The federal government often negotiated directly with county medical societies to arrange the fee schedules for relief recipients. The FERA medical care program was plagued by the same problems of regional irregularities, disparities, and racism in implementation that all New Deal programs experienced. Despite Federal Emergency Relief Administrator Harry Hopkins's official rule that African American doctors were to be included in medical relief work, African American physicians, for example, protested that they were being barred from participating in some states.[38]

Yet contemporary observers believed that the FERA medical program had a significant symbolic impact. Certainly many needy people received care, but it also brought to public authorities' attention just how many people never received any medical attention. In trying to carry out Hopkins's mandate, public agencies, social workers, and activists also "discovered" many communities where medical facilities and personnel were severely lacking. As Josephine Brown, a social worker, observed, "Perhaps the most valuable contribution . . . besides the immediate remedial measures . . . was the public awareness which it created of health needs. . . . This new awareness of health needs and the wide participation of citizens in the program did much to educate communities to their responsibilities."[39] The program ended with the termination of FERA in November 1935.

Other New Deal programs, while not specifically focused on health, found themselves drawn into offering health care. The Resettlement Administration (RA), successor to the Agricultural Adjustment Administration (AAA), assumed responsibility for rural relief and rehabilitation in 1935. In surveying loan defaults, the RA found that many farmers suffered from illness and poor health, which hampered their productivity and economic self-sufficiency. The RA negotiated with local medical societies for rural doctors' participation in a group prepayment plan funded through the federal loans made to struggling farm families. In two states, North Dakota and South Dakota, the RA worked in conjunction with local and state physician groups and public health agencies to establish statewide health programs based on farmers' mutual aid corporations. Through these programs, families on relief could obtain comprehensive medical care, hospitalization, nursing care, and emergency dental services. Each plan also provided for preventive services such as immunizations and pre- and postnatal care for women and infants. The Works Progress Administration (WPA) contributed to health issues by putting people to work on public health projects such as mass inoculations, health checkups for schoolchildren, and dental hygiene education. The massive National Health Survey of 1935 was originally proposed when Hopkins asked Falk to recommend some public works projects. These New Deal programs raised the public's consciousness about medical care, stirring employee associations, consumer groups, and trade unions to demand more permanent health policies from the state and to develop community programs.[40]

But when New Dealers began designing a long-range structure for economic security, with emphasis on an omnibus economic security bill, health insurance was cut out of the deal. In 1934 Franklin Roosevelt established the CES to design a permanent, long-range economic security program. The CES was staffed by an all-white, almost all-male group of social welfare activists whose policy focus was social insurance.[41] A new generation of health insurance advocates believed this project would be their opportunity to translate what they had learned into public policy. After its first meeting, in August 1934, the CES announced that its work would include "all forms of social insurance (accident insurance, health insurance, invalidity insurance, unemployment insurance, retirement annuities, survivors' insurance, family endowment, and maternity benefits) and also problems of providing work . . . for the unemployed and training them for jobs that are likely to become available." The CES established a technical committee for each specialty—unemployment, old age, medical care, and public employment and relief. Two labor economists, Harry A. Millis and William Leiserson, sat on the technical committee for medical care along with Edgar Sydenstricker and his colleague at the Milbank Fund, I. S. Falk. Sydenstricker and Falk did the bulk of the work of drafting a health insurance proposal.[42] These health reformers had long before abandoned issues of public health, and since the CCMC study their primary focus had been on health insurance for individual medical therapeutic services.

Roosevelt and his close advisers saw health insurance measures as expendable. As soon as CES announced the initiation of a health insurance study, letters and telegrams of protest from the medical profession began pouring into Roosevelt's office. Although Sydenstricker set up a Medical Advisory Committee for physicians, it refused to endorse any health insurance proposals. For Secretary of Labor Frances Perkins, President Roosevelt, and CES Chairman Edwin Witte the most important issues at the moment were unemployment and old-age security. Although Harry Hopkins saw health insurance as a high priority, neither Witte nor Perkins was willing to back it up in the face of controversy. They decided it was not worth a fight, which they believed could sabotage unemployment insurance and old-age benefits. Moreover, while the Townsendites were marching in the streets and flooding Congress with petitions, fledgling experiments in group hospitalization and other health plans had not generated a politically visible movement. In the end, not only did the CES exclude health insurance proposals from the Economic Security Bill but the administration suppressed the technical committee report drafted by Sydenstricker and Falk in the spring of 1935 and prevented it from being publicly released. The Roosevelt administration was not even willing to stand behind language in the Economic Security Bill to the effect that the newly created SSB would reserve health insurance for future study. Instead, the Social Security Act conferred on the SSB the responsibility for future study of "related subjects."[43]

The older, Progressive Era health reformers, including women social work activists, were somewhat more successful in getting their health proposals accepted. While social insurance for disability or medical care was swiftly eliminated from the CES Economic Security Bill, more traditional public health measures succeeded in making it into the Social Security Act. Public health still had its Progressive Era legitimacy, perhaps because it did not appear to challenge the distribution of economic resources. Katherine Lenroot and Grace Abbott, of the Children's Bureau, drafted a small maternal and child health program, to be administered by the Children's Bureau. The Medical Advisory Committee and the AMA officially opposed this program as well, condemning it as "lay control of medicine." But since both reformers and Congress saw it as reestablishing the Sheppard-Towner Act, proponents soon muted medical opposition, and the measure easily passed.[44] The Social Security Act also included direct federal funding for public health measures. Under Title VI the PHS could allocate funds to state health departments for a variety of programs, including occupational health and safety programs. These grants did have an impact. Prior to the passage of the Social Security Act only five state departments of health had a division for industrial hygiene (i.e., occupational health and safety). By 1938 twenty-five states had established such units, prodded by the PHS and enticed by new federal funding.[45] Edwin Witte considered the public health titles a source of strength for the bill, especially because of the emphasis on public health spending for southern states. Since public health and clinical medicine had long occupied distinct realms, and since public health held second-class status compared with private medicine, no one, including the AMA, objected to the public health proposals.[46]

Other New Deal health care projects continued too. Although the Farm Security Administration (FSA) replaced the RA in the summer of 1937, the new agency not only continued the RA health initiatives but significantly expanded them. The FSA actively helped establish medical care cooperatives by engaging in local negotiations with farmers, community residents, and county medical societies. As an incorporated health association, the FSA medical care cooperative relied on the group service model. Families paid annual membership dues, budgeted out of their rural rehabilitation loans and based on family size and ability to pay, and received routine medical care, surgery, obstetrical care, and some hospitalization. Patients could receive medical care at physicians' offices or at home. As part of the FSA's rehabilitation program, loan recipients also received the services of visiting nurses and home sanitary engineers. Medical care cooperatives distributed health manuals and handbooks, and the FSA recruited farmers to participate in health promotion activities. Farmers had a voice in determining which medical services were covered by the plan, and in some locales they even sat on billing review committees. Thus for the FSA, good health, economic independence, and participatory democracy were integrally linked.[47]

Although African Americans were excluded from the new social insurance programs, they did gain from the New Deal's public health programs. Under FERA, the Public Works Administration (PWA), and the Civil Works Administration (CWA), African American relief recipients received some public health services, mainly through federal grants for antimalarial work, water and sewage projects, and visiting nurses. The WPA funded medical inspections of schools, care of handicapped children, and child nutrition programs. Under Social Security, the PHS set up southern programs to train African American public health nurses. The maternal and child health titles of the Social Security Act also reached black southerners. Social Security funds in particular helped set up local health departments in the South and funded traveling maternity and infant clinics. African American physicians and patients participated in FSA medical care cooperatives and traveling clinics, as did Latinos. In many ways, though, as Susan Smith has concluded, New Deal programs reached African Americans through the voluntary public health work and community activism of African Americans themselves—activists who had been building these programs long before the New Deal. Nor would these programs, which trained black nurses to go into black neighborhoods, for example, challenge the segregation status quo; universal health insurance, on the other hand, just might, because it would draw patients into institutions such as hospitals. Thus, again, public health measures were a safer political bet for New Deal Democrats than health insurance.[48]

More generally, the Social Security Act narrowed the scope of economic security from the plans originally spelled out by the CES. For example, public works and job training had been entirely eliminated from the Economic Security Bill; employment relief would end up being diverted into temporary or emergency legislation rather than permanent programs. The Social Security Act fell short when dealing with economic insecurity arising from health issues. Alice Kessler-Harris and other historians have pointed out that the act included conservative and traditionalist assumptions. It privileged waged labor over nonwaged labor, men over women, and whites over blacks. It did not provide an ongoing system of mass relief to all citizens or residents.[49]

Nonetheless, the Social Security Act, along with other New Deal social support and labor programs, launched a transformation in the nation's political culture. *Security* had gained cardinal political legitimacy. It legitimized working-class demands for economic security and advanced workers' ability to make a greater claim on national resources. As one trade unionist expressed it, "The public proclamation of President Roosevelt making the first objective of his Administration the realizing of security has crystallized fundamental aspirations of workers throughout the country."[50] In turn, the politics of security stimulated a vigorous national debate over what it included. Did social security just entail old-age benefits? If the state had now established a *right* to support when one could not participate in the labor market owing to old

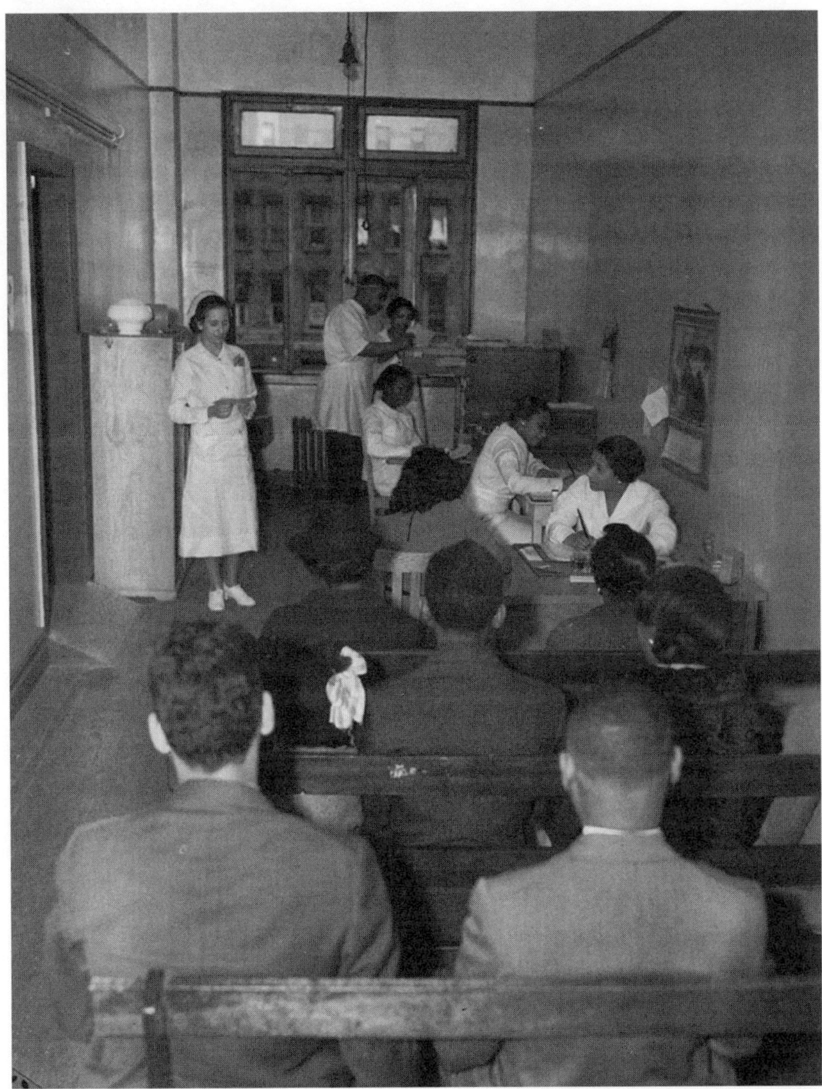

5. New Deal Medicine: The Lower Harlem Chest Clinic. Through programs such as the Works Progress Administration, the New Deal sponsored direct medical care or made public health funds available to communities for vaccinations and diagnostic tests. Courtesy of the National Archives and Records Administration.

age, why not when an individual could not earn wages for other reasons, such as disability or illness? Should there be health care services for impoverished mothers and children and not others, and why should those be so limited? The Social Security Act produced both a new agency, the SSB, that could officially promote the ideology of security and a dynamic set of expectations and demands that would further mobilize New Deal supporters.

The first annual report of the SSB opened with a treatise, "Security for a People." The treatise identified security as a grand national project, linking it to the promises of the Declaration of Independence ("to provide new guards for a future security") and the U.S. Constitution. In its first official report to Congress and the nation, the SSB staked out the political ideology embodied in the Social Security Act: "The security of a people is a great cooperative enterprise. The citizens, the economic system, and the government are partners in this national provision." The SSB gently reminded Congress in ecumenical language that the Social Security Act itself should be seen as a first step in building a comprehensive security program. "As we have met the exigencies which changing times have brought, the domain of security has been enriched and enlarged. As the way opens ahead, we must secure its wider opportunities."[51] Until the Supreme Court ruled on the constitutionality of social insurance, however, the board spoke in very general terms about the future course of Social Security.

Others were more specific about next steps in security, stating in particular that those next steps should include some sort of health insurance. Certainly, the group of reformers who had been advocating health insurance since the days of the CCMC believed their turn was next. Paul Douglas and John Andrews, labor reform activists, immediately called for this expansion of Social Security. At the end of 1936 Douglas wrote to the SSB outlining his suggestions for adding health coverages to the Social Security Act, particularly recommending hospitalization insurance. Douglas added, "I am anxious that we should include under our health insurance system a much broader group than those under unemployment and old age insurance."[52] Harry Millis, a labor economist trained by John R. Commons at the University of Wisconsin, wrote in *Sickness and Insurance* that the Social Security Act represented "an acceptable beginning" dealing with workers' economic needs, but New Dealers had to follow up with "a corresponding attack upon the problem of sickness." Millis had in mind health and disability insurance as much as occupational safety and occupational health measures. At its annual convention in 1935 the AFL resolved that "whereas even in normal times sickness is one of the greatest hazards confronting wage earners . . . the Social Security Act completely ignores it."[53]

CCMC veterans quickly linked health insurance with the Social Security project. Louis Reed could not have put it more forthrightly than in the title of his 1937 book: *Health Insurance: The Next Step In Social Security*. In discussing the Social Security Act, Reed wrote that "all of this is part and parcel of a broad philosophic attitude concerning the relation of the state, i.e. the organized community, towards its members." With regard to medical care he argued that "private initiative and enterprise have failed to make good medical care available to everyone. . . . [Therefore,] government action, on a scale far greater than at present, is required." Reflecting the New Deal ethos embodied in legislation such as the NIRA and the AAA, Reed saw medical and health issues as "a problem of industrial organization." It was up to the state to foster order and efficiency where there was disorder and lack of coordination of these particular economic activities. Organized cooperation meant more than pooling risks through national social insurance; organized cooperation also applied to the delivery of services at the local level.[54] This would take some prodding from public policy, however. As I. S. Falk wrote in his 1936 book, *Sickness against Security*, "The reorganization of medical practice which is badly needed will not come of itself, the product of laissez-faire. It will come—if at all—only as the fruit of strong and directed labors." The administration of medical services should involve joint action by professional and lay activists and intervention by the state.[55]

These New Deal intellectuals and reformers soon took a closer look at European public health insurance programs. They did not want to imitate the European models outright. Most of the European plans had begun as cash sickness programs, providing cash benefits to workers only for wage loss. In recent decades programs had begun to add medical benefits to the same fund, yet it appeared to American observers that the financing mechanisms had not been recalibrated. This transition had been especially difficult because almost all European national programs had initially been designed for the poor and low-wage workers. While their contributions could cover the cost of partial reimbursement of their own wages during sickness, they could not pay for regular medical services. The result, American reformers believed, was either substandard, "poor man's" insurance care or the need to bring in a greater pool over which to spread risk and resources. Because medical service benefits needed to provide support for the patient and adequate remuneration for the doctor, they required a different type of administration and funding than disability insurance offered.

Health insurance reformers inferred their own ideas from the European experience. First, as Falk wrote, "patching up old laws to meet new requirements is often a painful and ineffective procedure." Therefore, attempts to turn American workmen's compensation into health insurance for medical services would not work. Second, they had to determine the extent to which doctors would co-opt the program to serve their own prerogatives. In France, physicians dictated the fundamental tenets of the health program. Patients had to pay the doctor directly and then apply to the state for partial reimbursement. The state fund (*caisse*), however, established a much more limited fee schedule than did the doctors, who operated independently of the insurance system. Consequently, the difference between what the doctor charged and what the insurance system reimbursed was always quite large. If New Dealers planned to pursue legislation for medical care coverage, warned Harry Millis, "We must avoid passing any health insurance legislation that would make individual practice rather than group practice the legal foundation of the whole system . . . this has been one of the great pitfalls faced by European compulsory insurance systems."[56]

These New Deal reformers, then, had a notion of social security that was both expansive and expandable. Social Security did not have only a negative function, propping up subsistence when other means had disappeared; it could also be used for positive goals, such as promoting health and economic viability. It was not that they believed health insurance or medical care was the sole answer to all social or economic problems. However, they had a tremendous sense of optimism about the Social Security Act, both about what they believed it had accomplished and about what it might achieve in the future. Reed wrote, "Awakening at long last from the spell of an individualistic philosophy suited to the conditions of an earlier day, this country has taken appropriate steps to solve the social problems of old age and unemployment. . . . But the problem of health has not yet been solved, or even attacked in any substantial manner." When labor economists wrote that sickness was obviously, in Harry Millis's words, the "largest problem in the area of social insurance,"[57] it did not represent myopia; rather, they believed that the nation had finally acknowledged that old age and structural unemployment were serious causes of social and economic insecurity and thus had to be confronted collectively. Reformers hoped that those in power would likewise recognize illness and disability. Millis's book *Labor's Risks and Social Insurance* was part of a three-volume work, *The Economics of Labor,* a comprehensive treatment of all issues confronting American workers; health was seen as one among many.

The advocacy of health insurance as the next step in social security, however, marked the beginning of a process that transformed health security from a broadly conceived social concept into a more narrow category: contributory social insurance for workers. In his 1936 book

Health Security and the American Public, Michael Davis, a New Deal insurance advocate, argued that "the problems of health security are much broader than those of medical care. Housing and working conditions, for instance, may be such as to promote health. . . . The nutrition of people . . . The trend and rate of population growth. . . . All measures which make for more regular employment or for larger and more stable earnings among the mass of the people are health measures in the same generic sense. They contribute to individual and social security, of which health security is a part." Yet, added Davis, "in the more immediate sense of the words, health security for the American people means two things: financial security against the continuous economic risks and the occasional catastrophes due to sickness, and personal security against all that part of sickness itself which modern knowledge can now prevent or control."[58] Thus, the New Deal health insurance advocates comprehended that the politics of security was part of a comprehensive challenge to the control of economic resources and services by business corporations, insurance company executives, and physicians. Yet the remedy that these health security advocates would increasingly focus on, contributory social insurance, would circumscribe the expansive political potential of that challenge.

With a new institutional base in the SSB, the health insurance advocates gained more visibility in the formulation of New Deal health policy. Although the public health activists had secured much with the 1935 Social Security Act, their voices would become marginal in health policy debates after 1938. This became clear after Roosevelt's reelection in 1936, when the SSB decided that it was ready to start considering its next steps in security.

During the winter of 1936–37 the SSB acted on the mandate for further study included in the Social Security Act by augmenting the Bureau of Research and Statistics and putting its staff to work on new projects. The board now promoted the idea that the original programs in the Social Security Act were just the first step in building a wider program. The SSB hired I. S. Falk to set up a Division of Health and Disability Studies within the Bureau of Research and Statistics to work on proposals for disability and medical coverage. In 1937 Falk turned to his colleagues from the CCMC research staff in building his new unit. Those who joined the SSB to help design future policy thus already were committed to (1) the idea of health insurance to pay for medical services as a program distinct and separate from disability and (2) group practice plans. Falk's first assignment was to work on plans for disability benefits, yet he also put his staff to work researching medical care issues and medical service plans.

The SSB, however, could not so easily take over the social welfare functions of the federal government. President Roosevelt had also appointed an umbrella organization of executive agencies to formulate the next steps in Social Security. Roosevelt ordered this group to work on "a more nearly complete coordination of the activities of the government" in the fields of health and welfare. The Interdepartmental Committee to Coordinate Health and Welfare Activities, however, comprised agencies that were battling one another for exclusive jurisdiction over social welfare. Each saw its own agency as the best institutional base for expanding the new national welfare state. Representing the Progressive Era reformers, the PHS staked its claim as the traditional guardian of health generally, while the Children's Bureau advanced a claim based on its traditional jurisdiction over maternal and child health services. The Department of Labor asserted that all these issues were really workers' issues and therefore its responsibility. And SSB, the new member among the bunch, now elevated its stake on the basis that ensuring health was naturally a matter of social insurance. Although the Interdepartmental Committee's original charge in 1937 was rather general, New Dealers Arthur Altmeyer and Josephine Roche, the committee's director, urged the committee to focus on developing a national health program. They appointed a Technical Committee, run by Dr. Martha Eliot of the Children's Bureau, to produce yet another report. Falk and his staff worked on the Technical Committee too. Yet the bulk of the report concentrated on maternal and child health services and traditional public health projects such as controlling venereal disease and building tuberculosis sanitoriums. The Technical Committee relegated health and disability insurance to the final seven pages of the report, thereby reflecting the tensions among these groups. Nonetheless, the Interdepartmental Committee agreed that it would move forward with a "national health program."[59]

In order to organize public support for such a program, the Interdepartmental Committee invited activists, health professionals, and academics from all over the country to a National Health Conference in Washington, D.C., in the summer of 1938. More than 150 activists representing labor unions, farmers' groups, medical societies, hospital associations, social workers, government agencies, women's organizations, and philanthropic foundations attended. Businessmen from welfare capitalist firms such as Dennison Manufacturing, AT&T, Kodak, Metropolitan, and GM, as well as reform organizations, from the National Consumers' League to the General Federation of Women's Clubs to the NAACP, sent representatives. In addition to the steelworkers, the miners, and the garment workers who sent representatives, numerous farm and rural groups participated in the conference.

This National Health Conference marked a decline in the political importance of the public health progressives. The public health advocates calling for tuberculosis control, child welfare education, eradication of venereal disease, or services for crippled children seemed to stand alone. The number of speakers who concentrated on varying forms of health insurance, whether to oppose or support it, far outnumbered those who called for public health projects. The minority of speakers who emphasized primarily public health initiatives represented older, Progressive Era institutions, such as the General Federation of Women's Clubs, the Children's Bureau, and state and municipal public health agencies. African American representatives also stressed public health initiatives. A few physicians likewise called for government policy to focus on public health.

The conference secured the clear ascendance of the idea that insurance was the key to better health. In contrast to the Technical Committee's proposal, which had highlighted public health, most of the discussion at the conference debated access to medical therapeutic services. Equally important, the new labor movement stamped its agenda on the health security debate, advancing an aggressive, sometimes radical set of ideas about citizenship, security, and the social wage. And most importantly, the conference produced a ripple effect in communities, unions, and government agencies across the country.[60]

The emotional center of the debate converged on questions of access to medical services for individuals and families. Trade unionists, farm representatives, progressive doctors, social insurance advocates, and social workers emphasized the crushing burden of medical costs, the need for assistance in paying for medical services, and, occasionally, the need for disability support. Others from labor and the health professions, including some doctors, called for government to build more clinics and hospitals to provide more medical services; those who were bolder contended that government should support health centers and group practice plans. Even medical and hospital representatives who opposed this agenda argued for voluntary insurance, although they denied the need for government intervention, claiming that there was no medical services crisis.[61]

The labor and farm activists, among the staunchest proponents of national health insurance present, brought to the conference the language of New Deal social citizenship and a broad conception of social security. As Mrs. H. W. Ahart, president of the Associated Women of the American Farm Bureau Federation, explained, "In our understanding of 'security' as applied to national well-being, health plays a paramount part. We look upon the protection of health and the conservation of physical well-being as a responsibility and duty jointly of citizens and government. Physical well-being . . . must inevitably become a part of the policies of the Nation toward its citizens."[62] William Green and Joseph Padaway of the AFL and Lee Pressman of the CIO, who fiercely fought each other over the National Labor Relations Board (NLRB) and in hearings before the new House Un-American Activities Committee (HUAC), made similar statements regarding health security.

The CIO unions, such as the United Automobile Workers (UAW) and the Steel Workers Organizing Committee, were represented largely by women activists. As Florence Greenberg, of the Council of Auxiliaries, Steel Workers Organizing Committee, told the conferees, "I speak to this Health Conference as the representative of the organized wives of workers." Greenberg explained the political impact of the New Deal on the working families of Chicago, how the politicalization of her community had raised expectations. "Only a few years ago, my people—the steel workers, the packinghouse workers, the International Harvester workers—did not know what it meant to demand that their needs, their lives, their happiness be considered. They were only half Americans with no voice in the Government, with no part in planning this democracy. But now these men and women are organized, and they have learned how to ask for what they want, how to demand what they need." Greenberg wanted not only compulsory health insurance but also "slum clearance and housing projects"; programs of popular health education; early detection and prevention of syphilis, tuberculosis, pneumonia, and cancer; well-enforced occupational hazards laws; and inclusion of African Americans and Mexicans. Further, she sided with those health reform experts who called for health centers. Greenberg demanded that a national health program support the "expansion of all clinic and dispensary services with the concentration of medical care in these people's health centers." Eve Stone of the UAW Women's Auxiliary, Elizabeth Johnstone of the Women's Auxiliary of the Amalgamated Association of the International Steel and Tin Workers, and Harriet Silverman of the People's National Health Committee also asked for government support in creating community health centers that would service "diagnostic, preventive, and curative needs." Stone, a noncommunist leftist, wanted WPA funds to build and maintain health centers because "such health centers would render medical care at first to Works Progress Administration, unemployed, and welfare groups but later to all people insured under the Social Security Act."[63]

The American Left played an extremely important role in this movement for health security and community-controlled health care. These women activists were communists or socialists whose presence at the National Health Conference reflected the Popular Front political culture of the late 1930s. Harriet Silverman, who had been working on behalf of workers' health issues since the 1920s, represented such politics quite well, declaring:

> I should like to say in passing that the Social Security Act, inadequate as it is, was the first real step in the direction of meeting some of the basic needs of the people. The slum clearance and home building program is also under way. The Fair Labor Standards Act is the latest measure in the series that will contribute to the maintenance of health standards by increasing and stabilizing employment and insuring minimum earnings. The Works Progress Administration, the Public Works Administration, the Resettlement Administration, and the Civilian Conservation Corps were, of course, indispensable as emergency measures during the lowest periods of catastrophic economic crisis. What is needed at present is the coordination of these various recovery measures into a coherent and permanent program for full social security.[64]

Silverman argued that Social Security should be extended to include old-age and disability and health coverage for "employed and unemployed, farm and domestic labor, itinerant workers, and others now excluded." Further, she offered a radical plan that eschewed the worker–social insurance model: "free medical care for all *families* having incomes of $2,000 or less a year" and free medical care for all pregnant women.[65] These women activists ratified the New Deal and sought to construct a broader base for working-class security and citizenship.

Labor activists also defended the idea of national standards for welfare and security. They challenged the timidity of government health reformers, who supported compulsory health insurance but refused to endorse a fully national health insurance program. Lee Pressman, the communist general counsel for the CIO, remarked, "It is always difficult to try to understand what is so Biblical about these State lines that we talk about. What are the so-called diversifications in local needs? What are we talking about when we mention the different kinds of state problems, or local problems, with regard to health? I always thought that if there was one problem which certainly did not give heed to State lines, it was the problem of the health of the people."[66] The Popular Front coalition sought to foreground the more social democratic elements of the New Deal. Paralleling the goals of the Fair Labor Standards Act (FLSA), they sought a nationwide floor that would raise the standard of living of the whole working class.

One of the most significant consequences of the National Health Conference was that labor activists had an opportunity to meet, or to hear from, experts in the field of prepaid health services. Health insurance experts such as Michael Davis, Falk, and Millis were present, along with physicians, administrators, and welfare activists who were actively engaged in building group health plans. Dr. Clifford Loos, of the Ross-Loos Medical Group, attended the conference, as did a physician from the Health Service System of San Francisco. People involved with AHA hospital plans came, as did a representative of the International Workers Order (IWO), a left-wing fraternal society, which had established its own health insurance plan. The FSA's Health Services staff attended also. Contact with these people offered activists such as Florence Greenberg or Eve Stone an opportunity to learn about how a health center or medical care cooperative would operate, how workers would pay for such services. Kingsley Roberts, a physician and director of the Bureau of Cooperative Medicine, recommended four essential principles for an effective group health plan: periodic prepayment, coordination of medical facilities, a health conservation program, and cooperative or democratic control. Roberts, like others, recommended the development of local medical centers under the administration of or in partnership with consumer groups.[67]

C.E.A. Winslow, a prominent academic long active in Progressive Era public health work, summed up the impact of the conference in a moving speech from the floor. He acknowledged the ascendance of the new coalition pushing for health security. He noted that although he had spent his entire career attending such conferences and meetings, he had never before "discussed [health reform issues] face to face with those great agencies that really represent the American people." Winslow declared their presence at the conference and activism "of the most profound significance" and hoped they were ready to return to their communities to build group health programs and prod the more reluctant health reformers and policymakers into action. Chastising the reluctance of the conferees to commit to a national health insurance program, Winslow suggested that they needed a shot of "vitamin CIO and vitamin AFL and whatever kind of vitamin they make in the Farm Bureau." The labor activists took his advice. As Florence Greenberg said, "We women who organize to make our lives and those of our families happier . . . promise that, not only are we willing to back these efforts further, but we intend to go home and organize to see that the recommendations passed upon here actually go into effect."[68]

The Interdepartmental Committee ultimately produced a proposal for a national health program, and Senator Robert Wagner introduced a national health bill in 1939. Unable to win endorsement from the president, Wagner's bill presented a rather comprehensive health program. The bill provided for the creation of a federal program to provide actual medical care to infants and mothers. It expanded the maternal education program and increased funds for PHS programs. New proposals included a federal program to build and maintain hospitals and medical centers. Without specifying "compulsory insurance," another title provided funds to the SSB to assist and supervise state government efforts to establish federally approved medical care programs. Each state would design its own program, including eligibility and benefits. Senator Wagner assured states that their plans could either apply only to those on public relief or have wide application, as they chose.

The ideas of the New Deal health insurance reformers had finally made it into a piece of legislation. Wagner's bill encouraged the kind of group arrangements Falk and the health insurance reformers supported, suggesting that "states should utilize and encourage cooperative arrangements with practitioner and welfare groups and organizations." The other title established temporary disability compensation along the same lines as the federal-state unemployment insurance system. Although these two health insurance provisions were very cautiously phrased, diluted even, the coalition of New Dealers supporting the bill clearly considered them essential features. The AMA, agitated first by the National Health Conference and then by Wagner's bill, offered to compromise. The physicians agreed not to fight Wagner's other proposals if the reformers would drop health insurance from the program. The reformers refused outright; clearly, by the late 1930s health insurance had become the essential component of a national health program.[69]

The work to develop the National Health Bill, however, was deliberately kept separate from the proposals to amend and revise the Social Security Act. Although the National Health Conference confirmed the emphasis on health insurance for medical care services and the idea that disability wages and medical care insurance had to be separate, neither the SSB nor the Roosevelt administration was willing to present it to Congress. During 1938 and 1939, as the leaders at SSB were drafting amendments to the Social Security Act, they never discussed insurance for medical care publicly. They discussed cash disability or sickness insurance only. The SSB leaders insisted on a complete separation between the review and assessment of "ongoing programs already enacted and in operation" and health security proposals.[70] After Falk drafted a proposal for permanent disability benefits, the SSB Advisory Council firmly advised against it. When it came time to present the Social Security amendments to Congress, Altmeyer backed away from disability benefits as too controversial.[71]

At the Senate Committee on Education and Labor hearings for the Wagner health bill in April, Altmeyer endorsed "the principal objectives proposed" but would not express an opinion as to the rapidity with which this program should be put into effect. Labor representatives testified in favor of the bill, although they wanted it to establish national, rather than state, health insurance. Labor leaders endorsed national welfare standards as citizenship rights. Matthew Woll, chairman of the AFL's new Committee on Social Security, stated that any health program must "bring equal benefits to the citizens of all our States no matter where situated and no matter how richly one State may find itself against the other." Dr. Louis Wright, of the NAACP, insisted that health care should be a right of citizenship for all Americans. Louisiana Senator Allen Ellender asked Wright: "You are interested, as I understand, in getting your race as well taken care of under this bill as the white race?" Dr. Wright responded: "They are all American citizens." Nor did labor or African American groups view such rights as being confined to social insurance. Once again, labor and African American activists called for augmented public health and occupational health and safety programs.[72] The Wagner bill, however, died in committee.

The AMA, which had opposed both compulsory and voluntary health insurance throughout the decade, decided that it would now have to offer some constructive alternative in response. The AMA House of Delegates endorsed hospital service plans on the condition that Blue Cross plans cover hospital expenses only and no medical fees. Previously the AMA had opposed any medical societies that formed their own service benefit plans, as well as group practice plans such as the Ross-Loos Medical Group in Los Angeles and the Group Health Association (GHA) in Washington, D.C., expelling doctors affiliated with these plans and others. In the wake of the National Health Bill, many doctors concluded that a plan controlled by medical societies would be preferable to compulsory insurance or lay-controlled prepayment plans. The AMA House of Delegates voted to allow local or state medical societies to establish "nonprofit medical expense indemnity insurance," what would later be called Blue Shield. Such insurance had to be based on cash indemnity and not medical service. There should be no interference with higher fees being charged to higher-income groups. Any family whose income was above a designated (modest) income would be charged on a strictly fee-for-service basis. Even those below the stipulated income level had to pay medical fees in addition to the annual subscriber fee. The plans did not use group enrollment to lower per capita costs. All aspects of the Blue Shield plan had to be under the control of the medical profession. The state medical societies prodded state governments into enacting legislation prohibiting nonprofit hospital service plans (i.e., Blue Cross plans) from being licensed to furnish coverage for medical services.

In 1939 and 1940 medical societies in California, Michigan, and New York formed the first medical indemnity plans, such as the California

Physicians' Service, to accept prepaid fees. Over the next two years medical societies in Massachusetts, Ohio, Colorado, and New Jersey prepared to inaugurate medical indemnity plans as well. All had trouble enrolling large numbers of people. Some medical society plans, such as the one in Buffalo, New York, had enrolled fewer than 6,000 persons after three years in business. Although formally "nonprofit agencies," medical society plans were essentially proprietary institutions.[73]

Pursuing Health Security: Organized Labor's Experiments in Health Care, 1936–1941

Inspired by the social democratic politics of the New Deal and the Popular Front era, activists began designing, constructing, or participating in community health programs. As the labor movement regained its strength and confidence in the late 1930s, the health security movement offered possibilities for breaking free of company doctors and employer welfare plans. The labor movement had traditionally supported the idea of "self-help," whereby workers would pay dues into a union insurance fund or mutual benefit association. Yet these funds generally paid some kind of disability wage or injury compensation. Like pre-Depression employer pension plans, union sickness funds did not use actuarial planning in assessing fees or premiums and thus had irregular, inadequate reserves. For medical care, workers had to rely on either company-sponsored medical programs, often just a doctor or nurse at the plant, or charity care from physicians and hospital wards. Under workmen's compensation an injured worker usually had to visit a doctor chosen by his or her insurer or company; even then care was dispensed only for occupational injuries. In the days of Samuel Gompers, self-help and union welfare funds were meant to be alternatives to government insurance programs, a means of avoiding state intrusion. In the New Deal era labor health security projects would be reconceptualized as complements to the welfare state.

Soon after the passage of the Social Security Act, the AFL joined the movement to bring health care within reach of the working class. Beginning in 1936 the *American Federationist* published editorials, articles, and even skits and cartoons promoting and explaining the Social Security Act and health security. William Green argued for the importance of group practice in pooling costs and producing economies that seemed to make possible a greater level of services for working families. The *Federationist* introduced readers to the new AHA hospitalization plans. Other articles discussed group practice clinics such as the Ross-Loos Medical Group in Los Angeles and the Milwaukee Medical

Center, as well as cooperatives such as the GHA in Washington, D.C. Thus, as early as 1936 the AFL counseled unions to consider these new mechanisms for obtaining health care.[74]

The 1938 National Health Conference further stimulated a grassroots health security movement. In Chicago, Florence Greenberg's hometown, trade unionists and social welfare reformers formed the Citizens' Committee for Adequate Medical Care, of which Greenberg became vice chairman. The committee held a mass meeting in Chicago to discuss health security, drawing representatives from AFL and CIO unions, Hull House, the Young Women's Christian Association, the Young Men's Christian Association, the National Negro Congress, the Chicago Association of Medical Students, and Chicago's Non-Partisan Labor League, as well as sponsorship from teachers, university professors, social workers, dentists, and some members of the medical profession. The committee declared three goals: (1) to promote the passage of national health legislation; (2) to effect improvement in the health facilities in Chicago; and (3) to cooperate with numerous civic and neighborhood organizations in health activities and in other fields of social legislation. In 1939 the committee began agitating for Cook County Hospital to establish outpatient clinics in working-class neighborhoods. Committee activists held conferences with officials of the hospital, the Cook County commissioner, and the city council's committee on health. Health activists teamed up with the Packinghouse Workers "to urge a municipal clinic in the stockyards district of Chicago." The committee also began pressing for expansion of New Deal health services, such as extending the dental care program provided by the WPA.[75]

Unions and other organized groups in Chicago launched a process of education, experimentation, and even enrollment in local health plans. The Chicago Teachers Union began an extensive study of health issues and insurance for medical services in the fall of 1938. Union activists studied the reports of the CCMC, as well as group health plans in different regions of the country. Already committed to the idea of joining a group medical practice, the union further decided that the plan should "emphasize preventive care instead of mere relief for those who are ill" and that members of the union should have a voice in administrative or economic aspects of the plan. The Teachers Union chose to enroll in a prepayment plan with the Civic Medical Center, a private group practice clinic. Subscribers paid a fixed monthly or annual fee and in return received full medical services and a full physical examination annually. Members could also select their own personal physician from the staff of the center; the physician would then refer them to specialists. Union members paid the group plan fee themselves; therefore enrollment was voluntary. The Chicago Post Office Clerks' Union also joined the Civic Medical Center. Petro Patras, a union official, explained why the union chose this group health plan. "When we compared the hospitalization plans with the total risk of illness, we saw that hospital plans covered just one item, *hospitalization in limited amounts.* . . . At the same time they do not guarantee good medical attention or preventive care which would keep us out of the hospital in many cases." Patras advised the labor movement to study the question of health security carefully and provide community (and national) leadership in promoting vital options.[76]

In Milwaukee, workers joined a similar program, the Milwaukee Medical Center, which catered to workers who earned between $1,600 and $2,400 a year. International Harvester, DuPont Company, and Stroh Die Casting Company employees joined, as did filling station employees and hosiery workers. Many of the members came from white-collar unions or organizations: postal clerks, teachers, and office workers, workers with steady, year-round incomes.[77]

Unions representing industrial workers whose employment was less secure did not feel that their workers could afford to pay a regular monthly fee. Packinghouse workers, for example, whose employment was seasonal and irregular and who as a group had wide income disparities owing to both seasonal work and variations in wage rates, decided that hospital service plans were too expensive. Since no prepaid insurance plan appeared viable, they decided to support public health insurance and public medical facilities.[78]

The defeat of the 1939 National Health Bill meant that labor unions and consumer groups would have to redouble their efforts to achieve health security at the local level. Beginning in 1939, local unions asked AFL headquarters for assistance in setting up sickness benefit funds that could pay for medical therapy or hospital care or for advice on enrolling in various local plans. Local officials would often send plans that had been presented to them by a local Blue Cross organization, insurance agencies, or even doctors and dentists offering their own prepayment schemes.[79] Consequently, the AFL research staff solicited advice from Blue Cross administrators, private foundations, health reform experts, the Bureau of Cooperative Medicine, and even the SSB.[80] Although still establishing its institutional legitimacy, the CIO resolved similarly at its 1941 annual convention that "the Executive Board study the various types of voluntary health insurance being offered to labor and make available to CIO unions information and guidance to enable them to analyze and judge such insurance plans."[81]

The AFL supported the group practice model but questioned employer financing. While acknowledging that an employer plan would reduce the burden on workers, the AFL warned of several pitfalls. "The worker loses his membership upon leaving the employ of the company. The prospect of this hardship would tend to keep him attached to the company, even though other working conditions might be unfavorable." The AFL advised that "any medical service plan should provide for administration of the service by employee organizations, not by the company or its personnel division. . . . Community or trade union health service plans would not so limit the worker."[82] The AFL rejected the tradition of company medical plans and sought alternatives free of company paternalism. Health security defined a relationship between citizens and the New Deal, not between employees and employers.

During this period of ferment and experimentation late in the 1930s, local unions, central labor councils, and employee associations joined a variety of health plans, ranging from loose, vaguely defined arrangements with local doctors to formal contracts with bureaucratically organized systems, such as Blue Cross. At the informal, loose end of the spectrum a union might organize a list of physicians, general practitioners, and specialists who agreed to furnish services to members at considerably reduced fees, such as the plan used by the United Office and Professional Workers. More organized was a plan established in New York City by the IWO. The IWO set up a system of seventy district physicians, each serving a section of the city. A district doctor was responsible for serving about two hundred to three hundred patients. The doctors agreed to supply home and office care to members without charge except for night calls, and members received an annual physical exam. Approved specialists treated patients at reduced fees when referred by a district physician. Families paid one low annual fee. Unions such as the CIO Wholesale and Warehouse Workers Union affiliated with the IWO health plan.[83]

The Transport Workers Union (TWU) in New York and the Retail Food Employees Union began similar plans of their own, free of charge to all union members. The TWU medical plan, supported by the union treasury and independent fundraising, engaged the full services of fifty-two district physicians and specialists, including surgeons, psychiatrists, and ophthalmologists. Each enrolled member was entitled to a general health examination by the district's general physician once a year. Doctors provided office treatments, home visits, hospital attendance, and consultations. The assigned general practitioner would treat industrial accidents and illness (compensation cases), as well as non-work-related health problems, thus further freeing workers from the exploitation of the company-doctor system. Appointments to see specialists and to receive laboratory or diagnostic tests had to be made by the general practitioner. The plan did not cover hospital costs or supplies; patients paid for those individually. Still, the TWU plan represented one of the most comprehensive medical programs of this period. The TWU medical plan, however, covered dues-paying workers only; family members were excluded. As unions like the TWU established their own medical programs, these experiments represented far more than the voluntarism of Samuel Gompers. John Santo, the communist union official in charge of the plan, placed these efforts within the larger, political, Social Security project: "While we believe that fundamentally this is an obligation which must be met by government agencies, we have no objection to blazing the path."[84] These experiments grew out of 1930s community unionism, a movement in which women and the Left played a vital part.[85]

Other unions tried to meet the problems of the working-class *community*. In 1941 the Cleveland Industrial Union Council, a group of CIO unions, developed a plan to build a labor clinic that would be a group practice center, a community service around which the city's unions could rally. Maintained by unions in various industries, the center would serve families of all unionized workers. This project failed for several reasons. First, bad planning failed to generate a regular financing mechanism. Second, the labor council did not establish a good relationship with the local doctors, many of whom were looking for regular, paying clients. One critic believed that if the union leadership had launched an educational campaign to "help doctors understand the role they were playing in the development of a workers' health program" and in eliminating charity medical care, it might have gained more cooperation. Finally, Ohio passed legislation, proposed by the Ohio State Medical Society, designed specifically "to thwart the efforts of labor to set up a group practice plan, such as the Cleveland Industrial Union Council had planned." The new law stated that "any prepayment medical care plan must have the approval of 50% or more of the local physicians before it could operate in any county."[86]

At the other end of the spectrum, employee organizations, mostly white collar, established cooperatives, consumer-controlled medical care programs. The health cooperative took the basic model of the Ross-Loos Medical Group plan and carried it a step further. Rather than being owned by doctors, it was a patient-led cooperative. In the case of the GHA, of Washington, D.C., formed by federal government employees in 1937, the members operated the organization. The cooperative chose the physicians and hired them to provide the medical services designated by the membership; physicians were a salaried staff. The membership had final authority over its policies. On a day-to-day basis an elected board of trustees handled administrative matters, while a salaried medical director supervised the medical staff and medical policy. In addition, an elected advisory council of about 150 persons from all the federal agencies represented in the health association served as a liaison between the board of trustees and the membership. The board, the advisory council, and the medical director maintained regular contact with the membership and reviewed suggestions and complaints. By 1941, 3,000 workers had joined the GHA; counting their dependents, the plan covered 7,000 people.

Cooperatives such as the GHA also faced numerous obstacles, but most formidable was the AMA, which repeatedly obstructed GHA access to hospitals and blacklisted or threatened cooperative doctors. The GHA filed an antitrust suit against the medical association. The Department of Justice backed up its claims, filing an indictment. The GHA eventually won the legal battle in 1943, with a lower federal court and the Supreme Court ruling that the AMA was guilty of conspiracy in restraint of trade, but it was a pyrrhic victory since the AMA continued to obstruct other cooperative plans. The Medical Service League, organized in 1938 by university professors and federal and state employees in Berkeley, California, encountered the same obstructionist tactics but did not survive the battle.[87]

A similar cooperative in New York City provided an example of what a not-for-profit, consumer-responsive plan might look like. The Group Health Cooperative received a license in 1941 to begin its prepayment medical plan, and by the end of 1943 it had 5,000 subscribers. Invoking Ross-Loos and the Roanoke Rapids Medical Service as models, the Group Health Cooperative offered all-inclusive coverage of doctors' bills for an annual membership fee. Subscribers could also buy a share in the plan, which entitled them to a vote in policy decisions. The general practitioners were paid on an annual per capita basis, although specialists would be remunerated on fee-for-service schedule. The plan clearly articulated the need for central controls in determining access to specialists. It contended that the combination of required annual physical examinations, preventive care, group sharing of facilities, and per capita remuneration would ultimately contain costs and provide good medical care. Patients had the right to transfer to a different panel of doctors. Finally, the cooperative involved subscribers in policy making. But with an annual fee of $18 for group members, $24 for individuals, and as high as $54 for families, this plan would only be affordable to the well-paid working class and the middle class, not to low-income groups.[88]

Many group clinics and cooperatives opened on the West Coast, where there was a tradition of contract medical care. As Rickey Hendricks, a historian of Kaiser Permanente, contends, "Workers and entrepreneurs who migrated west left familiar community networks and were compelled to create new ones. . . . Huge reclamation projects to bring water and power to burgeoning Los Angeles county in southern California and to other Pacific states stimulated innovation among doctors, laborers, and employers at desolate labor sites." In urban areas, new municipal agencies signed up their employees; for example, San Francisco enrolled all city workers in the new Health Service System in 1938. Beyond urban areas, hazardous conditions in extractive industries meant serious injuries from accidents and high disability rates. In the early 1930s almost 30 percent of doctors in Washington State were employed under contracts that served industrial workers. Moreover, radical western unions such as the Western Federation of Miners had a long-established network of mutual aid and hospitals in hard-rock mining areas. Where industrial workers were enrolled in contract group plans, they tended to be welfare capitalist programs, arranged and paid for by employers. During the New Deal, physicians in farming areas worked for the FSA farmer cooperatives and prepayment plans. FSA grants helped support the Agricultural Workers Health and Medical Association in California and Arizona.[89] Continuing through World War II, the Department of Agriculture gave financial assistance to several consumer-sponsored plans. Health insurance reformers often looked to western models when studying and recommending strategies for increasing access to medical care.

Despite AMA opposition, many doctors were eager to participate in new group plans. The majority of general practitioners had a difficult time maintaining a steady income. In midwestern and East Coast cities doctors in working-class or immigrant communities saw union plans, health centers, clinics, and cooperatives as an excellent opportunity to build up a stable clientele and earn a steady income. They believed they could strike a new path for medicine, one that socialized costs and benefits. As soon as the TWU announced its union health plan, doctors and dentists flooded the union with requests for applications to join the panel. Dentists were particularly eager to offer their services to the union. Most of those who applied to the TWU plan were Jewish and Italian, as were many of the physicians who would later become part of the municipal Health Insurance Plan of New York. They forwarded references from labor movement supporters. One Italian doctor in New York even had Congressman Vito Marcantonio write to the union on his behalf. A Jewish doctor had the American Labor Party write a recommendation in support of his application. A CIO union of physicians, Local 67 of the State, County, and Municipal Workers, asked for priority consideration as fellow members of the labor movement. "We are sure that most of our members could and would qualify well, both from the scientific and social standpoints, to act as physicians for your members under this plan. We feel that as brothers in the C.I.O. we are entitled to such consideration from you."[90] For doctors on the West Coast group practice plans proved equally attractive. In California, emergency-room surgeons in San Francisco hospitals earned less than electrical line workers, plumbers, and fire squad captains. In small southern towns where few could afford medical service, doctors even cooperated with the federal government to arrange prepaid services for poor white families. In all regions, medical students, worried about facing uncertain prospects upon graduation, saw the new programs as a way not only to earn a steady income but also to participate in a socially useful enterprise. One medical student asserted: "By taking an interested and sympathetic view towards the efforts of organized working people to better their health, medical students and practicing physicians will really benefit themselves and will aid one essential part of the country's national defense—the good health of its people."[91] The AMA clearly did not speak for all doctors.

Although the labor movement aspired to some of these comprehensive medical programs, most industrial workers could not afford them. They could afford to pay only for hospitalization coverage, and so numerous AFL and CIO locals signed group contracts for Blue Cross plans in the late 1930s and early 1940s. The Cincinnati Central Trades Council issued an endorsement report of Blue Cross in 1940 since so many locals had been signing up for the hospitalization plan there. Locals in Lima and Cleveland followed suit. By the spring of 1940 the Associated Hospital Service of Philadelphia, a Blue Cross plan, had 200,000 subscribers, half of whom came from AFL trade unions. In discussing the hospitalization plan, the Central Labor Union of Philadelphia repeatedly cast it as representing independence from employers, as the opposite of a welfare capitalist group insurance program, and as providing superior coverage. "Certain companies charge higher rates for females and for workers in certain hazardous occupations or industries," the report claimed. "The AHSP does not discriminate against these groups. The AHSP also charges proportionately less to the larger families. . . . The AHSP rates have been set so that the persons who can least afford hospital care pay least." The Associated Hospital Service rejected only 92 cases out of 10,000. The Central Labor Union portrayed union Blue Cross membership as being in sync with "the Principles of the Social Security Laws."[92]

The UAW Executive Board decided on two strategies: first, hospitalization insurance, and second, a UAW diagnostic health center to study industrial diseases. Acting quickly on the former, dozens of UAW locals enrolled in the Blue Cross Michigan Hospital Service Plan. In 1941 the

6. Patients receiving prepaid medical care at the Ross-Loos Clinic in Los Angeles, 1940. One of the early group practice medical plans, Ross-Loos was often upheld as a model health plan by health reformers and labor activists. Reprinted with permission of CIGNA Archives.

Chrysler Committee signed up all Chrysler employees for a plan that cost workers twelve dollars annually. GM locals joined as well, again carrying the cost themselves. By one 1942 estimate, the Michigan Hospital Service Plan covered 90,000 GM employees for twenty-one days of hospital care.[93]

Unions saw joining Blue Cross plans as an initial step toward achieving health security and broadening the scope of social security. These hospital plans certainly offered greater access to medical care than any earlier form of union self-help or mutual benefit fund. In addition, labor activists initially saw local Blue Cross plans as community, social service institutions. As the Central Labor Union of Philadelphia claimed, rather idealistically, "The AHSP is being conducted as a non-profit community health agency to further the community health and welfare."[94]

Unions and employee groups made these decisions to subscribe to a health plan independently of employers. On the whole, they were not part of a process of collective bargaining. Unions researched the available options, established contacts with local plans, and signed contracts directly with the local health plan. When the employees of the Southern California Telephone Company chose to join the Ross-Loos Clinic, the employees' association handled all of the negotiations, taking "responsibility for acquiring members from among the employees of the Company, for collecting payments, adjusting complaints, and working with the physicians of the clinic to make the service even more satisfactory than it is at present."[95] Even where enrollment relied on a payroll deduction scheme, the union and the health plan worked out the details first and then arranged with the employer to have members' dues forwarded to the health plan. When GM locals proceeded to sign up for the Michigan Blue Cross plan, the UAW persisted even in the face of alternative proposals from the company. From October 1940 to February 1941 the UAW Chrysler Committee negotiated with the Michigan Hospital Service for a service-based contract. As the Chrysler Corporation recognized the union's initiative, it tried to preempt these independent efforts by offering a company alternative, Aetna group insurance. The UAW refused. It saw Blue Cross and Blue Shield coverage as a *union service* to the membership.[96]

Moreover, labor saw health security as a public project with permeable boundaries between the state and voluntary institutions. In trying to offer such services, trade unionists regularly called on the expertise of the SSB. The SSB's Division of Health and Disability Studies collected detailed information from numerous prepayment plans across the country. Unions interested in setting up health and pension programs or enrolling in health insurance sent proposals to I. S. Falk for review.[97] Throughout the 1940s, staff of the SSB Bureau of Research and Statistics assessed the merits and drawbacks of available private health insurance plans and recommended group practice plans, in which "patients are much more likely to seek the physician in the early or ambulatory phases of an illness" and industrial workers received as much care as persons who were better off.[98]

Regardless of what type of health program it pursued, organized labor strove to have a voice in administrative decisions. As the *American Federationist* advised, "The first step in the realization of the enormous potentialities of group hospitalization is the assumption by the consumer of a strong place in the administration of well-established plans." Where labor joined established hospital or medical society plans, it worked to liberalize them or to get labor representatives a place on policymaking boards or committees. In Cleveland, Seattle, New York, Los Angeles, Buffalo, and other cities, labor health groups formed to reshape local health plans more in their interest. In Buffalo, where the

Medical Society of the State of New York dominated the medical prepayment plan, AFL and CIO unions pressured the plan to provide service-based contracts rather than individually charged fees and to allow their organizations to review fees. At a large public rally held in 1942, "the union representatives expressed the need and the desire, on labor's part, to participate in the benefits and in the administration of voluntary prepayment plans."[99] Labor activists did not see these plans as private programs walled off from public discussion and decision making.

In Detroit, Blue Cross did give union representatives a handful of seats on its administrative board, but the board remained dominated by hospital officials. Labor activists recognized that they would have to move beyond token representation in bureaucracies in order to achieve the kind of union health security programs they envisioned. Within two years of subscribing to the Michigan Blue Shield plan the UAW became exasperated with the operation of the plan even though it had union liaisons. The first step the union took was to insist on participation in remedial planning and a continued commitment to service benefits. Second, though, the UAW Hospitalization Committee requested permission from the UAW Executive Board to begin planning an independent UAW-CIO health program, one that would revolve around a health center.[100]

Other health center–based plans had built-in mechanisms for subscriber cooperation. Experiments such as the Ross-Loos Clinic, where doctors, patients, and labor worked together, allowed for some public input. At the Ross-Loos Clinic every subscriber group had an elected committee. The committee met regularly with the plan administrators and received monthly reports of the services rendered to the members of the group. The Civic Medical Center in Chicago operated similarly; each subscriber group had a committee working with the Medical Center.[101] Because these were seen as employee programs and not a management gift, employee representatives sought active decision-making roles.

Labor activists and liberal health reformers argued that while doctors were experts on medical care, they did not have exclusive knowledge relating to the economics of medical services and resource planning. Responding to an AMA critic, Lee Pressman contended that "the American people and organized labor are entitled to representation and responsibility in the administration of a program for improving the medical care of the American people." In envisioning health security, the labor movement adopted the ideas about health centers and group practice promoted by the CCMC health insurance reformers over the last decade and intended to push them further to the left. They wanted the health center to be more than just a proprietary institution run by the medical profession or by elite experts like CCMC or SSB professionals. At their most ambitious point, their initial impulses toward health security anticipated building community institutions, not just obtaining contract-bound dollar amounts of health insurance. This idea was reinforced by labor economists such as Harry Millis and health insurance reformers such as Michael Davis and Dr. Kingsley Roberts, a progressive physician. As Michael Davis wrote in support of labor's experiments, "Those who pay the bills should have a share in the say. . . . Self determined professional codes may rightly govern professional standards and procedures, but economic policies and public relations should be determined by participation of all groups concerned."[102]

During this initial phase of health insurance activism the labor movement saw health security as a two-tiered project: a federal government subsidy for insurance nationally and group practice plans at the community level. The labor activist Andrew Beimiller, an advocate of group practice plans, proposed a payroll tax to build an insurance fund for those covered by Social Security and to subsidize group clinic rates for lower-income persons. With national insurance and the subsidies, group plans "would be much fuller, including hospitals, medicine, and nursing at home, in addition to all other services, and those with incomes of less than $1800 would pay less than clinic rates for more service."[103] After its frustrating experience with the medical society's Blue Shield plan, the UAW suggested, among other options, "seeking Federal aid for the construction of a union-owned and operated medical center."[104] At its 1941 convention the CIO affirmed its support for universal national health insurance. In addition, it resolved that as a spur to the adoption of national health insurance, CIO unions should "assist in the formation of general medical cooperatives and other nonprofit medical insurance plans in their communities." Finally, the CIO urged unions to insist on labor participation in the control of any health insurance plans they recommended to their membership.[105] Thus, union activists saw national policy and community activism as linked. Citizens could build democratic institutions that would promote economic security.

Labor also saw health security as part of a broad economic security project. All of labor's policy proposals during these early years included occupational safety, industrial health, and public health demands. Indeed, the health security movement's emphasis on community-based models could have changed the American conception of health care in significant ways. Less focused on technologically intensive hospital care, they might have allocated resources and attention more equally between clinical medical services and policies addressing the economic and environmental factors that affect health. As the *American Federationist* proclaimed with great optimism: "The Social Security Act is the new basis for workers' security in the United States. It inadequately employs a limited instrumentality to the comprehensive problem of workers' insecurity. To realize security, workers must look beyond social insurance, they must 'let their minds be bold.' "[106]

5

Economic Security on the Home Front

HEALTH INSURANCE AND PENSIONS DURING WORLD WAR II

> In these few weeks, the American people will directly shape the outlines of the world they will live in for a long time to come. The big questions and the little questions, the broad problems of world security and the personal problems of individual security, seem to merge.
>
> —CIO Conference on Wages, Full Employment, and Political Action, 1944

World War II stimulated massive population upheavals, as workers and farmers uprooted themselves and migrated to new production centers. Twenty-five million Americans, one-fifth of the total population, moved to a new town, county, or state between 1940 and 1947. The intensified pace of production, as well as the pressures of overcrowding on housing and local services, brought new health problems and increased the risks of industrial accidents and diseases. Responding to the social demands of wartime mobilization, the federal government became an instrumental agent shaping the spatial and social relations of war boomtowns and communities, not only through military production contracts but through the direct provision of social services as well.[1]

During the war, the federal government expanded its involvement in health care, both directly and indirectly supporting health programs that were not intrinsically linked to a family-wage model of contributory social insurance. By the middle of the war government programs covered more than 800,000 persons for some kind of medical care services and actively promoted local health service experiments.[2] The policymakers who designed and directed some of these health programs hoped that the projects would become models for national health policy after the war. In fact, agencies such as the Children's Bureau and the FSA began paving the way for health policies based not on employment but on citizenship rights. Meanwhile, the SSB solidified its position as the premier federal agency responsible for social welfare. To ensure such jurisdictional control, the SSB emphasized that health policy should take the form of amendments to the Social Security Act's old-age pension and unemployment compensation programs. Consequently, the SSB helped suppress health policy alternatives to payroll-based contributory social insurance. While grass-roots health activists, particularly leftists and African Americans, saw medical care and health in community as well as individual terms, health insurance reformers, as proponents of social insurance, necessarily cast health care coverage as a wage earner's issue. Increasingly, they assumed that health insurance should be designed and implemented as compensation for the wage-earning individual.

The lines between public and private health security were not starkly drawn during the war and its aftermath. The absence of social insurance did not mean an absence of state-funded, state-directed, or state-encouraged health care. In some wartime programs the government became a third-party payer for privately dispensed medical care, while in other cases the government built new medical clinics, as in Taos County, New Mexico. Even when we consider the state's role in promoting private health plans, it is important to scrutinize closely what the state's representatives specifically encouraged or facilitated. In mining, the state helped create a uniquely independent union welfare and pension fund after the war, one that functioned outside of corporate control and unrestricted market relations. Trade unionists, community activists, and New Dealers continued to experiment with citizen-based models, hoping to solidify a connection between the state and communities. At a minimum, health activists intended to use the state to mitigate market-determined patterns of medical care delivery.

In the wake of the war, of course, industrial relations politics and corporate strategies would tip this public-private continuum toward public authority's being used to augment private market arrangements. But more than that, the alliance between the state and communities would be attenuated, foreclosing the possibility of a popular base of control over local health services. The federal government's wartime apparatus for managing war production and workplace issues fundamentally influenced the developmental course of industrial relations and the institutional development of the union movement. The government's policies, in particular those of the National War Labor Board (NWLB), militated against community-based, labor-run social projects. Labor unions had become engaged in a broad project of security on many fronts, stimulated by the Social Security Act. The policies of the NWLB, however, shifted the momentum for health security, as well as other social welfare benefits, to employers and channeled independent union initiatives into collective bargaining.

The war, however, did not shut the door on social democratic possibilities or on organized labor's attempt to tip the balance of class power. The politics of security still embodied a class challenge, a means of making a claim on those who owned and amassed great economic resources. Some historians have asserted that during the war, labor leaders and New Deal liberals ceded their power and their willingness to achieve universal economic security, as well as to advance any social democratic ideas.[3] But compelling business firms to hand over funds in excess of wage compensation, monies that could be used to build health centers, social services, and private or public social security, did entail redistribution of economic resources, as well as social democratic plans to link local programs and the national welfare state. As the war ended and the economy shifted to peacetime production, organized labor still sought strategies for socializing the costs of business cycles and economic insecurity.

Government Health Security Projects

During the war, the government continued the health plans sponsored by the FSA and the Department of Agriculture, offering a vital model that combined community-based, community-responsive health services and federal funding. Migrant farm workers, domestic and foreign, received medical care through the federal government's migrant camps. By 1945 the FSA operated a migrant health program in some form in almost every state in the country. FSA-sponsored medical cooperative plans existed in a third of all rural counties, covering well over a half-million poor farmers. The FSA held community meetings to involve farm families in identifying health care needs and negotiating with the local medical society for a prepayment plan. With 1,200 local medical plans in place in 1942, the FSA moved on to more ambitious experiments in financing and providing medical care. The agency launched seven countywide health plans and one multicounty health plan and extended eligibility to nonrelief (or FSA loan) residents of the area. Although the FSA wanted enrollment to be open to everyone, opposition by physicians forced it to scale back the program to cover low-income residents who met the terms of a means test. Each of the eight "experimental plans" included group prepayment through annual membership dues, local administration, income-adjusted dues, comprehensive medical care, and preventive health services. The FSA made grants to subsidize deficits in the plans. Moreover, it made an effort to combine medical care, public health initiatives, and democratic empowerment. In Taos, New Mexico, a poor, Hispanic community, about 40 percent of the county's entire population joined the new Taos

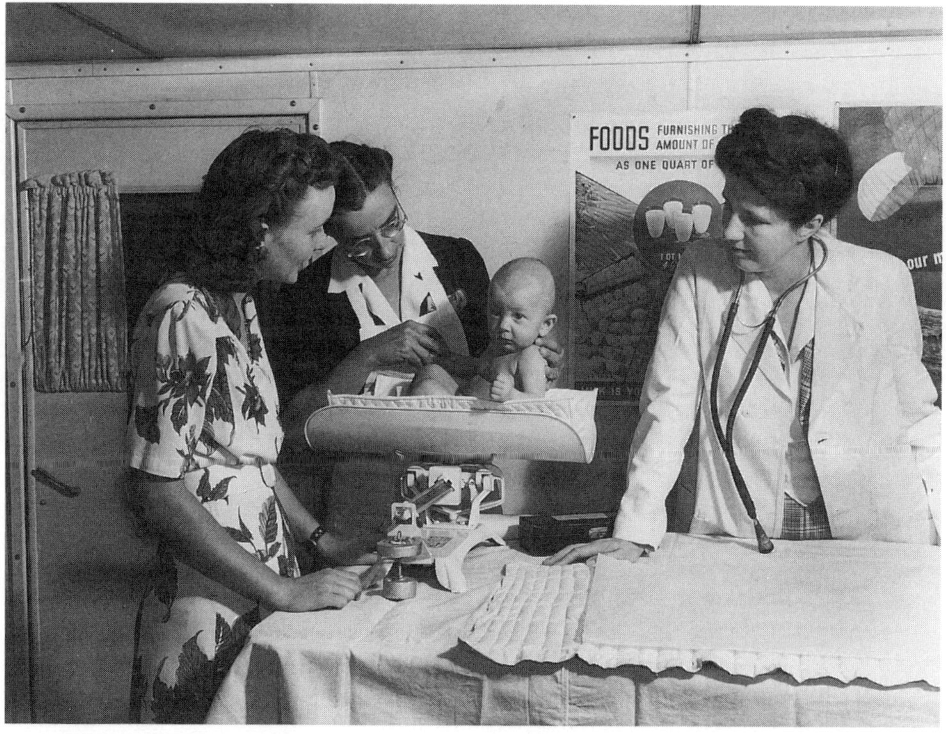

7. Mrs. George Davis having her child examined by Dr. Ann Kent, FSA Public Health Well Baby Clinic, Middle River, Baltimore, 1943. Photograph by John Collier. Courtesy of Library of Congress.

County Cooperative Health Association. The association provided childhood immunizations, nutritional counseling, and maternal programs in addition to general-practitioner care, surgery, laboratory testing, nursing services, and full obstetrical services. The FSA's New Dealers treated these experimental plans as a pilot program for federally funded health care after the war.[4]

The federal government also arranged medical care for war workers living in wartime government housing projects. In the booming California war production centers of San Francisco, San Pedro, Marin, San Diego, Contra Costa, and Alameda, the U.S. Public Housing Authority signed contracts with the California Physicians' Service for "full-coverage," prepaid medical care for housing project residents. Physicians and nurses worked for the Housing Authority on salary. In some cases the Housing Authority built and equipped medical centers in the public housing projects. Although it is unclear exactly how the plan was paid for, it seems that residents had to pay a monthly fee, with the Housing Authority also making some financial contribution. Participation in the plan was voluntary. In the fall of 1943 the California Physicians' Service broke its contracts and demanded a fee-for-service system. The Housing Authority appeared willing to acquiesce until housing residents at the Marin and Vallejo projects protested, forming tenant associations to negotiate directly with the physicians. They demanded a prepaid service plan, and they won. The new contracts, signed directly with the tenant council, covered 5,550 members in Marin and 12,000 in Vallejo. In San Diego, after the withdrawal of the Physicians' Service, the Linda Vista housing project signed a contract with a group practice organization. This plan, covering several thousand residents, became so successful that within a year the staff had increased to six physicians working in three medical centers, and plans were developed to add more specialists and health centers. Again, federal officials hoped these experiments would generate "permanent self-supporting prepayment plans."[5]

The most far-reaching government health program during World War II was Emergency Maternity and Infant Care (EMIC), run by the Children's Bureau. The Social Security Act had authorized a new program for maternal and infant health. Like the Sheppard-Towner Act of the 1920s, the Social Security Act's maternity and child health program (Title V) stressed information, education, and supervision. The core of the Children's Bureau's "preventive health policy" was educating pregnant women and mothers about sanitation, hygiene, stopping work outside the home, breastfeeding, and infant care. The Children's Bureau reformers, however, had always seen this infancy protection program as a starting point for a broader national health program. As the administrator of Title V, Dr. Martha Eliot, an assistant chief at the Children's Bureau, began expanding the section on disabled children to include medical care, hospitalization, and corrective surgery and therapy in the late 1930s.[6] During the war she seized on an opportunity to move further in this direction. As thousands of servicemen and their wives converged on new military bases, training camps, and towns, many women found themselves in places where they knew no one who could assist them during pregnancy or childbirth—neither family, nor midwife, nor doctor. Eliot, a physician, and her research assistant, Harry Becker, used this "crisis" situation to argue that the federal government had a responsibility to help servicemen's wives obtain medical or hospital care. Harry Becker later recalled that after visiting one such location to supervise the administration of the Social Security Act's maternal education program, they realized that "we could take our maternal and child health program and plunge it more deeply into medical care than we were able to [prior to] that time by concentrating on the problems of servicemen's dependents."[7]

In March 1943 Congress established the EMIC program with an appropriation of $1.2 million, and a year later Congress approved an additional $18.6 million. The program rested on an expansion of Title V funding, which enabled servicemen's wives to receive prenatal, obstetrical, and postpartum care from a physician of their choice in a hospital. The federal government paid the fees. In addition, infants received pediatric care for the first year of life. Physicians could not charge patients fees in excess of what the program paid. Becker and Eliot designed the hospital reimbursement formulas, methods of paying physicians, and the stipulations for postpartum examinations. They relied on state health departments to carry out the program. Yet EMIC was a purely federally funded program; states did not have to provide matching funds.[8]

So many women took advantage of EMIC that it grew rapidly. In many areas women applied public pressure to force recalcitrant state health departments and doctors to cooperate with the program. In turn, Congress authorized new appropriations throughout the war, the final one amounting to almost $43 million. According to Eliot, all but four states and Puerto Rico were participating in EMIC by 1944. The Children's Bureau estimated that at the height of the program one out of every seven births in the United States was paid for by this program. By 1946 EMIC had provided maternity care services to 1.2 million women and medical care to more than 230,000 infants. The program relied on a means test in the sense that only pregnant wives of servicemen in the lowest four pay grades qualified for benefits. And of course women received benefits as dependents of an employed male. Yet all who applied had to be given medical service benefits; the Children's Bureau prohibited states from using financial investigations or other tests of applicants. Martha Eliot stated firmly that "the Congress has made it clear that this is not a so-called 'charity' service, but that it is to be provided as the right of any wife of an enlisted man in the fourth, fifth, sixth, or seventh pay grades." And these grades represented a majority, not a minority, group. The people entitled to care constituted an estimated 75 percent of the Navy and 87 percent of the Army personnel. Because of its emphasis on medical service, EMIC represented a significant departure in health policy.[9]

In fact, EMIC appears to have given hundreds of thousands of poor women access to hospital and physician care for the first time. The EMIC administrator in New Mexico, for example, spoke of the program's reaching counties where "the Spanish speaking portion of the population is above 90% . . . [and] a vast majority of the families are living at a low income level." Under New Mexico's program, maternity service including prenatal, delivery, and postpartum care would be provided in either a hospital or a woman's home. The service included care of the newborn infant, a six-week checkup for both mother and baby, and care of infants under 1 year old for any illness. Because EMIC refused to cover maternity care by a midwife, the program contributed to the decline of midwifery and the increasing emphasis on the hospital as the site of both routine and acute medical care. Not only did the program bring more women to the hospital or to doctors. In the case of New Mexico, administrators found that doctors gladly accepted the program fees since they were now assured payment from a group that usually could not pay. The EMIC director, however, did not refer to the program as charity at all. Instead, he used the language of New Deal social citizenship: "The *people* of New Mexico have enjoyed a real benefit from this program. . . . Additional *social security* is made possible by this plan" (emphasis mine).[10]

Thus, EMIC enabled the New Dealers and health activists involved in this project to use the wartime emergency to bring women into the realm of national social citizenship that had been created for some men by the Social Security Act's social insurance programs. EMIC demonstrated the capacity of the state to handle the new entitlement to health care envisioned by the New Dealers and health activists. The Children's Bureau intended to build on the EMIC program and use it as a foundation for postwar national health care. In public addresses before welfare organizations and public health groups Martha Eliot reported on the administrative skills and institutions being developed through this program. She stressed the "efficient methods that are now being developed" in trying to run such a far-flung program of medical benefits. The Children's Bureau also insisted that beneficiaries could freely choose the type of care they would receive. According to Children's Bureau policy, each woman "should be equally free to select care in a clinic, health center, or a hospital, public or voluntary."[11] Patients could also call on the services of public health nurses, child health conferences, prenatal clinics, and medical social services. First, then, this open policy enabled the Children's Bureau health reformers to test the different forms of health care organizations emerging during the period. Second, to these Children's Bureau activists EMIC represented a way to "integrate basic public health concepts of prevention and detection with treatment and bring medical care and public health together."[12] The challenge before them at the war's close was how to translate this into a more permanent set of rights to health care.

In 1944 the New York Foundation and the Marshall Field Foundation commissioned a major research study of EMIC, "intended to contribute to the chief issue in public health economics, the organization and administration of a national health plan." The Children's Bureau gladly opened up its files, including correspondence, complaints, criticisms, financial data, plans submitted by the states, and administrative decisions, to the outside researchers. The researchers also visited local communities where the EMIC plan was in operation, interviewing participants and patients in southern, northeastern, midwestern, and western states. The final report carefully and extensively laid out the lessons for a national health plan learned from EMIC. On the one hand, the study concluded that one of the key reasons for EMIC's success was the Children's Bureau's ability to invoke patriotism and the imperatives of the war effort. The usual opponents to government medical programs, in particular the medical profession, were neutralized: "to oppose the program vigorously and publicly was to be accused of lack of patriotism, an unsympathetic attitude toward those who were doing the fighting." Even though the number of births did not increase significantly during the war, "under EMIC the antagonistic forces were canceled by the urge to contribute to the war efforts." On the other hand, the study contended that EMIC provided a general model exemplifying the federal government's ability to run successfully a massive administrative project, a social service that extended over many state boundaries, both political and geographical. The foundations' report concluded that contrary to the claims that profound geographical differences in health needs and living conditions impeded any national approach to health care, in fact medical needs were fundamentally similar everywhere; by allowing the states some flexibility within basic federal standards EMIC had discharged this argument. Finally, the study also endorsed the health activists' claim that the scientific aspects of medical care and the economics of financing and distributing medical care were separate issues. The foundations concluded that the latter was inherently a matter for public concern, community control, and social policy.[13]

As the war effort began to wind down, Democratic Senator Claude Pepper of Florida conducted wide-ranging hearings on the nation's health needs and health problems with a view to continuing wartime government health programs on a more permanent basis.[14] In July 1945 with the help of experts such as Martha Eliot and Harry Becker, Senator Pepper drafted the Maternal and Child Welfare Bill, a bill that would establish a permanent program of national maternal and health services for the entire country using federal grants-in-aid to the states. Senator Pepper's bill spelled out a remarkably progressive program that offered a sharp contrast to work-based social insurance. Under the proposed program the funding would come from general revenues, not a payroll tax. Becker was emphatic on this point. The Children's

Bureau explicitly rejected a social insurance, payroll tax approach. The bill eliminated the means test and called for each state to set up a program that provided physical and mental health care to all women "during the maternity period" and to children, "including medical, nursing, dental, hospital, . . . preventive health work and diagnostic services," until they reached adulthood. Moreover, while the SSB policymakers were willing to compromise on racial segregation to appease southerners, the Pepper bill included a nondiscrimination clause stating not only that "there will be no discrimination because of race, creed, color, or national origin" but also that there must be "no residence requirements." It also included a stipulation that women denied benefits had the right to a "fair hearing." Thus the Pepper bill offered a public social program that was not based on contributory social insurance or the contract-based social citizenship model preserved for wage earners. Instead, as the bill specifically stated, it provided social support as "the right of mothers and children."[15]

There were several motivations behind these choices. First, although this program would only serve pregnant women and children, the bill's proponents thought it would establish the principle of tax-supported health care from general revenues, thus creating a foundation for later additions. Second, Becker and Eliot wanted to avoid the insidious distinctions that payroll-tax social insurance created between supposedly public programs for the poor and insurance programs for those who were stably employed. In their policy proposal, all children and all expecting mothers who needed assistance would get medical care paid for by all the public. It gave women direct social rights from the state and eliminated the stress on benefits for wage earners only. Finally, Becker added, social insurance was aimed at boosting purchasing power; it was not a social service program in and of itself. By contrast, policies for public health and medical care should focus on the optimal distribution and organization of health services. This would simply not be accomplished by payroll-based social insurance, he believed. "We were quite convinced as a result of the EMIC program that it was folly to get large sums of federal funds and go into communities and just pay the doctors' bills and hospital bills for services rendered under the pattern then existing and under the pricing methods and so forth," Becker argued.[16]

Becker and Eliot sought to develop new patterns of organizing medical care and paying for services. Therefore, Becker also drew on another model: group practice medical centers. He joined the GHA, the federal employees' cooperative in Washington, D.C., and soon became active in its affairs, "trying to learn what was involved in organizing a team of doctors, paying for their services on a salary and providing comprehensive care to the families." Through GHA and EMIC, he found pediatricians receptive to experimental programs. The Maternal and Child Welfare Bill specified that the program would promote the use of health centers and clinics, as well as hospitals. It stipulated that physicians would be paid on a per capita or salary basis, using fee-for-service remuneration only in case of emergency visits or consultations. Finally, the bill mandated the establishment of a general advisory council in every state, composed of medical professionals, representatives of public agencies, and representatives of the public, paralleling the community or employee advisory councils found in the more progressive group practice health programs.[17]

Clearly, the Pepper Maternal and Child Welfare Bill offered an alternative to work-based social insurance, but did it merely replicate the child-centered welfare model of Aid to Dependent Children (ADC)? ADC, historians have noted, reflected the maternalist orientation and agenda of the women policymakers who created it. ADC represented reformers' maternalism not just in its content but also in its structure: because, as its architects believed, women were naturally and socially inclined to understand domestic welfare issues, cash aid should be accompanied by case work and social work intervention. Aid to single mothers aimed to provide children with subsistence but to encourage women to find a marriageable man—a man who earned a citizen's wage and a citizen's pension—soon. ADC offered women some support in their role as mothers, a politically necessary function of reproduction, but, as Gwendolyn Mink has argued, "without rights and resources for her own sake."[18] The Pepper bill was different. Granted, women would only receive health benefits because of their maternal reproductive role, but the program offered a set of benefits conferred directly on women. The bill removed the surveillance and morals testing that had characterized previous maternalist policies, thus eliminating the eligibility distinction between worthy and unworthy. There would be national standards and national oversight, as was the case for Social Security old-age pensions. The nondiscrimination clause would bring to women of color, often considered workers rather than mothers, recognition of their rights as mothers. Thus, in contrast to benefits centered on wage work or children, this health program offered an alternative claim to social benefits from the state.

One could argue that EMIC succeeded only because of the war emergency and thus was an unstable basis for permanent benefits. Yet given that old-age pensions also passed during a crisis period of emergency, there is no reason to conclude that this automatically doomed it in the long run. But the proposed postwar version offered women benefits independent of work history, contributions, or even men and hence challenged the ideological underpinnings of the welfare state being created by the SSB. Moreover, as the board's positions prevailed, women policymakers' social welfare base within the federal government—the Children's Bureau—had become increasingly weak and marginalized. Unwilling to link this health program to work-related social insurance, the Children's Bureau's attempt to influence health policy was quickly silenced.

The SSB, busy staking its turf, appears to have ignored entirely these wartime government experiments. During the war, the board's staff continued to draft new proposals for expanding the Social Security Act. But more than ever, health proposals focused on contributory social insurance. After the swift demise of the 1939 National Health Bill, the SSB decided that it needed to shift course somewhat. SSB leaders decided that their main mistake in 1939 had been the state-choice approach and the lack of commitment to a fully national insurance program. Furthermore, drawing on the staff's experience in trying to implement the state-federal unemployment compensation programs, the SSB decided that from now on all proposals should frankly call for a national social insurance program. Whatever the specific new social problem it took on next, contribution-based social insurance was clearly the best answer. These issues were best solved not only by social insurance but also, as Altmeyer and Wilbur Cohen argued, through "a unified social insurance program based on . . . a single insurance fund, and a single administrative office for all programs." A unified social insurance fund, however, would only "unify" the social needs and resources of some gainfully employed workers.[19]

In the spring of 1942 the SSB invited labor representatives to attend a Labor Research Group Conference to discuss health policy. The two-day conference focused on social insurance, which labor eagerly supported. Not discussed were other approaches to health security that could have accompanied social insurance as part of a national health policy—federal grants to community organizations that wanted to establish medical service plans, federally subsidized medical care cooperatives such as those being run by the FSA, or programs that would reach nonworkers. All discussion focused on payroll-based contributory social insurance for workers who qualified for Social Security benefits, although the SSB itself understood keenly the limitations of this proposal. SSB research staff had been studying options for extending Social Security to uncovered workers, including agricultural workers. The technical question would then be a matter of extending the payroll-based insurance enjoyed by one group of workers to other groups. Questions of coverage outside the employment relation and broader questions of democratic power over medical care and community health were not addressed.[20]

These plans for Social Security expansion were being laid amidst a very different economic context than the one before the war. With the booming war economy and surge in employment, Altmeyer and Cohen had to create new rationales for social insurance. As Edward Berkowitz has argued, they had to defend Social Security as contributing to the war effort and as having a role in healthy economic times. Altmeyer and Cohen chose a dual argument: that Social Security was anti-inflationary in the short run and boosted purchasing power in the long run. During the war, when employment and inflation were rising, new social insurance taxes would siphon off excess income and put it into forced savings. After the war, if economic hard times returned, the nation would have a large reserve fund from which to pay out social welfare benefits, buttress purchasing power, and recharge the economy. "Provided expansion is undertaken now, social insurance can play a dual role in the economic readjustment and reconstruction that will be necessary when the war ends," Altmeyer wrote, thereby promoting his agency's importance within federal policy making.[21] In his budget message to Congress, President Roosevelt himself adopted this argument. "From the inception of the social security program in 1935 it has been planned to increase the number of persons covered and to provide protection against hazards not initially included. By expanding the program now, we advance the organic development of our social security system and at the same time contribute to the anti-inflationary program."[22]

In order to proceed with a new health bill, the SSB decided to narrow the scope of the proposal to make it less controversial. Rather than proposing comprehensive medical insurance, the SSB would draft a bill for hospitalization benefits only. In the *Preliminary Report* on the 1939 National Health Bill, Falk contended that health insurance could not merely pay cash benefits into a fee-for-service medical system; federal policy should promote other arrangements for the delivery and payment of medical care. As the SSB prepared to draft a hospitalization bill in 1941 and 1942, Falk deliberately pushed his earlier arguments aside. In a memo to Altmeyer, Falk said that he believed that service-based benefits would be the "soundest and most desirable" in comparison with cash benefits or indemnity, but he guessed that such a policy would be very hard to sell politically. Therefore, Falk and Altmeyer decided to go with indemnity benefits. They proposed an expanded payroll tax that would fund benefits for reimbursement of a daily hospital rate. This benefit would be paid only to workers in industries covered by Social Security who had made contributions.[23]

Yet in drafting a program for hospitalization coverage, policymakers now had to contend with a new organized interest that had not been present in 1935 or even 1938–39: Blue Cross. Upon hearing of their plans, Rufus Rorem, of the AHA, immediately requested a meeting between the SSB and Blue Cross administrators. At least two such conferences took place in 1942. In general, Blue Cross representatives argued that since hospital service plans already covered 8 million persons, "in a short while it would be plainly evident that the plans were in effect 'covering the population of the country.'" The hospital administrators were no more satisfied with cash-indemnity than with guaranteed service benefits. Some, however, were shrewd enough to insist that if a government plan were enacted, "the program should be designed so as to encourage the growth and development of the Blue Cross plans on a voluntary basis," presumably at the expense of their competitors. Others added that beneficiaries should have no discretion in spending the cash benefit; it had to go directly to a hospital to pay whatever rate local hospitals chose to charge. The SSB did not seem to be getting across its main goal, namely, that "the worker is the beneficiary of the plan."[24]

In order to defend the hospital social insurance proposal from assaults by Blue Cross, the SSB invoked the supplementation argument. Arthur Altmeyer assured the Blue Cross representatives that the proposed government plan would offer only minimal provisions, "leaving room for supplementary insurance provisions to operate above the minimum." Altmeyer pointed to parallel fears expressed a decade earlier when old-age retirement benefits were proposed under the original Social Security Bill. "If a hospitalization program is adopted," Falk reasoned, "the [private] group hospitalization systems would presumably be adjusted to supplement the Federal Plan in much the same way as private group pension schemes were adjusted to supplement old age and survivor benefits." For example, social insurance benefits might cover enough for ward care in a hospital. Private insurance would cover semiprivate or private care or make up the difference between the ward and a private room. Supplementation was now being woven through the fabric of social security, becoming a new orthodoxy. This supplementation rationale, however, further encouraged the split between benefits for the worthy employed and the unworthy poor, perpetuating myths about what was earned and unearned. In addition, it raised the ambiguity of who would be supplementing whom: would private insurance supplement the government program, or vice versa? SSB policymakers also started using the defensive argument that government health insurance was necessary for particular groups, such as low-paid workers, indigents, and people with large families. This line of argument set up the premise that private insurance functioned fine for well-employed citizens, whereas other citizens would need a different level of health care.[25]

Both Roosevelt and the SSB staff thought hospitalization insurance might eliminate the doctors' opposition since the benefits would exclude all physicians' services. They were wrong. The AMA still voiced opposition, and now the hospital administrators and Blue Cross plans became part of the opposition as well. Nor was organized labor too happy since this proposal did not significantly contribute to health security or expand Social Security. The hospital bill went nowhere. Once again, the lesson the SSB staff drew from this experience was to redouble their efforts to enact health insurance through Social Security. In contrast to Roosevelt's opinion, they decided that the medical profession would oppose everything the SSB put forward and therefore they might as well go for the comprehensive package. Falk and Cohen went to work drafting a comprehensive health insurance program that included medical care, hospitalization, and disability. This plan became the Wagner-Murray-Dingell Bill, introduced without the consent of the president in 1943.[26]

The Wagner-Murray-Dingell Bill proposed the "single unified system of national social insurance" Cohen and Altmeyer had envisioned. The bill had twelve titles, including extension of old-age pensions to previously excluded groups, such as domestic and agricultural workers; permanent and temporary disability benefits; and maternity leave benefits. It would replace the state-federal unemployment insurance system with a fully national one. Although the bill included a title to increase funding for public assistance to "dependent persons"—the aged, the blind, and children—it left the administration of those programs to the states, again leaving the poor and women out of the unified social insurance system. Public health measures were now gone from the picture. Under the Wagner-Murray-Dingell Bill the social insurance programs would all be funded by one payroll tax: 6 percent from workers and 6 percent from employers. The bill designated that the PHS would handle any technical aspects of the health program, but the surgeon general would have to consult with the SSB and gain the approval of the head of the federal Security Administration. All administration and financial matters would be handled directly by the SSB. With this bill, the SSB would grab the whole social welfare field for itself, squeezing out other agencies.[27]

SSB policymakers do not appear to have considered other proposals. In fact, the SSB fought agencies that did and snubbed their proposals. SSB directors were especially hostile toward the Children's Bureau and its attempts to expand EMIC. Harry Becker and Martha Eliot found themselves continually in conflict with the members of the SSB. "EMIC was a threat to the social insurance concept somewhat . . . it was moving in a different direction than the social insurance boys would go," Becker concluded.[28] The highest-profile blueprint for postwar economic security was the National Resources Planning Board's 1943 report *Security, Work, and Relief Policies.* The NRPB proposed social welfare policies that would work in conjunction with full-employment policies, in essence reunifying the original goals of the CES's economic (social) security plan of 1934. The report grouped public assistance, social insurance, and public employment programs together as "public aid." Each program should provide at least the minimum wage set by the FLSA. No one program was more socially valid than the others, although the NRPB stressed the importance of public works and public employment. The report called for the permanent planning of such projects. Because of this full-employment view of security, the NRPB's plan entailed the reorganization of federal agency jurisdictions. For example, the board argued that a national employment service should collect all data about employment and employment trends, administer all work and training programs, and run the unemployment compensation program. The NRPB report challenged the preeminence of contributory social insurance as the centerpiece of the welfare state, and hence it too became mired in factional turf wars. Although Falk and his staff helped with some of the research for the NRPB report, Altmeyer repeatedly warned him not to get too close to the project. When the NRPB finished the report, Altmeyer recommended it as good background material for the SSB's own projects. As Falk admitted, "The Board didn't like anybody going around with Social Security programs independent of them."[29]

In drafting a national health insurance program, the SSB also let Falk's earlier ideas about the organization of medical care fall by the wayside. Despite all that Falk and the Bureau of Research and Statistics had learned about medical service plans, the Wagner-Murray-Dingell Bill equivocated on these points. The proposed insurance coverage included medical care by general practitioners, care by specialists, hospitalization, and laboratory tests. Practitioners could be remunerated on a fee-for-service, per capita, or salary basis. The bill left it to the medical practitioners to decide. Hospital benefits "might be" paid on a cash-indemnity basis, or the surgeon general might approve some service contracts. These points were written into the bill as bits that could easily be discarded at the slightest sign of opposition. The Wagner-Murray-Dingell Bill did not specifically discuss possible incentives for supporting the development of group practice plans or health centers. Nor did it include an occupational safety and industrial hygiene program. Nonetheless, organized labor and other progressives wholeheartedly supported the bill. As had happened with previous health bills,

Congress convened hearings on the bill, but it never made it out of committee. The basic Wagner-Murray-Dingell bill had a long life, however. The bill was resubmitted in 1945, and it formed the basis of all health insurance bills introduced in Congress from 1945 to 1950.[30]

Cohen and Falk quickly learned that winning any new legislation would be difficult, so they looked for other avenues through which to encourage economic security during the war. As anti-inflation became the dominant imperative for domestic economic management, they had to find ways in which they could encourage social welfare programs without violating the 1942 Emergency Price Control Act or the NWLB's wage freeze. As the NWLB confronted increasingly intricate questions regarding employee compensation, the SSB was one of the few institutions within the federal government that had expertise on such matters. Consequently, Falk and Cohen assisted the NWLB in working out its policies on employee benefits and group insurance. SSB staff had longstanding personal ties with industrial relations specialists such as Harry Millis and William Leiserson, and they developed new ones with a rising generation of industrial relations professionals, such as John Dunlop. Others who served on regional war labor boards, such as Edwin Witte, had very close ties to the SSB. Consequently, Falk and Cohen assisted the NWLB in working out its policies on employee benefits and group insurance. As Falk recalled, "The fringe benefit development during the period of manpower, wage, and salary freeze was also one of our programs. . . . We were living day in and day out with the problems of health insurance as a private benefit. . . . You see, [with] the manpower freeze and anti-inflation measures, the tax exemption, and the corporate income surcharge taxes and so on, . . . we were in the voluntary health insurance business with a bang at that time."[31]

Public Policy and Private Benefits

The National War Labor Board and Industrial Relations

Once the United States formally entered the war, the federal government sought to control more directly the movement of goods and workers. Starting in early 1941, unemployment dropped by a percentage point every month; nonfarm employment jumped from 35 million persons to 41 million by the end of 1941. Fifteen million Americans took advantage of tightening labor markets to move into new, better-paying jobs. Wage rates across the economy rose almost 20 percent. But as wartime inflation and war profiteering set in, workers became worried that they were not going to share in the prosperity. Furthermore, the federal government had been indiscriminately issuing defense contracts to employers who were clearly ignoring the nation's new labor laws protecting hours, wages, and the right to organize. The discontent generated by overwork, speedups, and inflation finally erupted into a strike wave involving AFL, CIO, and independent unions in 1941. Concerned that any such actions imperiled the national war effort, President Roosevelt ordered the establishment of the National Defense Mediation Board to ensure that national defense work continued unimpeded. This board, however, had little power, and its decisions were not binding; its purpose was to encourage mediation between disputing parties. The strike wave continued unabated. Consequently, Congress, especially the House of Representatives, repeatedly tried to pass a variety of bills restricting unions and outlawing strikes; it even considered a bill that would conscript industrial workers. The War Department demanded more than mediation. After the attack on Pearl Harbor, Sidney Hillman, the CIO's representative in the government's defense mobilization apparatus, gathered the forces of labor in Washington, where they agreed not to strike for the duration of the war. In return, the president replaced the National Defense Mediation Board with the NWLB in January 1942.[32]

The NWLB, a tripartite agency, had far more power to intervene directly in labor-management relations than any previous government agency, including the NLRB. Roosevelt authorized the twelve-member board to determine final settlements for labor disputes. While the NLRB ruled only on whether bargaining in good faith had taken place, the NWLB could decide the "actual settlement of disputes by 'mediation, voluntary arbitration, or arbitration.'" By 1943 the War Labor Disputes Act spelled out this jurisdiction even more explicitly, stating that the NWLB had the power to "decide the dispute and provide by order the wages and hours and all other terms and conditions . . . governing the relations between the parties." As the legal historian James Atleson has concluded, "Once the board assumed jurisdiction [of a particular case], its power to resolve the dispute was all-encompassing."[33]

Wages, hours, and conditions, of course, were matters that theoretically, under the terms of the Wagner National Labor Relations Act, should be decided by collective bargaining agreements between unions and management. Yet by the time the United States entered the war, there was still little federal law defining the scope of collective bargaining or the means by which negotiated labor-management contracts would be enforced. The constitutionality of the Wagner Act had been upheld only a few years earlier, in 1937. Most employers had refused to accept its provisions (regarding the rights of collective bargaining and independent unions) until that point, and hence unions, in particular CIO unions, spent much of the late 1930s simply fighting for basic recognition from employers. Nor did union recognition in these years necessarily result in a collective bargaining agreement. When employers such as GM and Firestone did agree to union recognition, they quickly turned their efforts to making sure this would not be a permanent state of affairs. The recession helped them along in this stonewalling effort, as layoffs and unemployment led to a drastic drop in CIO membership. While CIO unions fought for institutional survival, collective bargaining had little meaning in this period.[34]

After 1941, with the no-strike pledge in place, labor unions had to rely on the favor of state agencies to achieve wartime gains or protections. New Dealers promoted the rhetoric of collective bargaining during the war, yet they did not leave open avenues through which labor could realistically pursue independent bargaining. On the one hand, the NWLB was staffed by a group of lawyers and economists who believed that management had to accept the integral role of the trade union movement in ensuring social stability and smooth ("efficient") production. The maintenance of membership rulings early on served as evidence of this stance. On the other hand, the board increasingly saw its essential task as limiting strikes and fighting inflation. The board's rulings on nonwage compensation reflect both these imperatives.[35]

Labor relations experts and historians alike have long claimed that the NWLB initiated the spread of pecuniary fringe benefits, such as group insurance and pensions, but this axiom does not represent an accurate reading of the board's position. From 1942 to 1945 the NWLB issued a mixed bag of rulings on employee welfare benefits. The director of economic stabilization first established the policy that "insurance and pensions in a reasonable amount" would be excluded from wages and salaries under the stabilization program. It was not until April 1943 that the NWLB agreed to approve insurance plans, pensions, or sick leave plans if they did not exceed 5 percent of payroll. Although the board would not include insurance and pensions as wages, this policy by no means represented a victory for labor. The fear of inflation still pervaded the board's rulings on these issues, and it never agreed to a union's request for liberalization of an existing plan. Nor is this policy really the most important legacy of the NWLB.

In the majority of individual cases the national board ruled against labor unions that requested new benefit plans or improvements in existing plans. In general, the board took a rather conservative position regarding insurance benefits, contending that it would not order something that "would be a distinct innovation in the industry." In a 1942 case involving the Strand Baking Company the board also indicated that it would not endorse health insurance in cases where "the work is not characterized by extraordinary hazards." The case represented a particularly conservative position since the employees were asking simply that the employer deduct contributions to a hospital service plan from *employees'* paychecks. The board claimed that such deductions placed an undue burden on employers. Yet even when petitioning employees subsequently could make the case that they worked under particularly hazardous conditions, as in the case of munitions workers at U.S. Cartridge Company, the board denied their request for a compulsory insurance plan. These cases set a precedent that the board adhered to throughout the war: it would not order establishment of an insurance or other benefit plan in a dispute case. The NWLB frankly reaffirmed this position in the Basic Steel cases in 1944 and the U.S. Rubber case in 1945.[36]

In some cases the NWLB's ruling sent the parties back to the negotiating table to "continue to bargain collectively on this issue." This type of ruling usually amounted to a death knell for the issue. With the no-strike pledge and the Little Steel wage formula holding wage increases, unions' ability to bargain was limited; without the ability to strike, unions did not have much leverage to compel management to grant their demands. AFL and CIO leaders repeatedly expressed this frustration. As one CIO executive board member reported, "In our negotiations in several sections of the country we find the employers taking the attitude that they need not bargain on any single issue."[37] Because of labor's limited room to maneuver in collective bargaining, unions had to try to enlist the help of the state and the NWLB in order to achieve their demands. Yet the board would not take on the role of the union's heavy in forcing employers to liberalize existing group insurance plans. When employees of the Philadelphia Transportation Company petitioned the board to improve an already existing company pension plan, the board ruled that it would not order changes in existing pension plans.[38]

There was, however, one group of cases in which the NWLB consistently ruled in labor's favor: compelling management to guarantee already existing benefits. The board was willing to order companies that did provide insurance benefits to maintain them for the duration of the war. In early 1943 the NWLB asserted that the petitioning union was entitled to a written guarantee from Western Union Telegraph Company that it would neither alter nor abolish the existing pension and benefit plan. Western Union argued that since it had initiated the plan on its own and financed it fully, without employee contributions, management had the right to take any action it chose regarding the plan. Concerned that any modification of the plan during the war would "undermine the morale of employees," the board overruled this contention, determining that Western Union had to seek union approval prior to making any changes. Two months later the NWLB ruled that whether or not sick leave and vacation provisions were included in a negotiated contract, the benefits had to be maintained for the duration of the war. In subsequent cases the board went a step further and ordered employers to include sick leave, disability wage plans, and group insurance in labor-management contracts, arguing that these aspects of the employment relation belonged in written contracts. In the Tidewater Oil Company case a regional labor board ordered the company to incorporate into the contract a clause reading, "For the life of the present contract, employees shall receive wages during periods of physical disability . . . under the current terms and conditions of the company's Plan of Sickness Disability Payment." On appeal, the general counsel for the NWLB determined in January 1945 that as an "employment practice" the employer's refusal to incorporate the sickness (disability insurance) plan in a contract constituted a "refusal to bargain" under the terms of the Wagner Act. In a case similar to the Tidewater case but involving group insurance the board emphasized that the "directive order was intended to preserve in writing these insurance benefits which had in fact been in existence for the past five years."[39]

Such cases had several rationales. New Deal ideology supported the notion of industrial rights and economic security as essential components of citizenship. New Deal legislation, from the Wagner Act to the Social Security Act to the FLSA, had conferred rights on American workers, as well as corresponding duties on employers to participate in the new framework constructed to promote workers' security. Within this milieu the board on some level enforced the New Deal right to security, even if it took a rather circumscribed form. On the one hand, the board declared that "employers have no greater legal or moral obligation to pay insurance premiums for their employees than to pay their food, rent, or clothing bills." If, however, employers had decided to provide such benefits, they would have to follow through on their promises, at least in making sure the plan continued to exist. Arbitrary managerial power in this case was no more acceptable than spontaneous job actions by workers.

At the same time, the board's first priority was to keep war production going. On the most basic level, board members sought to keep employees from becoming disgruntled, striking, and interrupting production. Despite the official no-strike pledge, thousands of "job actions" erupted during the war. In the years 1942–45, 7 million workers took part in more than 14,000 strikes. The number of strikes rose by 25 percent in 1943 and increased again in 1944.[40] Any fear on the part of workers that they might be deprived of an existing benefit or privilege could trigger militant action by the rank and file. A written guarantee against arbitrary termination or reduction of a benefit plan appeared to eliminate this source of discontent. In return for workers' subordinating their interests to the imperatives of unlimited production, the state would enforce their rights.[41]

For the legal theorists and industrial relations experts who sat on the NWLB, workers' rights would be based upon the specific language in a contract, and the contract would function as a "constitution" or "a basic statute for the government of an industry or plant." Faith in bureaucratic procedures and contracts infused the board's rulings on welfare benefits (as well as many other issues), an ideology that would gain coherence after the war as *industrial pluralism.* The board and other consultants sought to channel labor disputes into administrative resolution mechanisms. They believed that by routinizing interactions between management and workers through collective bargaining contracts and bureaucratic grievance procedures, they would construct a dependable, rational system of industrial jurisprudence, hence eliminating labor-management strife. With a collective bargaining contract in place, labor lawyer Archibald Cox wrote, "the rule of law would be substituted for absolute authority."[42] In promoting this doctrine the NWLB defined industrial democracy as a formal process, rendering substantively fair outcomes less important. Only disputes about the language of a contract, whatever that language might be, would be resolved. In fact, the industrial pluralists mistakenly assumed that a contract in and of itself reflected some kind of just agreement or settlement between management and its workers rather than the balance of power in the industry.

This emphasis on contract as a marker of equality between labor and capital is the most important legacy of the NWLB. By sending unions the message that disputes should be settled by establishing contractual features rather than through workplace activism, the board encouraged an increasing reliance upon collective bargaining. As unions began to focus on getting social security demands included in a labor-management contract, as a concession extracted from management, the labor movement began to move away from the independent health projects initiated prior to the war. Labor-liberal support for social security through community projects and national policy aimed to compensate for the uncertainties of the employment relationship, as well as the arbitrary control over security exerted by employers prior to the New Deal era. The emphasis on social security through collective bargaining would, in the long run, refocus health security, and to some extent old-age security, on the employer and what the employer was willing to provide.

Tax Policy

The NWLB's policies regarding employment-based insurance and pension benefits mirrored Congress's policy choices on private pensions. The Treasury Department had put forward several suggestions in 1938 to prevent private pensions from becoming exclusively a tax-avoidance mechanism for highly paid executives. The 1938 Revenue Act, however, left out the key suggestions, enacting only a requirement that firms submit various documents to qualify a plan for tax relief and that they establish an irrevocable trust. Private pensions subsequently mushroomed in exactly the way the Treasury Department had warned against. The tax-sheltering benefit for top-tier management became even more flagrant as war heated up the economy and incomes began to rise significantly in 1940–42. Numerous small firms initiated pension plans for company owners only. Once the United States entered the war, the federal government became acutely concerned with revenue. Hence, when Congress took up the issue of wartime taxation in 1942, the Treasury Department was able to get pension reform back on the agenda.[43]

Undersecretary of the Treasury Randolph Paul crystallized the New Dealers' position: if pension plans were to receive tax preferences, they had to advance a social purpose, providing benefits to a wide range of employees. Paul therefore proposed four new requirements for private pensions receiving tax exemptions: full and immediate vesting; general employee participation and no discrimination against rank-and-file workers; a $7,500 cap on yearly allowances, to put a lid on tax sheltering; and minimum funding requirements to ensure that a tax-favored pension plan would have the money to pay out in the long run.[44]

These proposals met vigorous opposition from conservative legislators, insurance pension consultants, and corporate employers. Republican Senator Robert Taft accused the Roosevelt administration of using the tax code to advance its social program—in fact, an accurate charge. The debate involved some of the same players involved in the fight over the Clark Amendment seven years earlier. H. Walter Forster, the pension consultant who drafted the Clark Amendment, led the pension community in protesting the $7,500 cap on individual pension accounts. Many corporations' pension plans would have failed to meet such a restriction. AT&T led the corporate opposition to the proposed pension regulations; as in 1935–36, it threatened to terminate its pension plan if this legislation were enacted.[45]

Mandatory vesting, the issue in which the idea of citizenship rights was most manifest, encountered the most hostile, vociferous opposition. Without early vesting, an employee only had rights to pension money at the time he or she retired. In general, top-level company officers stayed with the company until retirement. Low-level employees usually left the firm well before meeting service requirements, and when they left, they forfeited their claims. Paul soon dropped his call for full and immediate vesting and changed it to mandatory vesting after fifteen years of service for employees over age 40. Employers still resisted. They claimed that early vesting would "facilitate quits" and hence undermine the industrial relations goals of their pension plans. Congress agreed and dropped the proposal, even though both the TNEC investigations of the late 1930s and the Treasury Department found that without vesting, most company pensions amounted to a shifting of a vast amount of tax-free income to top-level personnel. Mandatory vesting and pension maximums would not be enacted for another thirty years.[46]

Congress was most predisposed to the nondiscrimination clause. It agreed with the Roosevelt administration that the state should get a return for its tax favors. Congress wanted to ensure that private pensions would benefit those who needed old-age support, especially middle- or lower-middle-income employees. Legislators inserted new language stating that tax-exempt pension trusts were for "the exclusive benefit of employees or their beneficiaries." Under the 1942 Revenue Act, companies now had to ensure that participation in the plan extended to 70 percent of all full-time employees or 80 percent of employees in voluntary plans, with at least 70 percent of full-time employees eligible to participate. The Internal Revenue Service (IRS) would be allowed to review the plans in order to determine that they did not discriminate in favor of officers or highly compensated employees and that the plan applied to a "bona fide employee group."[47]

In addition to enacting the nondiscrimination clause, Congress also included in the Revenue Act of 1942 the first funding obligations on private pensions. In order for a company to gain tax-favored status, the cost of benefits accrued would have to be funded each year. The pay-as-you-go method or the strategy of trying to fund the obligations as employees retired would no longer be approved by the IRS for tax-favored status. The IRS would also monitor corporate plans to fund past-service liabilities in order to prevent claims of unfunded past liabilities from becoming a backdoor tax shelter. Most pension underwriters and consultants agreed with the costing and funding regulations included in the legislation. Insurance companies had long tried to convince employers to adhere to actuarial planning and funding.[48] Of course, the new requirements meant that premiums paid to insurance companies for unfunded past service or annuity credits would also come under IRS scrutiny. The IRS, in carrying out the mandate of the new law, began issuing its own regulations in an effort to transform employee pension plans into more permanent undertakings—much in line, of course, with the NWLB's rulings that employer-provided insurance benefits must be put into a written contract and hence "secured."

Thus, federal lawmakers, like the NWLB, sought to guarantee a minimum level of security, but without tipping the balance of power between management and workers, or without interfering with corporate power. The requirement that company pension plans enroll a majority of employees (and adhere to actuarially sound funding) marked a significant step, but it was as far as the government would go. This policy reflected an attempt to make the supplementary welfare state operate a bit more fairly, yet there would be no guarantee of actual pension benefits.

Organized Labor and Private Security

During the war, the two labor federations focused most of their attention on getting the Little Steel wage cap formula overturned or getting wages to rise, rather than exploiting stabilization loopholes to obtain group insurance or pensions. There was little discussion about fringe benefits. Labor leaders' main concern seems to have been that workers were not sharing in the prosperity of the war and receiving just compensation for their service to the war effort and that unions' ability to negotiate with employers had been curtailed by the no-strike pledge.[49]

Individual unions had a somewhat different response. With union recognition and membership now secure, and the state setting wages, they could move on to other issues. NWLB policy held that the board would approve group insurance or other benefit plans voluntarily agreed upon by unions and management as long as they did not exceed 5 percent of payroll. In addition, the NWLB occasionally allowed regional war labor boards to order establishment of a plan if such was standard practice in the industry or community and if workers endured hazardous working conditions. Some unions began to present demands for sick leave, vacation pay, disability wages, or group insurance as compensation in lieu of wage increases, strategically putting forth a demand for a wage increase first and insurance second. Unions invoked the language of social security, as they had prior to the war, but they began to link it to contracts signed with employers.[50]

Despite new tax policies and NWLB policies, organized labor still pursued independent health experiments. These included health centers, in-house or union insurance companies, and union diagnostic or industrial health research centers. *Medical Care* reported that labor groups in Seattle and Los Angeles were trying to set up their own group health projects. CIO unions in St. Louis established the Labor Health Institute in 1945, providing complete medical care to union members. In Detroit, the UAW Hospitalization Committee recommended that the union seek alternatives to the physician-controlled medical plan, including government support in "the construction of a union-owned and operated medical center." The UAW suggested that the full-employment conditions of the wartime economy perhaps offered a unique opportunity: "The committee believes that the exigencies of the war effort enhance the possibilities of [a] drive forward by the Union in the area of organized medical service. . . . The time is ripe for the UAW-CIO to apply its intelligence and energy to this task."[51]

As a first step toward this goal, in 1943 the union opened the UAW Health Institute, also referred to as the Medical Research Institute, a center for diagnosis and research on industrial accidents and diseases among autoworkers. According to their original vision, UAW social planners expected the Health Institute to function in three areas. It would provide physical examinations and diagnostic tests for individuals, as well as regular follow-up laboratory and physical exams. Doctors then provided workers with diagnoses and recommendations regarding change of job or shift. The UAW also intended the institute to carry on studies of work groups in shops affected by fumes, dusts, or other particular hazards and then make recommendations to alleviate or eliminate the hazards in each workplace and press for plant investigations by state boards of health or departments of labor. In addition, the institute would provide health and safety education for workers. Finally, the UAW intended the institute to develop specific health and safety clauses to be included in local contracts.[52] Thus, this union-initiated health project defined health care and health promotion in terms that extended beyond individual-based medical therapy.

In another search for union-linked social security, in 1943 the Amalgamated Clothing Workers inaugurated the nonprofit Amalgamated Life Insurance Company in New York and the Amalgamated Life and Health Insurance Company in Illinois to underwrite union welfare funds. The board of trustees of both the insurance company and the union benefits fund included union representatives only; management did not want to assume the financial responsibility of an insurance company. Instead, garment employers established an advisory committee. With its own insurance company, the Amalgamated Clothing Workers reaped the advantages of knowing all cost information, avoiding the added fees of middlemen and brokers, and being able to invest accumulated health and welfare funds in socially beneficial projects, such as workers' housing. The United Retail, Wholesale, and Department Store Workers (CIO) followed a similar route, creating the Trade Union Accident and Health Association of America (TUAHA). The company received an official insurance charter from the New York State Insurance Department in 1943 to negotiate and administer blanket accident and health protection policies on an indemnity basis. TUAHA also lent its underwriting, brokering, and consulting services to other unions pursuing the strategy of negotiating with employers for insurance benefits. The ILGWU augmented its long-established health center during the war by securing employer funding. Over the course of the 1940s, the ILGWU Health Center grew to occupy six stories of a building in the Garment District and employed more than two hundred medical and administrative personnel.[53]

But outside New York City such endeavors remained limited. Instead, local and international unions became more focused on placing nonwage benefits, including those established unilaterally by management, into negotiated contracts. Pointing to the long list of accident and injury statistics and the accompanying loss of production, UAW President R. J. Thomas declared that "the companies have done little or nothing about them. Therefore, we of the UAW-CIO must carry forward the battle for health and labor. We must insist upon collective bargaining for health!"[54] Unions such as the American Federation of Hosiery Workers resolved at their annual convention to bargain for employer contributions to accident, hospital, medical, and surgical insurance coverage.[55] International unions codified local bargaining on this issue. As the United Furniture Workers announced in October 1944, "The International Union has perfected a plan which meets the needs of every union member. It's the job of each local union to see that the benefits of the plan reach every member."[56] In this way unions also began to narrow the potential reach of health security, focusing more specifically on unionized workers rather than on the extended community.

Strategies for pursuing health security through collective bargaining were by no means uniform. In some cases, as with several needle trades unions, the union designed its own proposals for a health or social security program, presented it to employers, and asked for a percentage of the payroll paid to unions to administer the plan. In local economies based primarily on small-scale production or small employers such a route was politically possible. In many other cases, however, unions accepted the model suggested by the NWLB, offering no independent alternative but instead seeking to incorporate a preestablished plan into the contract. An industrial relations study at the end of the war found that numerous "local unions negotiating contracts insist on incorporating in these contracts [employer] provisions for group life insurance, accident and sickness, accidental death and dismemberment insurance, and hospitalization."[57] The United Electrical, Radio, and Machine Workers of America (UE) took the lead in this strategy. In December 1943 the UE's General Executive Board decided to demand that the electrical companies' life and sickness insurance plans be incorporated into labor contracts and that management pay the premium. Another strategy sought leverage over employer-provided benefits by insisting on a labor-oriented insurance carrier. Upon the first anniversary of their health plan sponsored by TUAHA, the general counsel for the Textile Workers of America contended that "group insurance, which is mutually agreed upon between the Union and the Employer and administered by an enlightened insurance carrier . . . is the finest medium for building morale among the workers and rendering a greatly needed social service."[58]

Walter Reuther, on the rise in the UAW, saw some potential for this route. Frustrated with the sluggish response of the Michigan Hospital Service (Blue Cross) to labor's demands, Reuther consulted with Leo Perlman, of TUAHA, several times in 1944 and 1945. Although Reuther rightly saw the health insurance program being offered by TUAHA as limited and inferior in benefits to Blue Cross, he thought TUAHA would offer him something other plans could not: union control and input. Perlman would help extract employer funds and place them in the trade union's insurance company, where he insisted that TUAHA would have "sole jurisdiction over the administration of all of the terms and provisions of the policy including the adjustment of all of the claims which may arise." Reuther thought that Perlman's company would not only thwart arbitrary control by employers but also open the door to union determination of the expenditure of funds. Reuther wrote to Perlman: "If we were to negotiate a satisfactory and comprehensive insurance contract with your firm, what basis of representation in the executive structure of your company would you offer to our union?"[59] Reuther mistakenly believed that the UAW would get to manage the reserves earned on its policies. Additionally, Reuther sought to convince Perlman to switch from cash-indemnity coverage to contracts with group service plans. But these labor insurance carriers were not really significant alternatives. They usually operated on traditional group insurance principles, providing limited cash indemnification, not service. Indeed, they often acted as brokers or intermediaries for the larger commercial insurance companies.

Including insurance benefits in collective bargaining stimulated the development of labor-friendly insurance consulting firms. Leo Perlman's TUAHA directly underwrote some insurance policies but more often assisted unions in obtaining advantageous policy packages from commercial insurance companies. In the case of the Hosiery Workers, the TUAHA plan was actually issued through the National Casualty Company. Even Perlman's proposed health plan for the UAW ultimately would have been "underwritten by [a] licensed commercial carrier." Perlman offered unions expertise in insurance calculations; he knew how insurance companies worked and how to put together premium estimates.[60] Perhaps the most influential labor insurance consultant to arise in this period was Martin Segal. During the 1930s Segal worked at both small insurance agencies and large insurance companies, becoming familiar with group insurance at Metropolitan. In 1939, well before the war or the NWLB ruling on fringe benefits, Segal opened his own agency and began soliciting employee and employer groups. His first major client, in 1940–41, was the Electronic Manufacturers' Association, a group of small employers who sought health and disability insurance coverage for workers who worked in the trade. Soon after that, however, Segal began putting together insurance packages for construction and building trades unions, maritime trades unions, and teachers' unions.

Segal acted as a consultant to the unions who were trying to purchase group insurance policies, but he was no ordinary insurance broker. Segal became an advocate for the unions. As he explained, "We take competitive bids [from different insurance companies], we analyze the bids, and we tell the client: here's what this all means. You decide. Now, in those days, insurance companies paid commissions [to brokers]. We tried to get the insurance companies to eliminate commissions. . . . where that was impossible, we used the insurance company commission to pay for the services provided to the client." This practice was very important for workers, for commissions were granted to brokers every time the group insurance contract was renewed (i.e., every year), and the commission was folded into the premium. Segal would tell his clients what the commissions were, a practice that was, Segal noted, "unheard of in the group insurance business—absolutely unheard of." By doing so, he enabled his clients to negotiate for better contracts. In fact, Segal eventually decided that the insurance companies were simply retaining too much money at the end of the year. Thus, he started promoting self-insurance, as well as Blue Cross coverage, to unions. Segal tended to represent AFL craft unions, and so the plans he set up were typically multi-employer health and pension programs. By the end of the war Segal's firm, the Trade Union Agency, was well on its way to gaining a national reputation as a labor-supportive insurance consultant.[61]

Segal not only collected the bids and interpreted them for unions; he participated in the negotiations and prepared all the public relations material for the union to distribute to members promoting the new insurance plans. Like Perlman, Segal encouraged unions to seek employer funding of the insurance or pension plan. He promoted the collective bargaining system taking shape during the war (off which he was of course making a good deal of money): "Formerly the worker found himself cut off from insurance protection, even under a group plan, during these periods when he was most in need of protection. By including these plans in collective bargaining agreements, provisions can be made—and should be made for these contingencies." Thus, Segal espoused the industrial pluralist outlook, namely, that the existence of a collective bargaining contract itself ensured security. He advised all labor organizations to "put the union demand in the proposed collective bargaining agreement." To help carry out this design, Segal's Trade Union Agency offered a standard clause to be inserted in all union contracts.[62]

As labor pressed management to negotiate health benefits, Michael Davis and other health insurance reformers appealed to unions to advocate group practice plans. A study conducted by the Princeton University Industrial Relations Section in 1945 raised a concern about cash benefits versus direct medical care. It found that among the unions and firms studied, "the programs established through collective bargaining [during the war] have provided for the former much more frequently and extensively than for the latter. A number of union sponsored plans . . . provide medical service and no cash benefits. They are, however, comparatively few in number and have not been stimulated to growth under the wartime conditions as have cash benefit plans."[63] The journal *Medical Care*, edited by Davis, highlighted emerging group service plans instead. It extolled, for example, the new Kaiser Permanente health program, initiated in the Bay Area of San Francisco, as a model both for policymakers designing legislation and for labor unions seeking voluntary arrangements for their members. In the fall of 1943 *Medical Care* reported enthusiastically, "Mr. Kaiser not only builds ships but has announced a medical discovery: first-rate medical care . . . can be supplied to people for $25 to $30 a year while paying good incomes to their doctors, maintaining excellent hospitals, and yielding a surplus over current expenses."[64]

The New Marriage of Group Practice Medicine and Employee Benefits

The Welfare Capitalism of Henry Kaiser

Kaiser Industries' health and medical care program for workers was developed by Dr. Sidney Garfield, who adapted the Ross-Loos Clinic group practice model to a welfare capitalist setting. During the 1930s Garfield ran his own hospital for workers employed on the southern California aqueduct project in the desert two hundred miles from Los Angeles. In order to ensure payment for his services, he hooked up with a local casualty insurance company and devised a prepay insurance plan. Garfield convinced project employers, among whom Kaiser was only one, to implement a payroll deduction plan for workers who wanted coverage. Still, Garfield needed a way to hire medical personnel and to integrate the insurance scheme with compensation for personnel and services. This developed when Kaiser won a contract for part of the Grand Coulee Dam construction in Washington. With the passage of the National Labor Relations Act and the Davis-Bacon Act, requiring that federal construction contractors pay their workers "prevailing wages," militant unionism surged up and down the Pacific Coast. Workers began organizing CIO unions and pressing charges against employers at the Colorado River Aqueduct and the Grand Coulee Dam for violation of Davis-Bacon minimum wage and PWA regulations. Because of the work's extreme danger and high accident rate, medical care became an intensely contested issue among these militant unions. Labor protested the shabby quality of company industrial medicine programs. While Henry Kaiser remained either oblivious or hostile to union activity in the 1930s, his son Edgar was determined to appease the unions in order to start off the project with friendly labor relations. He invited Sidney Garfield to set up a hospital and medical program at Grand Coulee for Kaiser employees. Garfield saw this invitation as an opportunity to experiment with ideas he had been developing on prepaid group practice.[65]

Eager to mollify disgruntled workers and unions, Henry and Edgar Kaiser allowed Garfield to expand and modernize the existing hospital at Grand Coulee. Garfield recruited general practitioners and specialists, hoping to create what he referred to as a "little Mayo clinic." Garfield then established a prepaid voluntary health plan based on weekly payroll deductions of 50¢ cents a week per person. These contributions would pay for nonoccupational health care, while Garfield relied on workmen's compensation to pay for all job-related health problems; there would be no additional charges at the time of service. Thus, as

Garfield argued, the one premium deduction paid for virtually "unlimited medical care." And for workers this was mostly true. Soon unions began to demand that family members be included in the prepaid plan, an unprecedented type of coverage for both Kaiser's company and Sidney Garfield. When the unions threatened to strike, they came up with family coverage. Unions leaders then became actively involved in promoting the plan among workers, and even though the plan was voluntary, 90 percent of families enrolled.[66]

With the start of World War II, Kaiser Industries moved from remote desert or mountain job sites to urban centers of ship construction. The vast Kaiser shipyards stimulated a massive population influx and altered the physical landscape of Bay Area towns and cities. Richmond, California, exploded in size during the war, and Oakland, now the headquarters for Kaiser Industries, grew by 20 percent. As new housing projects, transportation lines, and roads sprawled out to accommodate war workers and migrants, the wartime economy hastened the growth of a metropolitan region. The population explosion overwhelmed not only the housing stock but also services such as medical care. Kaiser war workers experienced great difficulty getting appointments with private doctors or a bed in the hospital. So late in 1941 Henry Kaiser asked Garfield to come to Richmond, where the Kaiser payroll had jumped from 4,000 employees to 30,000.[67] Previously Garfield had set up his group practice plans far removed from the scrutiny or interest of others in the profession. Now, although the lack of infrastructure and the crisis of war boomtowns still gave him room to experiment and set up a whole new system, it also brought him directly into conflict with the organized medical establishment.

Just as Kaiser Industries had thrived through New Deal largesse—from federal land reclamation projects and Public Works Administration projects of the 1930s to massive injections of federal spending during World War II—so too did Permanente. The first Kaiser medical center in the Bay Area opened its doors in March 1942. At first it provided industrial care: Garfield arranged with local insurance companies to be the exclusive provider of workmen's compensation care for the employees of Kaiser shipyards. In June 1942 Garfield launched the supplemental Permanente Health Plan, which would provide full medical services for nonoccupational injuries and illnesses under a payroll deduction plan. Together these programs covered 20,000 workers in Richmond and Oakland. For about $4.20 per month, workers' families received full care. Kaiser and Garfield also began construction of a new hospital to support the plan. The Federal Works Administration subsidized the construction of the Richmond Hospital, run by Permanente on rental agreement. That summer Henry Kaiser and Sidney Garfield established the Permanente Foundation, a nonprofit health care foundation, to raise funds for building more facilities. The Permanente Foundation opened another hospital in Oakland and one in Vancouver, Washington. The Federal Works Administration gave financial assistance to both of these hospitals. The foundation built a fourth hospital, or medical center, at Fontana in southern California. The National Urgency Committee approved an additional two hundred hospital beds for Kaiser hospitals in 1944—over the opposition of local authorities. The Permanente Foundation soon established clinics near wartime housing projects from Los Angeles to Vancouver.

The doctors recruited by Garfield worked for the Permanente Foundation on salary. Permanente furnished all equipment and uniforms. Permanente also employed 240 nurses. Once again, Henry Kaiser pulled strings in Washington to make sure his health program flourished. Kaiser secured draft deferments or exemptions not only for Sidney Garfield but also for numerous young doctors whom Garfield recruited. Kaiser made the case that ensuring workers' health was essential to the war production effort. Consequently, Permanente recruited many young, energetic doctors during the war who were willing to participate in group practice service plans. The doctors worked together in the Permanente hospitals and their accompanying outpatient clinic. As Garfield explained, "These outpatient clinics correspond to what is the doctor's office in the usual scheme of things. More important, it is the office of a number of doctors whose training and talents are pooled in group practice."[68] These doctors carried the Permanente Health Plan well beyond a simple industrial medicine program. In addition to providing general care for workers and families, they also launched public health–oriented programs during the war. These included a syphilis clinic, a tuberculosis treatment program, and special projects for research and treatment of pneumonia and pulmonary diseases. Garfield and his associates actively promoted an ethic of community service; a communitarian "corporate" culture developed in which doctors and staff were highly committed to the social principles and values of group practice medicine.

The new Permanente Health Plan focused on promoting health as much as it did on treating sickness. The plan paid attention to nutrition and conducted a survey of Bay Area diets and eating habits. Permanente also published articles on health in the shipyard house organ and gave lunchtime lectures on diet, vitamin supplements, and improving health. As more men went overseas and the workforce became older and more female, doctors again were instructed to be alert to the particular nutritional needs of women, the elderly, and disabled workers. It took Kaiser a while, however, to respond to the issues and needs of women workers. It was not until mid-1944 that Permanente covered childbirth expenses. Eventually, however, Kaiser established a child care program and child service centers and prepared take-home meals for working mothers. Permanente clinics also distributed birth-control information. In general, the program encouraged members to pay a visit to the medical center at the first sign of any health problem. As Henry Kaiser later described the program, "The plan works because of four basic principles . . . prepayment, group practice, well-planned, integrated facilities, and preventive medical care."[69]

Although participation in the Permanente Health Plan was voluntary, Kaiser Industries worked assiduously to ensure employee enrollment. According to Kaiser Permanente historian Rickey Hendricks, "Management bombarded workers with information." The company repeatedly sent letters and pamphlets to every employee explaining the plan and sign-up procedures, techniques that companies such as Metropolitan had long used to sell group insurance to employees. Management relied on the loudspeaker system throughout the shipyards, as well as the company newsletter, to issue perpetual reminders about the plan. Announcements invoked the rhetoric of national duty and patriotism to promote enrollment in the health plan. Maintaining health and reducing absenteeism were the patriotic duty of every war worker; management and workers would be partners in this process. By the end of 1944, 87 percent of Kaiser's 93,000 Bay Area shipyard workers had joined the plan in Richmond and Oakland. Overall membership during the war peaked at about 100,000 members. African American workers joined on the same terms as white workers and received the same benefits.[70]

Late in 1944 Kaiser decided to continue the medical care program after the war and open it up to the general public. During the last year of the war Garfield experimented with a health plan for non–Kaiser Industries employees at the Harbor Gate federal housing project in the East Bay area. Despite the vocal opposition of the medical societies, the Federal Housing Administration supervised the program and held Garfield to generous and inclusive standards, insisting, for example, that all children under 18, even if employed, had to be included in "family coverage." The Federal Housing Administration also insisted that the membership premium be held to an affordable amount. In the end, Garfield set up a family plan for $6.40 a month for a family of four, an affordable deal for working-class families. For about 3 percent of a worker's annual salary Permanente provided preventive and comprehensive care.

When the war ended, however, so many workers left the Kaiser shipyards that membership in the Permanente Health Plan sank. Thus, beginning in the summer of 1945 Garfield and associates began aggressively seeking new client groups. The postwar membership came from two groups—white-collar professionals and labor unions. Permanente first recruited federal and state civil service workers. In 1945 faculty and workers at the University of California, Mills College, and San Francisco State University joined the health plan. And in the Portland-Vancouver area Reed College faculty became one of the first new member groups. Then, as soon as the program was opened up to the general public, CIO and AFL unions signed up. In July 1945 it was the only health plan endorsed by the state CIO council. Union members joined the plan at a rate of 2,000 per month. In particular, the most radical and militant CIO unions joined Permanente: the International Longshoremen's and Warehousemen's Union (ILWU), the UE, and the Mine, Mill, and Smelter Workers. The ILWU newspaper recommended to all locals that they include demands for the Kaiser Permanente health plan in all future negotiations with employers. They stressed the importance of Permanente's preventive medicine program. In 1946 and 1947 steelworkers at the Bethlehem Pacific Coast Steel Company and the U.S. Steel Corporation's Columbia Geneva plant went on strike, demanding the comprehensive medical benefits of the Kaiser Permanente plan. It would take several years to win these battles, but by the end of the decade these unions would bring in tens of thousands of members to the Permanente program. Garfield eventually went to great lengths to satisfy the demands of unions such as the ILWU. UAW and United Steelworkers of America (USWA) locals in northern California also initiated self-administered plans with Kaiser Permanente. Permanente began to build numerous small clinics in areas where it had new members. Yet where Permanente could not set up facilities, it helped unions enroll in smaller, more local group practice plans. The leftist unions and the liberal university and civil service workers who joined reinforced the progressive, community service ethos of the program. After one year of open enrollment only 15 percent of the Permanente Health Plan's 40,000 members worked for Kaiser Industries.[71]

Though most members of the Permanente Health Plan were not Henry Kaiser's employees, they could not escape one crucial aspect of welfare capitalism: employer control. Subscriber groups did not have formal mechanisms for participating in administrative decisions. Except in the case of the very largest groups, the Permanente Foundation generally blocked consumer input in decisions on policy, management, and investment in facilities. Thus the Kaiser program offered many of the benefits of comprehensive medical care promised by group practice experiments of the 1930s, but it left out a crucial component labor and New Deal health reformers had hoped for: a consumer or patient voice in the economics of medical care and the definition of health promotion.

Garfield nevertheless promoted Permanente as a model that community groups anywhere in the nation could replicate. As Garfield told audiences, the press, and doctors returning from the military, "There is no reason, if the obstacles are fairly analyzed, why the equivalent to a Permanente Health Plan cannot be set up at once in almost every town in the nation. Such plans can be sponsored by doctors returning from the war, by existing group practice organizations, by hospitals, consumer and farm cooperatives, or by labor unions."[72] This was not mere grandiosity and self-importance. An AMA survey in 1944 found that "30% of the older men, who have now had the opportunity to compare practice under the traditional structure with group practice for the government, want full-time jobs in government service. Moreover, 53% of doctors of all ages want to go into the group form of private practice. Considering all age groups, 63% indicate a preference for a form of practice other than the traditional form of solo practice on a fee-for-service basis."[73] Kaiser and Garfield hoped to attract these doctors, particularly those coming home from the war and those now able to attend medical school under the G.I. Bill. They started investing heavily in new plant, equipment, and new research in order to promote Kaiser Permanente as an attractive, cutting-edge place to work that provided stable income (through prepayment), the most up-to-date equipment, and perpetual learning through exchange of information and research made possible by the group health center. Likewise, these facilities were beginning to attract middle-income members.

Now the medical societies of the AMA had something to worry about. The California Medical Association branded doctors who went to work for Kaiser or the other group plans in the state, such as Ross-Loos, as unethical, and the California State Board of Medical Examiners charged Garfield with violation of the state Medical Practice Act in 1946. Combining several charges, the board even revoked his medical license for one year and placed him on five years' probation. The county medical societies attacked other Kaiser Health Plan doctors as well and rejected their applications for membership, tarring them with the brush of "socialized medicine." Such denial also blocked Kaiser doctors from gaining certification by specialty boards in orthopedics, ophthalmology, and obstetrics. These boards required medical society membership for certification. Medical schools refused to cooperate with the Kaiser Health Plan. In the early 1950s Dr. Paul Foster, president of the Los Angeles County Medical Society, eager to stop Kaiser's growth, instigated a nationwide AMA effort to block prepaid group plans. In 1953, following a resolution written by Foster, the AMA voted to declare all group practice plans unethical, modifying that in 1954 to include only closed-panel plans. Organized medicine actively mobilized to prevent the Kaiser Permanente health plan from taking root outside of California.[74]

The Transition from War to Peace

Despite compromises organized labor made during the war to maintain its collaborative relationship with the Democratic Party, with the onset of postwar reconversion many union activists intended to push for social democratic corporatism in industry and an expansion of New Deal social rights. The labor movement emerged from the war with economic power that also was explicitly political. The question would be how labor could use New Deal and wartime political structures to transform economic relationships and realize labor's broader economic security goals. Immediately after the war, the working-class movement was poised to exert significant political power. American workers greatly feared that their wartime gains would soon be wiped out. A strike wave erupted as soon as V-J Day had passed, sweeping through all of basic industry. During the war, the number of unionized workers in the United States had risen from 9 million to 15 million—35 percent of the civilian labor force. More than 3 million of these workers participated in strikes from November 1945 to June 1946. The strikes were no longer wartime wildcat strikes; they were spirited and well organized, targeting powerful corporations.[75] In addition, labor's allies, including Popular Front leftist activists, labor journalists and intellectuals, and neighborhood activists, were still mobilized to press a broad agenda for working-class security, including extending economic and social rights to women and African Americans at work and in their communities.[76]

The first bold, comprehensive, and visible move was taken by the United Mine Workers (UMW). During the first postwar bargaining round, John L. Lewis demanded that coal operators finance a health and welfare plan. Since the mid-1930s, rank-and-file miners had actively demanded that the union replace the company-doctor system with a comprehensive disability, medical, and retirement program accountable to the workers. Lewis had generally brushed these requests aside, but in 1945 he was eager to push himself forward as a champion of trade union independence and militancy. While Lewis's response to miners' demands for security began as a confrontation with the New Deal state, its success ultimately depended on extensive cooperation between the UMW and the New Deal state. Determined to show that he was not beholden to "a corporate state and all its manifestations" and that the pro–Democratic Party CIO was headed down the wrong path, Lewis put a union-run, private social security program at the center of his postwar bargaining goals. When the coal operators balked, Lewis took the bituminous coal miners out on strike on 1 April 1946. Invoking the War Labor Disputes Act, President Truman seized the mines after six weeks of work stoppage. With the mines now officially under the jurisdiction of the Department of the Interior, the secretary of the interior took a seat at the negotiating table. The federal government would now be responsible for responding to each of the demands presented by the union, including a health and welfare fund.[77]

Secretary of the Interior Julius Krug was ready to make a deal, whereas the mine owners were not. Truman and Krug consulted with the Social Security Administration (SSA) on the issue of a union-run health and welfare fund. Arthur Altmeyer, director of the SSA, heartily endorsed the principle of a private, union-run, industrywide social security fund. He even offered the technical assistance of the SSA's Bureau of Research and Statistics in designing the fund. I. S. Falk stepped in and fashioned a plan for the UMW. On 29 May Krug and Lewis signed a contract that included a medical and hospital plan, a retirement fund, and provisions for coordinating the two.[78]

For Lewis, the most important element was union control. Miners had long been subject to payroll deductions for health care. These contributions, however, went to pay the salary of the company doctor, usually a crony of the mine owner who performed very little actual medical care and did so under substandard conditions. Now the UMW wanted to ensure that all monies went to funding high-quality medical care. After difficult negotiations, operators and the UMW struck an agreement. The operators would pay for a union welfare and retirement fund. The fund, however, would be run by a tripartite trusteeship, with one trustee chosen by the union, one chosen by the owners, and one neutral trustee. The fund would be financed by a royalty assessed on the amount of coal extracted by union workers. The royalty was initially set at 5¢ per ton, and it was soon raised to 10¢. Lewis eventually gained union control over the fund by controlling the choice of the third, "neutral" trustee. The owners conceded: it would be the union's fund.[79]

While the UMW story turned out to be rather unique—because of geography, industry, and personality—it is important for several reasons. Here the SSA and its policymakers actively facilitated the supplementation idea. Even after the May 1946 contract had been signed, the SSA asked to be involved in assisting the union to set up the various programs and monitor them. Falk recommended to Altmeyer that the

SSA should assist private health and pensions plans so that they would be "interlocked with proposed security legislation."[80] Second, and quite ironically, although Lewis set out to prove the UMW's independence from the New Deal state, his success in winning his goals certainly owed a great deal to the intervention of the state and sympathetic government officials. Publicly, Lewis continued to condemn government interference and legislative shackles. Yet, as Edward Berkowitz has written, "close ties between the government and the fund enabled the UMW to receive help from the Social Security Administration and the Public Health Service in recruiting staff for the fund." Physicians, public health experts, and industrial health experts came from the PHS and the FSA, which had run rural medical programs during the 1930s and World War II. In 1948 Josephine Roche, a Social Security and health insurance expert, chair of the 1938 National Health Conference, and the former assistant secretary of the treasury in charge of the PHS, became director of the UMW fund. A longtime friend of John L. Lewis's, Roche was the third trustee for many years.[81]

The New Dealers, government staff, and physicians whom Josephine Roche recruited were willing to participate in developing innovative programs to fulfill the social vision of the union. They had the opportunity to create a comprehensive health care plan from the ground up. In turn, these health reform experts and physicians helped train a generation of union officials, as well as Lewis, to run this private welfare system. The new UMW health program departed significantly from traditional, fee-for-service health care, turning instead to the models presented by the CCMC and health care reformers in the 1930s and early 1940s. They relied on group practice, managed care, closed panels of physicians, and treatment review to ensure that miners would get the most for their dollar. The fund immediately launched a rehabilitative program for thousands of severely handicapped miners who had been disabled by mining accidents and injuries, many of whom had not left their beds for years. The drama of carrying these bedridden miners down from the remote mining communities to modern hospitals for rehabilitation proved a powerful symbol to union members: the union would take care of its own.[82]

Although the UMW programs would not dispense benefits until the end of the 1940s, and wrangling over the details continued for several years, labor leaders were impressed by what Lewis and the UMW had done. Lewis may not have won precisely what he wanted, but CIO leaders perceived it as a victory on union terms. It appeared that the UMW had extracted resources from the coal operators that would be shifted into a true workers' security program, a program in which Lewis and his advisers could experiment. They would implement the ideas and practices of group practice medical centers and service plans; and they could build medical services that served community needs. Moreover, the settlement was industrywide. Neither CIO nor AFL unionists intended to abandon their support for an expanded welfare state, but they had the sense that Lewis had shown how labor could build on the collective bargaining regime fashioned by the NWLB and make it part of the broader politics of security. At the first postwar convention of the CIO, in November 1946, CIO leaders resolved to include social security programs in their collective bargaining demands.

In late 1946 the UAW instructed all locals to demand a social insurance program based on a straight employer contribution of 3 percent of employees' gross earnings—modeled, clearly, on the UMW royalty per ton of coal extracted, as well as the plans negotiated by AFL craft unions near the end of the war. The contributions would fund a comprehensive, integrated, union-run Workers' Security Program to provide disability, hospital, surgical, and medical benefits, plus maternity and survivors' benefits.[83] The UAW Social Security Department, which in 1947 hired Harry Becker, formerly of EMIC, spent the next few years formulating and more fully designing this ideal program. At this moment it appeared that the UMW model might be viable for other unions in various regions. In an important sense this strategy did attempt to shift power relations within the industry; it was intended to take security out of the realm of personnel policy, out of the realm of welfare capitalism.

Major business interests, however, were prepared to launch a counterattack on interventionist wartime labor policies. Although during the war the NAM usually reported that the NWLB would not order plans requested by unions, it obscured this record as the war came to a close. Instead, it cast the board as having imposed radical changes under the guise of a wartime emergency. Among the fringe issues "thrust upon industry," as the *NAM News* put it, the NAM listed vacations, shift differentials, paid holidays, sick leave, insurance plans, and severance pay. The NAM Industrial Relations Department urged employers to retrench on these benefits not merely because of the cost of the various sick leave plans and insurance policies. The NAM saw these developments in political terms. Not only had the NWLB's directives "alter[ed] industrial relations practices within the relatively short war emergency period" but, the NAM feared, they "may have the effect of determining industrial relations practices far into the future." Seeing security very much as a balance-of-power issue, the NAM advised employers to "examine and evaluate fringe increases with which you are now burdened. Develop sound support for claims that some or all of them must be 'shaded' or eliminated entirely in the event that favorable action is to be taken on a demand for a wage boost."[84]

At the war's end many business executives believed that organized labor had become an intrepid social movement about to break out beyond the boundaries of basic industry. American business executives therefore sought to "restore" and "preserve" their authority, to reestablish "the legitimate spheres of influence of labor and management," as Howell Harris has argued. Although they accepted the presence of unions in basic industry, they did not necessarily accept industrial pluralism or an expanded realm of negotiable issues.[85] In summarizing the impact of the NWLB on the "rights and responsibilities of management" and reviewing cases on fringe-benefit issues specifically, the NAM asserted, "With the termination of the War and the dissolution of the War Labor Board, the trend towards limitation of such rights must be changed, and many restrictions so imposed be cast off by negotiations during peace-time."[86]

Therefore, if the CIO movement was to succeed in its bold demands on the economic resources of an industry, it had to marshal political power as much as economic power, and in the later 1940s the political terrain was shifting, allowing conservative business, southern, and antilabor interests to reconfigure political possibilities. When Social Security policymakers first became involved in the UMW fund, Falk insisted to Altmeyer that "'a basic floor' of income and health protection should come from the government, and 'company or industry systems should be built on that floor.'"[87]

This, of course, was not the path of development the American welfare state would take after World War II. The federal Social Security System did prove its resilience during World War II, yet the expansion of Social Security during the war occurred involuntarily: employment in covered industries grew dramatically, and with more people paying in, the number of eligible retirees increased. Congress blocked, diluted, and delayed expansions in social insurance provisions requested by Presidents Roosevelt and Truman. Legislators deliberately kept veterans' programs separate from Social Security policy. Through much of the 1940s, Congress was not convinced by the arguments of the SSB or its successor, the SSA, that social welfare programs either fought inflation or boosted critical purchasing power. Congress voted against a planned OASI tax increase. After the war, with Dixiecrats more firmly allied with Congressional Republicans, an antilabor coalition that opposed further development of the welfare state emerged as a powerful check on New Deal programs and the Fair Deal agenda.[88]

But well before the final showdown on national health care later in the decade, the premier agency at the helm of the welfare state, the SSA, already promoted private social welfare arrangements. By the end of World War II Altmeyer and Cohen and their associates regularly advanced the basic welfare state–private supplementation position without hesitation. Once the Republicans took over Congress in November 1946, solidifying an anti–New Deal bloc of southern Democrats and conservative Republicans, the SSA ideologically capitulated. SSA members now spoke more regularly and more publicly about private-sector supplementation. As Commissioner for Social Security Arthur Altmeyer told American audiences: "Social Security recognizes that all a government program should do is establish a minimum basic protection against loss of income, on which the individual will be encouraged to build for himself a more attractive degree of well-being through well-known devices of individual savings, private insurance, and home ownership."[89] Of course, the ability to attain these "well-known devices" would depend upon the place one occupied in the labor market; federal policy would reinforce labor market segmentation, not compensate for it.

The NWLB may have encouraged bureaucratization and routinization, institutionalizing an ideology of industrial pluralism at variance with power relations and imbalances in industry. But as the war ended, labor still had a fight to fight. Labor leaders still had ideas and plans for tipping the balance of power and restructuring relations between capital and labor, management and workers. When we look closely at the particular way in which the big CIO unions and the UMW structured their health and pension demands—as independent programs that took a percentage of payroll and put it into union-run or union-determined social service programs—we see that these contests over security were about the balance of power. The UMW's apparent success in negotiating an employer-funded health and welfare program spurred other unions to pursue the strategy of bargaining for security. Yet what they wanted to follow was not the mere negotiation of a contract. Unionists in the UAW, the USWA, the UE, and the International Union of Electrical, Radio, and Machine Workers (IUE) were well aware of the limits of insurance and employer-provided pensions. But Lewis had negotiated a social welfare system run by the union that would be independent of management and subsidized by the state. This was no mere insurance contract.

With the New Deal and the war, many of the contests over work issues—compensation, working hours, days off, contractual obligations—had shifted to the political arena in Washington, where labor apparently had a political as well as an economic voice. In the context of the New Deal and the 1930s, security discourse had been part of a class challenge. Through the language of security, workers, both organized and unorganized, and progressive political activists could call into question the inequality of capital-labor relations. The politics of security embodied a challenge to the prerogatives of capital and an assertion of economic rights. Because the New Deal and the wartime state had so politicized the once insular realm of the workplace, labor liberals believed they could translate private security benefits into social security more broadly. The problem, however, was that as the Truman administration increasingly equivocated on labor issues, the balance of power in the political economy really did shift heavily toward business. Other unions did not have the real support of the state, for intervention of the state was crucial to Lewis's success, and collective bargaining only reinforced the balance of power at the level of the firm.

During the war, the CIO launched a massive voter-registration drive through its new Political Action Committee. The CIO Political Action Committee spread the political message that security abroad and security at home, casting a vote at the polls and casting a vote at work, were inextricably linked. By voting, by exercising their political citizenship, workers achieved greater rights and security in the workplace. A publication of the Greater New York CIO Political Action Committee told its members, "Insure Your Future, Register to Vote: For Peace—Jobs—Security. If You Register, You Can Vote For Collective Bargaining and Full Employment, Lasting Peace and Security." For the CIO, the job rights guaranteed by the Wagner Act were inseparable from the welfare measures of the Social Security Act.[90]

6

Managing Security

THE TRIUMPH OF GROUP INSURANCE AND THE STATE'S LEGITIMATION OF THE PUBLIC-PRIVATE WELFARE STATE, 1940–1960

> There is one topic which is essentially first on every agenda. It is of such vital importance that failure to give it proper place in a report of this sort is to neglect the one vital immediacy of our times and to invite the censure of posterity for so serious an omission. . . . For the first time a real beginning had been made to effectuate collective security. We have come now to the necessity of a new evaluation of the old ideal of self-reliance. In every land, the quest for security has begun; more markedly in some, but discernible in all. There is a growing conviction that, just as has been proven that completely self-reliant individuals cannot exist in a modern world, the same rule applies to people collectively, and that utter self-reliance cannot protect the nations of the earth from scheming aggressors.
>
> —*Security: A Report to the Life Insurance Association of America,* 7 May 1946

AMERICA'S PRIVATE social security system would reach full fruition after World War II. Threatened by the potential expansion of the New Deal state—its regulatory apparatus, its welfare support, and its endorsement of trade unionism—business firms acceded to the pervasive ideology of security and provided unprecedented levels of social welfare benefits. The private social security system flourished because of a political climate that simultaneously supported the New Deal welfare state but increasingly defended it as a basic system of support upon which private institutions would build.

The conventional narrative regarding the inclusion of fringe benefits in collective bargaining begins in 1943, with the NWLB's ruling that employer payments on insurance premiums would not violate the wartime wage freeze. As a result of that ruling, unions successfully sought a whole range of so-called benefits. The story then jumps to 1948–49, when the NLRB and a U.S. court of appeals ruled that managers had to negotiate with unions over pensions and insurance as "conditions of employment." Finally, this narrative points to the landmark contract signed in 1950 between GM and the UAW, which included pensions and partially financed health insurance for workers. Other unions marched onward and upward from there.[1]

An important struggle took place during these years, however, in which unions and health activists tried to influence the very nature of health insurance benefits—what they would cover, how services would be organized and financed, who would have a voice in determining premiums and benefits. As a result of experiences during the 1930s and early 1940s, organized labor became a vigorous advocate on behalf of service-based health plans, resisting the cash-indemnity, fee-for-service principle of the commercial insurance companies and the medical societies. When organized labor spoke of health security, it had in mind plans like Ross-Loos and the GHA; national health insurance would make possible the redistributive financing mechanism. As part of their larger struggle to establish broad-ranging social security and job rights—legacies of the New Deal—labor unions tried to promote health programs that would transcend the limits of firm-based collective bargaining and would have broken the links between benefits and the firm. Moreover, organized labor hoped to use the power of the federal government to bolster these efforts, tightening the connection between workers and the state.

After World War II, American employers fought to sever the links between workers and the state through both public and private strategies. The strength and organized response of the commercial insurance sector helped rejuvenate welfare capitalism. Although Blue Cross far surpassed insurance companies in the number of persons covered at the end of World War II, commercial cash-indemnity insurance became the dominant form of health financing by the mid-1950s,[2] predating the beginning of substantive bargaining over health benefits between national unions and management. Indeed, as of 1950, when such bargaining commenced, group insurance had already become well entrenched in many workplaces, and as a result of this growth it had begun to undercut the competitive conditions that enabled other health insurance alternatives to thrive. Group hospital and surgical insurance transformed the market for health insurance during a period when thousands of employers, including key firms in basic manufacturing, still implemented benefits unilaterally. The insurance industry successfully channeled both government and private health provision away from universalist, community-based, or service-oriented options that New Deal labor liberals demanded. The ascendance of cash-indemnity health benefits, then, was a function of politics and power: it served employers' goals in industrial relations, enabling them to offer the social benefits demanded by workers without ceding them power and without allowing benefits to become employment rights. Moreover, corporate leaders, through antilabor racketeering charges and legislative labor "reform," were able to shift the balance of power between business, the state, and labor. They could not restore the political economic order of the pre-Depression era, but in the 1950s business interests were able to alter the role of the state in industrial relations politics and in fact use it to sustain an increasingly insular, private, firm-centered definition of security.

As organized labor retreated from earlier ideas of independent social welfare institutions to collective bargaining over specifically demarcated benefit amounts, security became less of a broad political economic vision, less a challenge to inequality. Private welfare benefits became more like the paternalism of an earlier age. With each round of bargaining in the 1950s and 1960s, employers granted enumerated increases—adding on a few more surgical procedures, additional hospital days, visits to physicians' offices, maybe coverage for eyeglasses and root canals—within a limited framework that foreclosed labor's capacity to challenge any existing economic relationships, whether in industrial relations or in the delivery of health care. Thus as long as business executives faced a countervailing weight—unions or the state—the incentive to bargain upward remained. In the 1970s the tables turned, and bargaining started going in the other direction; "bargaining for security" became a downward spiral of concessions and losses.

In 1942 the Public Relations Committee of the NAM distributed the results of a survey entitled "What the Factory Worker Thinks about Free Enterprise" to executives at several leading American corporations. The survey found that "while believing in the system of private enterprise, the worker finds it wanting on several counts." Chief among the workers' complaints was the lack of economic and social security through employment. "*He wants more security.* The busiest bee in the worker's bonnet is that he never knows what is going to hit him. He wants better provision for old age. But even more, *he wants to know how he is going to live next month and next year.* . . . 63% say they would rather work on a government job than for a private employer, principally because of *greater security*" (emphasis in the original).[3] Indeed, observers from all quarters, from the NAM to the CIO, agreed that, in the words of one observer, "as a nation, we have become security conscious." This palpable concern with security arose out of the discourse generated by the Social Security Act of 1935.[4] All forms of private insurance benefits that proliferated in the late 1930s and 1940s built on the public social security foundation laid by the Progressives and the New Dealers. Insurers had quickly adapted to, and essentially taken over, the market for occupational injury reimbursement created by Progressive Era workmen's compensation laws. A generation later, insurers began referring to their new pensions, disability benefits, and nonoccupational health policies as supplemental Social Security, for as Equitable's Thomas Parkinson insisted, "We in the life insurance business are selling security and preaching security."[5]

By the 1940s life insurers believed that Social Security had been a tremendous boon to the sale of insurance and old-age pensions. Insurance executives instructed their agents to incorporate the new Social Security program in their sales pitch, emphasizing that federal old-age pensions would meet only the barest subsistence needs. As one Metropolitan supervisor said, "Now we sell an insurance program that will fit in and add to the social security protection the prospect already has."[6] Equitable's group insurance directors exhorted employers "to complete the protection afforded under the Social Security Act," reminding them that Equitable "specializes in all forms of group insurance: group life, group accident and health [disability], group accidental death and dismemberment, group hospitalization with surgical benefits, and group annuities." With federal pensions in place, individuals or employers could more easily purchase a retirement annuity worth one year's full salary for a small outlay.[7]

The life insurance industry called for expansion of Social Security in the 1940s. The *National Underwriter* and the *Spectator*, two key industry journals, regularly advocated extending coverage to previously excluded groups of workers. Some insurance men supported public disability coverage for incapacitated workers over 55 years of age until they qualified for Social Security benefits. Albert Linton, the president of Provident Mutual, concluded that "from a life insurance point of view, an expanded social security program on practical lines would undoubtedly be beneficial. Companies and agents have made good use of the social security plan as a foundation for life insurance programs."[8]

Yet the industry vehemently opposed attempts to expand the types of benefits offered through Social Security. Its leaders decried the Wagner health insurance bills of the 1940s, state and national temporary disability insurance proposals, and public local health plans, including

Mayor Fiorello LaGuardia's new Health Insurance Plan of New York (HIP).[9] But life insurance companies avoided actively lobbying against governmental programs, fearing that their agitation might lead to greater governmental scrutiny, regulation, or taxation of their own industry, issues that were indeed being raised in the late 1940s. As one insurance leader advised, "If the trend is toward extensive liberalization of social insurance measures in this country, it is more important to know that and to attempt to guide it into sensible channels rather than merely futilely trying to hold back the tide . . . by fighting every manifestation."[10] They would channel policies so that expansions of social insurance would apply only to indigents—who could not purchase insurance for themselves—and would not encroach upon their newest, fastest-growing field of business, health insurance. For insurers the war was an opportune moment.

The Development of Commercial Health Insurance

In order to understand insurers' wartime political stance and marketing strategies, we need to go back to the 1930s to trace the developmental course of this variant of voluntary health insurance. Life insurance companies had begun experimenting with hospital and surgical coverages during the 1930s, compelled by both the welfare capitalist motivations of their corporate group clients and their own desire to check the growth of state social insurance. The 1932 report of the CCMC, *Medical Care for the American People*, had stimulated insurance companies, as it had others, to experiment. For example, Metropolitan first offered hospital benefits to its home office workforce, primarily young women, on an experimental basis. Subsequently, insurance companies began to study the hospital service, or Blue Cross, programs that emerged in the first half of the 1930s. After reporting favorably in 1934 to the American Institute of Actuaries, the Health and Accident Underwriters Conference resolved that it would proceed to develop guidelines for hospitalization insurance on an indemnity basis. Within a year, Metropolitan was ready to offer its alternative to hospital service plans, a hospital reimbursement policy that would pay $3 per day for hospital room and board. Other group insurers followed suit, writing hospital benefits on the same basis. Still, for the rest of the decade these companies only issued policies on a closely controlled, experimental basis, usually as a supplement to a group accident and health policy.[11]

Organized as the Group Association, companies writing group insurance worked together through the late 1930s to develop disability and hospital coverages and reduce excessive frontloading charges. In 1937 they agreed upon a formula for surgical benefits, relying on statistics gathered by hospital benefit associations and service plans. All Group Association companies adopted the same rates. The payment would not be strictly a reimbursement but rather would be entirely independent of actual hospital charges.[12]

Independently, companies such as Equitable developed new health coverages at the request of particular employers. In the fall of 1935, after the passage of the Social Security Act, DuPont asked Equitable to design a plan of hospitalization and surgical benefits for employees and dependents. DuPont specified that the plan was for employees at their Buffalo, New York, plant and possibly some others, including one in Waynesboro, Virginia. As it turns out, the United Textile Workers of America had been trying to organize the Buffalo plant, a rayon plant, in 1934–35. The new local, Local 2055 of the United Textile Workers, had demanded that the company recognize it as the sole bargaining agent and convene negotiations with it. The company first turned the union down flat, but by the spring of 1935 DuPont management was becoming increasingly concerned about the militant activities of the workers.[13] Consequently, the company responded in typical welfare capitalist fashion. Rather than recognize independent representatives of the employees, they proceeded unilaterally to expand their insurance policies and welfare work. DuPont had long been an Equitable group life insurance policyholder, and more recently, had added disability coverage in the early years of the Depression. Now DuPont wanted hospital and surgical coverage too. After meeting with DuPont executives to work out the details of such a policy, Equitable's board of directors approved the issuance of hospitalization and surgical benefits for employees and dependents in 1936. It appears, however, that Equitable did not actually write such a policy for DuPont at that time, nor did it issue a hospitalization and surgical policy for dependent coverage until the end of the decade.[14] Nonetheless, Equitable had developed its next innovation in group insurance, hospital and surgical benefits, directly in response to the imperatives of welfare capitalism.

After 1939 Metropolitan's and Equitable's clientele for group disability and health policies began to expand. What group insurers found was that their longstanding group clients, particularly those in basic industry threatened by CIO organizing, were willing to build on group life policies with the new disability coverages. By the early 1940s, companies with group disability or hospital coverage included Republic Steel, Jones and Laughlin Steel, the Caterpillar Tractor Company, Armour and Company, GM, the American Can Company, the Signal Oil and Gas Company, the Okonite Company, and General Tire and Rubber.[15]

The burgeoning war economy offered insurers a tremendous opportunity to market their new wares. By 1941 industrial production had reached levels unseen since before the Depression, and American workers were on the move, heading toward the newly booming production centers of the South, the West, and the Midwest. This mass migration had several consequences for insurers. Prior to this period workers had bought primarily industrial insurance—burial or funeral policies purchased in small, weekly installments. Industrial insurance depended on a vast agency force to collect the premiums every week and maintain policy enrollment. But as workers relocated, many industrial policies lapsed. Industrial insurance had always been confined to the largest, most densely concentrated cities. Now either agents could not track their migratory clients or workers moved to locations where insurance companies had no agency infrastructure. As workers started taking home bigger paychecks, bringing the costs of a burial or funeral within the average family's reach, industrial insurance declined toward obsolescence. Insurance companies like Metropolitan, whose bread and butter had always been the industrial business, therefore needed new strategies for reaching workers and for meeting other nonburial life cycle needs. And employers needed strategies for keeping their new workforces in place. Group insurance fit the bill.[16]

So in 1941 and 1942 insurers stepped up their efforts to market group insurance to employers. Group insurance overcame the lapse problems of individual insurance policies because one annual decision by one policyholder, the employer, bought coverage for thousands of people. Indeed, workers could come and go, but the policy stayed in place as long as employers kept 75 percent of the workforce enrolled. Insurance companies soon realized that as a "fringe benefit" group policies were increasingly attractive. With the possibility of a government wage freeze imminent in 1942, the *National Underwriter* reported that "as a sales argument for corporations . . . , agents have found the imminence of a wage ceiling quite effective."[17] Insurers stressed the anti-inflationary impact of group insurance: it took money out of circulation and put it directly into savings. Meanwhile, insurers worked aggressively to convince employers that group insurance would enable them to keep workers from leaving and to meet the increased toll in accidents and sickness resulting from all-out production. It was the insurance companies, more than anyone else, who saw the potential in the NWLB ruling that employer contributions to insurance premiums did not violate wage stabilization guidelines. By 23 March 1943, when the NWLB issued its favorable decision on fringe benefits, group insurance sales had already increased during the war by over 80 percent.[18]

In order for employers to meet (or circumvent) the NWLB requirements, insurers advised them on how to select and manage particular insurance benefits. Metropolitan's PSB offered to conduct labor turnover analyses, set up internal health and safety programs, establish standardized hiring and firing procedures, and help with personnel recordkeeping for any group client. Companies like Metropolitan, Aetna, Prudential, and Equitable made it easier for employers to put a program in place swiftly before "getting the employees and perhaps the unions approval." During the war, insurers allowed employers to pay the first month's premium, announce that the policy had been put in place, and then let employees "sign up."[19] The large insurance companies also set up payroll deduction systems to cover the policies.

These changes were significant for several reasons. First, they allowed the perpetuation of a unilateral approach to employee compensation even when unions were demanding a negotiated one. Second, when unions brought grievances over fringe benefits to the NWLB, the board rarely ruled in the union's favor if the plan had already been unilaterally implemented by the employer. And ultimately, they helped establish, or in many cases reinforce, close relationships between insurers and employers. Such exclusive relationships would persist after the war had ended and complicate collective bargaining over insurance when unions made their big push for benefits in the late 1940s.

Insurers had another incentive for aggressively promoting such group policies. Even during the war liberal policymakers continued their efforts to expand New Deal social programs. In 1941 alone congressmen introduced more than 126 bills to liberalize various aspects of Social Security.[20] The federal government was actively involved in providing health care through programs such as EMIC, FSA rural health projects, and wartime public housing projects. In 1943 Senator Wagner introduced the first version of the Wagner-Murray-Dingell Bill for comprehensive health insurance through Social Security, while the SSB's Arthur Altmeyer and Wilbur Cohen generated new proposals for long-term and temporary disability insurance. Rhode Island actually passed a cash sickness (disability insurance) program. The most comprehensive proposal for an expanded American welfare state came from the NRPB, which in 1943 issued its own version of the Beveridge Report, Britain's blueprint for the postwar welfare state. Congress actually did enact many of these types of benefits for veterans in the Servicemen's Readjustment Act, or G.I. Bill, of 1944.

Insurers such as the Commercial and Metropolitan Casualty Company of New York realized they had to convince employers to buy more than group life insurance if either of them were to reap the benefits of private security. The Commercial Casualty Company called on insurers to use uniform disability and health contracts so they could mass market disability insurance. Condoning these efforts in an editorial entitled "Keeping Up with the Social Planners," the *National Underwriter* conceded that the advocates of a comprehensive Social Security program could legitimately claim that thus far insurers had not "measure[d] up to what the advanced social planners believe should be done through public schemes." The editorial implored insurers to find better ways to distribute policies besides life insurance, particularly disability and health policies, so that "its personnel and machinery might be utilized to do some of the things that the social planners desire to have done."[21] Insurance executives were happy to steer in this direction, for group casualty and health coverages brought in premiums three to four times those of group life. These efforts soon bore fruit: the number of persons covered by hospital insurance increased from 1 million before the war to 8.5 million by 1944.[22]

Still, insurers consciously made this pitch within the discursive framework of the New Deal. The Great-West Life Assurance Company invoked President Roosevelt's "Four Freedoms" speech in promoting its new accident and health policies and group insurance. "Let us not forget what we are fighting for," declared Great-West Life's 1944 ad campaign. "Freedom of Speech, Freedom of Worship, Freedom From Want, Freedom From Fear." It even identified its symbolic representative, the Great-West Life Man, with Roosevelt himself, proclaiming, "He showed us the way to Freedom From Fear."[23] Insurers sought to capture the political resonance of the New Deal's economic bill of rights and link it to commercial enterprises and the marketplace.

In planning for the postwar period, insurers believed that workers who earned less than $3,000 represented the largest untapped market for insurance of all kinds. As one Metropolitan executive proclaimed, "The great market ahead is the new aristocracy of America—the technical workers, those who are skillful with their hands. Seek that market."[24] Moreover, insurance journals emphasized that these workers, as part of a newly empowered working class, would be the engine driving postwar efforts to expand the welfare state. The editor of the *Spectator* advised his readers to heed "the new social order" in which the average worker "is one of millions who . . . have become a prime force in the social, economic, and political currents of democracy. Unless some assurance to his future is offered by private enterprise . . . he will demand a state agency to affect his objective." In this new social order the working voter would demand that government meet vital security needs that were not met through work and wages.[25]

The Struggle for Health Security

Insurance companies were not the only ones who sought to accommodate the new security consciousness. World War II had also seen the initiation of HIP in New York, the Group Health Cooperative in Seattle and Puget Sound, and the Kaiser Permanente Foundation in California. HIP, which would open after the war, was structured as a prepaid service plan, deliberately eschewing indemnity insurance, and as a non-profit entity with a corporatist board of directors. At the end of the war the St. Louis Joint Council of United Retail, Wholesale, and Department Store Employees prepared to launch its Health Institute, which would provide extensive medical services to employees and their dependents. Blue Cross flourished, as not only local unions but employers too enrolled; by the end of World War II it had 19 million subscribers.[26] Through the end of the war Americans continued to choose from a variety of experiments in health insurance.

Perceiving that national, public health insurance was a distant goal, yet not forsaking it, trade unionists redoubled their efforts to learn as much as they could about their private-sector options. Some of the larger CIO unions, such as the UAW, as well as the AFL central office, spent 1945 and 1946 conducting a massive educational effort: collecting information on insurance companies and medical plans from around the country, comparing their benefits, corresponding and meeting with Blue Cross representatives, devising their own group plans with labor insurance companies, and visiting hospitals. The UAW Social Security Department studied approximately 250 insurance companies, as well as Blue Cross, HIP, and Kaiser Permanente. Harry Becker, of the UAW's Social Security Department, corresponded continually with the Michigan Hospital Service (Blue Cross), while members of the Greater New York Industrial Council joined the board of the New York Blue Cross in the mid-1940s. In 1946 the AFL's research department still targeted its research on "prepaid medical plans, whether private or cooperative, that emphasize complete medical, surgical, and hospitalization directly as opposed to cash indemnity plans." The research department and the AFL Social Security Committee collected and dispensed information for the "many unions [in other locales] seeking plans that emphasize prevention as well as cure such as Group Health Association in Washington D.C. and Permanente Foundation in California."[27] By the time the CIO passed its official resolution calling for "Security Through Bargaining,"[28] the labor movement had developed an expertise on the possibilities for organizing and financing health care.

Now familiar with both service-based and indemnity-based health coverage, labor representatives astutely gauged the benefits of the former and the weaknesses of the latter. They preferred Blue Cross because in its original form it came rather close to being true social insurance. Members paid only one fee—a membership fee. Patients could be admitted to the hospital without delay, and they would incur few additional costs. Individuals who were not part of a group could join at an affordable price as individuals, or those who belonged to a group could convert their group coverage to an individual policy if they left their jobs. As a nonprofit institution, Blue Cross accepted applicants year-round. Blue Cross offered family coverage, whereas commercial insurance plans often did not. Most Blue Cross plans covered preexisting conditions and in some cases diagnostic care. And since everyone in the community who belonged to the hospital group paid the same rate, a community rate, those who were healthier helped subsidize those who needed services more often. Thus, community members shared the costs of sickness. Health activists, spanning the Popular Front spectrum from trade unionists to organized neighborhood women, were committed to the principle of community rating, mutual responsibility. Prepayment really did mean prepayment: Blue Cross coverage paid for more than 95 percent of the patient's hospital bill.[29]

Still, Blue Cross, as an alliance of hospitals, could only provide hospital services, and unions wanted more. For example, even when they were covered by Blue Cross, most UAW members could not pay for surgery or physician care outside of the hospital. As the UAW told Congress at the end of World War II, "About half of the membership of the Michigan Medical and Hospital Service comes from the ranks of the United Automobile Workers, Congress of Industrial Organizations. This is a plan which provides the workers with limited hospital service and limited payments for surgical procedures performed in hospitals. Experience with the plan indicates its inadequacies both from the standpoint of services offered and from the standpoint of the percentage of the population it is possible for the plan to reach."[30]

Thus, the labor movement argued that true "health security" also had to include prepayment of physicians' services, rehabilitative services, and preventive medicine. The best way to realize this goal would not be through the medical profession's Blue Shield plans, which essentially operated on a fee-for-service basis, rarely accepting plan enrollment as prepayment. Rather, labor health experts envisioned a nonprofit community plan in which a board of trustees or, as in the case of Kaiser Permanente, a nonprofit foundation contracted out for services. Public members and labor representatives, as well as health professionals, would have representation on the board. As presented in the UAW's model, groups of physicians, working in cooperation with hospitals, would sign a contract with a board of trustees made up of representatives from both the UAW and the community. For a monthly per capita fee, physicians rendered all services needed by the patient at clinics that had outpatient services, diagnostic labs, X-ray facilities, and specialists all together. In this way the doctors would be forced to contain or self-subsidize costs. Nor would the emphasis always revolve around expensive hospital care, as Blue Cross and hospital insurance did. Several plans of this type already existed, such as HIP of Greater New York, the Group Health Insurance Association of Puget Sound, the Arrowhead Health Association in Minnesota, and the Stowe-Lipsett Clinic in Oakland, California. According to Nelson Cruikshank, the AFL's leading spokesperson on health insurance, "These progressive programs are going in the direction we in the labor movement want to go." They offered "local, consumer-controlled, comprehensive medical services."[31]

In certain regions organized labor's preference for direct service plans over cash-indemnity insurance could be immediately realized. Lacking the political strength to achieve health insurance legislation and the capital to build a labor health system, West Coast labor leaders decided that Kaiser Permanente offered their best opportunity to achieve health security. While Seattle longshore workers joined the Group Health Cooperative of Puget Sound, in California the ILWU chose the Kaiser Permanente Health Plan for all members in California. ILWU workers in Portland and Vancouver followed suit. The AFL Retail Clerks Union, with 26,500 members in Los Angeles, signed up with Kaiser Permanente for a family medical program, and the 30,000-member Culinary Workers Union joined the Kaiser plan in northern California. The UAW signed its first negotiated health insurance agreement with the Kaiser-Frazer Corporation on 1 June 1948. This plan provided comprehensive medical care to 10,000 autoworkers. Financed entirely by the employer, the health plan would be administered by a board of trustees, on which the union and management had equal representation. Under this Kaiser agreement, the joint board would select the benefits and could improve and modify terms. John L. Lewis even tried to court Henry Kaiser to bring his program to the coal-mining regions of the East Coast. In New York City, unions enthusiastically responded when HIP, a group practice medical plan, finally opened its doors in March 1947. Moreover, Joshua Freeman has argued that because of the particular industrial structure of New York City—an economy based on an extraordinary heterogeneity of locally oriented small employers—and the breadth and sociopolitical strength of the New York labor movement, New York labor succeeded, at least up until

8. Organized labor experiments with community health care. In addition to regional union health centers, the International Ladies Garment Workers Union also sponsored this mobile diagnostic clinic. Courtesy of *The George Meany Memorial Archives.*

the late 1950s, in building health care systems rooted in working-class institutions.[32]

Further, progressive health care experts and organized labor hoped that federal social policy would soon financially support the development of group service programs and community medical centers. At the end of the war, the UAW argued that "a national health insurance plan on a compulsory basis with provision for varying experimentation in group techniques is necessary to provide all of the people with necessary medical care."[33] Through much of the 1940s labor leaders still asserted essential links between security, industrial relations, and an activist federal government.

As we have seen, public health reformers, liberal policymakers, and social insurance experts shifted away from Progressive Era income replacement schemes toward a strategy that provided actual medical services. They favored using public funds to train more doctors, build new hospitals, establish clinics and medical laboratories, and bring new services to rural areas. Health financing plans, therefore, would provide universal access to these newly expanded community-based services. Thus, President Truman's 1945 national health plan emphasized hospital construction, medical training and education, and more maternal and child health clinics, in addition to "universal" insurance coverage.[34] The Hill-Burton Act, which passed a year later, would dedicate federal money to building up substantially the medical infrastructure, especially hospitals, and training doctors; not included in this legislation was an economic security component.

Commercial indemnity insurance directly contradicted all of the activists' goals. Insurers designed health policies around the basic premise they used for all other lines of insurance: they insured something against loss. According to commercial underwriting, risk meant exposure to medical care or health services, and what was lost was the cash used to pay for them. "A necessary corollary," an Equitable actuary explained in 1940, "is that the happening of the event must not be subject to the control of the insured individual, or that there must be a strong incentive or normal desire on the part of the insured individual to avoid the happening of the event which is the subject of the insurance."[35] In short, the insured individual must avoid seeking medical care—routine medical care. Commercial insurance applied a variety of mechanisms to protect this principle. The more one used medical care, the higher the premium became, and the lower the net benefits. Those who had health problems and needed the services had to pay the most money. Insurers made the notion of risk an individualized one: "each insured will pay in accordance with the quality of his risk." Neighbors in the same community or workers in the same firm could pay significantly different rates based on their medical experience; this became known as experience rating, as opposed to community rating. By necessity, then, coverage had to be limited, and cash-indemnity plans covered only a fraction of the insured services, generally paying 45–55 percent of an individual's hospital expenses.[36] They excluded preexisting conditions. Patients shouldered an open-ended liability. Electrical workers complained that cash-indemnity plans at GE and Westinghouse continually left them with unexpected, hidden costs. David Fitzmaurice, president of an IUE local in Cleveland, groused that his members paid out-of-pocket expenses for X rays, drugs, and laboratory work dispensed in the hospital. "They are typical examples of the things GE employees do not like. They want full coverage under the GE plan," Fitzmaurice complained.[37]

Labor representatives recognized the inherently inflationary nature of cash-indemnity insurance. Instead of forcing service providers to contain costs and prices to what they took in in prepayment fees, insurance, by paying a percentage of anything doctors or hospitals charged, opened the way for swift inflation in medical prices. In addition, because there was no direct relationship between the indemnifier (insurers) and the service providers (hospitals or doctors), there was no structural mechanism to monitor and evaluate costs and care in order to ensure that beneficiaries received the most cost-effective services. Nelson Cruikshank expressed his dissatisfaction a few years later, saying that "the fact is as long as insurance benefits are paid in cash with no guarantee of the medical services they will actually purchase, this constant upward pressure on fees can be expected to continue. That is one of the major reasons why the service, rather than the cash-indemnity principle is so essential to constructive, effective health programs."[38]

In the postwar years, then, insurance companies faced competition not only from the state but also from a set of quasi-public, labor-oriented health care programs that had emerged in the late 1930s and early 1940s. Even *Fortune* magazine declared that "the achievements of the Ross-Loos, Permanente, and Washington Group Health [Association] plans seem to demonstrate that if a voluntary prepayment plan is to be broad enough in its benefits to affect materially the consumption of medical care, it must be based on group practice."[39] Insurers therefore directed much of their attention and planning in the immediate postwar years toward limiting the growth of Blue Cross and prepaid group plans, making inroads on their membership or territory, and eliminating the social or competitive conditions that enabled those other plans to survive. Insurers hoped to convince potential clients that "the 'not for profit' approach which formerly attracted many is . . . an anathema to more and more business men."[40] Insurers needed an alliance that would serve as a bulwark against the service providers' alliances.

Insurance companies found that ally in large employers, unionized and nonunionized alike. Since insurers did not provide the medical services and in fact initially had no relationship with service providers, they had to make sure that hospital groups and medical groups did not shut them out. Although Blue Cross was supposed to be an intermediary between patients and hospitals, it increasingly functioned as the advocate of the hospitals. Life companies selling hospital coverage at first had problems with their policies because "few of the [insurance] companies stand in well with the hospitals," especially if the hospitals were affiliated with Blue Cross. "They can cite case after case of hospitalization in which the hospital balked at dealing with the insurance company." Insurers also encountered initial problems with the local medical societies of the AMA. The AMA did not like the idea of commercial insurance any better than it liked the idea of national, public insurance; both seemed to threaten the financial and medical autonomy of private physicians. The AMA initially used its Council on Medical Service to deny "approval" to health plans devised by insurance companies.[41] If insurers were to gain any clout, they would have to represent large groups of potential patients. But who could deliver these large groups?

They looked to corporate employers, who by 1946 were quite receptive to the message. Employers wanted to restore the managerial prerogatives they saw under attack from both the New Deal state and unionized workers. They took unionism in basic industry as a given, but they wanted to take the offensive, on both the ideological and the economic level.[42] Employers certainly recognized that "the American employee of today is vitally interested not only in wages and working conditions, but in security against the hazards of illness, disability, old age and death." *Business Week* advised executives to respond quickly. "Management, for the first time, is faced with a broad social demand—the demand for security," a feature story opined. "But if management does not use it wisely, the worker is likely to transfer his demands from the bargaining table to the ballot box."[43] Business leaders clearly saw the aggressive health and welfare demands of union leaders such as John L. Lewis as having political ramifications. In *Industry's View* the NAM warned of the larger consequences of "the demands by the United Mine Workers for a royalty, or tax, of ten cents a ton": "This tax . . . is for the 'economic protection' of the mine workers, according to the demand. . . . [I]t would take little ingenuity to construe 'economic protection' to mean political activity, since economics and politics have definitely become partners."[44]

In many ways the state had made Lewis's gains possible, as it would make gains possible in the steel industry a few years later. Not only had the federal government forced the settlement of the contract but the settlement included the stipulation that the federal government would conduct a comprehensive survey of the available medical services and health care needs of miners and their families. This meant that federal surveyors would, and did, visit mining towns and mining camps to inspect the actual workings of the company-doctor system, testing the claims of coal operators that they were taking care of their employees. The federal government surveyed 260 mines employing 72,000 miners and found that in the majority of cases workers had very limited access and substandard care. Here was a direct and threatening intervention of the state into the employment relation. The government's report presented the evidence the UMW needed to bolster union claims for a major new health program. The next round of negotiations created the Welfare and Retirement Fund, which gave the cost of the program to the employers and control of it to the union. It called for a tripartite trusteeship to run the fund. To business, the whole affair smacked of European-style corporatism and "politicized bargaining." The link between union power and the federal government had to be severed.[45]

On one front, then, corporate employers sought to check the growth of the regulatory apparatus of the New Deal state and the national welfare state. If the state stepped in with taxation, business could lose control over any social spending. A bill to federalize unemployment compensation was already on the dockets by the end of the war. Social Security taxes would only go up, depending on the whim of the legislature, for as the NAM feared, "the domestic trend is toward creation of a Welfare state; the world trend is toward a Welfare World; the slogan of the hour is a Fair Deal for all." The NAM raised the specter of alarming increases in the Social Security taxes—20–26 percent of payroll; the actual tax rate held steady at 1 percent in those years. It would be far better for employers to structure their own policies.[46]

On the other front, employers feared that welfare benefits might further legitimize trade unionism. Union leaders, the U.S. Chamber of Commerce explained, "hope that the union treasury and the union leaders become the exclusive source of worker protection. . . . In other words, management . . . [is] being forced to finance health and welfare funds in order that unionism and union leadership may be more deeply entrenched." In an official policy statement the Chamber of Commerce urged employers to move as quickly as possible to install "voluntary" health coverages and thereby gain the moral high ground on the security issue.[47] The NAM agreed "that management should not surrender its initiative in this matter to the union."[48] This imperative seemed all the more acute in the wake of the great strike wave that swept the nation in 1946. Business managers now interpreted health and welfare demands as a fundamental challenge to managerial prerogatives. "Not only do these plans represent a heavy payroll burden, but they go right to the heart of management's relations with employees by driving a wedge which tends to make the employee feel that his bargaining agent is more sympathetically concerned with his wellbeing than is his employer."[49] Facing John L. Lewis on one side and Harry Truman's Fair Deal on the other, employer associations sought to accommodate these dual threats by developing a more sophisticated form of welfare capitalism to compete with the state and the unions.

Whether a redistributive social policy would be realized through social insurance, the Wagner National Labor Relations Act, or other corporatist means, it had to be stopped. Business interests had circulated blueprints for revising the Wagner Act throughout the first half of the

1940s. Their proposals focused on prohibiting unionization of foremen and supervisory employees, industrywide bargaining, the closed shop, and boycotts. They wanted affirmative declarations of management rights and restrictions on strikes. It was not until *after* the UMW went on strike for a union health and retirement program financed by employers that revisions of the NLRA came to include restrictions on union trust funds and welfare funds. At first, some business executives, such as GM's Charles Wilson, called for a provision explicitly excluding welfare and pension benefits from collective bargaining. While they were unable to get this outright ban, Congress did include in the Taft-Hartley Act a requirement that employers had to share equally in the administration of any welfare or retirement plan. Unions could not run them independently. They would have to undergo an annual audit of the fund, with results available to interested persons. The courts would appoint an impartial umpire in cases of deadlock between management and union. The new Taft-Hartley Act also restricted labor's ability to determine the uses to which monies deposited in social security funds could be put. Funds to be used for pensions or annuities had to be placed in a separate account. Unions had to provide management with a detailed plan of the way in which benefit payments would be made. Republican Senators Robert Taft and Joseph Ball made clear that these restrictions were meant to prevent unions from "indiscriminate use [of employer funds] for so-called welfare purposes." Preventing union control of social security for American workers clearly became an essential component of curbing union power. With the Taft-Hartley Act, employers had created a climate in which they could restore welfare capitalism.[50]

For employers, the unilateral purchase of commercial group insurance proved the key to containing union power and union political goals. Amid the postwar strike wave commercial group health sales surged, and steady growth continued for the next three decades. Between 1945 and 1947 the number of persons covered by commercial group hospital and surgical insurance doubled, rising from 7,804,000 in 1945 to 14,190,000 in 1947. Group accident and sickness insurance (disability wage) covered 9.5 million workers by 1948.[51] Unionized companies, such as GM, Ford Motors, Republic Steel, U.S. Rubber, Standard Oil, U.S. Steel, Socony-Vacuum, GE, International Harvester, and Westinghouse, all longtime policyholders with Equitable, Metropolitan, John Hancock, and Aetna, expanded their existing group policies to include coverage ranging from minimal disability to hospital-surgical plans. Inland Steel contracted with Equitable for the full complement of group life, disability, accidental death and dismemberment, hospital, and surgical insurance. In fact, by mid-1947 more than half of the employees in basic steel had group hospitalization insurance. Nonunionized companies, especially consumer goods industries with relatively stable employment patterns, purchased the most full scale health insurance packages. Johnson & Johnson, Kodak, the Upjohn Company, Bristol-Myers, the Borden Company, Colgate Palmolive, and Pillsbury Mills installed hospital, surgical, disability, and even limited medical insurance plans.[52]

The majority of these new group health insurance sales represented employer modification of existing policies without union input or union revision.[53] The major firms in the steel, rubber, auto, electrical, and oil industries repeatedly rejected union requests to negotiate over the actual substance of the benefits. At the end of the decade only 380 out of 2,200 collective bargaining agreements contained health insurance. "In one instance," the NAM reported with some satisfaction, "a clause had been written into a company contract which specifically stated that there was to be no bargaining about the company's employee benefit program."[54] Although the UAW, the USWA, and the UE asked employers to contribute to a Blue Cross plan in the 1940s, GM and GE responded with unilateral expansion of their Metropolitan group policies, Inland Steel and Westinghouse added on to their Equitable policies, and Ford Motors told the UAW that employees would be enrolled in a John Hancock group plan. A 1950 survey by NICB found that about one in three contracts provided for either new or revised group insurance plans. In the face of New Deal demands for social entitlements, these companies clung to an older tradition that defined health benefits as "gratuities given by employers to employees."[55]

At a 1947 NAM labor relations meeting that included representatives of International Harvester, the National Biscuit Company, Boeing, the American Screw Company, Standard Oil of New Jersey, Dodge Steel, and DuPont "there was a consensus that so long as management showed leadership in the establishment and administration of sound and adequate employee benefit plans, it would be in a position to exercise the initiative in this matter." In particular, employers in basic industry and consumer goods manufacturing were determined to oppose CIO requests for flat payroll deductions or a "royalty tax on product" that would be used to fund independent union social security programs. This issue was of far greater importance than even the question of contributory versus noncontributory financing. Many companies were willing to concede on the latter, but all were "unalterably opposed" to the UMW model or the proposed ideal UAW plan. By handing over the funds to an independent trust or welfare fund, "this practice . . . [was] permitting an outside agency—the union—to step in and constitute itself as the source from which benefits flow to employees." Leo Wolman, a Columbia University economist and industrial relations consultant, warned the American Iron and Steel Institute that even a jointly operated welfare fund would undermine managerial rights and prerogatives. "Joint operation very swiftly deteriorates, degenerates into operation of these welfare funds by unions."[56]

Commercial insurers made it possible for employers to resurrect welfare capitalism, "tailoring" health insurance policies to fit the needs of each employer. In order to make their product more competitive, insurers offered the purchaser of a group plan the opportunity to select exactly what it did and did not want. Employers could decide which hospital services would be covered, the percentage of reimbursement, and the amount of an employee's contribution. For medical plans, they could decide whether specialists would be included, whether benefits for physicians' care covered visits to the physician's office or only treatment in the hospital, and whether payments would start with the first visit. "Every Equitable Group plan is specifically tailored to meet your company's individual needs, eliminating the cost of superfluous coverage while protecting you from the danger of inadequate coverage," an Equitable promotion piece assured prospective clients. Metropolitan's Group Division published a booklet entitled, *Tailored to Fit: A Group Insurance Plan Designed for the Employees of Your Company.*[57] Insurers pitched tailoring as an advantageous substitute for Blue Cross, warning that "service plans offer only one or at the most a limited number of alternative plans which do not permit tailoring."[58] As a Massachusetts Mutual executive explained, "In practically all instances a plan is designed, originating in discussions between the insurer and the purchaser. In other words, the companies offering group health insurance of any type do not follow a format . . . or some prepared plan. . . . What you do is sit down and actually tailor make a program within the scope of your group underwriting plans to meet the particular need of that employer."[59] The Ohio Oil Company, an Equitable client, first introduced hospital and surgical benefits in 1940. From 1946 to 1949 Ohio Oil increased the daily hospital allowance, added surgical benefits for dependents, and altered some of the surgical benefits. A personnel manager for the company pointed out that "many of the above revisions were introduced at the suggestion of our insurance carrier."[60] Managers and insurers became partners in defining what constituted health security, shifting away from the New Deal emphasis on national standards and social solidarity and toward a multitude of isolated, firm-specific welfare sites.[61]

Insurers rarely met with either unions or workers' representatives during this formative period. A Federal Mediation and Conciliation

Service conciliator reported that during ten years of service "the insurance representatives made no attempt to reach an understanding with labor representatives." Indeed the *National Underwriter* confirmed that "it has been general practice to acquaint union officials with the provisions of a plan in advance of its general announcement, but the details have hitherto not been subject to union revision."[62]

By this time most American companies had developed the internal bureaucratic structure and personnel management policies that Metropolitan's PSB had so long claimed were necessary to sustain welfare capitalism. Since its earliest days, insurers had promoted group insurance as part of a firm-based industrial relations system. The late 1930s through the end of World War II proved to be a key period for the diffusion of bureaucratic personnel practices, including job evaluation systems, personnel departments, centralized employment procedures, and seniority. In addition, in the 1940s more firms began to use productivity bonuses, promotions, pensions, paid vacations, suggestion systems, and extensive communications programs. Metropolitan's PSB continued to lend assistance to group insurance clients on these matters, as well as to provide employers with leaflets and posters on the value of group insurance and welfare services provided by the employer. These in-house communications programs—magazines, newsletters, pamphlets, monthly letters home, films, bulletin boards—emphasized the employer's generosity, the symbolic importance of company welfare benefits, and a sense of corporate community. Suggestion systems, attitude surveys, and training programs for foremen and supervisors helped to monitor and adjust employee responses to company policies. As companies laid down rules and definite procedures on promotions, layoffs, compensated days off, retirement, and benefits or agreed to them with unions, welfare capitalism came to seem more efficacious and reliable than it had been in an earlier era. More than ever, group insurance and these personnel programs could highlight the difference between security inside the firm and insecurity in the outside labor market.[63]

Insurance tailoring infuriated labor leaders. They saw it as subverting their attempts to win universal benefits throughout an industry or region, and thereby broaden the number of people who would shoulder the risks of insecurity equally. When the USWA surveyed its members in the early 1950s, it found that "almost all the insurance programs negotiated in the different companies under contract with our union differ in some respect."[64] As Nelson Cruikshank later complained, "In industry today, thousands of different arrangements exist, whose variations in scope and benefits are not justified by any criteria, despite the prevalence of the appeal to fit the insurance benefits to the needs of a given group or industry. . . . This piecemeal approach means inequality of benefits even in the same community or neighborhood." Cruikshank argued that "tailoring" was a sham: workers' "needs are always comprehensive health services and medical care," regardless of company or industry.[65]

Besides leading to uneven benefits, tailoring also made it difficult for workers to know what they were getting for their money. Because the insurer dealt directly with the employer, unions or employee representation councils never knew just how much the premiums actually cost. As Joseph Swire, director of the IUE's Pension, Health, and Welfare Department, noted, "The employer is considered the customer and the only party to whom reports can be given."[66] Whether the compensation value of the policy represented the premium cost or the eventual net cost was not known. Swire complained that in the case of GE, which had Metropolitan group insurance, "the employees never have had a complete report, don't know how much Metropolitan keeps in retentions, what the exact costs were, how much commission or fees brokers get, whether or not improvements could be made for the same cost." Swire believed that were there competitive bidding, they could probably improve their insurance benefits by 25–30 percent.[67] Since premium rates and benefits varied from employer to employer and even within companies, attempts to estimate the cost were almost impossible, thus putting unions at a disadvantage during collective bargaining.

The true costs were even further obscured by the channeling of dividends. Insurance companies used the promise of dividends to promote their product. All mutual insurance companies purposely overcharged at the front end to make up for any possible miscalculations in "risk," or actual use of services. After covering administrative and other charges, insurers returned any extra premium money as a year-end dividend. Since the corporation was the legal policyholder, such dividends belonged solely to management. In the case of GM, dividends from Metropolitan often exceeded the company's premium payment for group disability and life insurance in the 1940s. Until 1948 GM did not even contribute to the premium for the hospital or surgical policies; still the company received dividends on the policy. Even after 1950, when the company paid half the premium, GM pocketed all of the dividends.[68] GE dividends amounted to $20–30 million in the years 1950–54. IUE officials estimated that workers actually paid for about 60 percent of the group policy, while receiving far more limited benefits than they would have if they had subscribed to Blue Cross.[69] The return of dividends also enabled insurers to convince employers that they were signing on to programs that initially seemed inexpensive. Companies like Westinghouse explicitly stated in their social insurance contracts that dividends would be used to reduce the company's (not the workers') contribution to the insurance plan. Moreover, as the Office Employes International Union found, such dividends were not used to improve the plan's coverage or benefits.[70] Companies thus received not only the credit for providing insurance but also the cash in hand for doing so—plus a tax break.

Martin Segal, who ran a pension and health insurance consulting firm for unions, advised clients to avoid employer group insurance policies for exactly these reasons. In a guide issued to unions by Segal's firm, Segal warned that with such policies, "employees pay all or a major portion of the cost of the insurance." He laid out explicitly the ways in which employers rather than workers benefited from these policies:

> Note the fact that the employer will frequently announce these plans being on a cooperative basis, with the employer and the employee sharing the cost. The fact is, however, that analyses of more than 300 plans show that these plans are cooperative in name only. The employer's contribution to the cost of the group insurance is deductible from his taxes as a necessary "business expense." . . . Furthermore, after tax deductions, the remainder of the employer's contribution is wholly or in part wiped out by the dividends or rate refunds which are returned to him by the insurance company. Rarely are these rate refunds divided with the employees in the same proportion that the employer and the employees contribute to the initial cost of the insurance. As a rule, therefore, after tax deductions and insurance company dividends or rate deductions, the employer's contribution is only nominal.[71]

Another selling point was that employers' premiums were based on the medical experience of each firm or group of workers. Premiums thus varied according to companies' accident or sickness experience. Lane Kirkland, then a social insurance expert with the AFL-CIO, commented that "experience rating raises a wall of isolation about each covered group. It conflicts with the principle of social insurance which calls for the pooling of risks and the spreading of costs over the widest possible area of population." Indeed, as an actuary from Equitable noted, "A sound basis of *selection* of lives to be insured is fundamental" (emphasis mine).[72] Experience rating then also meant that certain groups, such as retirees, would be selected out of coverage. Experience rating not only had an impact on the workers in each plant; it also directly affected the viability of the service plans. By selecting the better health risks, insurers left the community service plans with a higher-risk population. By the early 1950s the tremendous increase in group insurance had made it increasingly difficult for Blue Cross to underwrite plans based on the prepaid-service principle. Although experiencing significant growth as well, the Blues either increased rates continually or switched to cash-indemnity, fee-for-service underwriting in the 1950s.[73] Thus, by the time unions had won the legal right to sit down and bargain over health benefits, insurers had already begun limiting the viable options, including those that led to a more universal system of relatively equitable, service-based care. AFL-CIO health experts became increasingly frustrated and concerned as Blue Cross plans shifted from community rating to insurance-type experience rating in the mid- and late 1950s, thereby pursuing "commercial insurance principles" over "social insurance and medical care principles."[74]

The institutional connections between the welfare entrepreneurs and their clients, American corporations, can be seen more clearly by looking at the sinews of American capitalism, capital flows. In the first few years after the war life insurance companies accumulated about $3.5 billion a year in new assets, for a total of $50 billion in total surplus—a significant amount of money in the 1940s. The life insurance industry found an outlet for its surplus capital in the booming auto, steel, telecommunications, oil, and aviation industries, as manufacturing companies sought to make long-postponed major capital improvements. Firms that had never sought outside financing before turned to new sources. And like GM, which borrowed an unprecedented $125 million in 1946, these capital-starved firms turned to life insurance companies.[75]

By the late 1940s, Equitable, New York Life, and Metropolitan stood at the center of the New York financial markets. Corporate borrowers increasingly turned to insurance companies because of "direct placement" loans, which enabled corporations to avoid the taxes and public disclosure rules mandated by the Securities and Exchange Act of 1934. Unlike publicly distributed issues, privately or directly placed ones did not require registration with the Securities and Exchange Commission, so the borrowing firm could avoid unwelcome publicity. By 1948 private placement accounted for 73 percent of all new debt issues.[76] As key financial intermediaries, insurers solidified the institutional connections that would facilitate their role as welfare entrepreneurs. An Equitable vice president, commenting on the advantages of direct placement, noted that "it provides 'a ready outlet for the steady accumulation of institutional investment funds'; and it sets up a uniquely close relationship between borrower and lender, with obvious advantages to both."[77] Not unexpectedly, the boards of directors of life insurers, manufacturing companies, and commercial banks also overlapped. In a formal letter of complaint to GE, the IUE pointed to the exclusive relationship between the company and the insurance carrier as a hindrance to negotiating over health benefits. "GE gives all its business to Metropolitan Insurance. Two of GE's Board Members are also members of Metropolitan's Board of Directors."[78]

Insurance companies strengthened their relationship to manufacturing and retail firms through purchase-lease arrangements, in which they purchased real estate, stores, warehouses, and even equipment and leased it back to the company that originally owned or would later operate the facility. For example, in 1947 Equitable began building a new manufacturing plant in Chicago for Westinghouse. Westinghouse then contracted to lease the plant from Equitable for twenty-five years to house all of its manufacturing and repair activities in the Chicago area. In light of these connections, it is not surprising that unions could not get what they wanted. The IUE asked for Blue Cross coverage in every round of negotiations, but Westinghouse responded by offering Equitable insurance. These institutional relationships in the economy ultimately advantaged insurance companies as purveyors of both welfare benefits and capital.[79]

All of these factors—tailoring, undisclosed information on costs, dividends, experience rating, financial relationships—reinvigorated postwar welfare capitalism. The large eastern life insurance companies that dominated the market rarely sold group health plans to labor unions, farm organizations, community groups, or consumer cooperatives. More than 90 percent of group insurance policies were written for single employers or their subsidiaries. Labor unions or multiple-employer associations held fewer than 7 percent of all group policies. When the Taft-Hartley Act outlawed welfare funds run solely by unions, it encoded de jure what had already become the insurance industry's practice. In 1952, 38 million Americans had private disability coverage (accident and sickness insurance); fewer than 2,000 of those individuals received their policies through a union-administered plan or an employee mutual benefit association.[80] This private, employer-based welfare system linked health insurance to steady employment in a particular firm. Unlike Kaiser Permanente or the original Blue Cross, insurers made no attempt to allow an employee to convert from a group policy to an individual one if she or he left work. The insurance pioneer William Graham declared that group insurance "extends protection to employees over the term of their employment. That is all it does, all it was planned to do."[81] Equitable's group insurance promotional material made clear that "employee privileges on termination of employment" were "none."[82] Group insurance, then, retained two essential aspects of welfare capitalism. It tied workers to a particular company, and it made all other family members dependent on the worker. As William Graham explained, "Group insurance is a purely American plan of providing security by protecting the pay envelope at its source."[83]

Insurers and employers established employment-based health coverage on a white male model of participation in the workforce: the full-time, full-year worker. Two-thirds of women did not work for wages in the 1950s. Moreover, among 23 million employed women, two-thirds

1919 THEN ... BENEFITS ... 1969 NOW

9. "1919–1969 . . . Benefits . . . Then and Now." This cartoon promoting the continuity of company generosity through group insurance appeared in the fiftieth-anniversary edition of the *Hercules Mixer,* the employee magazine of the Hercules Chemical Corporation, a DuPont subsidiary. Courtesy of Hagley Museum and Library.

worked either in part-time jobs or in full-time jobs during one or two seasons of the year. Women who worked full time year-round were concentrated disproportionately in low-paying industries such as food service, sales, domestic labor, and administrative support. Facing few threats to the labor supply or control, employers in these sectors found that they could do without employee benefits. Any insurance coverage that employers did provide remained minimal, being generally confined to skeletal hospital coverage. Almost half of African American women worked as agricultural or domestic laborers, outside both the public and private social security systems. Because of interruptions in their workforce participation to raise children or care for ill family members, women switched jobs more often; this made them more vulnerable to preexisting-condition clauses. African Americans faced many of the same problems, complicated by the fact that many lived in nontraditional family structures.

Inequality inhered in coverage for family members, especially if they were not in the waged labor force. In most cases, even in unionized industries such as the automobile industry, workers had to pay out of their own pocket in order to extend their health coverage to their families, often limiting the amount of insurance coverage they received. Family members usually received lesser benefits, such as fewer days in the hospital and more excluded procedures, and faced stricter rules about preexisting conditions. By the 1950s most union plans provided maternity coverage, but only for delivery. Unionized industries employing predominantly women were more likely to provide some additional pre- or postnatal medical coverage, but comprehensive medical coverage was available only under service-based, group practice plans. Not only did women workers and spouses have to wait nine months before becoming eligible for maternity coverage—a requirement that has persisted into the present under many plans—but initially hospital plans, including Blue Cross, required women and men to be enrolled in a family or "husband-and-wife" contract to be eligible for maternity benefits, thereby reinforcing the patriarchal structure of access to health care. A nonemployed woman also risked losing any coverage if she divorced her spouse. Commercial insurers at that time did not cover medical care for newborn babies; since newborn infants might be susceptible to infections or emergency complications, they were classified as "uninsurable risks."[84] A study conducted by the San Francisco Labor Council in 1952 found that "coverage [in San Francisco] is available to dependents in only about half the programs and benefits are so sharply reduced that less than one-third of the health care needs of wives and children are included."[85] On the national level, the AFL determined that "coverage for family members is found to be spasmodic and generally less complete in scope of benefits than for employees."[86] At the end of the decade, the IUE still reported that "in many contracts, our members pay the full cost for dependent coverage at the hospital and for surgery."[87]

While the spread of hospital insurance among the population was striking, group insurance and Blue Cross still did not cover actual care from doctors. The number of persons who had any form of hospital insurance had risen from 6 million in 1939 to approximately 75 million by 1950 and 91 million by 1952. Yet, in 1950 only 21 percent of those covered had hospital and surgical coverage; 11 percent had hospital, surgical, and limited medical. Fewer than 3 percent had comprehensive medical care insurance (hospital, surgical, and complete medical).

In the southern states, from Maryland to Texas, only 7,622,000 people had medical coverage in 1952.[88] Among themselves, insurers complained regularly that they had yet to figure out how to successfully underwrite insurance policies that would actually cover medical and surgical services; a large percentage of the premium went into administration. Insurance benefits paid about one-tenth of the total private expenditures for physicians' services. A decade after their introduction, surgical insurance benefits still regularly fell short of costs. A study by the Health Information Foundation in the mid-1950s concluded that more than 7 million families went into debt each year because of medical bills and "'having or not having insurance had no appreciable effect on indebtedness' for medical care." Unions such as the UAW concluded that "the mere buying of group insurance does not mean a health security program."[89]

To forestall the unilateral imposition of insurance industry health care plans and pensions, the labor movement turned to the federal courts and the NLRB. The UAW, for example, had sought to negotiate over health insurance since the end of the war, but at the end of 1947 GM turned to Metropolitan for a new hospital and surgical insurance plan. The UAW filed a suit with the NLRB accusing GM of an unfair labor practice. As the *CIO News* reported, "The corporation's contract with the insurance company was consummated without notice to the union and without consultation and collective bargaining . . . to discredit . . . the union as representative of the employes."[90] The NLRB soon ruled in the UAW's favor, and GM agreed in the 1948 negotiating round that if a "court of last resort" declared benefits a subject of bargaining, they would initiate a joint union-management committee to resolve the issue. The union agreed, the injunction was lifted, and GM proceeded to sign more than 75 percent of its employees into the Metropolitan hospital and surgical policy.[91] The UAW would have to await the outcome of the USWA cases.

Meanwhile, the USWA had two cases pending, one against Inland Steel regarding pensions and one against W. W. Cross and Company regarding health and other social welfare benefits. The NLRB ruled against the companies in both cases in 1948, declaring that all these benefits, being "conditions of employment," were negotiable. Employers, however, took their case to the United States Court of Appeals and even the Supreme Court, a move some observers in the insurance industry advised against, claiming that a loss would make the ruling applicable in all industries. In fact, the United States Court of Appeals did rule against the companies, upholding the decisions of the NLRB; the Supreme Court denied certiorari in 1949, reinforcing the court of appeals. The Presidential Steel Fact Finding Board in steel now ordered the companies to recognize health insurance, pensions, and other welfare benefits as subjects of collective bargaining.[92]

As the decade came to a close the era of health bargaining commenced. Yet whereas in mining the state had helped settle and enforce the content of the negotiations, in this case the presidential board's ruling in steel paved the way for the state's withdrawal. The parties were sent back to the bargaining table, where liberals assumed they would now bargain as equals. The Truman administration believed that with this ruling it had established equilibrium and therefore no longer had a role.[93]

GM, Ford Motors, and U.S. Steel signed new contracts terminating the old group contracts and adding Blue Cross. Yet for all the fanfare that surrounded these landmark contract settlements of 1950, labor did not get what it wanted. The 1950 contracts would offer segments of the working-class increases in real income and social benefits. But the UAW's comprehensive Workers' Security Program was shelved—permanently.[94] These large oligopolistic firms refused to hand over a percentage of payroll to union-run social welfare programs. The five-year Treaty of Detroit, for example, provided an annual improvement-factor wage increase, COLA, and a pension of $125 per month. It also included group life insurance; group disability insurance, which paid temporary weekly disability benefits; permanent disability benefits; and Blue Cross and Blue Shield benefits. GM would pay only half of the premiums. Nor did the company make any concession to the union's desire to participate in the administration of the plans or to be informed of the financial and underwriting arrangements. These facts did not change during the 1955 round of negotiations. Each round of bargaining from that point on would revolve around raising the amount of group insurance, the number of hospital days, and the coverage of additional procedures. Although union leaders, contemporaries, and historians alike have long celebrated the Treaty of Detroit as a masterful victory, the social welfare provisions in fact represented a significant retreat from labor's and health care reformers' vision of security.[95]

The court cases pried collective bargaining open somewhat, but they did not make a significant difference in the way health insurance would be dispensed, administered, and financed. In the 1930s and early 1940s, when unions began designing health plans for their members, the whole idea of prepaid health coverage had been a novelty. Over the next decade, however, commercial insurance companies solidified relationships with employers, gained more than 50 percent of the hospital and medical insurance market, and undercut the viability of service plans through the spread of experience rating. During the

1950s the growth of cash-indemnity plans outpaced that of any other alternative, growing at twice the rate of Blue Cross. By 1953 commercial hospital insurance covered 51 million people, or about 32 percent of the American population.[96] The AMA, realizing that it could no longer hold back the tide of voluntary insurance, decided to promote the indemnity approach, albeit through its own institutions, the Blue Shield associations. It recognized that indemnity-based insurance, whether provided through Blue Shield or through insurance companies, offered doctors the most autonomy to determine rates and medical treatment. Medical societies now accepted insurance companies' overtures to instruct doctors in setting up cash-indemnity plans or to work in conjunction with insurance company plans. By the mid-1950s doctors and insurers had formalized their alliance by establishing the Health Insurance Council to entrench fee-for-service care through insurance and Blue Shield.[97]

Although labor's more comprehensive vision of health security never materialized, powerful unions like the UAW and the USWA did achieve some elements of the comprehensive program the UAW originally designed in the mid-1940s. GM extended temporary disability benefits to a record twenty-six weeks; the contract added surgery and other medical benefits. The USWA generally obtained Blue Cross over commercial insurance as well. U.S. Steel even picked up the tab for surgery insurance for dependents. The UAW refused all attempts to eliminate community rating or to institute deductibles and co-payments. In cities or regions where these unions held significant power in the community, such as Detroit and Pittsburgh, they preserved community rating and fought to maintain Blue Cross as a service-based plan, a strategy that benefited all members of the community. In areas where a direct service or group practice program existed, such as northern California, Seattle, or New York City, the UAW and the USWA successfully negotiated to enroll their members in Kaiser Permanente or HIP.[98]

Unions like the UAW or the USWA were large enough that they could also fulfill social democratic functions unmet by the state. They tried to fill the gaps in social policy—the lack of a national underpinning for universal health care—by working to create a national standard of Blue Cross service benefits, or what the UAW referred to as the "Auto Standard." The members of the UAW Social Security Department visited Blue Cross Associations and hospitals in every city or state in which the union had members, places where Blue Cross was just a fledgling operation or offered a basic package with far fewer benefits than that of the Michigan Hospital Service. They went to Pennsylvania, Illinois, Virginia, Alabama, Ohio, New Jersey, Tennessee, Louisiana, Kentucky, and North Carolina and continuously negotiated an improved level of benefits offered by Blue Cross plans in those locations. The UAW brought the basic hospital package of 120-day coverage to cities in Virginia, Utah, Tennessee, Iowa, and Minnesota. The Pittsburgh Blue Cross Association devised a uniform plan for the USWA and agreed to coordinate Blue Cross benefits throughout the United States, wherever there were steel plants.[99] Thus, in looking out primarily for its members, the UAW succeeded in improving Blue Cross benefits and standards for whoever lived in the same area.

After a decade of bargaining for welfare benefits, large unions in basic manufacturing even won equal benefits for workers and spouses, but at this point a wider gap opened between those in union and nonunion jobs. Among nonunionized sectors, the extent of coverage for family members persistently lagged behind that for workers.[100] The variations in coverage for nonworkers and workers in secondary economic sectors reflected the unevenness and inequity of this private welfare system most acutely.

In the early 1950s African Americans finally made the economic gains that would bring them within the coverage of the public Social Security System and possibly offer private supplemental security. After the war, African Americans moved into jobs in basic manufacturing and mining. Yet just as they had the possibility to obtain union-negotiated health insurance, life and disability insurance, and pensions—the price management had paid for industrial peace—employers embarked on a new labor strategy: automation and relocation. As auto companies pursued automation beginning in the mid-1950s, black workers bore the brunt of automation and layoffs. The same was true in mining, meatpacking, chemicals, and tobacco. In fact, in mining, the trade-off between jobs and welfare benefits was explicit: in return for the union health and welfare fund, Lewis accepted drastic cuts in employment in the long run. Companies such as GM and Ford Motors relocated plants to suburbs and small communities where blacks could not follow. In places such as Detroit, black unemployment had shot up to as high as 18 percent by 1960. Additionally, the regional and sectoral disparities of welfare capitalism persisted; health benefits payments and health care resources lagged in the Southeast and the Central Plains South of Texas, Oklahoma, and Louisiana. Health insurance coverage was rising generally during this period for those in the middle and upper third of the income distribution; likewise, their share of social insurance and transfer payments grew as well. For African Americans the limited welfare state and private supplementation would both mirror and solidify unequal patterns of economic opportunity.[101]

Overall, labor-management contract benefits remained closer to employment compensation and managerial employment policy than to a genuine workers' health security program, not to mention a national health care program. The autoworkers could not gain an equal voice with management on the full administration and distribution of costs for the health security program. Metropolitan continued to underwrite temporary and permanent disability insurance and in some cases medical insurance for GM, which never allowed the union to participate in the selection of the carrier. "Fact gathering is in the hands of the company," a UAW negotiator wrote. The company "gives us proposal for acceptance or rejection." In both the 1950 and 1955 contracts, GM retained the right to "receive and retain any divisible surplus, credits, or refunds, or reimbursements under whatever name made on any such contracts." Nor did the company provide any information about its financing arrangement with Metropolitan.[102] Even in the era of health bargaining, GM could still use private commercial insurance as a bulwark against union power and union attempts to gain economic security. Moreover, as much as they tried, unions simply could not overcome regional variations in benefits. And as they were keenly aware, benefits negotiated with employers left out all those who were not employed, such as retirees, the disabled, and family members. The more the labor movement tried to increase the reach of employment-based benefits by negotiating new contracts with employers or expanding the range of benefits therein, the more they foreclosed the possibility of constructing truly communal health programs because health financing became linked ever more tightly to a firm-centered structure.

The SSA, while continuing to support the Wagner-Murray-Dingell Bill, national health insurance, and further extensions of Social Security, promoted supplementation as a necessary corollary to its failure to expand social insurance. At a Conference on Union Health and Welfare Funds, sponsored by NICB, Arthur Altmeyer stated, "In a country as wealthy as ours, there are abundant opportunities for additional and supplementary protection beyond that provided in a basic social insurance system." The SSA and close allies criticized the Taft-Hartley Act's restrictions upon union health and welfare plans as violating the spirit of supplementation. Congress had limited the ability of workers' organizations to develop comprehensive private social security programs that supplemented public provisions in areas unions thought were most necessary. By the early 1950s Wilbur Cohen often invoked what he referred to as the "three layer cake analogy: the first layer being minimum subsistence; the second layer providing a more adequate standard supplemental to minimum subsistence; and the third luxury 'layer' being primarily a function of what the individual can do for himself." Cohen often stressed the consensus of labor, management, and SSA around this formulation. Moreover, because the SSA had spent so many years trying to convince Congress and the public that Social Security was merely a self-supporting insurance system, Congress had essentially come to view it as such. Thus, in the 1950 amendments to the Social Security Act legislators blocked a government subsidy from general revenues, which would have enabled the public program to expand beyond the level of subsistence benefits, or the first layer of the cake. By necessity, the second layer had to be developed further.[103]

But most of the labor movement could not follow in the UAW's footsteps. Indeed, the UAW represented the exception, not the model. What happened in the electrical industry is more typical. Despite the presence of a union and the appearance of bargaining, electrical workers could not penetrate the links between their employers and commercial insurance companies; hence, they could not obtain the health benefits they thought best for workers and their families. Whether they were represented by the communist-influenced UE or the anticommunist IUE, the result was the same. GE and Westinghouse, whose ties to Metropolitan and Equitable stretched back to the early 1920s, refused to grant union requests for Blue Cross coverage or community-based group plans. At every bargaining round in the 1950s, the companies refused to divulge the costs of the commercial plan or how much the firm paid. They unilaterally chose the carrier, perpetuating the same group policies they had had since before World War II, in some cases since before the New Deal, but offering some new benefits each year.

Health insurance functioned as a chip not only in the contest between management and labor but also in the fratricidal contest between the UE and the IUE. While the electrical unions fought and refought battles over organization and representation, electrical manufacturers moved to expand their group life insurance policies to include group disability, group hospital insurance, and in some cases group surgical coverage, intending to preempt the union. The UE, anxious to settle a contract before the IUE could come in, call for new representation elections, and supplant it, accepted group insurance policies chosen unilaterally by employers in a number of plants. But once the IUE came in, the new union found the situation equally difficult. It had neither the power nor the internal resources to compel employers to substitute Blue Cross for their cash-indemnity plans.

Following GE Vice President for Labor Relations Lemuel Boulware's strategy of "Truth In Bargaining," GE listened to union demands and then responded publicly with fully worked out contract provisions, provisions that could not be changed.[104] Boulwarism's "take or leave it" approach accurately characterized the health benefits situation, both before and after the *Inland Steel* and *W. W. Cross* cases. The IUE repeatedly criticized the UE for accepting employer-chosen, contributory cash-indemnity health insurance and signing contracts that barred the union from making any requests for changes or modifications.[105] When the IUE began negotiations for a new contract at GE in the summer of 1950, the upstart union boasted that it would do everything differently. It would force GE to negotiate and give IUE members Blue Cross service plans and coverage for dependents, fully paid for by the company, and union representation in administration. The IUE demanded Blue Cross and Blue Shield from GE, but GE refused, offering only Metropolitan group hospital and surgical insurance, with benefit levels much lower than those won in the auto industry. Nor did this plan cover dependents. After two weeks on strike, ended by the Federal Mediation and Conciliation Service, the IUE had to accept the Metropolitan cash-indemnity plan, which essentially represented additions to a group policy GE had held for almost thirty years. GE informed the union that it could not reopen the negotiations or change the plan at any time. The IUE did not report this part of the story to its membership. The *IUE-NEWS* simply proclaimed victory in settling unprecedented wage raises and COLA adjustments, barring reductions. The next round of labor-management negotiations took place in the summer of 1952. Again the IUE asked for Blue Cross; again GE refused, offering only Metropolitan group insurance. GE, in conjunction with Metropolitan, decided on new benefits, increasing hospital and surgical coverage. In the 1955 bargaining round Joseph Swire, the IUE's principal benefits negotiator, again contested "the fact that Metropolitan got its business without a bid," but to no avail.[106]

Labor remained frustrated not only because it could not win the type of benefits health activists and experts promoted but also because what it did achieve remained veiled and off-limits. As George Meany charged before the Senate's Special Labor-Management Rackets Committee, "The company maintains 'a consistent policy of secrecy.' "[107] The union never knew exactly what the premium cost, nor how much the dividends amounted to. Consequently, it never knew what percentage was being borne by the workers or how high a price was being paid for benefits that could be obtained more cheaply through other plans. Regarding dividends, Swire charged that "GE tries, by twisting words, to hide what actually happens" but said that "our union is fighting for full information."[108] The IUE estimated that GE probably received several million dollars a year in dividends. "Not only does GE keep dividends on its own contributions," the union complained, "but also the dividends on contributions by workers for their programs and on contributions for dependents on which GE does not pay one cent." In a formal letter of complaint to GE the IUE pinpointed the problem as the exclusive relationship between the company and the insurance carrier.[109]

GE, according to the company's carefully orchestrated policy of "Doing Right Voluntarily,"[110] responded by saying in 1955 that it would now give the union a choice. Instead of the traditional hospital insurance or surgical insurance, which followed a defined benefit schedule for each service, workers could now choose Metropolitan's new policy: catastrophic health insurance. According to this new policy, employees paid all "minor" medical expenses up to a given deductible; the insurer then paid 75–85 percent of the rest of the covered expenses. The splitting of the cost was known as coinsurance. A press release to Metropolitan employees, which included a photograph of Metropolitan's president shaking hands with Lemuel Boulware, proudly declared the two companies "partners in progress and protection."[111] Life insurers and business firms were partners in a post–New Deal project of private, management-controlled *security*.

GE's Employee and Plant Community Relations Department distributed pamphlets, posters, and newsletters claiming sole company credit for social welfare benefits and workers' security. All such benefits were said to result from company generosity, not from union pressure. In fact, GE literature argued that the union, rather than contributing to workers' welfare and security, only took from workers. The title of a GE newsletter to employees boasted: "*GE* Extra *Benefits—IUE* Extra *Assessments.*" While union leaders would be collecting strike funds from workers, which would go straight to Washington headquarters, GE would be paying out in "'the dreams-come-true' area—the new house, helping the kids go to college, retirement, and leisure." GE explicitly placed recent developments in the context of its history of welfare capitalism. Hospitalization coverage was yet another step "in fifty years of seeking what we could do in this benefits area." Moreover, recent additions to the welfare program resulted not from organized pressure by the workers, through their unions, but from the company's "doing right voluntarily." GE claimed that "whenever our studies suggest appropriate improvements, we have always made them voluntarily." According to this perpetual message of welfare capitalism, workers' security emanated from the business firm; "outside" institutions could only interfere with this finely tuned security program.[112]

The same scenario existed at Westinghouse and RCA. In the fall of 1950 Westinghouse expanded the hospital and surgical insurance that Equitable, its Chicago landlord and financier, had underwritten since 1939. Westinghouse offered a new policy underwritten by Equitable in conjunction with Metropolitan and Travelers Insurance Company. Hospital and disability payments were far lower than those of GM. Nor did they cover any medical services in the hospital other than surgery. In

10. "The GE Caravan," 1961. The GE Caravan was part of a campaign begun in 1960 to educate IUE members about the pension and economic security issues GE employees would face in the 1963 GE contract negotiations. A trailer forty-seven feet long included twenty-five exhibits. Courtesy of Records of the IUE, Special Collections and University Archives, Rutgers University.

1955 Westinghouse too offered a new "choice," Equitable's major medical plan, the equivalent of Metropolitan's catastrophic plan.[113] The IUE Pension, Health, and Welfare Department staff deeply distrusted major medical plans, referring to them in private correspondence as "complete frauds" and "gimmicky devices." Union leaders, however, wanting only to report victory in collective bargaining, refused to admit to the membership that the commercial policies fell far short of what they had demanded. The *IUE News* reported these settlements, which differed from firm to firm, as "comprehensive care."[114] Yet health benefits in the electrical industry remained nonstandardized and unequal. By clinging to commercial, cash-indemnity insurance, employers found ways to sidestep the NLRB's court-endorsed directive to expand the scope of collective bargaining.

Although unions signed onto collective bargaining agreements such as the ones offered by GE and Westinghouse, organized labor continued to expose the shortcomings of commercial health insurance and to call for both public and private alternatives. While private insurance benefits per family had nearly doubled between 1953 and 1958, private insurance still only met 24 percent of the total medical costs of insured families.[115] The AFL-CIO sent its social insurance experts around the country in the 1950s to educate people on the possibilities for organizing prepaid, group practice plans in their communities. Throughout the 1950s organized labor called on Congress to support legislation establishing federal long-term, low-interest loans that would enable local consumer groups to construct such independent group health plans and facilities.[116] Labor's representatives repeatedly tried to show that the continuous, annual increases in premiums reflected serious underlying flaws in the way insurance was being written; it was not merely a matter of "natural" inflation. Blue Cross and insurance companies struggled unsuccessfully to control costs, but Kaiser Permanente, organized along group practice lines, was so financially successful that it generated surpluses, which were quickly reinvested in medical plant, education, and research. Unions in cities such as Baltimore and Philadelphia still sought to build labor-based medical health plans offering outpatient medical and surgical services and preventive medical service regardless of age or physical condition. After purchasing the Metropolitan Hospital in Detroit, the UAW launched the Community Health Association in 1960 as a prepaid group medical program, running the program for twelve years, until Blue Cross–Blue Shield took it over.[117] Organized labor also lobbied in support of Medicare legislation for the elderly. In collective bargaining, unions that had sufficient leverage split up coverages. Life insurance, disability, and pensions went to insurance companies; the hospitalization contract went to Blue Cross, and the surgical contract went to Blue Shield. Unions instructed members and community leaders to lobby doctors to push Blue Shield toward the original Blue Cross service model.

Still, they could not alter the way in which health care would be organized and financed. Two forces finally thwarted their efforts and completed the triumph of cash-indemnity insurance over more progressive health insurance programs in the late 1950s: the continued opposition of the AMA and the arrival of major medical policies. The AMA vehemently fought all attempts to reorganize the practice of medicine. They rejected prepayment group practice plans in any form, even those run by physicians. The UAW denounced the AMA's "sordid fight against prepayment." The AFL-CIO accused doctors of illegal restrictive practices designed to discourage the development of alternatives to fee-for-service medicine. "The action of the Pennsylvania Medical Society is typical, and in essence, it provides that no physician can remain in good standing in his society if he is reimbursed for professional services on any other than a fee-for-service basis."[118]

Moreover, the physicians' medical societies blocked the development of group service plans, especially on the closed panel and cooperative models, by lobbying states to pass strict enabling statutes. State enabling acts established the terms and procedures under which collective health plans could be lawfully organized. Such legislation authorized the establishment and control of prepayment medical care organizations. In 1945 and 1946 fifteen states passed enabling acts, and another five states amended existing ones. The fifteen states that passed enabling acts followed the precedent set by New Jersey, Ohio, and Pennsylvania, where the legislation was formulated by medical societies to deliberately exclude nonprofit organizations. Under these laws, any group wishing to form a nonprofit corporation had to receive the approval of the state medical society. Eleven of the states required medical society supervision and participation. In Illinois, Florida, Rhode Island, and Tennessee, for example, the law required that the majority of the board of directors of an approved medical plan had to be physicians. Other states went so far as to pass legislation limiting prepaid medical plans to Blue Shield plans only. By the end of the 1950s twenty-six states had such restrictive acts. Forty states had enabling statutes for medical service plans. The American Labor Health Association warned labor unions and progressives of the devastating effect these laws had had on the group health movement. "Organized medicine is intent upon using these enabling acts for political purposes. . . . If none of these enabling acts had ever appeared on the American scene, both lay and profession sponsored plans would have developed unabated. . . . If organized medicine had not intervened by urging the passage of these acts, the probability is that the growth of the group health movement would have been far more rapid and health centers would now be widespread."[119]

Major medical, however, was the key strategic innovation that enabled insurers to solve the remaining problems they faced in selling group insurance. First, insurers believed it met the demands for comprehensive coverage. Major medical provided blanket coverage; it eliminated the distinction between hospital, surgical, and medical insurance. Major medical could be used for any of these services. Employers could offer major medical as their only policy, or they could use it to supplement other kinds of policies, including Blue Cross. Major medical thus solved the problem of split union contracts because now, instead of having to buy separate policies for each service, employers could buy one package. Equitable proudly stated, "In Major Medical Expense insurance and Care plans we have the answer to competition of Blue Cross and Blue Shield."[120] Finally, major medical confronted the problem of cost control. All insurance companies had experienced "spiraling costs" since the late 1940s. Despite the return of dividends and the ostensible competition among insurance companies, premiums never did go down. An Equitable report on group insurance admitted that "premium rates are being forced ever-upwards." Insurers devised the deductible and coinsurance to force patients to control their spending on medical care. Insurance coverage did not activate until the patient had spent his or her own money on services up to a specified amount, the deductible. After the deductible, insurers then split the cost of the medical bill: insurance paid 75–80 percent of the bill, and the patient paid the remainder. By making the insured take greater responsibility for their expenses, insurers would control "abuse," which they had concluded was the main problem with health insurance.[121]

Major medical spread instantly, growing 32-fold in five years. This type of health plan covered just over 500,000 individuals in 1952. By 1956 that number had grown to almost 7 million, and three years later coverage reached 22 million. Prominent nonunion companies such as Kodak enrolled in major medical plans, offering nonunionized employees the closest thing to comprehensive benefits commercial insurance had yet come up with. Its share of the market increased from 3 percent to 32 percent in four years as mass purchasers of group insurance aspired to obtain comprehensive coverage.[122]

But major medical was seriously flawed: it was not comprehensive, and it did not control costs. Organized labor recognized these problems immediately. Because of the deductible, these new insurance plans, like their predecessors, discouraged early diagnosis, treatment of early symptoms, and regular physical exams. As Jerome Pollack, a labor social insurance consultant, noted when major medical first appeared, "It abandons preventive care as a covered benefit."[123] But even more significantly, this policy left families without coverage for most of their medical expenses since the bulk of the care needed by the average person fell within the deductible range. Although major medical was sold as comprehensive coverage, in fact the deductible reduced benefits. "Co-insurance and deductible are a move in the wrong direction," the UAW argued throughout this period, "since they shift the cost to the workers when they are least able to afford it." Indeed, this form of insurance placed controls only on the consumer, in a sense punishing individuals for using medical services. Yet it left those who actually had some control over the costs—the doctors and hospitals—unhampered in setting prices. It was a policy that relied on the assumed self-restraint of the medical profession, a restraint it ultimately did not show.[124]

In fact, major medical's open-ended coinsurance only intensified the inflationary effects of insurers' earlier policies. Doctors and hospitals could charge any price they wanted without having to meet any standards of quality. In one case, a West Coast aircraft manufacturer abandoned the set fee schedule in favor of a major medical policy for workers. Within three months average surgical fees in that locale had increased by 17 percent. The insurers suffered an unexpected loss of $2 million and thus had to raise premiums and deductibles in turn. Even though employers offered expanded policies to their workers over the next two decades, the dramatic surge in medical prices and premiums often undercut the gains. In addition, under these policies, employers paid the premiums for active workers in about a third of the plans; workers for the most part paid for dependents' coverage. Insurers themselves soon realized the inflationary nature of the major medical policy. An Equitable executive admitted to a group of insurance representatives in 1958 that "we were enthusiastic about the potentials of this new coverage and dismissed rather lightly the possible pitfalls. . . . Today, in sharp contrast, we find ourselves in the very sobering position of seriously questioning how we can live financially with this coverage."[125] In 1960 the U.S. Department of Labor reported that "considerable statistical evidence has been compiled by insurers, medical societies, unions, and consultants" in support of major medical's inflationary impact on medical costs.[126] Insurers knew they had created a monster, but they refused to admit it to the public.

Although more than 79 percent of the population had some form of private health coverage by the mid-1960s, true health security remained elusive. American health care became the most expensive in the industrialized world. From the late 1950s through the 1970s the broadest statistic provided by the Health Insurance Association of America on coverage in fact referred to hospital benefits. Far fewer Americans had comprehensive medical benefits. About 60 percent of Americans under age 65 had medical expense benefits, but about half of that group had coverage against physicians' care in the hospital only. Of all the benefits paid out by insurance companies only one-third went into surgical, medical, and dental care. By 1980 private health insurance paid only 44 percent of total private expenditures on medical care. More revealing perhaps is that no more than one-third of American workers have ever had employee disability benefits, replacement of income during sickness or short-term disability. While the American health insurance system may pay for some hospital and medical care, individuals can never loosen their dependence on market forces; they cannot stop working.[127]

Pensions and Private Security

The story of private pensions essentially mirrors that of health insurance. Unions wanted not only the right to negotiate over pensions with employers; they also wanted to participate in the administration of the funds. As with health insurance, the labor movement at first sought entirely independent pension funds. After losing on this issue, they often supported the idea of a jointly run board of trustees on which management and labor had equal representation. Most corporations managed to block even this goal, for as management saw it, pensions involved the investment of *company* assets (not workers' compensation) over an extended period of time. Even the UAW had to make significant concessions and accommodations to managerial control. Throughout the 1950s and 1960s union demands for access to pension plan information and control were fiercely resisted and denied by management. As with health insurance, unions or workers' representatives usually had to depend on employer-provided cost estimates, budget and forecasting, and benefit formulas. An asymmetric distribution of bargaining power and information characterized private pension arrangements.[128]

Employers' discretion in pensions extended not only to benefits but also to investment of the pension reserves as well. Only a handful of unions—the Amalgamated Clothing Workers and its successor, the Amalgamated Textile and Clothing Workers, the ILGWU, the UMW, and the International Brotherhood of Teamsters—obtained sufficient control over jointly trusteed pension funds. These few unions have been able not only to voice decisions about benefits but also to direct investment of the funds into social purposes supported by the union movement. Thus, for example, the ILGWU instructed the Chase Manhattan Bank to use its pension fund reserves to grant mortgages to working-class applicants. Consequently, it is important to keep in mind that charges of "corruption" or "incompetence" may also represent political attacks against labor's exercising a broader role in economic investment decisions. For the first few years of welfare bargaining the UAW tried to force GM and Ford to allow the union to participate in these decisions, but it surrendered this struggle after 1955. After losing the contest over investment, unions retrenched from broader, classwide goals for economic security and focused instead on improving benefits for covered workers and lowering vesting standards for those within the bounds of the negotiated contract. Private supplementation would be confined to a fixed base of the economy.[129]

In order to get the most out of welfare state subsidization of welfare capitalism, employers initially integrated their pensions with Social Security benefits, a practice labor leaders went along with when pensions came under collective bargaining. Rank-and-file workers (and their spouses), however, soon became openly resentful of this integration, as well as its essential component, the Social Security offset. As the wife of a steelworker wrote to USWA President Philip Murray, "I would like to call your attention to this pension plan. Under the existing plan, the entire amount of the social security is deducted by the steel company. For instance, if my husband were to receive a $100 a month pension from the steel company and social security of $60, the steel company deducts the entire $60, costing the steel company only $40." She suggested there was a certain injustice to this, since the contract promised a company pension of $100. Many workers already perceived company pensions in terms of a somewhat reluctant trade-off: they had traded wage increases for future pension benefits. The Social Security offset, however, seemed to allow employers to cheat on this deal. Workers protested vociferously when company deductions immediately accompanied the Social Security increases of 1950 and 1952, essentially wiping out the gains they would have gotten from the public pension. Disgruntlement became so palpable at DuPont (in both unionized and nonunionized shops) that management decided to conduct a major review of the pension program in 1953. "Ever since Social Security benefits were first integrated with Company benefit formulas in 1941," concluded the report, "there has been serious employee dissatisfaction. Individual employees have firmly expressed their opinion that the direct integration is unfair and unjustifiable." Consequently, DuPont announced at the end of 1953 that the company was terminating its offset policy. In the mid-1950s CIO union officials began pushing in contract negotiations for severing the Social Security tie-in. Employee dissent and pressure thus forced some degree of liberalization in the terms of supplementation.[130]

Yet even within labor's realm of privately bargained social security, workers received vastly different benefits depending on local power and politics. As Joseph Swire, of the IUE, reported, "We bargain pretty much according to situation. We have different programs with each company." Not only pension amounts and service requirements but also the general range of benefits for retirees differed. In some places, pensioners received hospital insurance, while in others they received only life insurance. Sperry Gyroscope and Philco provided $1,000 insurance, but the Radio Corporation of America (RCA) provided $2,000. The union remained perpetually frustrated and thwarted at Westinghouse, which continually offered lower benefits. Swire lamented that "Westinghouse has always lagged behind, . . . while Westinghouse claims that GE is its major competitor, it has never approximated GE in pension benefits . . . or in granting medical benefits to pensioners or even to present employees."[131] In the latter half of the 1950s, in fact, rather than accept a "post-war social compact" with labor, Westinghouse embarked on a major plan of automation and shifting work and capital investment away from unionized plants and communities.[132]

The labor movement did push employers to commit to stiffer funding standards, to open pensions up to blue-collar workers, and to make the pensions noncontributory. But employers made these changes within the larger skeleton of preexisting employer plans. The ground rules of welfare capitalism remained in place: employers maintained control over benefit formulas, final eligibility rules, long-term service requirements for vesting, and how the pension would be funded. Although coverage had certainly expanded, the actual benefits of company pensions continued to be skewed toward long-tenured workers with unbroken service and higher wages; other workers paid into these funds without being eligible for benefits. Many companies continued the practice of firings and layoffs right before vesting. Women workers remained particularly vulnerable to these practices. Amid the recession of the late 1950s, for example, female electrical workers in Schenectady who had thirteen and fourteen years of service were "obliged to transfer to Office Cleaning where they are affected by short work schedules," that is, a work week of fewer than thirty-five hours. According to the collective bargaining agreement, an employee had to have an unbroken service record of working more than thirty-five hours a week for fifteen years in order to qualify for "minimum pension rights." Even labor-negotiated pensions remained "notoriously under funded." Unions, however, developed such a stake in the private pension system that they became partners in employers' strategies to keep the valuation of pension promises vague, using the ambiguity of private pensions to imply that collective bargaining had won a greater degree of old-age security for members than the system really offered.[133]

The Politics of Private Security

In the late 1950s liberals put the final stamp of ratification on the private, employment-based insurance system. Liberal Democrats, heirs of the New Deal, accepted a rather altered role for the federal government in issues related to workers' economic security. It was not simply that the state would no longer participate in industrial relations issues. The state instead would facilitate employers' control of private security through welfare capitalism, and public policy would, for the most part, supplement the gaps in private coverage. An extensive round of Senate hearings on many of the shortcomings of private employee benefits would ultimately fully legitimize this system in the name of "free" collective bargaining.

In the 1950s, congressional conservatives opened a new assault on the New Deal political economic order—backed by an increasingly militant alliance of medium-sized manufacturing firms, usually in more competitive markets, southern textile companies, and California agriculture. While Cold War red-baiting waxed and waned, a vigorous attack on corruption and racketeering in the labor movement and the purported ascendant, authoritarian power of the labor "bosses" increasingly occupied Congress. The Senate and House alternated organized crime probes in the early 1950s, even taking their show on the road, holding labor racketeering hearings in Detroit, Kansas City, and Cleveland.[134] As part of this new pattern of congressional investigations of union corruption, the Senate Committee on Labor and Welfare convened yet another corruption investigation in 1954—the same year that Elia Kazan's film *On the Waterfront* appeared—one specifically targeted at union welfare funds.

Emerging from this ripe political obsession with racketeering, subversion, and criminal conspiracies, the 1954 Senate inquiry on private welfare funds focused exclusively on collectively bargained union health and welfare plans, or jointly managed plans, so-called Taft-Hartley plans. Conducted by a subcommittee of the Committee on Labor and Public Welfare, these hearings' primary purpose was to expose corruption within the ranks of organized labor. And certainly, the subcommittee found some egregious cases of corruption and wrongdoing, as well as instances of mismanagement and waste. Mob-connected welfare fund consultants and directors in the Laundry Workers Union and the Distillery Workers Union, for instance, embezzled substantial amounts of money and raided funds. Yet some senators began to sense that problems could "spring from ignorance rather than venality" among union officials as insurance brokers seemed to take advantage of public ignorance of how insurance worked. In most of the cases where malfeasance was found, a member of the insurance industry was involved in the wrongdoing. Perhaps the questions to ask pertained more to the conduct of the group insurance trade than to a widespread corruption of labor leadership.[135]

After the Democrats regained the Senate in the 1954 elections, the probe continued, but with a shift in emphasis and objectives. Control of the subcommittee now shifted from Republican Senator Irving Ives to the New Deal labor liberal Senator Paul Douglas. A friend of organized labor and a welfare state advocate, Douglas resumed the hearings in 1955. But this time the inquiry would be broadened to include employer welfare plans, pension plans, insurance company practices, and other types of employee security programs. After all, as Chairman Douglas now made clear, what the committee was in fact dealing with was "a private social security system." Within this private social security system 91 percent of employee benefit plans were administered by employers; unions ran about 2.5 percent of the plans, and 6.5 percent were jointly administered, Taft-Hartley plans. Douglas invoked the private plans' importance, first, as the "underpinning of our economic security, broadening and supplementing the various governmental programs," and second, as huge aggregates of both investment capital and retirement savings, "involving enormous economic power and affecting the ultimate security of great numbers of our population."[136] Thus, under Paul Douglas the Senate probe shifted its emphasis away from one of labor corruption or labor racketeering to broader questions about the public's claim on private social security.

Through field investigators and hearings the new Senate inquiry concluded that "many of the worst abuses involved certain insurance industry practices." Insurance companies relied on independent brokers and agents to bring in new group business, especially from unions and smaller employers. As the market for private health insurance, disability coverage, life insurance, and annuities surged in the 1950s, competition among brokers, agents, and group insurance companies intensified dramatically, and they began to use a host of dubious tactics to secure new groups. The hearings revealed practices such as exorbitantly high commissions, excessive administrative charges, fictitious fees, unequal treatment of policyholders, and even outright embezzlement of premiums by brokers, sometimes in collusion with management or union officials. Insurance companies as well as brokers and agents retained unduly large shares of the premium payment, sometimes diverting as much 25 percent of the premium into service fees. While state insurance laws often required insurers to pay a commission to brokers for securing a new contract, insurers devised means of paying them perpetual commissions every year, or even a separate commission on each type of insurance the group carried. Insurers also allowed these intermediaries to be paid administrative fees out of the premium even though either the insurance company, the union, or the employer did most of the service work involved in maintaining the policy. Finally, brokers engaged in a game of extortion: they would threaten to take the group to another insurance company unless the insurers continued to pay such fees, or they would repeatedly switch carriers in order to continue earning high first-year commissions. This was where the collusion with union officials or managers came in. Insurance representatives would pay various types of bribes or kickbacks to union officials or personnel managers in return for their help in playing this game; or they would shake down the union by threatening to drop the business. Not surprisingly, as the committee lamented, "the effect of such commission payments was to reduce the dollars available for benefits and deprive employee-beneficiaries of protection rightfully theirs."[137]

By looking at plans that were unilaterally administered by employers, Douglas's subcommittee was able to consider issues more broadly related to private, employment-linked security than to union practices per se. "Management," the committee's report stated firmly, "shares the responsibility of the serious problems and abuses of employee welfare and pension plans." Management, however, did not so easily accept this claim. Companies did not intend to cooperate with this line of investigation, revealing the underlying power struggle over security. When asked to disclose such information to the committee, employers balked. At first most companies refused to turn over any financial or administrative information about their employee benefit plans, adamantly maintaining that "the costs of these benefits are private business costs, have no relation to employee compensation, and are therefore of no concern to employees or others." Even companies that had signed union contracts insisted that these were "private company matters."[138]

Using what information it could obtain through independent investigation, the subcommittee shined a light on practices that would not have been considered illegal or corrupt but nonetheless seemed to jeopardize workers' security: how and whether companies actually funded pension obligations, the absence of vesting provisions, the investment of funds, and the lack of a substantive union voice in any of these decisions. The Douglas committee found that GM consistently hid from workers the level of reserves and returned dividends on hourly workers' insurance plans and suggested that the workers had been literally cheated out of these dividends and hence forced to pay more for benefits. Examination of the steel industry pointed to disparities in insurance benefits among smaller companies and those outside of basic steel. Presciently, the committee's report criticized the fact that a number of pension plans had invested in "the securities and properties of the employing company," a point evidently forgotten in recent corporate debacles.[139]

Douglas countered employer recalcitrance by trying to recast these private plans as matters of public security and public interest, and in so doing he claimed an array of new employees' rights. Using the politically resonant language of rights to transcend the bald power struggle, Douglas went beyond the claim that workers and their beneficiaries had a right to the payout of pecuniary benefits. Douglas explicitly asserted that "employees accordingly have a right to know the cost of the program, how the money is spent, the reserves maintained, and how the programs are managed. . . . Employees have a right to know the financial details of such plans as well as have their interest in such plans protected."[140] Liberal senators bolstered this claim in two ways: by equating fringe benefits with wages, thereby asserting a property right, and by highlighting the hidden tax subsidies. Democrats reminded everyone repeatedly that "under existing laws, these companies obtain tax concessions in return for welfare and pension plan contributions in lieu of wages. . . . It is [therefore] impossible for the committee to accept the policy of secrecy. . . . Public welfare demands that this policy be discontinued."[141]

Although labor's supporters tried to claim workers' rights to security, by now legislators and unions were clearly dealing with private assets cordoned off from unions' reach. Rights talk not withstanding, labor did not have the economic or social power at the bargaining table to compel management to treat welfare benefits as such. In fact, Douglas articulated organized labor's frustrations with collective bargaining for welfare benefits, leveling charges against employers and insurers for the "attitude of secrecy [that] usually prevails" and for offering "little or no account of their stewardship."[142] The Senate report contained the whole roster of labor's complaints, including employers' not disclosing their actual contribution to the insurance premium; management's keeping the dividends or experience rating refunds and not using them to reduce workers' contributions or improve benefits. Despite the tremendous growth of fringe benefit plans, individual unions could not translate firm-based collective bargaining into social security, especially as much of the country settled into a recession in 1957.

Yet, given the legislative remedy that eventually came out of this investigation—the Welfare and Pension Plans Disclosure Act—the state, it seemed, had very little leverage to transform private welfare plans into public security. After all that the hearings uncovered, the subcommittee recommended that every union and employer benefit program file a registration statement and annual reports disclosing financial details; these would be held at the Department of Labor, available for public viewing. The proposal for a disclosure law came from the liberals, from Paul Douglas himself: "Let us let the light of day shine in on the operation of this great private security system of welfare and pension plans."[143] Organized labor quickly agreed to endorse the disclosure proposal; in fact it had already instituted such a policy internally at the 1955 AFL-CIO convention.[144] Douglas's 1957 bill offered something extra: employers would have to disclose too. Still, it involved no federal regulation, no standard requirements for funding, eligibility, or security of benefits.

But for political and ideological reasons this was as far as Democrats were willing to go for labor in 1957–58. The antilabor smear campaign did not let up but entered its most successful and sensationalist phase yet with the convening of the Select Committee on Improper Activities, otherwise known as the McClellan Committee. With the help of an extensive, questionable use of wiretapping, eight field offices, and television, the McClellan Committee kept the public tuned in to images of greedy, self-serving labor leaders betraying and double-crossing American workers. As labor's public credibility plunged, Democrats feared the political ramifications of getting too close to labor. Senate Democrats led by Lyndon Johnson had no intention of appearing to be under the thumb of the "labor bosses."[145] The Welfare and Pension Plans Disclosure Act, especially in its final, rather toothless form, enabled the Democrats to step in to protect workers' interests, while keeping labor at arm's length.

The disclosure remedy also made perfect ideological sense within the framework of industrial pluralism. If bargaining among industrial interest groups kept the self-governing democracy of the workplace on an even keel, then government had only to encourage collective bargaining and ensure its procedural regularity. The state should not intervene directly in disputes or compel particular resolutions.[146] And certainly by the mid-1950s Democrats of all stripes believed the state should not step in to tip the balance in industrial relations. Disclosure offered a "neutral" intervention of the state that would allow private labor-management arrangements to work better. If each side had the information it needed to make informed decisions during contract negotiations, then firm-based collective bargaining would continue smoothly, the system would provide security for workers, and sources of labor strife would be eliminated. The objective of disclosure was to bring order and stability to labor relations and the private welfare system "without impairing their voluntary or free bargaining character."[147]

Yet within this politics of "free" bargaining and "labor reform" of the late 1950s, liberal Democrats found they had to navigate within a very narrow channel of political options, one full of potential mines. With years of seniority under their belts, southern conservatives anchored the party; an ambitious Lyndon Johnson let them hold sway, for the most part, while sidelining the liberals. The Dixiecrats were only too willing to cooperate with conservative westerners such as Barry Goldwater of Arizona, Karl Mundt of South Dakota, William Knowland of California, and Carl Curtis of Nebraska, who were generating a range of so-called labor reforms, including a nationwide ban on the union shop. In fact, of the eight senators on the committee six came from states that had outlawed the union shop. What would soon become the Landrum-Griffin Bill began to take shape: disclosure but also heavy-handed government monitoring of union affairs, including union finances, elections, political activities, and individual "rights" vis-à-vis group rights.[148] The Democrats' Welfare and Pension Plans Disclosure Act, then, seemed to offer a safe alternative to the conservatives' increasingly strident and harsh proposals for labor reform. Labor-liberal Democrats hoped to head off the punitive Landrum-Griffin proposals, which intended to use the power of the state to control unions and limit the range of their activities. These Democrats engaged in a delicate political balancing act. They wanted to defend labor and, more importantly, the private welfare regime that was now necessary to supplement the stalled public welfare state, and yet the conservatives' bill, which aimed to punish and regulate unions, was deeply threatening to the labor movement. The best route appeared to be to try to bolster "free collective bargaining," which nominally offered federal protection of a right to security, but with minimal state intrusion.

In the end, Congress passed a bill that, while acknowledging "federal responsibility" for employee security, failed to do either: it neither protected workers nor prevented passage of the more punitive Landrum-Griffin Bill. After being hammered by House members in the joint conference committee, the bill stripped the secretary of labor of any enforcement powers, such as the ability to set requirements for disclosure and reporting, to conduct follow-up investigations of irregularities, or even to initiate judicial proceedings. The 1958 Welfare and Pension Plans Disclosure Act included employers as well as unions but called for only a general, summary disclosure rather than full disclosure; it put no requirements on insurance brokers. Summaries would reside at the Department of Labor. If employees thought there was a problem with their welfare or pension plan, they could travel to Washington, D.C., look up the report at the Department of Labor, and perhaps take independent action at court. Once the act was in place, thousands of groups flouted it. Tens of thousands of benefit plans—more than 25 percent—failed to file a statement or to report at all. Those who did file offered only superficial "summary" information about the plans. Amendments to plans were never submitted. Benefits remained within the realm of managerial prerogatives. As one labor lawyer observed, "The worst aspect of the legislation is that it fails to bring federal power to bear on the problem, while purporting to exercise it."[149]

After John F. Kennedy, a member of the original committee, became president and Arthur Goldberg became secretary of labor, they brought the issue of private welfare plans and employee security back to the Congress. Self-policing had not worked, Goldberg told Congress. Invoking the words of former Labor Secretary James P. Mitchell, California Congressmen James Roosevelt stated that for "the millions of Americans who have a right to a sense of security," the government had to amend the law. Congress estimated that almost 90 million Americans (workers and family members) now depended on some form of employee welfare benefits, including group life insurance, disability benefits, hospital insurance, surgical and medical benefits, supplemental unemployment insurance, or retirement pensions. Annual contributions to these plans exceeded $9.4 billion, and assets in funds and reserves had grown to $58 billion. While the Chamber of Commerce and the NAM insisted that no changes needed to be made, labor came back to Congress with the same list of frustrations over collective bargaining. After a year of wrangling and debate, Congress passed amendments in 1962 to shore up the enforcement mechanisms of the act. The secretary of labor could now establish regulations requiring specific types of information in disclosure reports. Annual reports would have to include the amount contributed by each employer, contributions by employees, the amount of benefits paid, and a detailed report of salaries, fees, and commissions charged to the plan. In addition to a statement of liabilities, a statement of fund assets had to specify in full the total amount held in various investment instruments. The amendments also carried the emphatic statement that "nothing contained in this Act shall be so construed or applied as to authorize the Secretary to regulate, or interfere in the management of, any employee welfare or pension benefit plan."[150] Private security, for the most part, was a private matter of employment.

Liberal policies would rely on private supplementation and the basic welfare state. The argument that benefits constituted deferred wages and hence a property right fit the supplementation model perfectly, as did, of course, the idea that the federal government granted tax favors in return for the public welfare. In the American welfare state only those who earned full-time wages received social insurance benefits. This was shored up by the 1954 and 1958 Social Security amendments, which linked a necessary subsistence increase in OASI to a payroll tax increase, making sure the pension program would neither draw on the general treasury for revenue nor blur the lines between federal welfare and social insurance programs. The private welfare state replicated this pattern, enforcing the notion that social welfare benefits were merely an extension of wages for deserving breadwinners rather than public benefits compensating for wage fluctuation or the lack of wages. The disclosure policy, along with the Landrum-Griffin Act, narrowed the scope of security even further by defining the reliability and accessibility of private welfare plans as a narrow issue of the individual beneficiary's procedural rights: if an individual could seek his own remedies, he could possibly ensure his own security.[151] The broad class challenge once embodied in the politics of security had been winnowed away.

As a result of the corruption controversies, labor's lack of bargaining power, and the legislative weakness of labor-liberal Democrats, organized labor accepted private insurance and welfare capitalism. At this point, many unions made their peace with experience rating. With experience rating, reserves, and experience-based refunds disclosed, unions could see how or where their members benefited from this policy. A couple of years later, Medicare essentially removed unions' experience rating problem by taking the older, sicker members out of the pool and having the state insure them. Turning inward, unions henceforth saw experience rating as another employee benefit for their own shrinking constituency. It seemed to give unions some minimal measure of control over the private security benefits that encompassed their members.

Historians have to rethink the consensus regarding collective bargaining and social welfare. Scholars have generally agreed that organized labor won optimal benefits for their members because they had collective bargaining, while those outside of unionized sectors suffered. Often, however, labor lost out in collective bargaining too because unions could not win the kinds of programs they wanted, programs that would have been much better at delivering more equitably priced and distributed services to entire communities. When unions lost out on these options, all Americans lost the chance for programs that would have charged all customers equally, provided more comprehensive coverage of medical services, regulated costs more effectively, and possibly even promoted a vision of health linked to social-environmental factors as well. Instead, health care access remains a marketable commodity whose distribution is still determined by insurers and employers. In a larger sense, collective bargaining and the particular industrial relations system that emerged from World War II helped dislodge health security from the broader issues of social and economic justice. Collective bargaining did not even the balance of power; it reflected the imbalance of power.

In 1960, after ten years of health bargaining, the USWA conducted a sweeping review of the medical care insurance benefits the union had negotiated for its membership. By 1960 more than two-thirds of the USWA members had health insurance for themselves and their dependents. Moreover, in 1960 they won noncontributory, full-employer financing throughout the basic steel industry. Clearly they had one of the best-negotiated programs in any major industry, including all hospitalization costs, surgical fees, and outpatient medical benefits. "Nevertheless," the USWA concluded, "we cannot be satisfied with the present plan or its method of operation. . . . [O]ur present programs do not guarantee the quality of the medical care received nor do they adequately cover the full range of services required by our members and their families. . . . The Union is deeply concerned over shortcomings of the health insurance benefits. Also, the costs of insurance keep rising rapidly, without improvement in benefits."[152]

The USWA was in an excellent position to conduct such a study. Its membership of more than 1 million had negotiated contracts for all three primary forms of health: commercial group insurance, Blue Cross–Blue Shield, and group practice service plans. Commercial group insurance, provided by companies such as Inland Steel and Republic Steel, covered 625,000 persons in the steel industry. Other companies, including U.S. Steel, had Blue Cross and Blue Shield coverage. The USWA also had contracts with the Kaiser Foundation Health Plans covering 39,000 persons, some of whom worked directly for the Kaiser Steel Corporation and others who had arranged contracts with Kaiser Permanente for direct service. Thus the USWA could systematically compare and evaluate the costs and benefits experienced by persons of roughly the same income under indemnity and service plans, although it admitted that the commercial insurance carriers were not cooperative in releasing information about premiums and costs. The USWA brought in I. S. Falk, formerly of the SSA, as a consultant.

The study determined that commercial insurance benefits were consistently inadequate. "The Steelworker standard plan covers on the average something less than 41% of total family health costs." In the case of Blue Cross and Blue Shield, the standard USWA package paid slightly more than 43 percent of the total cost per family. Yet even in this first decade of health plans workers experienced perpetually "skyrocketing costs." In addition to the inadequate coverage, these types of insurance did not use their health care dollars very efficiently. The union repeatedly criticized these plans for overutilization of expensive hospital care and surgery, a total lack of cost management, and the absence of financial or structural incentives against unnecessary hospitalization. Without effective control of rising costs, the higher costs were not translating into more comprehensive care. Hence, the USWA concluded that "little progress can be made toward our goal by the purchase of additional benefits from the standard insurance carriers" or "through additional purchases of insurance from Blue Cross–Blue Shield."[153]

Steelworkers participating in group practice service plans did not seem to be experiencing these problems. The study concluded that "the more comprehensive benefits of the group practice prepayment plan go much further: They are actually offering protection against 80–84% of private health costs." Union members and dependents had coverage for comprehensive hospitalization, but they received most of their medical care services in "well-equipped clinics (or offices)" rather than in hospitals. The plan covered general and specialist medical care, laboratory diagnostic services, physical therapy, and other technical services—all for about $15 more per person. Yet "we found that KFHP [Kaiser Foundation Health Plan] costs had been held down mainly by their much lower rates of hospitalization and their more extensive resources for serving patients in well-equipped clinics. Moreover, the services provided by KFHP were not only coordinated but, despite the economies of the group practice, were apparently of high quality."[154]

The small minority of the membership who had such coverage mirrored the proportions in the nation as a whole (by 1960 commercial group health insurance and Blue Cross–Blue Shield accounted for 95% of all coverage, and independent group practice plans covered 4.5% of the insured population) and prompted the USWA to comment, "We are far from having this full range of coordinated services and it is hard to see how we can get it under the present pattern of purchased insurance benefits."[155] At the very moment when the union won its best contract ever, union leaders were painfully aware that they had not achieved health security.

Yet the union's debate over security in 1960 occurred on a much smaller and narrower ideological terrain. The next steps toward achieving security, the USWA concluded, had to be further "cooperation" between unions and management, a joint project resting on the willingness of the employer. Security was no longer a political venture; it had floated loose from its moorings in the New Deal state. In laying out the USWA's course of action, the report never mentioned government; it offered no public policy suggestions. Instead, it contended that "the development of the [new, progressive group] program would require new achievements through collective bargaining."[156] Collective bargaining, however, had reached its limits. Indeed, after another ten years of collective bargaining, all the USWA ended up with was a major medical plan in 1970. The community group health programs the USWA now called for, or any other extension of health coverage among the population more generally, required a frontal assault on numerous structures of power and economic relationships. The depoliticized, firm-centered system of industrial relations was incapable of mounting such a challenge. Welfare capitalism was aimed at preserving power relations between owners and workers. It had created islands of security within the economy, with high waters all around.

Epilogue

The Limits of Private Security, 1960s–1990s

> The employee's urge for security is stronger than ever, and every company has a responsibility to make maximum provision, consistent with its ability, to cushion employees against the economic hazards of sickness, disability, old age, and death.
>
> —National Association of Manufacturers, 1948

> Time was when Americans savored freedom's uncertainties and considered 'security' an unworthy goal for a free people.
>
> —George F. Will, *Washington Post*, 22 February 1996

For two generations the public and the private welfare systems grew in tandem, offering a growing level of benefits to millions of Americans. Private pensions, firm-based unemployment benefits, and some forms of disability compensation supplemented the Social Security System. In some areas, supplementation actually became substitution. In the 1950s, private health insurance became the primary means for obtaining medical and hospital care; subsequent developments in health policy and public programs would supplement the private, employment-based system. Between 1945 and 1970, participation in private pensions increased from 19 percent to 45 percent. Most of that growth actually occurred between 1945 and 1960. The reach of the private pension system peaked in the late 1970s, at which point private pensions covered 49 percent of the private wage and salary workforce (40 million people). From the mid-1950s until 1980, pensions were a minor source of conflict between labor and management. At the level of the firm, pensions for the most part became noncontributory, and participation was nearly universal. In the 1960s, private health insurance finally reached two-thirds of the wage and salary workforce under 65 years of age. (Not all of that coverage was provided by employers; about 60% of those with health insurance received it from their employers.) Health insurance became a universal feature of middle-class employment. Among those Americans who worked in firms with more than one hundred employees and earned more than $50,000 a year, coverage levels were approximately 90 percent. At the height of this system and of labor's collective bargaining strength, 40 million unionized workers and family members received health insurance benefits. Union members were more likely to have major medical coverage or full physicians' benefits. Between the mid-1950s and mid-1960s employers increased their contributions to health and welfare plans from 47 percent to about 65–70 percent of all contributions. The proportion of hospital services paid by cash-indemnity insurance doubled, finally rising to more than half of the total hospital expenses. A broad swath of the American population had access to the private security system.[1] After 1979 this trend would reverse.

The public welfare state expanded too, although more slowly and in more circumscribed ways. The Social Security amendments of 1950 increased retirement benefits (OASI) and added new groups of beneficiaries. The only major development in Social Security in the 1950s was total permanent disability compensation for those over 50 years of age who were permanently removed from the workforce. These benefits would be supplemental to workers' compensation; that is, any benefits from workers' compensation would be subtracted from the Social Security amount. The state, however, would provide no short-term disability or paid maternity leave. In the early 1960s Social Security pensions still stood at about the same level as in 1950. The average OASI benefit replaced only 30 percent of the average American wage. In families with a nonworking spouse the minimum spousal allowance brought the replacement rate to 45 percent of household income. Women on their own after the death of a breadwinner faced greater economic insecurity because of the persistent widow's gap in survivors' benefits.[2]

During Lyndon Johnson's Great Society program, Congress enacted the first major extensions of the New Deal welfare state in a generation. While Johnson's policies included public housing, education funding and college loans, the Job Corps, and community action support, the most successful economic security and antipoverty programs were the Social Security amendments of 1965 establishing Medicare and Medicaid and the major expansion of Social Security allowances. Twenty-two years after the first appearance of the Wagner-Murray-Dingell Bill, the federal government took on subsidizing and socializing the costs of hospital care. Medicare established compulsory hospital insurance for nearly all persons over 65, financed by contributions to the Social Security System. Since health insurance for most working persons did not cover physician expenses, the federal Medicare program would subsidize voluntary insurance for the elderly to cover physician and surgical fees (Part B); government and the beneficiary would split the premium. The government's contribution to Part B would come from general revenues. Finally, the bill included a program for poor people, regardless of age: Medicaid, a means-tested public assistance program. If a state decided to participate in the program, it would receive federal matching grants to provide medical care for welfare recipients and the medically indigent. These programs substantially reduced the number of elderly persons living below the poverty line, lowered the infant mortality rate, and improved access to medical care for poor people. Medicare hospital coverage soon reached almost the entire elderly population. Medicaid offers the indigent, including the elderly poor, specific medical services, even dental and optometry services and prescription drugs. Nonetheless, these programs endeavored to compensate the gaps in privately provided health insurance. In addition, by accommodating private insurance companies and the traditional organization of American medicine, public policies yet again fueled the profits of private insurers, doctors, and hospitals, igniting rapid medical inflation as well.[3]

The 1960s and early 1970s also brought substantial increases in retirees' and survivors' benefits under OASI, the addition of cost-of-living adjustments beginning in 1972, and enactment of Supplemental Security Income. Supplemental Security Income replaced the federal-state assistance to the blind, the disabled, and the indigent aged with a federal, guaranteed income. The new program offered much higher benefits than the states had. Even Aid to Families with Dependent Children (AFDC) expanded in scope and benefits during these years, although a proposal to offer this group of aid recipients (poor women) a guaranteed minimum income failed. This expansionary phase of the public welfare state also peaked in the late 1970s, reversing course in the subsequent decade.

Most of the public policies enacted in the past twenty-five years, however, have been aimed at propping up or patching up the leaky private welfare system. Even when the private benefits system reached its heyday in the 1960s, many observers were concerned about its apparent shortcomings. The first sense of serious crisis over private pensions was triggered by the collapse of the Studebaker Corporation in 1964. Here was a model welfare capitalist firm with a negotiated pension contract signed by the responsible, trendsetting UAW. Yet when Studebaker closed its doors on 1 November 1964, the pension plan was found to be millions of dollars short. Seven thousand workers received little or nothing from the company. Public alarm over this high-profile incident sparked congressional hearings, which found that a high percentage of workers fell through the cracks when it actually came to receiving pension benefits. Unreasonably high vesting thresholds still prevented even long-service workers from qualifying for benefits. Pension plan rules defined "unbroken" service in extremely narrow terms; thus, in numerous cases in which a worker had been temporarily reassigned to a different classification, employers considered this reassignment a disqualifying break in service. Pension plans all reserved the employer's exclusive right to alter, reduce, or deny benefits or eliminate pensions at will, and courts upheld these practices. Employers also avoided liability by asserting in plan documents that workers' claims were against the plan, not against the assets of the corporation. In 1974 Congress passed the Employee Retirement Income Security Act (ERISA) to eliminate these abuses through greater federal regulation and federal guarantees.

ERISA represented the culmination of the disclosure act struggle, as well as the persistent liberal commitment to a private benefits system. Stemming from the ineffectiveness of the disclosure act in protecting individuals' work-based benefits, ERISA legally mandated that all employees participating in pension plans would be vested after ten years. It established federal participation rules and funding standards, created a new Pension Benefit Guaranty Corporation (PBGC, similar to the Federal Deposit Insurance Corporation [FDIC]) to insure vested funds, and stiffened corporate liability. Employers would also have to provide workers with more specific details about the finances of the pension fund. ERISA forced employers to make their welfare capitalist promises more explicit and more reliable. It conferred upon workers some minimal legal rights to employer-provided old-age security. ERISA was followed in the 1980s with the 1984 Retirement Equity Act and the Pension Reform Act of 1987, reflecting, on the one hand, continued commitment to tightening up the loopholes and gaps in the private pension system and, on the other hand, their unshakeable persistence. Moreover, another section of ERISA exempted employers with self-insured health plans from state-level insurance regulations regarding benefits, coverage, quality standards, or posting of sufficient reserves. This preemption, as Marie Gottschalk has recently shown, created a regulatory vacuum for a growing number of group health plans, including Taft-Hartley plans, and also further entrenched a set of stakeholders (unions as well as employers) against broad-based social reform or even state-level political experimentation. As unions, employers, and, later, health maintenance organizations (HMOs) became wedded to their ERISA exemptions, they reinforced the logic of the private benefits system and the public-private split in American social welfare.[4]

The American welfare state also continued to rely on the "passive" mechanism of tax exemptions and deductions to convince companies to provide employee welfare benefits. Since 1942, federal laws have treated employer payments to group insurance and pensions funds as business expenses. Thus, employee compensation in the form of health care benefits is not subject to federal income taxes. Monies diverted to pension trusts are tax exempt or tax deferred. In the postwar era, Congress has repeatedly adjusted and extended these tax supports. For example, the Keogh Act of 1962 allowed the self-employed and unincorporated small businesses tax-favored status for retirement plans. This meant that doctors, lawyers, and other professionals now had tax-subsidized retirement income. In 1981 new legislation expanded individual retirement accounts (IRAs) and Keogh plans by raising contribution limits and extended IRA coverage to workers already participating in employer plans. These tax policies have disproportionately benefited high-income Americans.

In health care too, the primary policy developments have been laws that attempt to goad market-based health insurance toward reaching more people and reining in costs. In the late 1960s and early 1970s legislators, academics, policymakers, and miscellaneous health reformers were disturbed by the ever-escalating cost of hospital and medical services and the persistence of an intractable block of uninsured Americans. This time they rejected entirely any consideration of government's paying for health insurance. Instead, each presidential administration in the 1970s supported, and secured, passage of laws offering federal loans and subsidies to prepaid group service plans, now recast by health economists as HMOs. Federal policymakers believed that under the HMO policy, the government would provide modest startup aid to HMOs, enough to make them attractive to private investors. Soon private capital would be injected, and because of its inherently self-regulating quality, a newly structured health industry would take off. Since lawmakers did not want to have to spend too much money on a new health policy, several key consequences followed. First, for-profit HMOs were to be encouraged. Second, *minimal* regulations and requirements would be imposed by the state; each HMO had to be given "flexibility" to decide on its basic package of services. Nor would there be any requirements regarding subscriber participation in administrative decisions. Congress, the presidents, the economists, and the Department of Health, Education, and Welfare (HEW) believed that they were simply enhancing markets.[5] A decade later it was clear that unless an individual had a secure position in the labor market, health insurance of any type remained out of reach. Congress thus enacted the Consolidated Omnibus Budget Reconciliation Act, or COBRA, in the 1980s, enabling individuals to continue their group insurance policy for one year after leaving employment. Individuals pay the full premium, including the portion previously paid by the employer. In 1996 Congress passed a more muscular version of the same law: the Kennedy-Kassebaum Bill, or the Health Insurance Portability and Accountability Act (HIPAA). Again, Congress enacted this law to assist workers who have lost or changed jobs to buy insurance for themselves and their families. The law prohibits insurers from denying coverage to someone based on preexisting conditions. (It also includes a new round of tax breaks: increased tax deductions for health insurance for self-employed persons and for long-term care insurance, as well as a number of experimental tax-exempt medical savings accounts.) Ironically, after 1965 private coverage would be considered the foundation around which public programs would mop up. In general, whenever flaws in the private benefits system have been exposed, the policy response has consistently been to regulate some other aspect of the private system rather than to augment the public Social Security program.[6]

Despite these improvements and adjustments, the American political system has not developed either the means or the political will to provide universal economic security. On the public side of the picture, Medicare has become almost universal. The primary title provided hospital insurance. For medical benefits, recipients had to purchase supplementary coverage through additional payments, but by the 1990s the beneficiary's share of the premium had declined to 25 percent. By the mid-1990s just about everyone who had Medicare hospital coverage also had Part B medical coverage. Yet neither plan covers long-term care, prescription drugs, or physicians' full fees. Medicare pays only 55 percent of elderly persons' total health costs. While many rely on privately purchased (tax-subsidized) Medigap policies or employer-provided retirement benefits to make up for these gaps, one-third of the elderly have no such supplemental coverage. The latter tend to be lower-income Americans, who end up spending a large chunk of their subsistence income on health care. Hence, once again the tax system is used to subsidize the private insurance market and particular income groups (at the expense of others). As for Medicaid, because it sets reimbursement fees so low, numerous doctors, particularly specialists, refuse to participate. Thus the poor often end up receiving care from hospital emergency rooms or practitioners in marginal facilities. States have discouraged applications to the program by requiring excessively complicated application procedures. Benefit amounts have varied significantly from state to state and more recently have included increased co-payments for medications and emergency room care. Medicaid replicated the split between social insurance and welfare contained within the original Social Security Act: between benefits for worthy citizens and charity for the unworthy poor. Left out of these programs entirely were the working poor, those least likely to receive health insurance on the job. Americans just above the poverty line received no benefits from the program. The federal Children's Health Insurance Program, begun in 1997, has since extended health insurance coverage to 2 million children, yet in the majority of states a person without children can be impoverished and still not qualify for federally subsidized health coverage. For the lower strata of the working class, covered by neither public nor private benefits, supplementation has meant nothing.[7]

Nor have the policies regulating the private sphere expanded the reach of coverage or eradicated the inequalities of private, employment-based benefits. These policies reveal both the ideological and political triumph of welfare capitalism and its economic and social inadequacy. By 1990 only 43 percent of men and 32 percent of women were vested and eligible for future benefits. Pension regulation still allows plans that have highly regressive earnings-related formulas, that exempt contingent workers, and that allow Social Security to be deducted from the intended amount. The problems that characterized private pensions in the 1950s have persisted. Although pension funds are vast, benefits per person often amount to very little. Private pensions rarely provide adequate retirement income. For example, at GE, once considered one of the more generous welfare capitalist employers, pension benefits replace only 32 percent of a retiring worker's annual wages.[8] Employers and unions often deliberately inflate workers' estimation of what their pensions will be when they retire, creating a dramatic gap between workers' expectations and the real costs and benefits. The gaps that have always plagued the system still do. The industries that did not provide pensions at midcentury still do not provide them. Despite the Retirement Equity Act of 1984, the gender bias of the private pension system remains in place. In the public sector, where employees are heavily unionized, women workers have rather high rates of participation, although still lagging behind those of men. In the private sector women are only half as likely to receive pensions as men, and those who do, receive only half as much as men. Minimum age and service requirements still hinder most women from ever actually qualifying for benefits. They receive only 22 percent of total private pension income. Those who need supplementation of public Social Security payments the most are not getting much supplementary support either.[9]

Broad changes in the political economy have exacerbated the instability of private social security. The decline of the labor movement, deregulation, and the North American Free Trade Agreement (NAFTA) have provided business firms with the social and political power to withdraw from their commitment to social welfare benefits. The ascendance of a well-organized, politicized business class in the late 1970s and 1980s, acting through groups such as the Business Roundtable and the Business Council, initiated an aggressive political and legislative assault on labor laws, business regulation, and consumer protection, leading a capitalist class offensive against the idea of security. The number of terminations and reversions of pension funds steadily increased from the late 1970s throughout the 1980s, precisely when the labor movement and the New Deal state declined. Federal regulation had not changed the fact that at the level of the firm corporate employers retained much initiative and discretion in social welfare administrative and financial matters. Although ERISA tightened employer liability, it still allowed firms to terminate pension plans even when the firm was not facing failure. And in fact, in the 1980s pension terminations were more prevalent than ever, particularly in unionized sectors of the economy. Privatized, firm-level collective bargaining, isolated from political support, ultimately could not sustain family welfare and security. Much as the savings and loan industry abused the FDIC, employers have been dumping unfunded or unwanted liabilities on the PBGC. In particular, corporations have been terminating collectively bargained plans—often as they packed their bags for Mexico or Asia—and forcing workers to file claims with the PBGC. (Union-negotiated plans accounted for 95% of the $200 million increase in claims.) At the turn of the twenty-first century the steel industry was the major beneficiary of the PBGC. Consequently, private pension coverage has fallen precipitously. After dropping to 38 percent of the private-sector workforce in 1980, coverage had fallen to 31 percent by 1987 and to below 30 percent in the 1990s. Thus, as the New Deal state is dismantled, only one-third of Americans receive private old-age pensions from their employers.[10]

Business firms have also been curtailing their contributions to social welfare by discontinuing company-paid pension plans and instead turning to worker-funded 401(k) plans. These plans are basically tax-preferred savings plans into which workers divert their own wages. After their inception in 1978, employers cut their contributions to defined benefit pension plans from $61 billion to $18.9 billion in 1990. By 2002, 88 percent of current workers allegedly covered by company pensions were enrolled in 401(k), profit-sharing, or stock-option plans, and workers were paying the majority of the contributions. Thus behind the veil of 401(k) retirement savings accounts, employers substantially, and in some senses invisibly, reduced their contributions to employee social security. Since a 401(k) plan is primarily an employee investment plan, to which the employer may or may not contribute, and since the amount of retirement income will depend on the value of the individual's investments, it shifts the risk back to employees.[11] An employer-based pension system by necessity is primarily responsive to the imperatives of profit seeking by the firm, more than to the social welfare needs of American citizens and workers.

Another pillar of public policy for private benefits has been tax breaks. Not only has tax policy failed to compel more universal coverage but it deprives the public system of funds that could go into universal public schemes, into Social Security. First, according to Congressional Budget Office estimates, health insurance tax breaks amounted to $75 billion in forgone revenue per year in the mid-1990s. In the case of pensions, the government loses about $50 billion a year in potential revenue because tax savings are deferred. Yet less than half of the nation's workforce is covered by these pensions. Only 9 percent of the nation's retirement income comes from private pensions, while Social Security serves a majority of the population. Second, the tax code privileges employers: the tax subsidy only applies to the purchase of health insurance by an *employer,* denying such support to other groups, such as community-based groups not linked to employment. Third, those with the highest incomes reap more generous after-tax benefits. Thus, tax favoritism for company pension plans violates basic principles of tax equity and social utility.[12]

Neither private health insurance nor private pensions have moved closer to universal coverage; nor will they. Private health insurance has never covered more than 69.6 percent of the nonelderly population, and that percentage refers primarily to hospitalization coverage. Benefits for physicians' services have never covered more than 66 percent. The system represents a surrender—a political decision to allow 16 percent of the nonelderly population to be uninsured. In countries such as Canada, Germany, France, Australia, and Great Britain health insurance covers 99 percent of the whole population. These countries have found a way to make sure that everyone receives "all 'medically necessary' hospital and physicians services." Moreover, instead of expanding, health coverage in the United States has been steadily shrinking. During the 1980s the number of uninsured increased by 25 percent. At the end of the 1980s, 37 million Americans had no coverage. By the time President Clinton took office in 1993, 40 million Americans had no insurance, and after the failure of Clinton's Health Security Bill another 3 million Americans joined the uninsured. The number of uninsured dipped minimally in 1999 and 2000, but by 2001 it had climbed back up to 41 million. Not only has the number of uninsured Americans remained significantly high, even through periods of record economic growth, but more than half of the uninsured are year-round or full-time workers. In New York state 73 percent of the uninsured population have jobs.[13]

Regardless of the innovations in coverage and underwriting, cash-indemnity policies ascendant in the 1950s perpetuated the problems inherent in employment-based insurance. Workers lost coverage when they moved or lost their jobs. Variations in coverage persisted across economic sectors and geographic regions. Deductibles ranged from $100 to $500, depending on the employer's willingness at any particular time to pay for a more expensive policy. By the 1990s, families without group insurance found that they had to purchase policies with deductibles as high as $10,000 or $15,000. While employers in basic manufacturing were willing to make this accord with employees for a while, employers in more casual sectors often were not. Health insurance coverage grew more uneven within the working class during the 1960s. Coverage for working women, nonworking family members, and people of color has continued to lag behind that of white men. In 1980, 65 percent of working men received private health insurance through their jobs, while 49 percent of women received such coverage. Throughout the 1990s the number of uninsured women grew steadily, rising to 21.3 million by 1998. Among older workers (age 55–64) in the 1990s, working women with health problems were most likely to lack health insurance, and the decline in employer-provided insurance has been greatest for older women workers generally. It took until the end of the twentieth century for 50 percent of African Americans to receive private, employment-related health insurance, but they were still the group most likely to rely on public health insurance. About 42 percent of Latinos in the United States have employment-based coverage, but 37 percent have neither public nor private health insurance of any kind. The distribution of health coverage remained tied to the distribution of good jobs, and the distribution of good jobs has not changed sufficiently for women, African Americans, and Latinos. As long as labor markets remain segmented, private, employment-based social welfare will not compensate for those inequalities; it reinforces them.[14]

COBRA and HIPAA have, predictably, been a bust. Only one in five people eligible for COBRA have enrolled; at any one time COBRA extends coverage to about 4.5 million persons. Employers with fewer than 20 employees do not have to comply with it. HIPAA included no price controls on premiums, especially for those who needed to purchase individual coverage. So while insurers cannot deny coverage to persons with health problems, they can certainly charge them an extortionate rate. A report issued by the General Accounting Office in March 1998 determined that people who exercised their rights under the new law were often charged premiums ranging from 140 percent to 600 percent above the standard rate; in other words. premiums may be $10,000 to $15,000 a year or more. Insurers have also intimidated agents, telling them that they would not receive commissions for policies sold to individuals with medical problems.[15] Despite a new public policy, insurers have priced these people right out of the market, which is not surprising given that insurers profit by screening out undesirable risks.

The essential premises of welfare capitalism, then, still apply. Employee benefits in the private sector are terminated by layoff or dismissal. More than ever, welfare capitalism heightens the risk of leaving a job and the cost of being left out of the system. In sum, none of these policies makes the provision of social welfare benefits a general legal requirement binding on all employers. Instead, such programs remain what they have always been since the 1920s: employer-determined, voluntary bestowals by individual, profit-driven enterprises. Indeed, reviving the practices of early-twentieth-century welfare capitalism, employers have overwhelmingly returned to self-insurance, in part to avoid state premium taxes and state mandates for minimum benefits and in part as an anxious attempt to control escalating insurance costs. Self-insurance became a dominant form of private group coverage in the 1980s, a development that utterly fractured any project of sharing social risks broadly and moved private benefits even farther away from the solidarity principles of social insurance.[16] Americans have come to accept this link between insurance and employment as natural and immutable, and yet it was the result of specific historical struggles and of the persistent pattern of American industrial relations.

This firm-centered social welfare system is faltering. Yet these recent deteriorations are only more glaring symptoms of a health insurance system that was flawed from the very beginning. Under the terms of fee-for-service and cash-indemnity benefits the insurers created an unsustainable system. By the 1980s the two firms that pioneered group insurance and created cash-indemnity health insurance, Metropolitan and Equitable, found the financial strain to be so great as to threaten their viability. Briefly in the late 1980s both firms converted their group health insurance operations into HMO-style subsidiaries, offering service-based contracts and adopting some of the very mechanisms they had spurned in the 1940s. Still they could not survive, and both eventually sold their health interests to HMOs. At Equitable, the various health and pension schemes almost bankrupted the entire firm. Today, Equitable is out of the group insurance business entirely. Neither Equitable nor Metropolitan offers health coverage any longer. They have also reconverted from mutual companies back to stock companies.[17]

The HMOs that took over the market in the 1990s did not fill in the gaps left by the absence of national health insurance. The legislation of the 1970s left out crucial guarantees of standards. Senator Edward Kennedy originally demanded that if HMOs were to receive federal support, they would have to offer something better than the status quo; the law had to ensure that they would provide more services to more people. Kennedy tried to advance a bill that required HMOs to offer the full range of services of a national health plan, a national quality control committee, consumer review, and health education and service centers. He lost on all of these points. The HMOs that received the federal government's stamp of approval did not resemble the Kaiser Permanente system, or the Group Health Association of Washington, D.C., or the Group Health Cooperative of Puget Sound. Instead, policymakers took some of the ideas, extrapolated bits and pieces, and created a theoretical hybrid that unfortunately deviated in critical ways from the existing, "real-life" models. HEW allowed the new HMOs to equivocate on community rating. After 1976 HEW even waived community rating entirely "for the first four years." Fee-for-service groups were allowed to qualify as HMOs. And at numerous junctures, Congress and HEW reduced minimum standards and medical care requirements and yet increased federal aid. The new HMOs also engaged in reckless underpricing to squeeze out insurance competitors. As Lawrence Brown has argued, they allowed market-oriented, cost-containment goals to take precedence over development-oriented, social goals.[18] It was a policy concerned with fortifying employee benefits rather than expanding social rights.

The managed care revolution of the 1990s reorganized the delivery and financing of health care, a reorganization that organized labor forty years ago predicted would be necessary. But now, for-profit HMOs use the original design of the service plan to restrict medical services, augment executives' salaries, and divert resources away from patients to stockholders. When HMOs and managed care surfaced in the 1970s and proliferated in the 1980s the HMO concept appeared to the public to be an entirely new idea, and a rather disastrous and distasteful one at that. Yet the idea existed earlier, of course. In its original form, health reformers viewed it as a community organization in which consumers and their representative organizations had a voice in determining the economic and medical practices that would promote and maintain health. At that time its purpose was seen as being entirely contrary to that of a profit-making institution. When health insurance reformers first recommended group service plans in the early 1930s, they explicitly stated:

> The danger which physicians and dentists principally fear, namely that lay groups organized for profit will control medical practice is a real one. Such groups, they believe, will place the practitioner in subservient positions, will deny them proper equipment and professional opportunities, and or in other ways will prevent them from rendering service of a high quality or from receiving adequate compensation. Such groups add to the cost of service without contributing any essential element which cannot be provided equally well by non-profit professional or community groups. . . . *The Committee [on the Costs of Medical Care] believes that lay groups organized for profit have no legitimate place in the provision of this vital public service.*[19]

The original, progressive version of the HMO has been lost in its latest incarnation as a profit-making enterprise that promotes shareholders' dividends over just medical care. In the 1990s for-profit HMOs overtook nonprofit HMOs as the dominant force in managed care. The cost-cutting, intensive competition of corporations seeking large profits in health care has escalated the worst trends and problems of private insurance. For-profit HMOs also have been underpricing traditional group practice plans like Kaiser, thus undercutting the competitive conditions under which they could survive as progressive service-oriented plans. The aggressive expansion of for-profit HMOs forced the rest of the system to emulate their practices. Since 1997 Congress has even pushed Medicare and Medicaid to be more like private managed care. Yet ultimately, HMOs did not contain health care costs; medical inflation is back. Once a hopeful alternative, the for-profit managed care plans have obstructed any possibility for health security.[20]

A renewed sense of crisis about market-based health insurance and insecurity over employee benefits emerged in the early 1990s. When President Bill Clinton took office, he offered the last major new social policy initiative of the twentieth century: national health insurance. In 1993 it seemed that conditions were right for national health reform. After Harris Wofford's surprising victory in the 1991 Pennsylvania Senate race, in which he made universal health insurance a primary issue, health security gained a prominent place on the national political agenda. Leading congressional Democrats, such as Jay Rockefeller, of West Virginia, circulated versions of "play or pay," while Republicans, fearing that some type of reform was inevitable, patched together incremental incentives to modify private health markets. The traditional opposition seemed to weaken. Big business, increasingly burdened by uncompetitive health care costs, sought federal relief. The AMA, the most longstanding opponent to national health insurance, even presented its own plan for universally guaranteed health insurance. By the time President Clinton unveiled his health insurance program in September 1993, public support for federal reform stood at 59 percent. Just under one year later the grand health security project lay in ruin.

Here was the most important opportunity in a generation to overcome the failures of the fragmented, employment-based social welfare system, and yet Clinton remained rhetorically and programmatically trapped by it. Although welfare state policies are supposed to compensate for the inequalities of the market, Bill Clinton promoted his most important social policy initiative in market terms, as "guaranteed private insurance." He devised rhetorical contortions to obscure the actual government role in his health security plan. By speaking as if his plan relied solely on competition in the marketplace, Clinton helped delegitimize the very foundation and rationale for national health reform and guaranteed security. Clinton should have buttressed the public's confidence in the public sector and defended the role of government in promoting social justice and economic security. At stake was a fundamental element of the New Deal: economic security as a legitimate responsibility of the government. The Republicans certainly recognized what was at stake and openly attacked this principle relentlessly.[21]

At the same time, as advocates of single-payer plans pointed out, the Clinton plan still relied on the employer-based system of health insurance, the very structure that had left so many uninsured or underinsured. Despite "subsidies" for the unemployed and "the poor," it was not clear whether managed competition would cover Americans whose links to the labor force were irregular: the underemployed, the seasonally employed, those looking for work, or those doing care work at home. Nor was it clear whether the undefined "subsidies" for the unemployed would apply only to those who qualify for unemployment compensation, whereas most of the people who work in low-wage labor markets, especially women and minorities, rarely qualify for unemployment benefits. The Clinton health plan would not have overcome the systematic racial and gender biases of the existing employment-based health insurance system.

Because the Clinton plan did not challenge the traditional linkage between benefits and jobs, the same struggle over employers' inclusion in, or exemption from, the legislated plan played out again. As in the 1930s, the 1940s, and the 1950s, the fate of social welfare policy was linked to the balance of power in the political economy. Historically, the United States has deferred to employers when it came to benefits for able-bodied Americans, and these political choices have buttressed low-wage labor markets. Low-wage firms did not have to pay into a public health plan, but neither did they have to pay for private benefit plans. If they chose, they could either shift the costs of sickness, medical needs, and temporary disability onto others (for example, having other firms pick up the costs through family coverage) or simply leave people out. By the end of the twentieth century large, relatively higher-wage companies or unionized companies were no longer willing to carry that burden. The question, however, was whether they had the political power to compel cost-shifting employers or small employers to "play or pay" while at the same time exempting their own firms from public oversight (either through ERISA exemptions or through Clinton plan exemptions for firms with more than 5,000 employees). They did not. Hence, during the legislative markup period in 1994, exemptions widened at the bottom (to include firms with fewer than 100 employees), cost shifting therefore increased, and finally, some congressmen even put the curbing of ERISA waivers on the table. To whom were legislators listening? Most visibly, the National Federation of Independent Business (NFIB) had successfully mobilized their small business members and organized an overwhelming activist opposition campaign. Yet behind the scenes House Republicans such as Dennis Hastert, of Illinois, were meeting with companies like Pizza Hut, Pepsico, the Marriot Corporation, and Wal-Mart,[22] service-based or labor-intensive firms that rely heavily on part-time work and low wages and that represent a much larger segment of the economy than in the 1940s or 1960s. These companies, determined to keep their workforces insulated from outside forces that might drive up labor's compensation, were unalterably opposed to employer mandates and government intervention. The NFIB had considerable clout because it also reflected the opinion of very large players like Pepsico, companies who had the power to neither play nor pay. The NFIB had become a stand-in for the new power in the economy: large, nonunionized firms that undermine the social wage established by the New Dealers and organized labor at midcentury.

Finally, the ideology of supplementation had devolved back to the ideal of the market. Clinton pitched his message toward consumers rather than toward citizens. As Clinton tried to assuage an imagined middle class, Americans were imagined as consumers of health services rather than as citizens contributing to a system of shared savings. This market construct could only undermine social solidarity, for defined as consumers, individuals thought in terms of individual gain or loss. The Clinton Democrats were incapable of framing health care as a public good, and economic security as a social project. Instead, they emphasized maximizing the consumer dollar, purchasing health insurance or health care as one would purchase any other commodity in the market. But health care is not just another commodity; a person with pneumonia needs treatment regardless of his or her margin of disposable income.[23] Clinton's policymakers and advisers showed utter disregard for the basic principle of the Social Security program: it is a system of shared responsibility and social solidarity. Although Clinton used the term *security,* it had absolutely no political content; its meaning had been entirely eviscerated. Consequently, the Clinton Democrats helped open the way for Social Security to be put on the privatization chopping block as well.

And in fact, soon after the demise of health security, Social Security became the next subject for "reform," although all of the proposals for reform involved partial, if not full, privatization. The idea that Social Security *must* in some way be privatized has become a mainstream position. Under President George W. Bush, former Democratic Senator Daniel Patrick Moynihan presides over the president's euphemistically titled Commission to Strengthen Social Security, a group that backs the president's official call for privatization. Secretary of the Treasury Paul O'Neill, formerly the chief executive officer of ALCOA, has made public appearances before groups such as the Coalition for American Financial Security, a financial services industry group that has been eagerly hanging on to his promises to carve out private investment accounts from Social Security. Indeed, O'Neill has questioned why we need any public social insurance programs at all. "Able-bodied adults should save enough on a regular basis," asserted O'Neill, "so that they can provide for their own retirement and for that matter for their health and medical needs."[24]

Given that the Social Security System is sound, that it has successfully kept the elderly population out of poverty, and that it has improved the standard of living for those who do not have to support aging parents or grandparents, we need to recognize that these jeremiads and privatization proposals represent an attempt to transform the meaning, the definition, of security, of social security. Social Security is a social project that we all participate in to make sure that everyone has a minimum, decent standard of living when they can no longer work. By recasting it in terms of how much money each individual could theoretically make in his or her own investment account, the privatizers throw the idea of security in old age back onto the fortunes of the individual, removing not only the "social" from "social security" but the "security" as well. Incredibly, the first privatization bill marked up by the House of Representatives in July 2001 entailed both increases in payroll taxes and cuts in benefits. Clearly, this is no less than an assault on the notion of public, shared, collective security, cloaked in terms of "fiscal realism" and demographic inevitabilities.

Similar inevitability arguments are being used to undermine security at work. We are told that downsizing and layoffs, wage stagnation, and reduction of health benefits are the inevitable consequences of the inexorable globalization of the economy; employers have to break their social contract with employees if they are to compete. The New Capitalism equals the End of History.

It is the political choices that historical actors make, however, and the political struggles that ensue that determine the outcomes. There was no "implicit" social contract between firms and workers that has suddenly broken down. It took political pressure to compel business firms to assume a share of the social security burden for their workers. Business firms increase their commitment to corporate social welfare programs when the government is expanding its role in social welfare and labor relations. When the state recedes from involvement, business has the political and ideological space to reduce its commitment as well. Public and private security are unraveling together.

For a few decades of the postwar era, business acknowledged the political legitimacy of security, although it tried to dislodge its connections to politics. A new generation of conservatives and opponents of the New Deal have delegitimized even the idea of security. Since the 1960s, free-market conservatives have tirelessly circulated the idea that if freedom is the fundamental principle of American citizenship, then security cannot be a facet of citizenship as well: they are ideological antitheses. As William F. Buckley wrote in *Up From Liberalism* in 1959, "Security does not equal freedom." Here Buckley spelled out the agenda for a New Conservatism: "If the people announce that they feel freer by virtue of the securities extended by the welfare state, we must be prepared to concede what they authoritatively tell us about their state of mind—yet insist, doggedly, that we strive after an objectively free society."[25] By the 1980s the new conservatives had managed to invert the New Deal era's meaning of security. In our contemporary political discourse, security conflicts with economic growth and economic opportunity. Security is literally equated with the term *personal responsibility* (the name attached to both the revocation of AFDC and recent Social Security privatization proposals)—with the clear ideological message that this means personal responsibility to oneself only. The essence of American citizenship, as opponents of the welfare state and the New Deal's ordering of political economy conceive of it, is the privilege to participate in unfettered market relations and face economic risks on one's own.

Welfare states protect citizens from the risks and insecurity of market forces and offset the inequalities generated by labor markets. In the United States, the basic welfare state, anchored by the Social Security Act, does have a redistributive aspect that gives a greater return to low-income wage earners than they would be able to obtain on their own. Yet because of the essential design of the Social Security Act, the American welfare state also reinforces the inequalities of labor market segmentation. Private supplementation follows in the same mold. Private benefits were supposed to be supplementary to the welfare state—a welfare state that held central political legitimacy from the 1930s through the 1960s. The theory of supplementation was a political and social rationale for private benefits. It also had the effect of limiting the growth of public social welfare. The more American politicians and business leaders defined public security benefits as supplementable, the more the rhetoric of supplementation ceded legitimacy back to the private sector. The efforts of both policymakers and labor leaders became increasingly focused on improving and protecting private security.

Now the dominant political discourse sees the welfare state only as a net drain on individual resources, money that could be maximized in individual investment accounts. The political and economic enfranchisement of the working class in the 1930s and 1940s enabled Americans to force the polity to guarantee a decent standard of living. Society as a whole could and would provide security against the economic difficulties of old age, unemployment, death of a breadwinner, or disability. An individual's political citizenship would be linked to social responsibility and social entitlements; profit-seeking enterprises were legitimate only insofar as they participated in this web of social obligations. Freedom and security, work and welfare, were compatible ideas, not competing ones. The politics of security was an attempt by labor and social progressives to make a just claim, a *social* claim, on the economic resources of the nation. We need to reclaim the language of economic dissent—of just alternatives to "the market"—that makes progressive changes possible.

Notes

In citing works in the notes, short titles are generally used after the first, full citation in a chapter. Works frequently cited are identified by the following abbreviations:

Addes Papers	UAW Secretary-Treasurer's Office Collection/George Addes Files, WPR
Cohen Papers	Wilbur J. Cohen Papers, 1930–1987, Mss 789, State Historical Society of Wisconsin, Madison
Cruikshank Papers	Nelson Cruikshank Papers, M66–15, State Historical Society of Wisconsin, Madison
ELAS	Equitable Life Assurance Society of the United States
ELAS Archives	Equitable Life Assurance Society of the United States Archives, New York
Graham Papers	William J. Graham Papers, acc. 1984-050, RG 4, Historical Collection, ELAS Archives
Harrington Papers	Willis Harrington Papers, acc. 1813, E. I. DuPont de Nemours & Company Records, HML
HML	Hagley Museum and Library, Wilmington, Delaware
IUE Records	Records of the International Union of Electrical, Radio, and Machine Workers, Special Collections and University Archives, Rutgers University, New Brunswick, New Jersey
MLIC	Metropolitan Life Insurance Company
MLIC Archives	Metropolitan Life Insurance Company Archives, New York
NA-DC	National Archives, Washington, D.C.
NAM Records	National Association of Manufacturers Records, HML
Rosenfeld Papers	Henry Rosenfeld Papers, acc. 1984-050, RG 4, Historical Collection, ELAS Archives
Saul Mills Papers	Saul Mills Papers, W 75, ser. 2, Robert F. Wagner Labor Archives, Tamiment Institute Library, New York University
SSB Records	Records of the Social Security Board, RG 47, National Archives, College Park, Maryland
Thorne Papers	Florence Thorne / Director of Research Papers, Mss 117A, Records of the American Federation of Labor, State Historical Society of Wisconsin, Madison
UAW SSD	United Automobile Workers Social Security Department Collection, acc. 317, pt. 2, WPR
WPR	Walter P. Reuther Library of Labor and Urban Affairs, Wayne State University, Detroit, Michigan

Introduction

1. *New York Times,* 20 Jan. 2002, sec. 3, p. 7.

2. *Houston Chronicle,* 18, 19 Dec. 2001; ibid., 4 Dec. 2001, letters. Under Enron's retirement savings program the company would only match employee contributions with Enron stock. Moreover, Enron set up an incentive structure that encouraged employees to put their own contributions into company stock (see *New York Times,* 20 Jan. 2002).

3. *New York Times,* 14, 20 Jan. 2002; *Christian Science Monitor,* 19 Dec. 2001.

4. Generally, the historical work on welfare capitalism fixes this phenomenon in time, seeing it as one point along a modernization trajectory. According to such interpretations, welfare capitalist programs proliferated among large employers during the 1910s and 1920s but collapsed during the Great Depression. The modern welfare state supplanted premodern welfare capitalism (see, e.g., Stuart Brandes, *American Welfare Capitalism, 1880–1940* [Chicago: University of Chicago Press, 1976]; David Brody, "The Rise and Decline of Welfare Capitalism," in *Workers in Industrial America: Essays on the Twentieth Century Struggle,* 2d ed. [New York: Oxford University Press, 1993]; Irving Bernstein, *The Lean Years: A History of the American Worker, 1920–1933* [Boston: Houghton Mifflin, 1960], 144–88; Roy Lubove, *The Struggle for Social Security, 1900–1935* [Cambridge: Harvard University Press, 1968]; James Patterson, *America's Struggle against Poverty, 1900–1994,* 3d ed. [Cambridge: Harvard University Press, 1994]; and Lizabeth Cohen, *Making a New Deal: Industrial Workers in Chicago, 1919–1939* [(New York: Cambridge University Press, 1990]). More recently, Sanford Jacoby and Elizabeth Fones-Wolf have shown how welfare capitalism flourished after the New Deal and World War II (Sanford M. Jacoby, *Modern Manors: Welfare Capitalism since the New Deal* [Princeton: Princeton University Press, 1997]; Elizabeth Fones-Wolf, *Selling Free Enterprise: The Business Assault on Labor and Liberalism, 1945–1960* [Urbana: University of Illinois Press, 1994]). Andrea Tone, whose book covers the Progressive Era and ends in the 1920s, argues similarly that welfare capitalism needs to be seen as a political strategy to counter state expansion (Andrea Tone, *The Business of Benevolence: Industrial Paternalism in Progressive America* [Ithaca: Cornell University Press, 1997]).

5. U.S. Congress, House, Committee on Ways and Means, *Overview of Entitlement Programs: 1994 Greenbook,* 103d Cong., 2d sess., 15 July 1994, 295; "Employer Spending on Benefits, 2000," *www.ebri.org/facts/0402bfact.*

6. This history of the private welfare state builds on the groundwork of Beth Stevens, Edward Berkowitz, and Kim McQuaid and joins the new work of Marie Gottschalk and Steven Sass. See Beth Stevens, *Complementing the Welfare State: The Development of Private Pensions, Health Insurance, and Other Employee Benefits in the United States,* Labour-Management Relations Series, 65 (Geneva: International Labour Organisation, 1986); Edward D. Berkowitz and Kim McQuaid, *Creating the Welfare State: The Political Economy of Twentieth Century Reform,* 2d ed. (New York: Praeger, 1988); Marie Gottschalk, *The Shadow Welfare State: Labor, Business, and the Politics of Health Care in the United States* (Ithaca: ILR Press, Cornell University Press, 2000); and Steven A. Sass, *The Promise of Private Pensions: The First Hundred Years* (Cambridge: Harvard University Press, 1997).

7. Jacoby, *Modern Manors.*

8. Cohen, *Making a New Deal*; Nelson Lichtenstein, *The Most Dangerous Man in Detroit: Walter Reuther and the Fate of American Labor* (New York: Basic Books, 1995); Gail Radford, *Modern Housing for America: Policy Struggles in the New Deal Era* (Chicago: University of Chicago Press, 1996); Landon R. Y. Storrs, *Civilizing Capitalism: National Consumers' League, Women's Activism, and Labor Standards in the New Deal Era* (Chapel Hill: University of North Carolina Press, 2000).

9. Thomas Spates, "The Competition for Leadership in a Welfare Economy," address to the Personnel Conference, American Management Association, Chicago, 15 Feb. 1949, box 18, acc. 1412, NAM Records.

10. Izzet Sahin, *Private Pensions and Employee Mobility: A Comprehensive Approach to Pension Policy* (New York: Quorum Books, 1989), 1; Health Insurance Association of America, *Source Book of Health Insurance Data, 1980–1981* (Washington, D.C.: Health Insurance Institute, [1981]).

11. Judith Stein, *Running Steel, Running America: Race, Economic Policy, and the Decline of Liberalism* (Chapel Hill: University of North Carolina Press, 1998), 311; Lichtenstein, *Most Dangerous Man in Detroit*; David Plotke, *Building a Democratic Political Order: Reshaping American Liberalism in the 1930s and 1940s* (New York: Cambridge University Press, 1996).

12. Gary Gerstle has shown how the term *Americanism* functioned "as a political language, a set of words, phrases, and concepts that individuals used—either by choice or necessity to articulate their political beliefs and press their political demands." Those who controlled this language could gain "an advantage in their bid for power" (Gary Gerstle, *Working-Class Americanism: The Politics of Labor in a Textile City, 1914–1960* [New York: Cambridge University Press, 1989], 8, 14; see also Robert Reich, ed., *The Power of Pubic Ideas* [Cambridge, Mass.: Ballinger, 1988], esp. "Beyond Self-Interest," by Garry Orren, 13–30, and "What Sort of Ideas Become Public Ideas?" by Mark H. Moore, 55–84).

13. *Annual Report of the Social Security Board, Letter from the Social Security Board Transmitting First Annual Report of the Social Security Board for the Fiscal Year Ended June 30, 1936* (Washington, D.C.: Government Printing Office, 1937), foreword.

14. U.S. Congress, Senate, Committee on Labor and Public Welfare, *Welfare and Pension Plans Investigation: Final Report Submitted to the Committee on Labor and Public Welfare by Its Subcommittee on Welfare and Pension Funds Pursuant to S. Res. 40 as Extended by S. Res. 200 and S. Res. 232*, 84th Cong., 2d sess., 16 Apr. 1956, 7, 158–59.

15. Nelson Lichtenstein, "Great Expectations: The Promise of Industrial Jurisprudence and Its Demise, 1930–1960," in *Industrial Democracy in America: The Ambiguous Promise*, ed. Nelson Lichtenstein and Howell John Harris, Woodrow Wilson Center Series (New York: Cambridge University Press, 1993), 115–40; James B. Atleson, "Wartime Labor Regulation, the Industrial Pluralists, and the Law of Collective Bargaining," in ibid., 142–75; Katherine Van Wezel Stone, "The Post-War Paradigm in American Labor Law," *Yale Law Journal* 90 (June 1981); Lichtenstein, *Most Dangerous Man in Detroit*, chap. 13; David L. Stebenne, *Arthur J. Goldberg: New Deal Liberal* (New York: Oxford University Press, 1996); Mike Davis, *Prisoners of the American Dream* (London: Verso, 1986).

16. See, e.g., Robert H. Zieger, *American Workers, American Unions*, 2d ed.

(Baltimore: Johns Hopkins University Press, 1994), chap. 5; idem, *The CIO, 1935–1955* (Chapel Hill: University of North Carolina Press, 1995); and Beth Stevens, "Labor Unions, Employee Benefits, and the Privatization of the American Welfare State," *Journal of Policy History* 2, no. 3 (1990): 233–60.

17. Elizabeth Faue, *Community of Suffering and Struggle: Women, Men, and the Labor Movement in Minneapolis, 1915–1945* (Chapel Hill: University of North Carolina Press, 1991); Annelise Orleck, *Common Sense and a Little Fire: Women and Working-Class Politics in the United States, 1915–1945* (Chapel Hill: University of North Carolina Press, 1995), chaps. 5–6; Joshua B. Freeman, *Working-Class New York* (New York: New Press, 2000).

18. On social citizenship, see T. H. Marshall, *Class, Citizenship, and Social Development: Essays by T. H. Marshall*, ed. Seymour Martin Lipset, 3d ed. (New York: Anchor Books, 1965); and Nancy Fraser and Linda Gordon, "Contract versus Charity: Why Is There No Social Citizenship in the U.S.?" *Socialist Review* 92, no. 3 (1992): 45–67.

19. Theda Skocpol and John Ikenberry, "The Political Formation of the American Welfare State in Historical and Comparative Perspective," *Comparative Social Research* 6 (1983): 92–119; Theda Skocpol, "Bringing the State Back In: Strategies of Analysis in Current Research," in *Bringing the State Back In*, ed. Peter Evans, Dietrich Rueschmeyer, and Theda Skocpol (New York: Cambridge University Press, 1985), 3–37; Ann Shola Orloff, "The Political Origins of America's Belated Welfare State," in *The Politics of Social Policy in the United States*, ed. Margaret Weir, Ann Shola Orloff, and Theda Skocpol (Princeton: Princeton University Press, 1988); Theda Skocpol, "The Limits of the New Deal System and the Roots of Contemporary Welfare Dilemmas," ibid.; Sven Steinmo and Jon Watts, "It's the Institutions Stupid! Why Comprehensive National Health Insurance Always Fails in America," *Journal of Health Politics, Policy, and Law* 20, no. 2 (1995): 329–72. See also Linda Gordon's critique, "Gender, State, and Society: A Debate with Theda Skocpol," *Contention* 2, no. 3 (spring 1993).

20. Jill Quadagno, *The Transformation of Old Age Security: Class and Politics in the American Welfare State* (Chicago: University of Chicago Press, 1988); Gosta Esping-Andersen, *The Three Worlds of Welfare Capitalism* (Princeton: Princeton University Press, 1990); Martin Rein and Lee Rainwater, "From Welfare State to Welfare Society," in *The Rise and Fall of Policy Regimes*, ed. Martin Rein, Gosta Esping-Andersen, and Lee Rainwater (Armonk, N.Y.: Sharpe, 1987).

21. Margaret Weir, Ann Shola Orloff, and Theda Skocpol, "Introduction: Understanding American Social Politics," in Weir, Orloff, and Skocpol, *The Politics of Social Policy in the United States*, 3–16; Colin Gordon, *New Deals: Business, Labor, and Politics in America, 1920–1935* (New York: Cambridge University Press, 1994); Cathie Jo Martin, *Stuck in Neutral: Business and the Politics of Human Capital Investment Policy* (Princeton: Princeton University Press, 2000).

22. Linda Gordon, *Pitied But Not Entitled: Single Mothers and the History of Welfare* (Cambridge: Harvard University Press, 1994); Eileen Boris, *Home to Work: Motherhood and the Politics of Industrial Homework in the United States* (New York: Cambridge University Press, 1994), 7; Kathryn Kish Sklar, *Florence Kelley and the Nation's Work* (New Haven: Yale University Press, 1995); Gwendolyn Mink, *The Wages of Motherhood: Maternalist Social Policy and Women's Inequality in the Welfare*

State, 1917–1942 (Ithaca: Cornell University Press, 1995); Suzanne Mettler, *Dividing Citizens: Gender and Federalism in New Deal Public Policy* (Ithaca: Cornell University Press, 1998); Alice Kessler-Harris, "Designing Women and Old Fools: The Construction of the Social Security Amendments of 1939," in *U.S. History as Women's History*, ed. Linda K. Kerber, Alice Kessler-Harris, and Kathryn Kish Sklar (Chapel Hill: University of North Carolina Press, 1995), 87–106; Michael K. Brown, *Race, Money, and the American Welfare State* (Ithaca: Cornell University Press, 1999); Robert C. Lieberman, *Shifting the Color Line: Race and the American Welfare State* (Cambridge: Harvard University Press, 1998).

23. Esping-Andersen, *Three Worlds of Welfare Capitalism*, 16; Gottschalk, *The Shadow Welfare State.*

24. For some of this literature, see Quadagno, *Transformation of Old Age Security*; Gordon, *New Deals*, chaps. 7–8; Alan Dawley, review of *New Deals*, by Colin Gordon, *International Labor and Working Class History* 50 (fall 1995): 219–21; Berkowitz and McQuaid, *Creating the Welfare State*; and Edward D. Berkowitz, *America's Welfare State: From Roosevelt to Reagan* (Baltimore: Johns Hopkins University Press, 1991).

25. There is an extensive literature on health insurance issues representing a variety of perspectives. The most comprehensive history of medical care and medical policy is Paul Starr, *The Social Transformation of American Medicine: The Rise of a Sovereign Profession and the Making of a Vast Industry* (New York: Basic Books, 1982). On labor and health insurance, see Raymond Munts, *Bargaining for Health: Labor Unions, Health Insurance, and Medical Care* (Madison: University of Wisconsin Press, 1967); Alan Derickson, "The United Steelworkers of America and Health Insurance, 1937–1962," in *American Labor in the Era of World War II*, ed. Sally M. Miller and Daniel A. Cormford (Westport, Conn.: Praeger, 1995), 69–85; Gerald Markowitz and David Rosner, "Seeking Common Ground: A History of Labor and Blue Cross," in *Between Public and Private: A Half Century of Blue Cross and Blue Shield in New York*, special issue of *Journal of Health Politics, Policy, and Law* 16, no. 4 (1991): 695–718; and Ivana Krajcinovic, *From Company Doctors to Managed Care: The United Mine Workers' Noble Experiment* (Ithaca: ILR Press, Cornell University Press, 1997). On particular programs, see Sylvia A. Law, *Blue Cross: What Went Wrong?* (New Haven: Yale University Press, 1974); Rickey Hendricks, *A Model for National Health Care: The History of Kaiser Permanente* (New Brunswick, N.J.: Rutgers University Press, 1993); *Between Public and Private: A Half Century of Blue Cross and Blue Shield in New York*, special issue of *Journal of Health Politics, Policy, and Law* 16, no. 4 (1991); and Freeman, *Working-Class New York*, chap. 7, on the Health Insurance Plan of New York.

26. See Alan Derickson, "Health Security for All? Social Unionism and Universal Health Insurance, 1935–1958," *Journal of American History* 80 (Mar. 1994): 1333–56; and Stevens, "Labor Unions, Employee Benefits."

27. For some of the literature on the history of health insurance policy, see, e.g., Daniel Hirshfield, *The Lost Reform: The Campaign for Compulsory Health Insurance in the United States from 1932 to 1943* (Cambridge: Harvard University Press, 1970); Ronald L. Numbers, ed., *Compulsory Health Insurance: The Continuing American Debate* (Westport, Conn.: Greenwood Press, 1982); Daniel M. Fox, *Health Policies, Health Politics: The British and American Experience, 1911–1965*

(Princeton: Princeton University Press, 1986); James A. Morone and Gary S. Belkin, eds., *The Politics of Health Care Reform: Lessons from the Past, Prospects for the Future* (Durham, N.C.: Duke University Press, 1994); Theodore R. Marmor, *The Politics of Medicare*, 2d ed. (New York: Aldine De Gruyter, 2000); Colin Gordon, "Why No National Health Insurance in the U.S.? The Limits of Social Provision in War and Peace, 1941–1948," *Journal of Policy History* 9, no. 3 (1997): 277–310; Michael R. Grey, *New Deal Medicine: The Rural Health Programs of the Farm Security Administration* (Baltimore: Johns Hopkins University Press, 1999); and Beatrix Hoffman, *The Wages of Sickness: The Politics of Health Insurance in Progressive America* (Chapel Hill: University of North Carolina Press, 2001).

28. W. A. Milliman, quoted in *Eastern Underwriter*, 17 May 1940.

29. U.S. Congress, Senate, Committee on Labor and Public Welfare, *Health Insurance Plans in the United States*, 82d Cong., 1st sess., 1951, S. Rept. 359; Deborah A. Stone, "The Struggle for the Soul of Health Insurance," in Morone and Belkin, *Politics of Health Care Reform*, 33–39.

30. Sahin, *Private Pensions and Employee Mobility*; William Glaser, *Health Insurance Plans in Practice: International Variations in Financing, Benefits, and Problems* (San Francisco: Jossey-Bass, 1991).

31. *New York Times*, 14 Jan. 2002, A12.

Chapter 1
Mass Marketing Private Insurance

1. Stuart Brandes, *American Welfare Capitalism, 1880–1940* (Chicago: University of Chicago Press, 1976); Daniel Nelson, *Managers and Workers: Origins of the New Factory System in the United States, 1880–1920* (Madison: University of Wisconsin Press, 1975), chap. 6; David Brody, "The Rise and Fall of Welfare Capitalism," in *Workers in Industrial America: Essays on the Twentieth Century Struggle*, 2d ed. (New York: Oxford University Press, 1993), 48–81; Gerald Zahavi, "Negotiated Loyalty: Welfare Capitalism and the Shoeworkers of Endicott Johnson, 1920–1940," *Journal of American History* 70 (Dec. 1983): 602–20. Zahavi argues that welfare capitalism established a compact between management and worker based on mutual loyalties, expectations, and obligations.

2. Nelson Lichtenstein and Howell John Harris, eds., *Industrial Democracy in America: The Ambiguous Promise*, Woodrow Wilson Center Series (New York: Cambridge University Press, 1993), chap. 1; Steven Fraser, "The Labor Question," in *The Rise and Fall of the New Deal Order*, ed. Steven Fraser and Gary Gerstle (Princeton: Princeton University Press, 1989), 55–84.

3. Mary Van Kleeck, quoted in Guy Alchon, *The Invisible Hand of Planning: Capitalism, Social Science, and the State in the 1920s* (Princeton: Princeton University Press, 1985), 44.

4. R. Carlyle Buley, *The Equitable Life Assurance Society of the United States, 1859–1964*, 2 vols. (New York: ELAS, 1967), vols. 1, chap. 7, and 2, chap. 8; Morton Keller, *The Life Insurance Enterprise, 1885–1910: A Study of the Limits of Corporate Power* (Cambridge: Harvard University Press, Belknap Press, 1963), chap. 25.

5. Equitable thereafter published public reports on its finances. The com-

pany divested itself of bank and trust holdings. Morton then launched Equitable on the process of mutualization, dissolving the large stock holdings and drafting a constitution that turned all policyholders into shareholders.

6. Roy Lubove, *The Struggle for Social Security, 1900–1935* (Cambridge: Harvard University Press, 1968), 29–44; Ann Shola Orloff, "The Political Origins of America's Belated Welfare State," in *The Politics of Social Policy in the United States*, ed. Margaret Weir, Ann Shola Orloff, and Theda Skocpol (Princeton: Princeton University Press, 1988), 37–80.

7. Hugh Heclo, *Modern Social Politics in Britain and Sweden: From Relief to Maintenance* (New Haven: Yale University Press, 1974), 78–92; Theda Skocpol and Gretchen Ritter, "Gender and the Origins of Modern Social Policies in Britain and the United States," *Studies in American Political Development* 5 (spring 1991): 36–93; Lubove, *Struggle for Social Security*.

8. Henry Rosenfeld to President William Day, 6 Sept. 1915, file 7, box 58A, Rosenfeld Papers; Paul Morton, speech, 26 July 1909, file 10, ibid.; Buley, *Equitable Life Assurance Society*, 2:756.

9. F. C. Schwedtman to Rosenfeld, 29 June 1910, file 8, box 58A, Rosenfeld Papers; Minutes of the Committee on Insurance meeting, 3 Apr. 1911, and Report of the Committee, 20 Apr. 1911, file 7, ibid.

10. Robert Asher, "Failure and Fulfillment: Agitation for Employers' Liability Legislation and the Origins of Workmen's Compensation in New York State, 1876–1910," *Labor History* 24 (spring 1983): 198–222; Karen Orren, *Belated Feudalism: Labor, the Law, and Liberal Development in the United States* (New York: Cambridge University Press, 1991), 110–11; Julian Go III, "Inventing Industrial Accidents and Their Insurance: Discourse and Workers' Compensation in the United States, 1880s–1910s," *Social Science History* 20 (fall 1996): 409–11.

11. Go, "Inventing Industrial Accidents," 409–10.

12. Schwedtman to Rosenfeld, 14 Mar. 1911, file 8, box 58A, Rosenfeld Papers.

13. Historians generally agree that by 1910 business supported workers' compensation laws (see Robert Asher, "Workmen's Compensation in the United States, 1880–1935" [Ph.D. diss., University of Michigan, 1971]; idem, "Failure and Fulfillment"; Lubove, *Struggle for Social Security*, chap. 3; Edward D. Berkowitz and Kim McQuaid, *Creating the Welfare State: The Political Economy of Twentieth Century Reform*, 2d ed. [New York: Praeger, 1988], 43–51; and Go, "Inventing Industrial Accidents").

14. Schwedtman to Rosenfeld, 14 Mar. 1911.

15. William Day, "Group Insurance—Its Aims and Its Field," address to the annual meeting of the Association of Life Insurance Presidents, New York, 11 Dec. 1913, file 10, box 58A, Rosenfeld Papers.

16. Henry Rosenfeld, "Cooperation and Compensation versus Compulsion and Compromise in Employers' Liability," address at the annual meeting of the NAM, 17 May 1910, file 7, ibid.

17. Illinois and Missouri had both passed workers' compensation laws in 1910.

18. Henry Rosenfeld, "Memorandum for the President, In re: Montgomery Ward Group Insurance," 17 Apr. 1912, file 7, box 58A, Rosenfeld Papers; Re-

port of the Committee, 20 Apr. 1911; Buley, *Equitable Life Assurance Society*, 2:776–85.

19. Montgomery Ward & Co. Inc., *Announcement of Insurance Plan of Montgomery Ward & Co*, 1912; idem, *Regulations of the Insurance Division of Montgomery Ward & Co. Inc.*, 4 Dec. 1918; ELAS, *Montgomery Ward: Statement of Benefits*, n.d.; and Joseph Zook, to William J. Graham, 12 Nov. 1918, all in file 12, box 58A, Rosenfeld Papers.

20. Henry Rosenfeld, "Group Insurance," 24 July 1913, file 4, ibid.; idem, "Memorandum for the President," 18 Apr. 1912, file 9, ibid.; Rosenfeld to the Agency Force of the Society, 1 Apr. 1918, file 8, ibid.; John Rousmaniere, *The Life and Times of the Equitable* (New York: Equitable Companies, 1995), 130.

21. Day, "Group Insurance—Its Aims and Its Field"; Henry Rosenfeld, "Life Insurance as a Factor in the Solution of Sociological Problems," 1912, file 9, box 58A, Rosenfeld Papers; Department of Group Insurance, ELAS, *Suggestions for Selling Group Insurance* (New York: ELAS, 1921), file 4, box 55C, Publicity and Sales Material—Group, acc. 1984-050, RG 4, ELAS Archives; "Nationally Known Members of the Equitable Group Family," 1922, file 3, ibid.; Angel Kwolek-Folland, "Gender, Self, and Work in the Life Insurance Industry, 1880–1930," in *Work Engendered: Toward a New History of American Labor*, ed. Ava Baron (Ithaca: Cornell University Press, 1991), 168–90. Kowlek-Folland uses the term *corporate motherhood* to describe the life insurance industry's use of images of family protection, motherhood, and children as part of sales and public relations strategies for life insurance. See also Andrea Tone, *The Business of Benevolence: Industrial Paternalism in Progressive America* (Ithaca: Cornell University Press, 1997), 141–71.

22. *Annual Dividends or Refunds Paid By the Equitable Life Assurance Society* (New York: ELAS, 1924), file 3, box 55C, Publicity and Sales Material—Group, acc. 1984-050, RG 4, ELAS Archives; *General Summary of Group Insurance Rules and Procedure* (New York: ELAS, n.d.), file 8, box 58A, Rosenfeld Papers.

23. Joseph A. McCartin, *Labor's Great War: The Struggle for Industrial Democracy and the Origins of Modern American Labor Relations, 1912–1921* (Chapel Hill: University of North Carolina Press, 1997); Brody, "Rise and Fall of Welfare Capitalism."

24. Jill Quadagno, *The Transformation of Old Age Security: Class and Politics in the American Welfare State* (Chicago: University of Chicago Press, 1988). The *National Underwriter* reported on 21 December 1923 that the New York State Federation of Labor had castigated group insurance as mere "paper protection." All citations of the *National Underwriter* are to the Life Insurance edition.

25. Quotation from testimony of William Day, in U.S. Department of Labor, Bureau of Labor Statistics, *Proceedings of the Conference on Social Insurance, Dec. 5–9, 1916* (Washington, D.C.: Government Printing Office, 1917), 421. See also "Equitable Life to Engage in Health and Accident," *Eastern Underwriter*, 16 Aug. 1918; *Group Accident and Health Insurance Protects the Pay Envelope*, n.d., file 6, box 55C, Publicity and Sales Material—Group, acc. 1984-050, RG 4, ELAS Archives; NICB, *Industrial Group Insurance* (New York, 1927); and Beatrix Hoffman, *The Wages of Sickness: The Politics of Health Insurance in Progressive America* (Chapel Hill: University of North Carolina Press, 2001), 29, 106–13.

26. "Nationally Known Members of the Equitable Group Family"; *Annual Dividends or Refunds Paid by the Equitable Life Assurance Society*; "Low Cost Results on Groups One to Fourteen Years in Force under the Equitable Merit Rating Plan," Dec. 1927, file 6, box 55C, Publicity and Sales Material—Group, acc. 1984-050, RG 4, ELAS Archives; Buley, *Equitable Life Assurance Society*, 2:795–96; Rousmaniere, *Life and Times of the Equitable*, 131–32.

27. Olivier Zunz, *Making America Corporate, 1870–1920* (Chicago: University of Chicago Press, 1990), 92–97; Louis I. Dublin, *A Family of Thirty Million: The Story of the Metropolitan Life Insurance Company* (New York: MLIC, 1943), 122.

28. Marquis James, *The Metropolitan Life: A Study in Business Growth* (New York: Viking Press, 1947), 168 and chap. 9.

29. Haley Fiske and Raymond V. Carpenter, *An Epoch in Life Insurance: A Third of a Century of Achievement, Thirty-three Years of Administration of the Metropolitan Life Insurance Company* (New York: MLIC, 1924), 205.

30. Zunz, *Making America Corporate*, 243.

31. James, *Metropolitan Life*, 200.

32. Louise Wolters Ilse, *Group Insurance and Employee Retirement Plans* (New York: Prentice-Hall, 1953), 53–58, quotation from 57–58.

33. Haley Fiske, "Industrial Relations," address delivered to the chamber of commerce, Cleveland, Ohio, 20 Apr. 1926, 9, file 4, box 13 04 05, Publications and Speeches by Officers—Haley Fiske, Subject Files, MLIC Archives.

34. Price V. Fishback and Shawn Everett Kantor, "Insurance Rationing and the Origins of Workers' Compensation," National Bureau of Economic Research, Inc., Working Paper Series no. 4943, Dec. 1994, 23–24. On racialist bases of actuarial calculation and insurance racism, see Hoffman, *Wages of Sickness*, 60–65; and Deborah A. Stone, "The Struggle for the Soul of Health Insurance," in *The Politics of Health Care Reform: Lessons from the Past, Prospects for the Future*, ed. James A. Morone and Gary S. Belkin (Durham, N.C.: Duke University Press, 1994), 35–38.

35. Henry Bruere, "The Service of a Modern Life Insurance Company," address to the National Wholesale Grocers' Association, 21 July 1926, box 13 01 06, Publications and Speeches by Officers—Henry Bruere, Subject Files, MLIC Archives; Stone.

36. William J. Barrett, "The History of the Policyholders Service Bureau," 1, box 17 05 02, ibid.

37. Ibid., 2.

38. Fiske and Carpenter, *Epoch in Life Insurance*, 167.

39. Gary Gerstle, "The Protean Character of American Liberalism," *American Historical Review* 99 (Oct. 1994): 1050–55; Alchon, *Invisible Hand of Planning*; Ellis W. Hawley, "Herbert Hoover, the Commerce Secretariat, and the Vision of an Associative State, 1921–1928," *Journal of American History* 61 (June 1974): 116–40.

40. McCartin, *Labor's Great War*, chaps. 6–7; Dana Frank, *Purchasing Power: Consumer Organizing, Gender, and the Seattle Labor Movement, 1919–1929* (New York: Cambridge University Press, 1994).

41. Dublin, *Family of Thirty Million*, 173; Fiske and Carpenter, *Epoch in Life Insurance*, 151. To make it easier to sell group insurance, Metropolitan and

other companies writing group insurance had it written into the law that group insurance could be sold without medical exams.

42. Fiske and Carpenter, *Epoch in Life Insurance*, 165, 152, 41.

43. Ronald W. Schatz, *The Electrical Workers: A History of Labor at General Electric and Westinghouse, 1923–1960* (Urbana: University of Illinois Press, 1983), 20–23 and chap. 1; David F. Noble, *America by Design: Science, Technology, and the Rise of Corporate Capitalism* (New York: Oxford University Press, 1977), 290–303; Sanford Jacoby, "Employers and the Welfare State: The Role of Marion Folsom," *Journal of American History* 80 (Sept. 1993): 533.

44. Henry Bruere, "New Business Pool Urged as Means to Prosperity," *New York Times*, 26 Aug. 1923, box 13 01 06, Publications and Speeches by Officers—Henry Bruere, Subject Files, MLIC Archives.

45. Fiske and Carpenter, *Epoch in Life Insurance*, 159–60.

46. Hoffman, *Wages of Sickness*, 106–13; Paul Starr, *The Social Transformation of American Medicine: The Rise of a Sovereign Profession and the Making of a Vast Industry* (New York: Basic Books, 1982), 252–53; Daniel S. Hirshfield, *The Lost Reform: The Campaign for Compulsory Health Insurance in the United States from 1932 to 1943* (Cambridge: Harvard University Press, 1970), 21–22.

47. Robyn Muncy, *Creating a Female Dominion in American Reform, 1890–1935* (New York: Oxford University Press, 1991), 106–23; Eileen Boris, *Home to Work: Motherhood and the Politics of Industrial Homework in the United States* (New York: Cambridge University Press, 1994), pt. 2; Kathryn Kish Sklar, "Two Political Cultures in the Progressive Era: The National Consumer's League and the American Association for Labor Legislation," in *U.S. History as Women's History*, ed. Linda K. Kerber, Alice Kessler-Harris, and Kathryn Kish Sklar (Chapel Hill: University of North Carolina Press, 1995), 36–62.

48. Steven Fraser, *Labor Will Rule: Sidney Hillman and the Rise of American Labor* (New York: Free Press, 1991), 215–16, 220.

49. Irving Bernstein, *The Lean Years: A History of the American Worker, 1920–1933* (Boston: Houghton Mifflin, 1960), 104.

50. PSB, *Annual Report of the Policyholders' Service Bureau for 1923* (New York: MLIC, 1923), 13–14, box 17 05 01, MLIC Archives.

51. "Metropolitan Life Issues Community Insurance, Including Life, Health, and Accident," *Canadian Insurance and Office and Field*, n.d., file 1, box 19 06 03, Group Insurance, Subject Files, MLIC Archives; James, *Metropolitan Life*, 222–25.

52. James Kavanaugh to Superintendents, 2 Oct. 1919, as quoted in Barrett, "History of the Policyholders Service Bureau," 3.

53. Jacoby, "Employers and the Welfare State," 529. See also Alan Derickson, "'On the Dump Heap': Employee Medical Screening in the Tri-State Zinc-Lead Industry, 1924–1932," *Business History Review* 62 (winter 1988): 656–77.

54. MLIC, "The Metropolitan Group Life Insurance Plan," n.d., box 19 06 03, Group Insurance, Subject Files, MLIC Archives; Tone, *Business of Benevolence*, 57, 80–101.

55. MLIC, "Metropolitan Group Life Insurance Plan," n.d., box 19 06 03, Group Insurance, Subject Files, MLIC Archives.

56. Lizabeth Cohen, *Making a New Deal: Industrial Workers in Chicago, 1919–1939* (New York: Cambridge University Press, 1990), 193–94.

57. PSB, Group Insurance Division, *Helping to Keep Old Customers and to Make New Ones: A Summary of the Work of the Policyholders Service Bureau in 1934 as an Adjunct to Sales of Group Insurance* (New York: MLIC, 1935), 1, box 17 05 01, Subject Files, MLIC Archives.

58. Department of Group Insurance, ELAS, *Suggestions for Selling Group Insurance; Group Accident and Health Insurance Protects the Pay Envelope*, 1927; *Annual Dividends or Refunds Paid by the Equitable Life Assurance Society*, files 3, 4, 6.

59. Mary Van Kleeck, "Some Problems of Sickness Insurance for Women," in Department of Labor, Bureau of Labor Statistics, *Proceedings of the Conference on Social Insurance*, 594, 589.

60. Bruere, "New Business Pool Urged"; *New York Times* Oral History Project, *The Reminiscences of Henry Bruere* (New York, 1972), 16; Sanford M. Jacoby, *Employing Bureaucracy: Managers, Unions, and the Transformation of Work in American Industry, 1900–1945* (New York: Columbia University Press, 1985), 59.

61. Barrett, "History of the Policyholders Service Bureau," 5.

62. *New York Times* Oral History Project, *Reminiscences of Henry Bruere*, 101, 137, 57. Henry's brother, Robert Bruere, was a well-known figure in labor reform circles. Robert was a member of the Taylor Society and founder of the Bureau of Industrial Research (Jacoby, *Employing Bureaucracy*, 103; Fraser, *Labor Will Rule*, 173).

63. Fiske and Carpenter, *Epoch in Life Insurance*, 162; Barrett, "History of the Policyholders Service Bureau," 10.

64. Gale Johnston to Henry Bruere, 8 Sept. 1925, included in Barrett, "History of the Policyholders Service Bureau," 21.

65. Henry Bruere, as quoted in Barrett, "History of the Policyholders Service Bureau," 8.

66. PSB, *The Use of Psychological Tests in the Selection of Clerical Employees* (New York: MLIC, n.d.), 21–22, Vertical Files, MLIC Archives.

67. Angel Kwolek-Folland, *Engendering Business: Men and Women in the Corporate Office, 1870–1930* (Baltimore: Johns Hopkins University Press, 1994), chap. 4; Ilene Devault, *Sons and Daughters of Labor: Class and Clerical Work in Turn of the Century Pittsburgh* (Ithaca: Cornell University Press, 1990), 176; Sharon Hartman-Strom, *Beyond the Typewriter: Gender, Class, and the Origins of Modern American Office Work, 1900–1930* (Urbana: University of Illinois Press, 1992); Zunz, *Making America Corporate.* Metropolitan's employee magazine, *The Home Office*, published a monthly list of promotions.

68. *A List of Metropolitan Group Insurance Policyholders, Classified by Industry* (New York: Group Division, MLIC, 1 July 1925), box 19 06 03, Group Insurance, Subject Files, MLIC Archives; *A List of Metropolitan Group Policyholders, Classified Alphabetically, Industrially, and Geographically* (New York: PSB, MLIC, 1934); Fiske and Carpenter, *Epoch in Life Insurance*, 152.

69. *Short Talks on Personnel Problems with the Business Executive* (New York: MLIC, 1925); PSB, *Use of Psychological Tests*; idem, *Promoting Laundry Employees* (New York: MLIC, n.d.), Vertical Files, MLIC Archives.

70. PSB, *Annual Report of the Policyholders' Service Bureau for 1923*; Tone, *Business of Benevolence*, 226.

71. Jurgen Kocka, *White Collar Workers in America, 1890–1940: A Social Political History in International Perspective*, trans. Maura Kealey (Beverly Hills, Calif.: Sage, 1980), 97, 123.

72. PSB, *The "Why" of a Vacation* (New York: MLIC, 1925), 1, Vertical Files, MLIC Archives.

73. PSB, *The Job Blueprint* (New York: MLIC, 1925), 2, ibid.; Fiske and Carpenter, *Epoch in Life Insurance*, 223.

74. PSB, *The Use of Research in Employment Stabilization: A Report on Applying Research to Steady Personnel* (New York: MLIC, n.d.), 30, 28, Vertical Files, MLIC Archives.

75. McCartin, *Labor's Great War*, 218.

76. Jacoby, "Employers and the Welfare State," 535; Brian Gratton, "A Triumph in Modern Philanthropy: Age Criteria in Labor Management at the Pennsylvania Railroad, 1875–1930," *Business History Review* 64 (winter 1990): 643; David Brody, "Rise and Decline of Welfare Capitalism," in *Workers in Industrial America: Essays on the Twentieth Century Struggle*, 2d ed. (New York: Oxford University Press, 1993), 52–54.

77. David Rosner and Gerald Markowitz, "Safety and Health as a Class Issue: The Workers' Health Bureau of America during the 1920s," in *Dying for Work: Workers' Safety and Health in Twentieth Century America*, ed. David Rosner and Gerald Markowitz (Bloomington: Indiana University Press, 1987), 53–54; Claudia Clark, *Radium Girls: Women and Industrial Health Reform, 1910–1935* (Chapel Hill: University of North Carolina Press, 1997), 150–52, 67, 93; Grace Burnham to Charlotte Todes, 15 Sept. 1927, Burnham to Brother [union affiliates], 1 May 1928, and other misc. correspondence, file: WHB, box 1, Correspondence, 1925–1928, Charlotte Todes Stern Papers, Tamiment Institute Library, New York University.

78. PSB, *Use of Research in Employment Stabilization*, 28; Fiske and Carpenter, *Epoch in Life Insurance*, 163.

79. Alchon, *Invisible Hand of Planning*; Fraser, *Labor Will Rule*, chap. 5.

80. PSB, *Annual Report of the Policyholders' Service Bureau for 1923*, 7; Fiske and Carpenter, *Epoch in Life Insurance*, 176–77.

81. Robert Zieger, *Republicans and Labor, 1919–1929* (Lexington: University of Kentucky Press, 1969), 117–19, 191, and chap. 6.

82. Henry Bruere, "Personnel and Public Relations," *Official Proceedings of the Western Railway Club* 36 (Oct. 1923): 21–22, box 13 01 06, Publications and Speeches by Officers—Henry Bruere, Subject Files, MLIC Archives; PSB, *Annual Report of the Policyholders' Service Bureau for 1923*, 7; Interstate Commerce Commission, *Hearings: Intangible Values*, valuation docket 367, testimony of Henry Bruere, 11 May 1925, box 13 01 06, Publications and Speeches by Officers—Henry Bruere, Subject Files, MLIC Archives; Henry Bruere, "When 2,000,000 Men Pull Together: The Power of Employee Cooperation on the Railroads," *Railway Age*, Mar. 1924, reprinted by MLIC, ibid.

83. Gratton, "Triumph in Modern Philanthropy," 656.

84. PSB, "Survey of the Policyholders Service Bureau," Aug. 1932, Vertical Files, MLIC Archives.

85. Alfred D. Chandler Jr., *The Visible Hand: The Managerial Revolution in American Business* (Cambridge: Harvard University Press, Belknap Press, 1977), 457–63.

86. James, *Metropolitan Life*, 264, 266; PSB, "Survey of the Policyholders Service Bureau."

87. Clark, *Radium Girls*, 150–51; David Rosner and Gerald Markowitz, "A Gift of God? The Public Health Controversy over Leaded Gasoline during the 1920s," in Rosner and Markowitz, *Dying for Work*.

88. MLIC, *Editorial Comment on General Motors Group Insurance* (New York, 1928), box 19 06 04, Group Insurance, Subject Files, MLIC Archives.

89. Richard Gillespie, *Manufacturing Knowledge: A History of the Hawthorne Experiments* (New York: Cambridge University Press, 1991), 267, 98–105; Ronald Schatz, "From Commons to Dunlop: Rethinking the Field and Theory of Industrial Relations," in Lichtenstein and Harris, *Industrial Democracy in America*, 92.

90. PSB, *A Personnel Program, Illustrated with Record Forms* (New York: MLIC, 1923), 11, Vertical Files, MLIC Archives; Howell John Harris, "Industrial Democracy and Liberal Capitalism, 1890–1925," in Lichtenstein and Harris, *Industrial Democracy in America*; Gillespie, *Manufacturing Knowledge*, 267–68; Schatz, "From Commons to Dunlop," 104; Nelson Lichtenstein, *The Most Dangerous Man in Detroit: Walter Reuther and the Fate of American Labor* (New York: Basic Books, 1995).

91. NICB, *Industrial Group Insurance*; idem, *Recent Developments in Industrial Group Insurance* (New York, 1933); Cohen, *Making a New Deal*, 193–94.

Chapter 2
Industrial Pensions

1. Robert H. Zieger, *The CIO, 1935–1955* (Chapel Hill: University of North Carolina Press, 1995), 13; Linda Gordon, *Pitied But Not Entitled: Single Mothers and the History of Welfare* (Cambridge: Harvard University Press, 1994), chaps. 7–8; Lizabeth Cohen, *Making a New Deal: Industrial Workers in Chicago, 1919–1939* (New York: Cambridge University Press, 1990).

2. Daniel Nelson, *Unemployment Insurance: The American Experience, 1915–1935* (Madison: University of Wisconsin Press, 1969); Roy Lubove, *The Struggle for Social Security, 1900–1935* (Cambridge: Harvard University Press, 1968). For a somewhat different interpretation, one that argues that the AALL did in fact emphasize security, see David Moss, *Socializing Security: Progressive-Era Economists and the Origins of American Social Policy* (Cambridge: Harvard University Press, 1996). The emphasis on prevention of accidents and unemployment over compensation or relief would, in the AALL's view, secure the opportunity to work regularly and earn a sufficient income.

3. Walter S. Nichols, "Fraternal Insurance in the United States," *Annals of the American Academy of Political and Social Science* 70 (Mar. 1917); Charles Knight, "Fraternal Life Insurance," ibid. 130 (Mar. 1927); Jill Quadagno, *The Transfor-*

mation of Old Age Security: Class and Politics in the American Welfare State (Chicago: University of Chicago Press, 1988), 65. On ethnic lodges' affiliating with fraternals, see Cohen, *Making a New Deal,* 56–71.

4. The quotation is from John Sibley Butler, *Entrepreneurship and Self-Help Among Black Americans: A Reconsideration of Race and Economics* (Albany: State University of New York Press, 1987), 99. See also M. S. Stuart, *An Economic Detour: A History of Insurance in the Lives of American Negroes* (College Park, Md.: McGrath, 1969), 14, 15, 36, 44–45; and Robert E. Weems Jr., *Black Business in the Black Metropolis: The Chicago Metropolitan Assurance Company, 1925–1985* (Bloomington: Indiana University Press, 1996), introduction.

5. Mardsen G. Scott, in U.S. Department of Labor, Bureau of Labor Statistics, *Proceedings of the Conference on Social Insurance, Dec. 5–9, 1916* (Washington, D.C.: Government Printing Office, 1917), 754–55.

6. Murray Webb Latimer, *Trade Union Pension Systems and Other Superannuation and Permanent and Total Disability Benefits in the United States and Canada* (New York: Industrial Relations Counselors, 1932), 98 (quotation), 11, 35; Quadagno, *Transformation of Old Age Security,* 56–60. Unions also tried to provide old-age security by building old-age homes, but very few workers chose to live in them. Old-age homes seemed to symbolize everything that was unpleasant about old age: poverty, idleness, and isolation from family and community (William Graebner, *A History of Retirement: The Meaning and Function of An American Institution* [New Haven: Yale University Press, 1980], 139–47).

7. Murray Webb Latimer, *Industrial Pension Systems in the United States,* 2 vols. (New York: Industrial Relations Counselors, 1932), 1:26–28, 55–58; Brian Gratton, "A Triumph in Modern Philanthropy: Age Criteria in Labor Management at the Pennsylvania Railroad, 1875–1930," *Business History Review* 64 (winter 1990): 634–35; Graebner, *History of Retirement,* 155.

8. *McNevin v. Solvay Process Company* (New York Supreme Court, Appellate Division, 1898), 32 App. Div. 610, 612–123; *Dolge v. Dolge* (New York Supreme Court, Appellate Division, 1902), 70 App. Div., 517; *Clark v. New England Telephone Company* (1918), 229, Mass. 1, 8; *Cowles v. Morris and Company* (1928), 330 Ill., 11; *Strecker v. Consolidated Gas Company* (New York Supreme Court, Appellate Division, 1929), 227 App. Div., 820; and *Eiszner Company v. Wilson and Company Inc.*, Docket No. Equity 30–119, Federal Court, Southern District of New York, Mar. 1929, all cited in Latimer, *Industrial Pension Systems,* 2:682–97.

9. Ingalls Kimball to William J. Graham, 30 Oct. 1924, box 19 06 04, Group Insurance, Subject Files, MLIC Archives.

10. G. Powell Hamilton, "Essentials of a Pension Plan," Mar. 1929, file: Speeches—General, box 3, Insurance Affairs/Group Operations, acc. 82-45, RG 4, ELAS Archives; Latimer, *Industrial Pension Systems,* 2:572, 272, 581–610; "Workmen's Compensation and Social Insurance: Problems of Old-Age Pensions in Industry," *Monthly Labor Review* 24 (Mar. 1927): 53; Gratton, "Triumph in Modern Philanthropy," 630–56.

11. NICB, *Industrial Pensions in the United States* (New York, 1925), 14; "Workmen's Compensation and Social Insurance," 52–54; Latimer, *Industrial Pension Systems,* 1:36–54, 402–3, 441–43; Colin Gordon, *New Deals: Business, Labor, and*

Politics in America, 1920–1935 (New York: Cambridge University Press, 1994), 247–50.

12. NICB, *Industrial Pensions in the United States*, 44.

13. Sanford M. Jacoby, *Employing Bureaucracy: Managers, Unions, and the Transformation of Work in American Industry, 1900–1945* (New York: Columbia University Press, 1985), 197; Latimer, *Industrial Pension Systems*, 1:126; N. R. Danelian, *AT&T: The Story of Industrial Conquest* (New York: Vanguard Press, 1939), 233–34; Quadagno, *Transformation of Old Age Security*, 85–87. Danelian obtained much of his information from Congress's Temporary National Economic Committee (TNEC) hearings, which focused on monopolistic practices and economic concentration.

14. Danelian, *AT&T*, 224; W. R. Williamson to Wilbur Cohen, 30 Mar. 1939, file 050.112, box 23, SSB Records. Williamson, a consulting actuary for the SSB, quotes from a preliminary report prepared by the Federal Communications Commission on the Bell System. See also Latimer, *Industrial Pension Systems*, 2:665, 761–63; and Gordon, *New Deals*, 218–19.

15. NICB, *Industrial Pensions in the United States*, 44, 27.

16. Latimer, *Industrial Pension Systems*, 2:706.

17. Theda Skocpol, *Protecting Soldiers and Mothers: The Political Origins of Social Policy in the United States* (Cambridge: Harvard University Press, 1992); Ann Shola Orloff, "The Political Origins of America's Belated Welfare State," in *The Politics of Social Policy in the United States*, ed. Margaret Weir, Ann Shola Orloff, and Theda Skocpol (Princeton: Princeton University Press, 1988), 37–80.

18. Ellis W. Hawley, "Herbert Hoover, the Commerce Secretariat, and the Vision of an Associative State, 1921–1928," *Journal of American History* 61 (June 1974): 116–40.

19. Employers could make sure these programs "paid" quite literally. Through enforced employee "contributions," profit sharing, stock-option plans, and pensions enabled employers to generate capital internally through their workers. AT&T invested more than 95% of pension reserves in AT&T securities (see Edward D. Berkowitz and Kim McQuaid, *Creating the Welfare State: The Political Economy of Twentieth Century Reform*, 2d ed. [Lawrence: University Press of Kansas, 1992], chap. 1; Jacoby, *Employing Bureaucracy*, 180–82, 196–99; and Gordon, *New Deals*. Gordon argues that welfare capitalist programs had more than an ideological rationale; they also had an economic component that could enable companies to raise money without going back to capital markets. On AT&T see Williamson to Cohen, 30 Mar. 1939).

20. Graebner, *History of Retirement*.

21. Roderic Olzendam, "What Industry Is Doing with the Older Worker," address delivered at the annual meeting of the NAM, New York, 15 Oct. 1929, file 2, box 18D, Graham Papers.

22. Noel Sargent, "Industrial Care of the Long-Service Worker," address at the annual meeting of the NAM, New York, 15 Oct. 1929, ibid.; Latimer, *Industrial Pension Systems*, 2:749.

23. W. P. Fuller Jr., *Pensions and the Employer* (New York: MLIC, [1932]), box 19 06 04, Group Insurance, Subject Files, MLIC Archives; A. C. Campbell, "Selling Group Retirement Plans—A Field Man's Opportunity," address at the an-

nual convention of managers, MLIC, New York, 26–28 Apr. 1932, MLIC Archives; William J. Graham, *Industrial Pensioning*, two lectures delivered at summer conference course in industrial relations, Princeton University, 21 Sept. 1931, file 1, box 18D, Graham Papers.

24. Jacoby, *Employing Bureaucracy*, 199; "Industrial Pensions for Old Age and Disability," *Monthly Labor Review* 22 (Jan. 1926): 24–44, 52; Latimer, *Industrial Pension Systems*, 2:611–14, chaps. 14–15, 902–6; Charles K. Seymour, "Are Present Plant Pension Plans Adequate?" speech delivered as part of "The Older Worker in Industry," roundtable discussion at the annual meeting of the NAM, New York, 15 Oct. 1929, file 2, box 18D, Graham Papers. See also Sargent, "Industrial Care of the Long-Service Worker"; and Hamilton, "Essentials of a Pension Plan."

25. Olzendam, "What Industry Is Doing with the Older Worker."

26. William J. Graham, "Group Insurance and Plant Pension Plans as a Cause of Old Age Hiring Limits," address delivered as part of "The Older Worker in Industry," file 2, box 18D, Graham Papers.

27. Latimer, *Industrial Pension Systems*, 2:816–18.

28. Graebner, *History of Retirement*, 125; Carole Haber and Brian Gratton, *Old Age and the Search for Security* (Bloomington: Indiana University Press, 1994), 96–99, 105–11.

29. NICB, *Elements of Industrial Pension Plans* (New York, 1931), 3–4, 43–44; Gratton, "Triumph in Modern Philanthropy," 648 (quotation), 652, 656.

30. Latimer, *Industrial Pension Systems*, 2:945; "Workmen's Compensation and Social Insurance," 520; Latimer, *Industrial Pension Systems*, 1:215–17.

31. Latimer, *Trade Union Pension Systems*, 102–24.

32. Quadagno, *Transformation of Old Age Security*, 64–75; Lubove, *Struggle for Social Security*, 124–43; Louis Leotta, "Abraham Epstein and the Movement for Old Age Security," *Labor History* 16 (summer 1975): 359–77.

33. Jackson K. Putnam, *Old Age Politics in California: From Richardson to Reagan* (Stanford: Stanford University Press, 1970), 7–9, 13–14; Haber and Gratton, *Old Age and the Search for Security*, 42–43; Caroline Manning, "The Industrial Woman Looks at Economic Old Age," *American Labor Legislation Review* 20 (Dec. 1930): 445–47; Jill Quadagno, "Welfare Capitalism and the Social Security Act of 1935," *American Sociological Review* 49 (Oct. 1984): 640.

34. Gordon, *Pitied But Not Entitled*, 223.

35. Quadagno, "Welfare Capitalism"; idem, *Transformation of Old Age Security*; Putnam, *Old Age Politics in California*.

36. Gordon, *Pitied But Not Entitled*, 224–27; Putnam, *Old Age Politics in California*, chap. 3.

37. William E. Leuchtenberg, *Franklin D. Roosevelt and the New Deal* (New York: Harper Torchbooks, 1963), 104, 114–15; Gordon, *Pitied But Not Entitled*, 228–33; Putnam, *Old Age Politics in California*, 50–59.

38. Gordon, *Pitied But Not Entitled*, 236–41; Robert C. Lieberman, *Shifting the Color Line: Race and the American Welfare State* (Cambridge: Harvard University Press, 1998), 60.

39. *Report of the Proceedings of the Fiftieth Annual Convention of the American Federation of Labor* (Washington, D.C.: Labor Law Printing, 1930), 115–16, 338; *Re-*

port of the Proceedings of the Fifty-first Annual Convention of the American Federation of Labor (Washington, D.C.: Labor Law Printing, 1931), 122, 412; *Report of the Proceedings of the Fifty-second Annual Convention of the American Federation of Labor* (Washington, D.C.: Labor Law Printing, 1932); *Report of the Proceedings of the Fifty-third Annual Convention of the American Federation of Labor* (Washington, D.C.: Labor Law Printing, 1933), 110–11, 452.

40. Graebner, *History of Retirement*, 135.

41. Christopher Howard, *The Hidden Welfare State: Tax Expenditures and Social Policy in the United States* (Princeton: Princeton University Press, 1997), 141.

42. Latimer's survey found a total of forty-five plans, covering just over 100,000 workers, discontinued (Latimer, *Industrial Pension Systems*, 2:843–46). Most of the discontinuations occurred in small firms or in declining sectors such as street railways. Others ended because of mergers. The percentage of discontinued plans was quite low in manufacturing (5.3%) and in banking and insurance (6%). Still, the number of employees eligible for pensions declined overall because employment levels dropped and employers closed existing plans to new employees. Overall, there was a movement toward retrenchment. But equally important, and perhaps more so for the long run, there was also a movement toward pensions with sound financing and more guarantees to employees.

43. William B. Foster to Willis F. Harrington, 12 Apr. 1933, file 11, box 15, Harrington Papers; "Annual Out of Pocket Costs of the Industrial Relations Plans," Sept. 1936, file 8, box 22, ibid.

44. NICB, *Elements of Industrial Pension Plans: Employees' Retirement Annuities* (Washington, D.C.: Chamber of Commerce of the United States, 1932).

45. NICB, *Elements of Industrial Pension Plans*, 45.

46. Ibid., 12.

47. P. Tecumseh Sherman, "Public Old Age Pensions Unsound," 23, address delivered as part of "The Older Worker in Industry," file 2, box 18D, Graham Papers.

48. Fuller, *Pensions and the Employer*; Campbell, "Selling Group Retirement Plans."

49. "Some Reasons Why Life Insurance Has Weathered the Business Storm," *Metropolitan Underwriter* 1 (Dec. 1931), MLIC Archives; "Give Your Job All That It Deserves," ibid.

50. "Give Your Job All That It Deserves," ibid.

51. The National Industrial Recovery Act of 1933 sought to restructure and rejuvenate American industry by allowing government-sponsored cartelization to stabilize prices and production levels. Section 7a guaranteed workers the right to organize independent unions and engage in collective bargaining with employers.

52. "Collective Bargaining through Employee Representation Plans," 1933, MLIC Archives. On employee representation plans generally see Daniel Nelson, *Managers and Workers: Origins of the New Factory System in the United States, 1880–1920* (Madison: University of Wisconsin Press, 1975); Jacoby, *Employing Bureaucracy*, 226–28; and Gordon, *New Deals*, 122–24. Metropolitan vigorously resisted union attempts to organize its field force. The company argued that its employees did not fall under the jurisdiction of the New York State Labor

Relations Board, which ruled in favor of a representation election for insurance agents. Although the company lost the legal battle, it so intimidated agents that they eventually told the board they no longer wanted union representation (Louis I. Dublin, *A Family of Thirty Million: The Story of the Metropolitan Life Insurance Company* [New York: MLIC, 1943], 112–13).

53. PSB, "Survey of the Policyholders Service Bureau," Aug. 1932, Vertical Files, MLIC Archives.

54. Campbell, "Selling Group Retirement Plans," 51; William J. Barrett to Metropolitan Group Policyholders, memorandum, 26 Dec. 1935, Vertical Files, MLIC; PSB, Group Insurance Division, *Helping to Keep Old Customers and to Make New Ones: A Summary of the Work of the Policyholders Service Bureau in 1934 as an Adjunct to Sales of Group Insurance* (New York, MLIC, 1935), 3, box 17 05 01, Subject Files, MLIC Archives.

55. Graham, "Industrial Pensioning."

56. Hamilton, "Essentials of a Pension Plan."

57. Workers could receive cash surrender values or already paid up deferred annuities in the case of terminated, reinsured plans. See William J. Graham, *Planned Financial Security for Industrial Workers*, address at the fourth annual conference course in industrial relations, Princeton University, 1934, file 1, box 18D, Graham Papers; idem, "Complete Group Protection for Employees: Its Need and the Prospect of Achievement," file 11, box 33B, ibid.; Birchard E. Wyatt, *Private Group Retirement Plans* (Washington, D.C.: Graphic Arts Press, 1936), 24–25; Graham to Irenee duPont, Jan. 1933, with insert by Graham, "1932—Paid for New Group Insurance," file 221, box 49, acc. 1304, Irenee duPont Papers, HML; Rainard B. Robbins, "Preliminary Report on the Status of Industrial Pension Plans as Affected by Old Age Benefits Sections of the Social Security Act," 21 Mar. 1936, 6, prepared for the Committee on Social Security of the Social Science Research Council, box 122, SEN 74A-F8, Senate Finance Committee Papers, NA-DC.

58. PSB, "Survey of the Policyholders Service Bureau."

59. Latimer, *Industrial Pension Systems*, 2:848–49, 583.

60. Gosta Esping-Andersen, *The Three Worlds of Welfare Capitalism* (Princeton: Princeton University Press, 1990), 64.

61. William J. Graham, "Group Insurance," *Annals of the American Academy of Political and Social Science* 161 (May 1932): 44.

62. "Industrial Pensions for Old Age and Disability," 52–53; *Report of the Proceedings of the Fifty-third Annual Convention of the American Federation of Labor*, 526.

63. Vermont Marble Company, "Letter to Our Employees," in *Retirement Plan for Employes of Vermont Marble Company*, 23 May 1932, file 6, box 32A, acc. 1984-050, RG 4, ELAS Archives.

Chapter 3
The New Deal Struggle

1. For contrasting views on the impact of social movements, see Edward D. Berkowitz, *America's Welfare State: From Roosevelt to Reagan* (Baltimore: Johns Hopkins University Press, 1991); and Linda Gordon, *Pitied But Not Entitled: Sin-*

gle Mothers and the History of Welfare (Cambridge: Harvard University Press, 1994), chaps. 7–8.

2. *Spectator: The Business Paper of Insurance* (hereafter *Spectator*), 11 June 1936.

3. Here I am building on Sanford Jacoby's argument that key welfare capitalist businessmen, such as Marion Folsom of Kodak, supported the concept of "the basic welfare state," wherein the state provided a minimal, basic level of protection that would not cover all needs and thus left the rest to private institutions (see Sanford Jacoby, "Employers and the Welfare State: The Role of Marion Folsom," *Journal of American History* 80 [Sept. 1993]: 525–56).

4. Franklin D. Roosevelt, "Message to the Congress Reviewing Broad Objectives and Accomplishments of the Administration, June 8, 1934," "The Initiation of Studies to Achieve a Program of National Social and Economic Security, Executive Order No. 6757, June 29, 1934," and "Address to Advisory Council of the Committee on Economic Security on the Problems of Economic and Social Security, November 14, 1934," all in *Public Papers and Addresses of President Franklin D. Roosevelt*, vol. 3 (New York: Random House, 1938).

5. I. M. Rubinow, *The Quest for Security* (New York: Henry Holt and Co., 1934), 279; Jackson K. Putnam, *Old Age Politics in California: From Richardson to Reagan* (Stanford: Stanford University Press, 1970), 26; Louis Leotta, "Abraham Epstein and the Movement for Old Age Security," *Labor History* 16 (summer 1975): 359–77; Henry J. Pratt, *The Gray Lobby* (Chicago: University of Chicago Press, 1976), 15.

6. Although he called for comprehensive economic security, Epstein perceived the security/insecurity dichotomy within a patriarchal framework; in his view the worker was definitely male and his wife was dependent. Even though he was one of the more radical social reformers, he still viewed social provision as necessarily linked to waged participation in the labor force. Consonant with the construct of the family wage, social security meant protecting the continuity of the male breadwinner's wage (Abraham Epstein, *Insecurity: A Challenge to America. A Study of Social Insurance in the United States and Abroad* [New York: Random House, 1933]; Gordon, *Pitied But Not Entitled*, 28, 178).

7. Rubinow, *Quest for Security*, 524, 548.

8. Mary Van Kleeck, "Security for Americans, Part IV: The Workers' Bill for Unemployment and Social Insurance," *New Republic*, 12 Dec. 1934, 123. In fact, Van Kleeck went so far as to say that "social insurance cannot ensure security; it can only ensure compensation for insecurity." See also George Soule, "Security for Americans, Part VII: Can We Provide Security?" ibid., 16 Jan. 1935, 16. For other articles in the series, see ibid., 21, 28 Nov.; 5, 19 Dec. 1934; and 2 Jan. 1935.

9. See, e.g., the following from *The Survey*: Gertrude Springer, "For Welfare and Security," Mar. 1934, 67–68; Mary Van Kleeck, "Our Illusions Regarding Government," June 1934, 190–93; A. J. Muse and I. M. Rubinow, "The Lundeen Bill," Dec. 1934, 376–80; "From Slogans to Action," Jan. 1935, 17; Paul Kellogg, "Fifteen Weeks and Insecurity," Feb. 1935; Barbara Armstrong, "Old Age in the Security Program," Mar. 1935, 70–72; and Marietta Stevenson, "A New Grist of Social Legislation," May 1935.

10. Raymond Gram Swing, "Social Security in a Hurry," *Nation*, 19 Sept. 1934, 318–20.

11. "Defeat the Wagner-Lewis Bill," ibid., 17 Apr. 1935.

12. Franklin D. Roosevelt, second "fireside chat" of 1934, "We Are Moving Forward to Greater Freedom, to Greater Security for the Average Man," 30 Sept. 1934, *Public Papers and Addresses of President Franklin D. Roosevelt*, vol. 3.

13. Franklin Roosevelt, "Address to Advisory Council of the Committee on Economic Security on the Problems of Economic Security," 14 Nov. 1934, ibid.; idem, "A Greater Future Economic Security of the American People—A Message to the Congress on Social Security," 17 Jan. 1935, ibid.; "White House Statement Summarizing Report from the President's Committee on Economic Security (Excerpts)," 17 Jan. 1935, *Public Papers and Addresses of President Franklin D. Roosevelt*, vol. 4 (New York: Random House, 1938); Arthur J. Altmeyer, *The Formative Years of Social Security: A Chronicle of Social Security Legislation and Administration, 1934–1954* (Madison: University of Wisconsin Press, 1966), 13; "A Letter from the President's Committee on Economic Security," 17 Jan. 1935, *Public Papers and Addresses of President Franklin D. Roosevelt*, vol. 4; Edwin E. Witte, "Preliminary Outline of the Work of the Staff," 13 Aug. 1934, as quoted in Witte, *The Development of the Social Security Act: A Memorandum on the History of the Committee on Economic Security and Drafting and Legislative History of the Social Security Act* (Madison: University of Wisconsin Press, 1963), 21–22; "Not Found Threat to Life Insurance . . . Witte Gives His View," *National Underwriter*, 15 Mar. 1935; Barbara Armstrong, "Old Age in the Security Program," *Survey*, Mar. 1935; W. R. Williamson, address to the American Management Association Insurance Conference, Atlantic City, N.J., 8–9 Apr. 1935, in *Social Insurance Legislation* (New York: American Management Association, 1935); "Linton Views Security Act," *National Underwriter*, 26 Apr. 1935; M. Albert Linton, "The Federal Old Age Security Program," in *Proceedings of the Thirtieth Annual Meeting of the American Life Convention* (Chicago: American Life Convention, 1935).

14. William J. Graham, *Planned Financial Security for Industrial Workers*, address at the fourth annual conference course in industrial relations, Princeton University, 1934, file 1, box 18D, Graham Papers.

15. Ibid.; Graham to Group Patrons, 28 Feb. 1935, file 18, closed files, Sterling Pierson Files, ELAS Archives.

16. William J. Graham, "Complete Group Protection for Employees: Its Need and the Prospect of Achievement," 3–4, file 11, box 33B, Graham Papers.

17. T.J.V. Cullen, "Social Insurance Limitations," *Spectator*, 8 Nov. 1934; "The Long Range View," ibid., 20 Dec. 1934, 8; Lincoln Lippincott, "A General System of Social Insurance Is Not a Practicable Ideal," ibid., 27 Dec. 1934; David Lunden-Moore, "The Annuity Situation," ibid., 21 Mar. 1935; T.J.V. Cullen, "The Annuity Viewpoint," ibid., 18 Apr. 1935; *Proceedings of the Twenty-ninth Annual Meeting of the American Life Convention* (Chicago: American Life Convention, 1934); "Colonel Robinson's Talk," *National Underwriter*, 17 May 1935; Martha Derthick, *Policymaking for Social Security* (Washington, D.C.: Brookings Institution, 1979), 136–39.

18. Edward D. Berkowitz, *Disabled Policy: America's Programs for the Handicapped* (New York: Cambridge University Press, 1987), chap. 1; *National Underwriter*, 14 Feb. 1935, 1; Derthick, *Policymaking for Social Security*, 136–42.

19. *Spectator*, 24 Jan. 1935; *Summary: Economic Security Proposals Now before Con-*

gress, Prepared for Group Patrons by Research Division, Group Department, 28 Feb. 1935, file 18, closed files, Pierson Files.

20. Gerhard Hirschfeld, "Social Insurance Viewed from an Economic Angle," *Spectator,* 5 July 1934. The National Association of Life Underwriters concurred (*National Underwriter,* 26 Sept. 1934). See also "Federal Social Security Plans Viewed by Actuary," *National Underwriter,* 12 Apr. 1935, 4; Williamson, in *Social Insurance Legislation,* 20–21; and *National Underwriter,* 21 Sept. 1934, 2, and 8 Feb. 1935.

21. *National Underwriter,* 24 Jan. 1935.

22. Ibid., 21 Sept. 1934, 2.

23. Ibid., 12 Apr., 8 Mar. 1935, 1; *Spectator,* 18 Apr. 1935, 6–10.

24. H. Walter Forster to Robert Doughton, 11 Feb. 1935, and Forster to E.W.G. Huffman, 11 Feb. 1935, file: Misc. Letters, 74th Cong., box 14118, HR 74A-F39.3, House Ways and Means Committee Papers, RG 233, NA-DC; H. Walter Forster, "Amendment to Permit Operation of Private Annuity Plans," 20 Feb. 1935, file 011.1, box 5, SSB Records; Arthur J. Altmeyer to Murray Webb Latimer, 26 Feb. 1935, ibid.; Witte, *Development of the Social Security Act,* 102–6, 151–61; Derthick, *Policymaking for Social Security,* 282.

25. Equitable's director and deputy director of the Pensions and Annuities Division, G. Powell Hamilton and Nathaniel E. Horelick, lobbied senators behind the scenes. Trying to encourage the fledgling trend away from in-house, self-insured pensions to annuities purchased from insurance companies, William Graham argued that the exemption should apply only to "corporations whose plans are or will be insured or soundly trusteed" (Graham to Leon Fisher, 16 Oct. 1935, file 18, closed files, Pierson Files. See also J. Douglas Brown, *An American Philosophy of Social Security: Evolution and Issues* [Princeton: Princeton University Press, 1972], 65; G. Powell Hamilton, address to American Management Association Insurance Conference, Atlantic City, N.J., 8–9 Apr. 1935, in *Social Insurance Legislation* [New York: American Management Association, 1935], 33–34; William J. Graham, "Financial Aspects of Social Legislation Now before Congress" (paper presented at meeting of the Academy of Political Science, New York, 16 Apr. 1935), file 6, box 18D, Graham Papers; "Social Security Is Viewed by Graham, Urges Substitution of Private Pension Plans in Bill before Congress," *National Underwriter,* 26 July 1935, 1; W. Ross McCain to Doughton, 29 June 1939, file: HR 7260, HR 74A-D38, House Ways and Means Committee Papers, RG 233, NA-DC; Frank Houston to Doughton, 1 Feb. 1935, file: Misc. Letters, 74th Cong., box 14118, HR 74A-F39.3, ibid.; and *National Underwriter,* 17 May, 28 June 1935, 6).

26. Paul H. Douglas, *Social Security in the United States: An Analysis and Appraisal of the Federal Social Security Act* (New York: Whittlesey House, McGraw Hill, 1936), 271–83; Leonard Calhoun, "Legislation to Encourage Private Pensions," Jan. 1936, box 122, SEN 74-F8, Senate Finance Committee Papers, NA-DC.

27. *Social Insurance Legislation; National Underwriter,* 26 Apr. 1935.

28. Latimer to Altmeyer, 21 Feb. 1935; Murray Webb Latimer, "Memorandum on Proposed Amendments to Economic Security Bill Permitting Employers with Private Pension Plans to Contract Out of the Government System"; and Altmeyer to Latimer, 26 Feb. 1935, all in file 011.1, box 5, SSB Records.

29. *Congressional Record*, 74th Cong., 1st sess., 1935, 79, pt. 12: 13255–57; Derthick, *Policymaking for Social Security*, 282; Witte, *Development of the Social Security Act*, 107–8.

30. U.S. Congress, Senate, Subcommittee on Finance, and House, Subcommittee on Ways and Means, *Private Pension Systems: Joint Hearings before a Subcommittee on Finance, United States Senate, and a Subcommittee of the Committee on Ways and Means, House of Representatives*, 74th Cong., 2d sess., 17 Jan., 30 Mar., 16 May 1936; U.S. Congress, Senate, *Report of the Proceedings: Hearings Held before a Subcommittee of the Committee on Finance, Senate, and a Subcommittee of the Committee on Ways and Means, House, on Private Pension Systems*, 74th Cong., 2d sess. (Washington, D.C.: Ward & Paul, Official Reporters, Earle Building, 30 Mar. 1936), 1:46–47; Senator Bennett "Champ" Clark, quoted in Senate Subcommittee on Finance and House Subcommittee on Ways and Means, *Private Pension Systems*, 17 Jan. 1936, 5KW; and Congressman Allen T. Treadway, quoted in ibid., all in box 122, SEN 74A-F8, NA-DC.

31. Altmeyer to Senator William H. King, 26 May 1936, file: 74th Congress, Study of Private Pensions, box 122, SEN 74A-F8, Senate Finance Committee Papers, NA-DC. For evidence of the SSB's initial stalling see Senate Subcommittee on Finance and House Subcommittee on Ways and Means, *Private Pension Systems*, 17 Jan., 30 Mar. 1936. See also John G. Winant, to Director, Bureau of the Budget, 18 May 1936; and Acting Director, Bureau of the Budget, to Altmeyer, 4 June 1936, both in file 011.1, box 5, SSB Records.

32. Derthick, *Policymaking for Social Security*, 7; Brian Balogh, "The Social Security Board as a Political Actor," in *Federal Social Policy: The Historical Dimension*, ed. Donald T. Critchlow and Ellis W. Hawley (University Park: Pennsylvania State University Press, 1988), 58–60, 64; Jerry Cates, *Insuring Inequality: Administrative Leadership in Social Security, 1935–54* (Ann Arbor: University of Michigan Press, 1983).

33. Rainard B. Robbins, "Preliminary Report on the Status of Industrial Pension Plans as Affected by Old Age Benefits Sections of the Social Security Act," 21 Mar. 1936, 2–5, 22, and idem, "Supplementary Report on the Proposed Substitute for the Clark Amendment," 27 May 1936, both prepared for the Committee on Social Security of the Social Science Research Council, in box 122, SEN 74A-F8, Senate Finance Committee Papers, NA-DC. Another witness told the joint committee that in cases where it appeared that an employer had discontinued an employee pension plan, in actuality the firm had discontinued its old plan in order to replace it with a new one designed to dovetail with Social Security (See testimony of W. H. Woodward, in Senate, *Report of the Proceedings*, 30 Mar. 1936, 49).

34. Harvey G. Ellerd to Felton M. Johnstone, 14 Mar. 1936; Thomas Spates to Johnston, 13 Mar. 1936; H. B. Bergen to Johnston, 5 Mar. 1936; F. W. Pierce to Johnston, 25 Feb. 1936; Marion Folsom to Johnston, 13 Feb. 1936; and Secretary, GE, to Johnston, 3 Feb. 1936, all in file: 74th Congress, Private Pensions, box 122, SEN 74-F8, Senate Finance Committee Papers, NA-DC. According to Sanford Jacoby, Folsom dropped his opposition to the Clark Amendment upon realizing that it would "bring undesirable scrutiny of private pension standards" (Jacoby, "Employers and the Welfare State," 542).

35. Woodward testimony, *Private Pensions Hearings,* 30 Mar. 1936, 23; testimony of Leonard Calhoun, ibid., 17 Jan. 1936; Calhoun, "Legislation to Encourage Private Pension Plans"; U.S. Senate, *Draft of a Bill to Amend the Social Security Act with Reference to Private Annuity Plans,* 15 May 1936, file 011.1, box 5, SSB Records.

36. James Little to Johnston, 7 Feb. 1936; Earl C. Henderson to Johnston, 3 Feb. 1936; Benedict D. Flynn to Johnston, 28 Jan. 1936; M. Albert Linton to Johnston, 31 Jan. 1936; James D. Craig to Johnston, 30 Jan. 1936; Aetna Vice President and Actuary to Johnston, 27 Jan. 1936, file: 74th Congress, Private Pensions, box 122, SEN 74-F8, Senate Finance Committee Papers, NA-DC. Graham to Johnston, 5 Mar. 1936, ibid.; Rainard B. Robbins, "Preliminary Report on the Status of Industrial Pension Plans as Affected by Old Age Benefits Sections of the Social Security Act," 21 Mar. 1936, 6–8, and idem, "Supplementary Report on the Proposed Substitute for the Clark Amendment," 27 May 1936, 4–6, both prepared for the Committee on Social Security of the Social Science Research Council, in box 122, SEN 74A-F8, Senate Finance Committee Papers, NA-DC. Equitable was the only large insurer in this group that would not fully give up on the exemption idea, although their support for it was more tepid in 1936 than earlier.

37. *National Underwriter,* 13 Sept. 1935, 2.

38. Ibid., 30 Aug. 1935, 1; 21 June 1935, 10; 7 June 1935, 3.

39. Mrs. W. Van Enam to Williamson, Oct. 1938, file 050.111, box 23, SSB Records. Van Enam conducted a study for SSB on private pensions.

40. Robbins, "Preliminary Report on the Status of Industrial Pension Plans," 6; Dorrance C. Bronson to Wilbur Cohen, 1 Feb. 1939, file 050.113, box 23A, SSB Records; "Group at Record, Parkinson States," *Spectator,* 9 Jan. 1936, 13; *National Underwriter,* 19 June 1936, 1.

41. *National Underwriter,* 13 Sept. 1935, 2; Craig to Johnston, 30 Jan. 1936.

42. N. E. Horelick to Sales and Service Staff of the Group Department, 19 Sept. 1939, file 4, box 35A, Group Insurance Research Division, acc. 1984-050, RG 4, ELAS Archives; William J. Graham, "Incidental Notes on a Group Annuity Retirement Plan to Supplement the Federal Old Age Benefits of the Social Security Act" (address to Milwaukee chapter, National Association of Cost Accountants, 1935, file 1, box 18D, Graham Papers).

43. Harold F. Browne, *The Social Security Act and Company Pension Policy,* Conference Board Information Service: Domestic Affairs Series, Memorandum 47 (New York: NICB, 10 Feb. 1936). In fact NICB suggested that one of the beneficial effects of the Social Security Act would be to finally force employers with unfunded company plans to drop them and augment the government plan "with a limited supplementary company plan established on a sound basis" (ibid., 17). See also Robbins, "Preliminary Report on the Status of Industrial Pension Plans," 22.

44. William J. Graham, "Social Security," radio address, 17 Dec. 1936, file 2, box 18D, Graham Papers.

45. *National Underwriter,* 27, 29 Sept. 1939, 10.

46. "Pension Program Outlined," ibid., 1 May 1936, 2; "Effect of the Security Act on Private Pension Plans," ibid., 24 Apr. 1936, 3; *Spectator,* 16 Apr. 1936, 34.

47. Graham, "Incidental Notes on a Group Annuity Retirement Plan."

48. Jacoby, "Employers and the Welfare State," 526–27; idem, *Modern Manors: Welfare Capitalism since the New Deal* (Princeton: Princeton University Press, 1997), 206–10.

49. "The Federal Pension Plan," box 1030, Jasper Crane Papers, ser. 2, pt. 2, DuPont Collection, HML; "Federal Grants," file 22, box 15, Harrington Papers. DuPont executives had numerous discussions among themselves about whether the employees considered these handouts propaganda; they even took regular surveys among the employees in order to gauge their reaction to the material.

50. E. G. Walker to King, 6 Apr. 1936; Clarence Teal to King, 21 Mar. 1936; Nelson Ross to Johnston, 13 Mar. 1936, with attachments (E. E. Richard to King, 19 Mar. 1936, and petition signatures); Thomas Flynn to King, 17 Mar. 1936; Catherine Akerr to Chairman, Senate Finance Committee, 3 Mar. 1936; and "Brief Submitted by the Association [of] Western Union Telegraph Employees in Support of Its Request That the Congress Enact Legislation Exempting the Western Union Company and Its Employees from the Operation of Titles II & VIII of the Social Security Act," 1936, all in file: Senator King Correspondence, box 122, SEN 74-F8, Senate Finance Committee Papers, NA-DC.

51. Altmeyer to Congressman John A. Martin, 30 Aug. 1938, file 050.112, box 23, SSB Records. On Western Union and its subsequent decision to discontinue the pension for any employees beginning work after 1936, see file 050.112, ibid.

52. Williamson to Altmeyer, 4 Dec. 1937; Williamson to Cohen, 30 Mar. 1939; R. B. White to Altmeyer, 6 Apr. 1938; Frank Bane, responding for Altmeyer, to White, 29 June 1938; and John J. Corson to John R. Campbell, 17 Jan. 1940, all in ibid. Danelian argued that AT&T was actually lucky that Social Security had come along. Once AT&T finally adjusted its pension plan to the Social Security Act, thereby reducing its payments by the amount of benefits received under Social Security, it saved itself from a dangerous employee relations problem (N. R. Danelian, *AT&T: The Story of Industrial Conquest* [New York: Vanguard Press, 1939], 227).

53. Danelian, *AT&T*, 200–206, 223–33.

54. John Dietrich to King, 3 Mar. 1936, file: Senator King Correspondence, box 122, SEN 74A-F8, Senate Finance Committee Papers, NA-DC.

55. Browne, *Social Security Act and Company Pension Policy*; *National Underwriter*, 26 June 1936, 1; Jacoby, "Employers and the Welfare State," 544.

56. Gordon, *Pitied But Not Entitled*, 223–42; Putnam, *Old Age Politics in California*, chap. 6.

57. *National Underwriter*, 17 Jan. 1936, 1.

58. W. C. Teagle, "Security—This Is More Like It," *Factory Management and Maintenance* 94 (Feb. 1936): 50; Alvin MacCauley, president, Packard Motor Company, "We Work toward Worker Security," ibid., no. 11 (Nov. 1936), 36–39.

59. J. Douglas Brown, "Provisions of Company Pension Plans As Adjusted to the Social Security Act: Excerpts from Recent Plans," Report no. 56, revised, Industrial Relations Section, Department of Economics, Princeton University (June 1939), 3, 5, 8, 15, 14, 28 (hereafter Brown Report), in file 050.112, box 23, SSB Records; "Coordination of the Federal Old Age and Survivors Insur-

ance System with Private Pension Systems," 19 Aug. 1940, in ibid. Both Jill Quadagno and Frank Dobbin contend that the number of company pensions increased rapidly in the period 1935–42 (Jill Quadagno, *The Transformation of Old Age Security: Class and Politics in the American Welfare State* [Chicago: University of Chicago Press, 1988], 117; Frank Dobbin, "The Origins of Private Social Insurance: Public Policy and Fringe Benefits in America, 1920–50," *American Journal of Sociology* 97 [Mar. 1992]: 1416–50).

60. Brown Report, 14.

61. Van Enam to Bronson, and Bronson to Cohen, both 1 May 1939, file 050.112, box 23, SSB Records; Actuary's Department to Ray D. Murphy, 7 July 1937, box: Correspondence and Office Files, Ray D. Murphy Files, acc. 84-14, RG 2, ELAS Archives.

62. Graham to Group Patrons, 27 Oct. 1939, and ELAS, *Summary: The Social Security Act Amendments of 1939, Prepared for Our Group Patrons By the Group Department* (New York, 1939), both in file 4, box 35A, Group Insurance Research Division, acc. 1984-050, ELAS Archives.

63. Brown Report. Among the companies who built upon their Metropolitan and Equitable group life insurance contracts were the American Meter Company, the Brown and Williamson Tobacco Corporation, the Borden Company, the Clark Thread Company, the B. F. Goodrich Company, the National Lead Company, the Union Carbide and Carbon Corporation, the Union Oil Company, Standard Oil of New Jersey and of Ohio, People's Drugstores, and the Chicago Daily News. Westinghouse Air Brake and the Barnsdall Corporation were among the companies that had held group life insurance with other insurance companies.

64. *Retirement Plan for Employees of the American Meter Company Inc.*, 1 Sept. 1938, file 050.112, box 23, SSB Records. For examples of Equitable clients who followed a similar path during the period 1918–39, see Piper Aircraft Corporation to Peter Bush, 17 Apr. 1939; Okonite Company to Equitable Life, 15 Jan. 1939; and People's Drugstores Inc. to Equitable Life, 9 Oct. 1939, all in Equitable Clients, acc. 1984-050, ELAS Archives.

65. NICB, *Company Pension Plans and the Social Security Act*, Studies in Personnel Policy, 16 (New York, Dec. 1939); Van Enam to Bronson, and Bronson to Cohen, both 1 May 1939; "Effects of Social Security Act on Company Pensions," *Monthly Labor Review* 50 (Mar. 1940): 642–47.

66. Graham, "Incidental Notes on a Group Annuity Retirement Plan"; NICB, *Company Pension Plans and the Social Security Act*, 24. As Marion Folsom, of Kodak, wrote, "We will arrange it so that the combined payments to the government and to the insurance company will provide a combined annuity practically the same as under the present company annuity plan" (Folsom, "Social Security Law Administration," *American Labor Legislation Review* 26 [Dec. 1936]: 173).

67. Suzanne Mettler, *Dividing Citizens: Gender and Federalism in New Deal Public Policy* (Ithaca: Cornell University Press, 1998), 68.

68. Van Enam to Bronson, 25 Apr. 1939, file 050.112, box 23, SSB Records; Bronson to Cohen, 1 May 1939; Brown Report, 7.

69. Brown Report, 5.

70. William Richter to Jasper E. Crane, 16 Nov. 1942, box 1030, Crane Papers, ser. 2, pt. 2; Graham, "Incidental Notes on Group Annuity Retirement Plan," 3.

71. GE to All Employees, "GE Company, Pensions," 6 Dec. 1936, file: 74th Congress, Private Pensions, box 122, SEN 74A-F8, Senate Finance Committee Papers, NA-DC.

72. *Retirement Plan for the Employees of Inland Steel Company and Its Subsidiaries*, 1 Jan. 1936, file 050.112, box 23, SSB Records; Island Steel's plan was somewhat unusual in specifying that pension benefits were for men. On the Campbell Soup Company, see Van Enam to Bronson, 25 Apr. 1939; on wages, Robert H. Zieger, *The CIO, 1935–1955* (Chapel Hill: University of North Carolina Press, 1995), 114–15.

73. Alfred P. Sloan Jr. to Holders of Common Stock, 29 Mar. 1940, and *General Motors Corporation Employees Contributory Retirement Plan*, 1 July 1940, both in box 1030, Crane Papers, ser. 2, pt. 2; Williamson to Winant and Altmeyer, 8 Feb. 1937, file 050.112, box 23, SSB Records.

74. Teresa Ghilarducci, *Labor's Capital: The Economics and Politics of Private Pensions* (Cambridge, Mass.: MIT Press, 1992), 21; Howell John Harris, *The Right to Manage: Industrial Relations Policies of American Business in the 1940s* (Madison: University of Wisconsin Press, 1982); Nelson Lichtenstein, "'The Man in the Middle': A Social History of Automobile Industry Foremen," in *On the Line: Essays in the History of Autowork*, ed. Nelson Lichtenstein and Stephen Meyer (Urbana: University of Illinois Press, 1989), 153–89; E. S. Cowdrick, "Report to Clients," 1937, 8, file: Special Conference Committee, box 28, Harrington Papers. Cowdrick reported that concerning nonwage benefits, "there has begun to grow up a community of interest between wage-earners and salaried employees. In some companies salaried workers have shown a desire for collective bargaining with employers, either through their own organizations or by use of the same agencies that serve wage earners" (9).

75. Henry Morgenthau, quoted in Christopher Howard, *The Hidden Welfare State: Tax Expenditures and Social Policy in the United States* (Princeton: Princeton University Press, 1997), 145.

76. Mark Leff, "Taxing the Forgotten Man: The Politics of Social Security Finance in the New Deal," *Journal of American History* 70 (Sept. 1983): 359–75; Alan Brinkley, *The End of Reform: New Deal Liberalism in Recession and War* (New York: Alfred A. Knopf, 1995), 99. Roosevelt and his close economic advisers chose government spending on the WPA and other public works projects and an easing of credit rather than Morgenthau's proposals for a balanced budget.

77. Eleanor Davis, memorandum on Social Security, pensions, and taxes, 21 Apr. 1937; E. L. Dulles to Ewan Clague, 21 Apr. 1937; Davis to Dulles, 17 Apr. 1937; Dulles to Clague, 27 Apr. 1937, file 011.1, box 5, SSB Records.

78. Quadagno, *Transformation of Old Age Security*, 159; Beth Stevens, "Blurring the Boundaries: How the Federal Government Has Influenced Welfare Benefits in the Private Sector," in *The Politics of Social Policy in the United States*, ed. Margaret Weir, Ann Shola Orloff, and Theda Skocpol (Princeton: Princeton University Press, 1988).

79. Michael K. Brown, *Race, Money, and the American Welfare State* (Ithaca: Cornell University Press, 1999), 64, 14–16; Robert C. Lieberman, *Shifting the*

Color Line: Race and the American Welfare State (Cambridge: Harvard University Press, 1998), 29–39; Mettler, *Dividing Citizens*, 69–73.

80. Mary Anderson, quoted in Mettler, *Dividing Citizens*, 80–82.

81. *Pension Plan with Death and Disability Benefits for the Employees of the Barnsdall Corporation and Associated and Operated Companies*, 1 Oct. 1934, box 122, SEN 74A-F8, Senate Finance Committee Papers, NA-DC. This company had previously held a group life insurance policy with Aetna, which was also underwriting the pension.

82. Williamson to Cohen, 19 Dec. 1939, file 050.111, box 23, SSB Records.

83. Richter to Crane, box 1030, Crane Papers, ser. 2, pt. 2; Zieger, *CIO*, 115; Jill Quadagno, "Women's Access to Pensions and the Structure of Eligibility Rules: Systems of Production and Reproduction," *Sociological Quarterly* 29, no. 4 (1988): 541–58; Alice Kessler-Harris, *Out to Work: A History of Wage-Earning Women in the United States* (New York: Oxford University Press, 1982), 238–39.

84. Lieberman, *Shifting the Color Line*, 192–93, 58–59, 44; M. S. Stuart, *An Economic Detour: A History of Insurance in the Lives of American Negroes* (College Park, Md.: McGrath, 1969); Robert E. Weems Jr., *Black Business in the Black Metropolis: The Chicago Metropolitan Assurance Company, 1925–1985* (Bloomington: Indiana University Press, 1996), chap. 5.

85. See *Retirement Plan for the Employees of the Inland Steel Company and Its Subsidiaries*, 1 Jan. 1936; *Contributory Plan for Annuities for Employees of the Ohio Oil Company and Affiliated Companies*, 1 Jan. 1936; *Summary of the 1940 Plan for Annuities and Insurance, Socony Vacuum Oil Company, Inc.*, 31 Dec. 1939; *Retirement Plan for Allegheny Ludlum Steel Corporation and Subsidiary Companies*, 7 Jan. 1941; and *Contributory Plan for Annuities for the Employees of Kentucky West Virginia Gas Company*, 1 July 1939, all in file 050.112, box 23, SSB Records. See also *Pension Plan with Death and Disability Benefits for the Employees of the Barnsdall Corporation.*

86. Albert Handy, "Private Pension Plans and the Federal Revenue Act," *New York University Law Quarterly Review* 16 (1939): 5; Arthur L. Berger to author, research memorandum, "Employee Rights in Benefit Plans," Aug. 2000; *T. C. Boase v. Lee Rubber & Tire Corp.*, 437 F. 2d 527 (1970); Jay Conison, "Suits for Benefits under ERISA," *University of Pittsburgh Law Review* 54 (fall 1992); Brown Report, 11.

87. Reinhard A. Hohaus, "Memorandum for Meeting with Social Security Advisory Council—Dec. 16, 1937," 8 Dec. 1937, file 011.1, box 6, SSB Records.

88. *Spectator*, 2 Mar. 1939; Linton, "Federal Old Age Security Program"; idem, "Annual Report," *Proceedings of the Thirtieth Annual Meeting of the American Life Convention*; T. W. Appleby, "Is Security a Delusion?" *Proceedings of the Thirty-second Annual Meeting of the American Life Convention* (Chicago: ALC, 1937); "Annual Report," *Proceedings of the Thirty-third Annual Meeting of the American Life Convention* (Chicago: ALC, 1938).

89. Brown, *American Philosophy of Social Security*, 67–68; Jacoby, "Employers and the Welfare State."

90. *National Underwriter*, 31 Mar. 1939, 12; Edward D. Berkowitz, "The First Advisory Council and the 1939 Amendments," in *Social Security after Fifty: Successes and Failures*, ed. Edward D. Berkowitz (Westport, Conn.: Greenwood Press, 1987), 62–67; Derthick, *Policymaking for Social Security*, 139–44.

91. Reinhard A. Hohaus, quoted in "Warn of Crushing Burden in Social

Security Outlook: Linton and Hohaus Urge Realistic Stand to Forestall Rude Awakening," *National Underwriter*, 21 Apr. 1939; Marion Folsom, quoted in Jacoby, "Employers and the Welfare State," 546 (Jacoby also writes about the importance of the supplementation argument); Lammot DuPont to Hon. George S. Williams, 9 June 1939, file 3, box 30, Harrington Papers; Cates, *Insuring Inequality*, 90.

92. Berkowitz, "First Advisory Council and the 1939 Amendments," 74; Cates, *Insuring Inequality*, 39; Leff, "Taxing the Forgotten Man," 375–81; Julian E. Zelizer, *Taxing America: Wilbur D. Mills, Congress, and the State, 1945–1975* (New York: Cambridge University Press, 1998), 61–63; Mettler, *Dividing Citizens*, 99–103.

93. Edwin E. Witte, "The Approaching Crisis in Old Age Security," *American Labor Legislation Review*, Sept. 1940, 115–23, idem, "Befuddled Social Security Finances," ibid., Dec. 1942, 149–52; ELAS, *Summary: The Social Security Act Amendments of 1939*, 5–6. Employers such as DuPont expressed their support for excluding employer contributions to welfare funds from the definition of taxable wages (see Lammot DuPont to Williams, 9 June 1939).

94. Linton to Altmeyer, 13 June 1939, file 011.1, box 5, SSB Records.

95. *National Underwriter*, 20 Oct. 1939, 10; 1 Aug. 1939, 12; 25 Aug. 1939, 2; 1 Sept. 1939; 15 Sept. 1939, 20; 25 Aug. 1939, 1; 15 Sept. 1939.

96. Cates, *Insuring Inequality*, 10–17, 32–37, 87–88. The SSB's actuarial advisers opposed Altmeyer's use of the insurance analogy, arguing that it misled the public, for the Social Security pension program and commercial insurance were not the same. One such consultant quipped that among the SSB insiders "there is lip-service to 'actuarial science' as a sort of mystic salvation" (Cates, *Insuring Inequality*, 88). Williamson repeatedly tried to stress the differences between insurance annuities and OASI (Williamson to Cohen, Corson, and I. S. Falk, 16 Oct. 1940, file 050.111, box 23, SSB Records). See also Andrew Achenbaum, *Social Security Visions and Revisions* (New York: Cambridge University Press, 1986), 28, 2–3, 125; Balogh, "Social Security Board as a Political Actor"; and Gordon, *Pitied But Not Entitled.*

97. Altmeyer to Senator Morris Sheppard, 13 May 1939; Robert J. Myers to Williamson, 29 Dec. 1936; Altmeyer to Tom Barnett, 19 Feb. 1940; and Williamson to Robert Shippey, 12 Feb. 1937, all in file 050.112, box 23, SSB Records.

98. Williamson, to Corson, Falk, Cohen, and Max Stern, 12 Oct. 1940; and Williamson to Cohen, Corson, and Falk, 15 Oct. 1940, both in file 050.111, box 23, SSB Records.

99. Brown, *American Philosophy of Social Security.*

100. Thomas Parkinson, "Opening of the Equitable Garden of Security at the New York World's Fair," 23 May 1939, file 7, box 20C, Thomas Parkinson Papers, acc. 1984-050, Historical Collection, RG 4, ELAS Archives.

Chapter 4
Organizing for Health Security

1. For literature on the development of individual private health programs, see, e.g., Sylvia A. Law, *Blue Cross: What Went Wrong?* (New Haven: Yale University Press, 1974); Alan Derickson, *Workers' Health, Workers' Democracy: The Western*

Federation of Miners' Struggle, 1891–1925 (Ithaca: Cornell University Press, 1988); Edward D. Berkowitz and Wendy Wolff, *Group Health Association: A Portrait of a Health Maintenance Organization* (Philadelphia: Temple University Press, 1988); *Between Public and Private: A Half Century of Blue Cross and Blue Shield in New York*, special issue of *Journal of Health Politics, Policy, and Law* 16, no. 4 (1991); Rickey Hendricks, *A Model for National Health Care: The History of Kaiser Permanente* (New Brunswick, N.J.: Rutgers University Press, 1993); Michael R. Grey, *New Deal Medicine: The Rural Health Programs of the Farm Security Administration* (Baltimore: Johns Hopkins University Press, 1999).

2. "Executive Council's Report to Tampa Convention," *American Federationist* 43 (Dec. 1936): 1263.

3. For a discussion of the term *community benefit*, see recent debates over managed care and health policy goals, for example, Mark Schlesinger and Bradford Gray, "A Broader Vision for Managed Care, Part 1: Measuring the Benefit to Communities," *Health Affairs* 17, no. 3 (May/June 1998): 152–68; and idem, "A Broader Vision for Managed Care, Part 2: A Typology of Community Benefits," ibid., no. 5 (Sept./Oct. 1998): 26–49.

4. Paul Starr, *The Social Transformation of American Medicine: The Rise of a Sovereign Profession and the Making of a Vast Industry* (New York: Basic Books, 1982), 193–94, 157; Michael M. Davis, interview, 16 Nov. 1965, 11–15, Columbia University Oral History, Social Security Project, Butler Library, Columbia University, New York; Daniel S. Hirshfield, *The Lost Reform: The Campaign for Compulsory Health Insurance in the United States from 1932 to 1943* (Cambridge: Harvard University Press, 1970), 28. For a more nuanced analysis of the relationship between public health, research science, and medical practice, see Judith Walzer Leavitt, "Typhoid Mary Strikes Back: Bacteriological Theory and Practice in Early Twentieth Century Public Health," in *Sickness and Health in America*, ed. Judith Walzer Leavitt and Ronald L. Numbers, 3d ed. (Madison: University of Wisconsin Press, 1997).

5. Starr, *Social Transformation of American Medicine*, 160–61, 258.

6. I. S. Falk, interview, 28 July 1965, 41–51, Columbia University Oral History, Social Security Project.

7. David Rosner and Gerald Markowitz, "The Early Movement for Occupational Safety and Health, 1900–1917," in Leavitt and Numbers, *Sickness and Health in America*, 467–81; Claudia Clark, *Radium Girls: Women and Industrial Health Reform, 1910–1935* (Chapel Hill: University of North Carolina Press, 1997), chaps. 3–4.

8. Daniel M. Fox, *Health Policies, Health Politics: The British and American Experience, 1911–1965* (Princeton: Princeton University Press, 1986), 38–42.

9. CCMC, *Medical Care for the American People: The Final Report of the Committee on the Costs of Medical Care* (Chicago: University of Chicago Press, 1932), 19; Falk interview, 28 July 1965, 41.

10. CCMC, *Medical Care for the American People*, 41; Falk interview, 28 July 1965, 41; Harry Moore, "Introductory Note," in *A Community Medical Service Organized under Industrial Auspices in Roanoke Rapids, North Carolina*, by I. S. Falk, Don M. Griswold, and Hazel Spicer, Publications of the Committee on the Costs of Medical Care, 20 (Chicago: University of Chicago Press, 1932).

11. CCMC, *Medical Care for the American People*, 10.

12. For a highly critical view of this group of reformers, see Fox, *Health Policies, Health Politics*, 45–51.

13. *The Layman's View about the Costs of Medical Care: Four Articles Reprinted from Current Popular Magazines* (Chicago: Julius Rosenwald Fund, Mar. 1935).

14. Falk, Griswold, and Spicer, *Community Medical Service*, 61.

15. Ibid., 43.

16. David Reisman, "Observations on Medical Service in Roanoke Rapids," ibid., 75–77.

17. Falk, Griswold, and Spicer, *Community Medical Service*, 2–3, 15, 20.

18. Ibid., 94, 104.

19. Starr, *Social Transformation of American Medicine*, 264.

20. Falk, Griswold, and Spicer, *Community Medical Service*, 76, 101.

21. Besides explicitly disavowing compulsory national health insurance, the Majority Report failed to galvanize any broad public consensus for health reform (Paul Starr, "Transformation in Defeat: The Changing Objectives of National Health Insurance 1915–1980," in *Compulsory Health Insurance: The Continuing American Debate*, ed. Ronald L. Numbers [Westport, Conn.: Greenwood Press, 1982], 124–28; Starr, *Social Transformation of American Medicine*, 264–65).

22. Starr, *Social Transformation of American Medicine*, 270; I. S. Falk, *Security against Sickness: A Study of Health Insurance* (New York: Doubleday, Doran, & Co., 1936), 344–47.

23. Falk interview, 28 July 1965; quotation from Falk, *Security against Sickness*, 347.

24. *Julius Rosenwald Fund: Eight Years' Work in Medical Economics, 1929–1936: Recent Trends and Next Moves in Medical Care* (Chicago: Julius Rosenwald Fund, 1937), 3, 2.

25. Ibid.; Davis interview, 11–15.

26. Mary Ross, *The Middle-Rate Plan for Hospital Patients: A Year's Experiment in Keokuk, Iowa* (Chicago: Julius Rosenwald Fund, 1931), 5; C. Rufus Rorem, Clyde Frost, and Elizabeth Richards, *How Do Physicians and Patients Like the Middle Rate Plan for Hospital Care? The Second Year's Experience of the Baker Memorial Unit of the Massachusetts General Hospital, Boston* (Chicago: Julius Rosenwald Fund, 1932).

27. C. Rufus Rorem and J. H. Musser, *Group Payment for Medical Care—The Stancola Employees' Medical and Hospital Association* (Chicago: Julius Rosenwald Fund, 1932); idem, *Private Group Medical Service—A Description of the Organization and Policies of a Private Clinic in a Mid-Western City* (Chicago: Julius Rosenwald Fund, 1937); Margaret Lovell Plumley, *Growth of Clinics in the United States* (Chicago: Julius Rosenwald Fund, 1932); C. Rufus Rorem, *Annual Medical Care Service in Private Group Clinics* (Chicago: Julius Rosenwald Fund, 1932); idem, *Sickness Insurance in the United States* (Chicago: Julius Rosenwald Fund, 1932); *Julius Rosenwald Fund: Eight Years' Work in Medical Economics*, 44–45.

28. Julius Rosenwald Fund, *New Plans for Medical Service: Examples of Organized Local Plans of Providing or Paying for Medical Service in the United States* (Chicago: Julius Rosenwald Fund, 1936); *Julius Rosenwald Fund: Eight Years' Work in Medical Economics*, 16.

29. Michael Davis and Rufus Rorem had written a book in 1932, *The Crisis in*

Hospital Finance (Chicago: University of Chicago Press, 1932), which they now drew on to construct a group hospitalization prepayment plan.

30. "Standards for Non-Profit Hospital Service Plans," app. B in Rufus Rorem, "Enabling Legislation for Non-Profit Hospital Service Plans," *Law and Contemporary Problems,* autumn 1939, box 2, ser. 8E, Thorne Papers.

31. Maurice Norby, "Hospital Plans: Their Contracts and Administration," *Law and Contemporary Problems,* autumn 1939, 548. The Commission on Hospital Service Standards stated that "the ultimate economic responsibility for service to subscribers enrolled within any given time should be assumed by the member hospitals through definite contractual agreement with the hospital service plan" (see Rorem, "Enabling Legislation for Non-Profit Hospital Service Plans"). See also Law, *Blue Cross.*

32. C. Rufus Rorem, *Non-Profit Hospital Service Plans: Historical and Critical Analysis of Group Hospitalization* (Chicago: Commission on Hospital Service, 1940), 7.

33. Ibid., 2, 7–8, 44–45, 72.

34. Mary Ross, "The Case of the Ross-Loos Clinic," *Survey Graphic,* June 1935, 304, 300; idem, "California Weighs Health Insurance," ibid., May 1935, 217; Julius Rosenwald Fund, *New Plans for Medical Service,* 56–58; Frank Taylor, "Group Medicine at Work," *American Mercury,* Aug. 1939, reprinted in SSB, Bureau of Research and Statistics, *Technical Publications Digest,* 7 Sept. 1939; Andrew J. Beimiller, "Medical Care for Wage Earning Groups," *American Federationist* 45 (Sept. 1938): 1055–56; Harry A. Millis, *Sickness and Insurance: A Study of the Sickness Problem and Health Insurance* (Chicago: University of Chicago Press, 1937), 34; William Trufant Foster, *Doctors, Dollars, and Disease* (New York: Public Affairs Committee, 1940), 17; Michael Davis, *America Organizes Medicine* (New York: Harper & Brothers, 1941), 160.

35. Mary Ross, "The Case of the Ross-Loos Clinic," *Survey Graphic,* June 1935, 304, 300; idem, "California Weighs Health Insurance," ibid., May 1935, 217; Taylor, "Group Medicine at Work"; Foster, *Doctors, Dollars, and Disease*; Michael Davis, "Health Insurance Plans under Medical Societies, Part I," *Medical Care* 3 (Aug. 1943): 223.

36. Starr, *Social Transformation of American Medicine,* 194–95; Millis, *Sickness and Insurance,* 33–34; *Julius Rosenwald Fund: Eight Years' Work in Medical Economics,* 5; Kingsley Roberts, address at National Health Conference, *Proceedings of the National Health Conference, July 18, 19, 20, 1938,* Interdepartmental Committee to Coordinate Health and Welfare Activities (Washington, D.C.: Government Printing Office, 1938), 114–15 (hereafter *National Health Conference*); Annie Goodrich, address, ibid., 70–72.

37. The quotation is from Robert E. Neff, address, *National Health Conference,* 78; David J. Rothman, "The Public Presentation of Blue Cross, 1935–1965," in *Between Public and Private: A Half Century of Blue Cross and Blue Shield in New York,* special issue of *Journal of Health Politics, Policy, and Law* 16, no. 4 (1991): 675–76, 684–89; Fox, *Health Policies, Health Politics.*

38. Edward H. Beardsley, *A History of Neglect: Health Care for Blacks and Mill Workers in the Twentieth Century South* (Knoxville: University of Tennessee Press, 1987), 158.

39. Nathan Sinai, Odin W. Anderson, and Melvin L. Dollar, *Health Insurance in the United States* (New York: Commonwealth Fund, 1946), 19–21; Josephine Brown, *Public Relief, 1929–1939* (New York: Henry Holt, 1940), 257.

40. Grey, *New Deal Medicine*, 40–44; Hirshfield, *Lost Reform*, 80–86; Sinai, Anderson, and Dollar, *Health Insurance in the United States*, 19–21; Brown, *Public Relief*, 257.

41. Linda Gordon, *Pitied But Not Entitled: Single Mothers and the History of Welfare* (Cambridge: Harvard University Press, 1994), 145–60.

42. Edwin E. Witte, *The Development of the Social Security Act: A Memorandum on the History of the Committee on Economic Security and Drafting and Legislative History of the Social Security Act* (Madison: University of Wisconsin Press, 1963), 21 (quotation), 23–25, 30–31, 171–77.

43. Ibid., 30–31, 173–89; Falk interview, 28 July 1965.

44. Witte, *Development of the Social Security Act*; Gordon, *Pitied But Not Entitled*, 255–58. Reformers in the Children's Bureau hoped that a child health program would be the first step toward enactment of a universal public health insurance program (ibid., 258).

45. David Rosner and Gerald Markowitz, "Research or Advocacy: Federal Occupational Safety and Health Policies during the New Deal," in *Dying for Work: Workers' Safety and Health in Twentieth Century America*, ed. David Rosner and Gerald Markowitz (Bloomington: Indiana University Press, 1987), 89.

46. Witte, *Development of the Social Security Act*, 171–73.

47. Grey, *New Deal Medicine*, chap. 2. In 1938 the FSA also became involved in providing medical care to migrant agricultural workers, first through federal clinics in migrant camps and then through formal regional and statewide agreements creating agricultural workers' health associations, comprehensive group service plans in which the federal government was the third-party insurer. The FSA negotiated the terms with the state medical society and picked up the costs. The plans offered acute care, maternity care, and preventive services to Mexicans, blacks, and whites (ibid., 81–87).

48. Beardsley, *History of Neglect*, 158–67; Grey, *New Deal Medicine*, 64, 76. The FSA established medical clinics and cooperatives for African Americans and Latinos, although it appears these were usually set up in communities that were predominantly African American or Latino; Susan Smith, *Sick and Tired of Being Sick and Tired: Black Women's Health Activism in America, 1890–1950* (Philadelphia: University of Pennsylvania Press, 1995), 58–59.

49. Jill Quadagno, "Welfare Capitalism and the Social Security Act of 1935," *American Sociological Review* 49 (Oct. 1984): 632–47; Gwendolyn Mink, *The Wages of Motherhood: Maternalist Social Policy and Women's Inequality in the Welfare State, 1917–1942* (Ithaca: Cornell University Press, 1995); Alice Kessler-Harris, "Designing Women and Old Fools: The Construction of the Social Security Amendments of 1939," in *U.S. History as Women's History*, ed. Linda K. Kerber, Alice Kessler-Harris, and Kathryn Kish Sklar (Chapel Hill: University of North Carolina Press, 1995), 87–106.

50. Harold November, "The Security of the American Worker," *American Federationist* 43 (June 1936): 602.

51. *Annual Report of the Social Security Board, Letter from the Social Security Board*

Transmitting First Annual Report of the Social Security Board for the Fiscal Year Ended June 30, 1936 (Washington, D.C.: Government Printing Office, 1937), foreword.

52. Paul Douglas to John G. Winant, 5 Dec. 1936, file 011.1, box 6, SSB Records; Paul H. Douglas, *Social Security in the United States: An Analysis and Appraisal of the Federal Social Security Act* (New York: Whittlesey House, McGraw Hill, 1936); John B. Andrews, "Health Insurance," *American Labor Legislation Review* 27 (June 1937): 59–60.

53. Millis, *Sickness and Insurance*, 143; Harry A. Millis and Royal E. Montgomery, *Labor's Risks and Social Insurance* (New York: McGraw Hill, 1938); "Executive Council's Report to Tampa Convention," 1262–63.

54. Louis S. Reed, *Health Insurance: The Next Step in Social Security* (New York: Harper & Brothers, 1937), 5, 44–46.

55. Falk, *Security against Sickness*, 333.

56. The description of the French health insurance system and Paul Douglas's statement are in ibid., 284 and 319, respectively. See also Millis, *Sickness and Insurance*, 127; and Falk, "Cash and Medical Benefits in Health Insurance," *American Labor Legislation Review* 43 (June 1936): 74.

57. Millis, *Sickness and Insurance*, 1.

58. Michael M. Davis, *Health Security and the American Public* (Chicago: Julius Rosenwald Fund, 1936), 11–12.

59. Interdepartmental Committee for the Coordination of Health and Welfare Activities, *The Need for a National Health Program: Report of the Technical Committee on Medical Care* (Washington, D.C., 1938); Hirshfield, *Lost Reform*, 102–10.

60. Historians usually discuss this event either as a euphoric moment that galvanized the health insurance advocates to push for compulsory health insurance legislation or as evidence of the reformers' cowardice (see Hirshfield, *Lost Reform*, 108–12; Starr, *Social Transformation of American Medicine*, 276–77; Alan Derickson, "Health Security for All? Social Unionism and Universal Health Insurance, 1935–1958," *Journal of American History* 80 [Mar. 1994]: 1333–56; and Fox, *Health Policies, Health Politics*).

61. *National Health Conference.*

62. Ibid., 17.

63. Florence Greenberg, address, ibid., 84–85; Harriet Silverman, address, ibid., 93–96; Eve Stone, address, ibid., 12.

64. Silverman address, ibid., 94.

65. Ibid., 95.

66. Lee Pressman, address, ibid., 105–6.

67. Roberts address, ibid., 115.

68. C.E.A. Winslow, address, ibid., 151, 149; Greenberg address, ibid., 86.

69. Senator Robert F. Wagner, "A Senate Investigation of Security against Sickness," *American Labor Legislation Review* 28 (June 1938): 77–78; "Mountain or Mouse?" ibid. 29 (Mar. 1939): 3; Senator Robert Wagner, "The National Health Bill," ibid. (Mar. 1939): 13–17; U.S. Congress, Senate, Committee on Education and Labor, *Establishing a National Health Program: Preliminary Report on S. 1620*, 76th Cong., 1st sess., 1939, S. Rept. 1139; Fox, *Health Policies, Health Politics*, 91–92.

70. I. S. Falk, interview, 23 Oct. 1968, 178–79, Columbia University Oral History, Social Security Project.

71. Arthur J. Altmeyer, *The Formative Years of Social Security: A Chronicle of Social Security Legislation and Administration, 1934–1954* (Madison: University of Wisconsin Press, 1966), 98, 103; "Proposed Changes in the Social Security Act: A Report of the Social Security Board to the President of the United States, Dec. 30, 1938," in *Social Security Bulletin* 2 (Jan. 1939): 7; Edward D. Berkowitz, "The First Advisory Council and the 1939 Amendments," in *Social Security after Fifty: Successes and Failures,* ed. Edward D. Berkowitz (Westport, Conn.: Greenwood Press, 1987), 70–72. On policy planning for disability, see idem, *Disabled Policy: America's Programs for the Handicapped* (New York: Cambridge University Press, 1987).

72. U.S. Congress, Senate, Subcommittee of the Committee on Education and Labor, *To Establish a National Health Program: Hearings on S. 1620,* 76th Cong., 1st sess., 1939; Arthur J. Altmeyer, testimony, ibid., pt. 3:702; Mathew Woll, testimony, ibid., pt. 1:227; Dr. Lewis T. Wright, testimony, ibid., pt. 1:240; Lee Pressman, testimony, ibid., pt. 1:209. Pressman also called for a nondiscrimination clause to ensure equal treatment for African Americans. See also *Report of the Proceedings of the Fifty-ninth Annual Convention of the American Federation of Labor* (Washington, D.C.: Labor Law Printing, 1939), 194; and Derickson, "Health Security for All?" 15.

73. Starr, *Social Transformation of American Medicine,* 304–7; Leonard M. Gardner, "The Progress of Nonprofit Hospital and Medical Insurance Plans in the State of New York," and "Comments on Mr. Gardner's Article," *Medical Care* 1 (spring 1941): 111–22; "Health Insurance," ibid. 2 (Jan. 1942): 68–69; Michael Davis, "Health Insurance Plans under Medical Societies, Part I," ibid. 3 (Aug. 1943): 217–26.

74. William Green, editorials, *American Federationist* 43 (Feb. 1936): 134–35, (Mar. 1936): 216, 246; William Trufant Foster, "Hospital Care in the Workers' Budget," ibid. (Apr. 1936): 390–93; November, "Security of the American Worker," 602–15; "Executive Council's Report to Tampa Convention," 1258–63; William Green, editorial, "Toward Social Security," *American Federationist* 44 (Feb. 1937): 131; Beimiller, "Medical Care for Wage Earning Groups," 1054–59; editorial, *American Federationist* 43 (June 1936): 578; Derickson, "Health Security for All?" 1338; Raymond Munts, *Bargaining for Health: Labor Unions, Health Insurance, and Medical Care* (Madison: University of Wisconsin Press, 1967), 5; David Rosner and Gerald Markowitz, "Hospitals, Insurance, and the American Labor Movement," *Journal of Policy History* 9, no. 1 (1997).

75. Mary Gerstel, "Chicago Committee for Adequate Medical Care," in "Local Initiative for Organized Medical Care: A Chicago Symposium," *Medical Care* 1 (Apr. 1941): 164–65; Senate Subcommittee on Education and Labor, *To Establish a National Health Insurance Program,* testimony of Florence Greenberg, pt. 3: 877.

76. M. C. Crew and Elmer Daniels, "The Chicago Teachers Union Medical Center Plan," and Petro Lewis Patras, "Search for Health Security," both in "Local Initiative for Organized Medical Care: A Chicago Symposium," *Medical Care* 1 (Apr. 1941): 162–64, 159–61.

77. Beimiller, "Medical Care for Wage Earning Groups," 1056.

78. Leslie Orear, "Chicago Packinghouse Workers and Their Problem of Medical Care," *Medical Care* 1 (Apr. 1941): 157–59.

79. William Green to C. O. Van Horn, 20 Nov. 1939, including letter from Falk to Green; Green to Ralph Benthein, 29 Jan. 1940; Anthony Pareso to Green, 11 Apr. 1940; Green to Pareso, 15 Apr. 1940; Roy Keehn to Green, 14 Nov. 1940; Green to Keehn, 5 Dec. 1940; Alfred Murphy to Green, 20 Jan. 1941; Oregon State Federation of Labor to Green, 26 May 1941; Frederick Mapes to Green, 9 July 1941; and Green to Mapes, 11 July 1941, all in box 3, ser. 8E, Thorne Papers.

80. Florence Thorne to Harold Maslow, 23 Feb. 1940, 1; Maslow to Thorne, 13 Jan., 3 May 1940; C. Rufus Rorem to Thorne, 14 Feb. 1940; W. H. McGreevy to Green, 8 Mar. 1940; Martin Brown to Green, 5 June 1940; Brown to Pareso, 5 June 1940; Kingsley Roberts, M.D., to Green, 5 Mar. 1941; and Percy S. Brown to Green, 2 Dec. 1941, all in ibid.

81. CIO resolution, quoted in "Health Insurance," *Medical Care* 2 (Jan. 1942): 71.

82. AFL, "Cooperative Hospitalization and Medical Insurance Plans," Jan. 1940, L-100 Medical Plan, 1939, Transport Workers Union Collection, Robert F. Wagner Labor Archives, Tamiment Institute Library, New York University; Green to Benthein, 29 Jan. 1940.

83. "Health Insurance," *Medical Care* 2 (Jan. 1942): 72; Thomas L. Perry Jr., "A Medical Student Looks at Trade Union Health Plans," ibid., 84–85.

84. *Medical Plan, Transport Workers Union of Greater New York,* 1939, 2; TWU-CIO press release, "Transport Workers Union Inaugurates Free Medical Service," 15 May 1939; and J. J. Fitzsimon to All Sections in TWU, Local 100, all in file titled "Announcement of Medical Plan," L-100 Medical Plan, 1939, Transport Workers Union Collection; Joshua B. Freeman, *In Transit: The Transport Workers Union in New York City, 1933–1966* (New York: Oxford University Press, 1989), 114–17.

85. Elizabeth Faue discusses the idea of a "community-based unionism," which emphasized "local autonomy and community organization" and "connections with local institutions and especially city-wide labor organizations." She argues that this type of 1930s CIO unionism would soon be displaced by bureaucratic, contract-oriented unionism that focused solely on workers at the workplace (Elizabeth Faue, *Community of Suffering and Struggle: Women, Men, and the Labor Movement in Minneapolis, 1915–1945* [Chapel Hill: University of North Carolina Press, 1991], 4; see also Annelise Orleck, *Common Sense and a Little Fire: Women and Working-Class Politics in the United States, 1900–1965* [Chapel Hill: University of North Carolina Press, 1995], chap. 6).

86. "Labor Union Plans," *Medical Care* 2 (Apr. 1942): 170; Helga Weigert, "Labor's Health Programs in Three Cities," ibid. 3 (May 1943): 11–116.

87. "Washington, D.C.: Group Health Association," one of two articles under the heading "How Subscribers to Group Health Plans Cooperate with Physicians," *Medical Care* 1 (July 1941): 226–27; Starr, *Social Transformation of American Medicine,* 305; Hendricks, *Model for National Health Care,* 7; Medical Service League of California, "An Open Letter to the Members of the Alameda County

Medical Association," 1 Aug. 1942, file: Hospitalization and Health, box 3, series 8E, Thorne Papers; Hubert Person to American Federationist, 21 Dec. 1942, ibid.

88. Helen Hershfield, *Report on Investigation Preliminary to the Establishment of Insurance Plan for the Group Health Cooperative, Inc.* (New York, Apr. 1941), 25, 17, 67, 72. The Group Health Cooperative was eventually subsumed by the city's Health Insurance Plan of New York (HIP) later in the decade.

89. Hendricks, *Model for National Health Care,* 5, 13, 14; Margaret Klem, "Some Recent Developments in Voluntary Health Insurance," *Social Security Bulletin* 5 (Aug. 1942): 14–16.

90. S. Locke, M.D., to John Santo, 24 May 1939, L-100 Medical Plan, 1939, Transport Workers Union Collection. For other letters, see L-100 Medical Plan, 1939, and L-100 Benefits, 1937–39, ibid. Apparently, so many Jewish, Italian, and other immigrant or ethnic doctors serviced the union plan that one doctor, Dr. J. Ruckin Dallas, wanted to resign because of it. Dr. Dallas apparently told a union member, "It's too bad there are so many refs (refugees) in the Plan. . . . There being only four Christians out of forty-one physicians in the plan" (James Caroll to George Rooney, 28 June 1940, L-100 Medical Plan, 1940, ibid.).

91. On the West Coast, see Hendricks, *Model for National Health Care,* 19. See also Klem, "Some Recent Developments in Voluntary Health Insurance"; and Perry, "A Medical Student Looks at Trade Union Health Plans."

92. Central Labor Union of Philadelphia and Vicinity, AFL, *Executive Board Report on the Associated Hospital Service of Philadelphia,* Mar. 1940, box 3, ser. 8E, Thorne Papers; Maslow to Thorne, 3 May 1940, ibid.; Maslow to Wilbur Cohen, 17 May 1940, file: Health Insurance, file 056.1, box 35, SSB Records. On New York, see Gerald Markowitz and David Rosner, "Seeking Common Ground: A History of Labor and Blue Cross," in *Between Public and Private: A Half Century of Blue Cross and Blue Shield in New York,* special issue of *Journal of Health Politics, Policy, and Law* 16, no. 4 (1991): 695–718. In New York City, union contracts spurred the growth of the Associated Hospital Service, which covered more than 1,250,000 individuals by 1940.

93. UAW-CIO, *Group Hospitalization Report by Chrysler Committee,* Feb. 1941, file 14, box 99, UAW SSD; George F. Addes to All Local Unions Affiliated with the International Union, 11 Oct. 1940, file 5, box 31, Addes Papers; Addes to All Employees, 11 Oct. 1940, ibid.; "Complete Hospital Care—Complete Surgical Care, for Employees and Their Families", ibid.; "Hospital and Surgical Plan Questions and Answers," ibid. The UAW explained that although it would have preferred to build a union health center, the union was not yet stable enough to pursue such a large and complicated project (UAW-CIO Hospitalization Committee to R. J. Thomas, 17 Apr. 1942, file 1, box 29, ibid.). See also "Health Insurance," *Medical Care* 2 (Jan. 1942): 70; and Robert William Dvorsky, "The Development of Negotiated Health Insurance and Sickness Benefit Plans of the Steel, Automobile, and Electrical Equipment Industries" (Ph.D. diss, University of Pittsburgh, 1956). Ford locals chose a John Hancock policy because Ford refused to make the payroll deduction to Michigan Hospital Service Plan (see "Labor Union Plans," *Medical Care* 2 [Apr. 1942]: 170–71).

94. Central Labor Union of Philadelphia and Vicinity, AFL, *Executive Board Report on The Associated Hospital Service of Philadelphia.*

95. Robert J. Clarke, "Los Angeles, California: Ross-Loss Clinic," one of two articles under the heading "How Subscribers to Group Health Plans Cooperate with Physicians," *Medical Care* 1 (July 1941): 222–26.

96. Special board meeting, International Executive Board, 27 Apr. 1941, 5, file 2, box 14, pt. 1, Addes Papers; and Art Hughes, "It Began in 1940–41: U.A.W. Chrysler Pre-Pay Hospital-Medical-Surgical Drug-Dental-Vision-Hearing Aid Plans," 18 July 1977, 3, file 14, box 99, UAW SSD.

97. The AFL, for example, sent Falk a proposal from the Associated Family Service, a health plan starting up in Fort Wayne, Indiana. See Falk to Elizabeth Paschal, 17 Nov. 1939, and Paschal to Falk, 20 Nov. 1939, file: Hospital and Health, box 3, ser. 8E, Thorne Papers; and SSB to Richard Neustadt, 25 May 1940, file 056.1, box 35, SSB Records.

98. Barkev Sanders and Margaret Klem, "Services and Costs in a Prepayment Medical Care Plan: Comparison with Other Plans and with the General Population," *Medical Care* 2 (July 1942): 221; Margaret Klem, *Prepayment Medical Care Organizations,* SSB, Bureau of Research and Statistics, memorandum 55 (Washington, D.C.: Government Printing Office, 1945). As will be discussed in chapter 5, the UMW and the UAW consulted directly with Falk and the SSB in designing their "trade union social security" programs (see Falk to Walter Reuther, 15 Oct. 1946, including a fifteen-page analysis of the UAW program, file 2, box 46, Cohen Papers; and on the UMW, see Edward D. Berkowitz, "Growth of the U.S. Social Welfare System in the Post–World War II Era: The UMW, Rehabilitation, and the Federal Government," *Research in Economic History* 5 [1980]: 233–47).

99. Michael M. Davis, "Health Insurance Plans under Medical Societies, Part II," *Medical Care* 4 (Feb. 1944); quotation from Weigert, "Labor's Health Programs in Three Cities," 104–5.

100. UAW-CIO Hospitalization Committee to Thomas, 17 Apr. 1942; Memorandum to Thomas, n.d., file 1, box 29, Addes Papers; Weigert, "Labor's Health Programs in Three Cities," 106–11. On steelworkers' efforts to gain union control or at least input, see Alan Derickson, "The United Steelworkers of America and Health Insurance, 1937–1962," in *American Labor in the Era of World War II,* ed. Sally M. Miller and Daniel A. Cornford (Westport, Conn.: Praeger, 1995), 69–85.

101. Clarke, "Los Angeles, California: Ross-Loos Clinic."

102. Senate Subcommittee on Education and Labor, *To Establish a National Health Program,* testimony of Lee Pressman, pt. 1:209; "Democratic Experimentation," *Medical Care* 1 (Apr. 1941): 167–68.

103. Beimiller, "Medical Care for Wage Earning Groups," 1057.

104. UAW-CIO Hospitalization Committee to Thomas, 17 Apr. 1942, 3.

105. CIO resolution, quoted in "Health Insurance," *Medical Care* 2 (Jan. 1942): 71.

106. November, "Security of the American Worker," 615.

Chapter 5
Economic Security on the Home Front

Epigraph: pamphlet, file 15, box 2, Saul Mills Papers.

1. Marilynn S. Johnson, *The Second Gold Rush: Oakland and the East Bay in World War II* (Berkeley: University of California Press, 1993), 2–4; Sally M. Miller and Daniel A. Cornford, eds., *American Labor in the Era of World War II* (Westport, Conn.: Praeger, 1995), introduction.

2. Margaret Klem, "Voluntary Medical Insurance Plans: Their Extent and Limitations," *Medical Care* 4 (Nov. 1944): 264. Government programs even provided dental care.

3. Steven Fraser, *Labor Will Rule: Sidney Hillman and the Rise of American Labor* (New York: Free Press, 1991), 502; Alan Brinkley, *The End of Reform: New Deal Liberalism in Recession and War* (New York: Alfred A. Knopf, 1995); Christopher Tomlins, *The State and the Unions: Labor Relations, Law, and the Organized Labor Movement, 1880–1960* (New York: Cambridge University Press, 1985).

4. Margaret Klem, "Some Recent Developments in Voluntary Health Insurance," *Social Security Bulletin* 5 (Aug. 1942): 15–16; idem, "Voluntary Medical Insurance Plans," 264; Michael R. Grey, *New Deal Medicine: The Rural Health Programs of the Farm Security Administration* (Baltimore: Johns Hopkins University Press, 1999), 5, 69, 80, and chap. 4; Nathan Sinai and Odin W. Anderson, *EMIC: A Study of Administrative Experience*, Bureau of Health Economics, Research Series no. 3 (Ann Arbor: University of Michigan School of Public Health, 1948), 2–3. The FSA subsidized the bulk of the operating costs for the experimental plans. According to Grey, Congress began attacking the programs and reducing the FSA budget after 1943. As physicians became more prosperous with the war and the spread voluntary health insurance, they became increasingly reluctant to participate in these federally sponsored programs, accept heavily discounted fees, and respond to community input and review. FSA leaders and staff became victims of red-baiting from both Congress and the AMA. In 1946 Congress dismantled the agency, and the experimental health plans were ended (see Grey, *New Deal Medicine*).

5. "Medical Care in California Public Housing Projects," *Medical Care* 4 (May 1944): 119–22; "Voluntary Health Insurance Plans," ibid. 3 (Feb. 1943): 360–61; Michael M. Davis, "Health Insurance Plans under Medical Societies, Part II," ibid. 4 (Feb. 1944): 20–21. The one major California war production town where the Housing Authority could not establish a plan was Richmond. There, of course, most workers were employed by Kaiser Industries and hence enrolled in the Kaiser Permanente plan. Permanente at this time did provide comprehensive prepaid medical care, but only for Kaiser employees.

6. Title V, which Eliot helped draft, originally included four sections: Maternal and Child Health Services; Services for Crippled Children; Child Welfare Services; and Aid to Dependent Children. Aid to Dependent Children was later spun off into a separate title, IV, and given to the new SSB to administer (see *Interview with Martha May Eliot, M.D.*, Schlesinger-Rockefeller Oral History Project, Nov. 1973–May 1974 [Cambridge, Mass.: Radcliffe College, 1976], 72–77, 83–88; Gwendolyn Mink, *The Wages of Motherhood: Maternalist Social Policy and*

Women's Inequality in the Welfare State, 1917–1942 [Ithaca: Cornell University Press, 1995], 66–72; and Linda Gordon, *Pitied But Not Entitled: Single Mothers and the History of Welfare* [Cambridge: Harvard University Press, 1994], 256–63).

7. Harry Becker, interview, 21 Nov. 1967, 18, Columbia University Oral History, Social Security Project, Butler Library, Columbia University, New York.

8. *Interview with Martha May Eliot, M.D.*, 104–8.

9. Martha M. Eliot, M.D., "Experience with the Administration of a Medical Care Program for Wives and Infants of Enlisted Men," *American Journal of Public Health* 34 (Jan. 1944): 36; Nathan Sinai, Odin W. Anderson, and Melvin L. Dollar, *Health Insurance in the United States* (New York: Commonwealth Fund, 1946), 21; Sinai and Anderson, *EMIC*, 83, 175, 110. Sinai and Anderson found, for example, that in Nebraska during the war 88% of the births to servicemen's wives, and 16% of the total births in the state, were covered by EMIC. Sinai and Anderson did not see EMIC as employing a means test. As they concluded, "With such a great majority included in EMIC, the program did not experience the usual public reaction toward publicly supported or 'free' medical service" (ibid., 114).

10. Stuart Adler, M.D., "Medical Care for Dependents of Men in the Military Service," *American Journal of Public Health* 33 (June 1943): 645–50, quotation on 650. Adler was director of the Division of Maternal and Child Health at the New Mexico Department of Public Health in Santa Fe.

11. Eliot, "Experience with the Administration of a Medical Care Program," 36.

12. Becker interview, 7.

13. Sinai and Anderson, *EMIC*, 176–77, 181.

14. U.S. Congress, Senate, Subcommittee of the Committee on Education and Labor, *Hearings: Wartime Health and Education*, 78th Cong., 2d sess., pt. 5, 10–12 July 1944, and pt. 6, 18–20 Sept. 1944.

15. *Maternal and Child Health Services*, 79th Cong., 1st sess., S. 1318, 4–7, 22; Becker interview; nondiscrimination clause quoted from Michael M. Davis, "Babies on the Doorstep," *Survey Graphic*, Nov. 1945, 438–39.

16. Becker interview, 7, 5–6.

17. *Maternal and Child Health Services*, 6; *Hearings, Wartime Health and Education*, pt. 6, Sept. 1944, pp. 1920–1921; Becker interview, 7, 13, 6, 24, 26–27.

18. Mink, *Wages of Motherhood*, 13, 8; Gordon, *Pitied But Not Entitled*, 7, chap. 9. Eileen Boris has argued that among other agencies and programs, there were women who offered policy alternatives not based on maternalism (Boris, "Mothers, Work, and Social Policy: De-centering Maternalism" [paper presented at the annual meeting of the Organization of American Historians, Toronto, Apr. 1999]).

19. "Extending the Social Security Program," *Social Security Bulletin* 6 (Mar. 1943): 8; Arthur J. Altmeyer, "Social Insurance for Permanently Disabled Workers," ibid. 4 (Mar. 1941): 10, 3; Summary of discussions, Labor Research Group meeting, 3–4 Mar. 1942, Tuesday afternoon session, 3 Mar., pp. 4–5, box 3, ser. 8E, Thorne Papers.

20. Agenda and summary of discussions, Labor Research Group meeting, 3–4 Mar. 1942, and Ida Merriam to Elizabeth Paschal, 23 Mar. 1942, both in box 3, ser. 8E, Thorne Papers.

21. Edward D. Berkowitz, *Mr. Social Security: The Life of Wilbur J. Cohen* (Lawrence: University Press of Kansas, 1995), 50; Arthur J. Altmeyer, "The Desirability of Expanding the Social Insurance Program Now," *Social Security Bulletin* 5 (Nov. 1942): 6.

22. Arthur J. Altmeyer, quoted in SSB, "Hospitalization Payments under Old Age and Survivors Insurance," approved summary of the discussion between SSB and AHA representatives, Washington, D.C., 3, 4 Sept. 1942, file 4, box 52, Cohen Papers.

23. U.S. Congress, Senate, Committee on Education and Labor, *Establishing a National Health Program: Preliminary Report on S. 1620,* 76th Cong., 1st sess., 1939, S. Rept. 1139. I. S. Falk to Arthur J. Altmeyer, 23 May 1941; I. S. Falk, "Preliminary Notes *Re* Hospital Benefits in a Revised Social Insurance Program," 23 May 1941; "Hospitalization Payments: Social Security for the Costs of Hospital Care," 2 Feb. 1942; and I. S. Falk, "Some Notes Summarizing the Conference between the Board and Representatives of Group Hospitalization Plans," 14 Jan. 1942, all in file 4, box 52, Cohen Papers.

24. I. S. Falk, "Some Notes Summarizing the Conference between the Board and Representatives of Group Hospitalization Plans"; SSB, "Hospitalization Payments under Old Age and Survivors Insurance"; S. S. Goldwater, M.D., to William Green, 24 Feb. 1942, box 3, ser. 8E, Thorne Papers; resolution adopted by the Assembly of Presidents and Secretaries of State and Provincial Hospital Associations, 14 Feb. 1942, ibid.

25. Falk, "Some Notes Summarizing the Conference between the Board and the Representatives of Group Hospitalization Plans," 2; SSB, "Hospitalization Payments under Old Age and Survivors Insurance," 7; Falk, quoted in summary of discussions, Labor Research Group Meeting, 3–4 Mar. 1942, Tuesday afternoon session, 3 Mar., 9.

26. Daniel S. Hirshfield, *The Lost Reform: The Campaign for Compulsory Health Insurance in the United States from 1932 to 1943* (Cambridge: Harvard University Press, 1970), 163–64.

27. "Medical Care for a Hundred Million People: A Summary of the Wagner-Murray-Dingell Bill, S. 1611 and H.R. 2861," *Medical Care* 3 (Aug. 1943): 239–55.

28. Becker interview, 19, 24. Martha Eliot also discussed conflicts between Altmeyer and the Children's Bureau. It seems that Altmeyer continually tried to issue orders to Katherine Lenroot and Martha Eliot and to subordinate the Children's Bureau's administration of EMIC and other welfare programs to SSB oversight (*Interview with Martha May Eliot, M.D.*, 93–94). Perhaps one reason their maternal and children's health bill fell so flat was that the SSB and its allies, such as Nelson Cruikshank, refused to endorse it and even wrote letters asking people to oppose it (see, e.g., Nelson Cruikshank to Mathew Woll, memorandum, 21 May 1946, file 24, box 45, ser. 1, Legislation Department Records, 1906–1978, RG 21-001, AFL Collection, George Meany Memorial Archives, Silver Spring, Md.).

29. Falk interview, 23 Oct. 1968, 250; Edwin Amenta and Theda Skocpol, "Redefining the New Deal: World War II and the Development of Social Provi-

sion in the United States," in *The Politics of Social Policy in the United States*, ed. Margaret Weir, Ann Shola Orloff, and Theda Skocpol (Princeton: Princeton University Press, 1988), 87–89, 106–8; Margaret Weir, "The Federal Government and Unemployment: The Frustration of Policy Innovation from the New Deal to the Great Society," ibid. Altmeyer's statement that the report provided "background" material comes from Berkowitz, *Mr. Social Security*, 51; Berkowitz argues, however, that the SSB supported the NRPB report.

30. "Medical Care for a Hundred Million People," 246–48; Martha Derthick, *Policymaking for Social Security* (Washington, D.C.: Brookings Institution, 1979), 84–86, 26.

31. Falk interview, 23 Oct. 1968, 239–40. Falk, however, may have had some reservations about the impact that this encouragement of private benefits might have on future attempts to expand Social Security.

32. Fraser, *Labor Will Rule*, 455–57, 459, 463–68; James B. Atleson, *Labor and the Wartime State: Labor Relations and Law during World War II* (Urbana: University of Illinois Press, 1998), 8, 20–33; Nelson Lichtenstein, *The Most Dangerous Man in Detroit: Walter Reuther and the Fate of American Labor* (New York: Basic Books, 1995), chap. 8.

33. War Labor Disputes Act, quoted in Atleson, *Labor and the Wartime State*, 46, 45–46.

34. Ibid., 5–7, 11–12, 59; Fraser, *Labor Will Rule*, 344; Robert H. Zieger, *The CIO, 1935–1955* (Chapel Hill: University of North Carolina Press, 1995), 82.

35. Lichtenstein, *Most Dangerous Man in Detroit*, 180; Atleson, *Labor and the Wartime State*, 59.

36. See *Strand Baking Company Case No. 3107-AR* (17 Nov. 1942) (the first set of WLB decisions that involved employee benefits did not pertain to the wage stabilization issue); *U.S. Cartridge Company Case No. 111-1445-D* (30 Nov. 1943); and *Basic Steel Cases, Carnegie-Illinois Steel Corporation et al. Case No. 111-6230-D* (25 Nov. 1944), as reported in National War Labor Board, *Termination Report of the National War Labor Board, Jan. 12, 1942–Dec. 31, 1945*, 3 vols. (Washington, D.C.: Government Printing Office, 1947), vol. 1, chap. 33, "Insurance Plans." See also Clarence O. Skinner, alternate industry member, "The Fringe Issues," in *Trends in Union Demands* (New York: American Management Association, 1945). Concerning insurance plans, Skinner stated that "some have been negotiated with unions, but most have been established by unilateral application. The Board has never ordered a sick-leave or insurance plan when one did not exist."

37. CIO, *Proceedings of the Executive Board*, Washington, D.C., 16–18 June 1944, George Meany Memorial Archives; *Associated Fur Coat and Trimming Manufacturers Case No. 111-6849-D* (14 Nov. 1944), in National War Labor Board, *Termination Report*, vol. 1, chap. 33.

38. *Philadelphia Transportation Company Case No. 3056-AR* (11 Feb. 1943), in National War Labor Board, *Termination Report*, 1:384; Atleson, *Labor and the Wartime State*, 72.

39. See *Western Union Company Case No. 2516-CS-D* (18 Jan. 1943); *West Coast Airframe Cases No. 2301–CS-D* (3 Mar. 1943); *Tidewater Oil Company Case No.*

111-5206-D (24 Jan. 1945); *Davis Engineering Corporation Case No. 111-7172-HO* (7 Feb. 1945); and *Edison Sault Electric Company Case No. 111-7549-D* (6 Mar. 1945), all in National War Labor Board, *Termination Report,* 1:384, 2:1190–92.

40. Zieger, *CIO,* 150.

41. Atleson, *Labor and the Wartime State,* 59; Lichtenstein, *Most Dangerous Man in Detroit.*

42. Archibald Cox, quoted in Katherine Van Wezel Stone, "The Post-War Paradigm in American Labor Law," *Yale Law Journal* 90 (June 1981): 1514; Atleson, *Labor and the Wartime State,* 55–59; Lichtenstein, *Most Dangerous Man in Detroit,* 181–82.

43. Steven A. Sass, *The Promise of Private Pensions: The First Hundred Years* (Cambridge: Harvard University Press, 1997), 103–12; Christopher Howard, *The Hidden Welfare State: Tax Expenditures and Social Policy in the United States* (Princeton: Princeton University Press, 1997).

44. Insurance companies, however, were not part of this opposition: they favored vesting (Sass, *Promise of Private Pensions,* 104–7).

45. Ibid.

46. Ibid., 105–6, 108, 110, 284; Teresa Ghilarducci, *Labor's Capital: The Economics and Politics of Private Pensions* (Cambridge, Mass.: MIT Press, 1992); Sanford M. Jacoby, *Modern Manors: Welfare Capitalism since the New Deal* (Princeton: Princeton University Press, 1997).

47. Sass, *Promise of Private Pensions,* 107; Beth Stevens, "Blurring the Boundaries: How the Federal Government Has Influenced Welfare Benefits in the Private Sector," in Weir, Orloff, and Skocpol, *Politics of Social Policy in the United States,* 123–48.

48. Sass, *Promise of Private Pensions,* 108–9.

49. See, e.g., CIO, *Proceedings of the Executive Board,* Nov. 1943, Jan., June 1944; *Minutes of Meetings of the AFL Executive Council,* vol. 89, 17–22 May 1943, and vol. 90A, 1944, George Meany Memorial Archives.

50. National War Labor Board, *Termination Report,* 1:381–83; Helen Baker and Dorothy Dahl, *Group Health Insurance and Sickness Benefit Plans in Collective Bargaining* (Princeton: Industrial Relations Section, Princeton University, 1945), 18–22.

51. Memorandum to R. J. Thomas, RE: UAW-CIO Health Program, Committee on Hospitalization, n.d., file 1, box 29, Addes Papers.

52. Health Institute of the UAW-CIO, "Program and Affiliation," 10 Mar. 1944, file 5, box 26, ibid.; "1943: An Editorial Review," *Medical Care* 4 (Feb. 1944): 10.

53. Raymond Munts, *Bargaining for Health: Labor Unions, Health Insurance, and Medical Care* (Madison: University of Wisconsin Press, 1967), chap. 2 and pp. 23–25; "Union Health Activities," *Medical Care* 3 (Nov. 1943): 364; Joshua B. Freeman, *Working-Class New York* (New York: New Press, 2000), 130.

54. R. J. Thomas, address at the second annual health conference sponsored by the Medical Research Institute, UAW-CIO, Detroit, Mich., 10 Mar. 1944, file 5, box 26, Addes Papers.

55. William Smith to Dr. Leo Perlman, 8 Dec. 1944, file 1, box 11, ser. 3, Addes Papers.

56. *Furniture Workers Press*, Oct. 1994, 5, quoted in Baker and Dahl, *Group Health Insurance and Sickness Benefit Plans*, 31. On the increasing centralization and bureaucratization of unions, see Elizabeth Faue, "Paths of Unionization: Community, Bureaucracy, and Gender in the Minneapolis Labor Movement of the 1930s," in *Work Engendered: Toward a New History of American Labor*, ed. Ava Baron (Ithaca: Cornell University Press, 1991); Atleson, *Labor and Wartime State*; Fraser, *Labor Will Rule*; Nelson Lichtenstein, *Labor's War at Home: The CIO in World War II* (New York: Cambridge University Press, 1982); and Ghilarducci, *Labor's Capital*, 37.

57. Baker and Dahl, *Group Health Insurance and Sickness Benefit Plans*, 42.

58. Isadore Katz to Perlman, 3 Nov. 1944, file 1, box 11, ser. 3, pt. 2, Addes Papers; Smith to Perlman, 8 Dec. 1944.

59. Reuther to Perlman, 17 Oct. 1944, file 1, box 11, Addes Papers; Reuther to All Members of the International Executive Board, UAW, 16 Jan. 1945, ibid. Reuther, at that time a vice president, did not necessarily have the endorsement of other UAW officials in pursuing this avenue. George Addes, Leslie Anderson, and others in Addes's camp opposed these efforts. Perlman himself wrote Reuther to say that Reuther was misleading the UAW in the way he described the plan to the executive council (Perlman to Reuther, 27 Apr. 1945, ibid.).

60. Perlman to Reuther, 27 Apr. 1945.

61. Martin Segal, interview, 3 Mar. 1994, 7, 12, 12–16, Robert F. Wagner Labor Archives; Roberts to Addes, 23 Aug. 1945, file 6, box 10, Addes Papers; *National Underwriter*, 2 July 1943, 4. In negotiations, Segal tried to ensure that dividends on group insurance policies went toward the workers' share of the premium.

62. See *Blueprinting a Health and Group Insurance Plan* (New York: Trade Union Agency, 1946), file 6, box 5, Saul Mills Papers.

63. Baker and Dahl, *Group Health Insurance and Sickness Benefit Plans*, 79.

64. "Mr. Kaiser Demonstrates Group Practice," *Medical Care* 3 (Nov. 1943).

65. Rickey Hendricks, *A Model for National Health Care: The History of Kaiser Permanente* (New Brunswick, N.J.: Rutgers University Press, 1993), 20–33; U.S. Congress, House, Committee on Interstate and Foreign Commerce, *Hearings: Health Inquiry (Voluntary Health Plans)*, 83d Cong., 2d sess., testimony of Henry J. Kaiser, 11 Jan. 1954, pt. 6: 1342 (hereafter *Health Inquiry*).

66. Hendricks, *Model for National Health Care*, 35–37.

67. Ibid., 46–47; Johnson, *Second Gold Rush*, 28–33, 8.

68. Sidney Garfield, "The Plan That Kaiser Built," *Survey Graphic*, Dec. 1945, 480.

69. Hendricks, *Model for National Health Care*, 50–51; Garfield, "Plan That Kaiser Built," 482; testimony of Henry Kaiser, *Health Inquiry*, 1343–44.

70. "U.S. Medicine in Transition," *Fortune*, Dec. 1944, 162; Garfield, "Plan That Kaiser Built"; Hendricks, *Model for National Health Care*, 51.

71. Hendricks, *Model for National Health Care*, 63–76, 115; testimony of Henry Kaiser, *Health Inquiry*, 1343.

72. Garfield, "Plan That Kaiser Built," 481.

73. "U.S. Medicine in Transition," 157.

74. Hendricks, *Model for National Health Care*, chaps. 4–5; Paul Starr, *The Social Transformation of American Medicine: The Rise of a Sovereign Profession and the Making of a Vast Industry* (New York: Basic Books, 1982), 320–27.

75. Lichtenstein, *Most Dangerous Man in Detroit*, 218; Nelson Lichtenstein, "Class Politics and the State during World War Two," *International Labor and Working Class History* 58 (fall 2000): 263–64.

76. Daniel Horowitz, *Betty Friedan and the Making of the Feminine Mystique: The American Left, the Cold War, and Modern American Feminism* (Amherst: University of Massachusetts Press, 1998), chaps. 6–8.

77. Alan Derickson, "Health Security for All? Social Unionism and Universal Health Insurance, 1935–1958," *Journal of American History* 80 (Mar. 1994): 1345; John L. Lewis, quoted in Fraser, *Labor Will Rule*, 563; Munts, *Bargaining for Health*, 30–41; Edward D. Berkowitz, "Growth of the U.S. Social Welfare System in the Post–World War II Era: The UMW, Rehabilitation, and the Federal Government," *Research in Economic History* 5 (1980): 236; Melvyn Dubofsky and Warren Van Tine, *John L. Lewis: A Biography* (New York: Quadrangle New York Times Book Co., 1977), 458–68.

78. Berkowitz, "Growth of the U.S. Social Welfare System," 236.

79. Ivana Krajcinovic, *From Company Doctors to Managed Care: The United Mine Workers' Noble Experiment* (Ithaca: ILR Press, Cornell University Press, 1997), 29–38.

80. I. S. Falk, quoted in Berkowitz, "Growth of the U.S. Social Welfare System," 236.

81. Berkowitz, "Growth of the U.S. Social Welfare System," 236–37; Krajcinovic, *From Company Doctors to Managed Care*, 54. Moreover, Berkowitz writes that eventually "the UMW sought to shift the financial burden of caring for disabled miners from the private to the public sector by referring all applicants for cash disability benefits and all recipients of emergency medical care to the public program. The greater a miner's disability, the more eager the fund was to have the public program pay for his rehabilitation counseling and training" (240).

82. Krajcinovic, *From Company Doctors to Managed Care*, 51–54. Krajcinovic also discusses the sacrifices Lewis had to make to gain union control of the fund, for example, acquiescing to mechanization, consolidation of the industry in the hands of large operators, and overall decline in employment. On the UMW disability and rehabilitation program, see Berkowitz, "Growth of the U.S. Social Welfare System," 238–39.

83. *CIO News*, 9 Dec. 1946, 2.

84. *NAM News*, Industrial Relations section, 25 Aug. 1945, box 3, Industrial Relations Division, acc. 1412, NAM Records; "Statement of NWLB's Industry Members with Reference to Wage Report of Public Members," 10 Mar. 1945, box 19, ibid.; "Minutes, Subcommittee of NAM Labor Negotiations Committee on the Subject of Union Encroachment," minutes of meeting at the Hotel Biltmore, New York, 22 Oct. 1945, box 3, ibid.

85. Howell John Harris, *The Right to Manage: Industrial Relations Policies of American Business in the 1940s* (Madison: University of Wisconsin Press, 1982), chap. 3, quotation on 96; Fraser, *Labor Will Rule*, 565; Jacoby, *Modern Manors*, 35–46; Andrew Workman, "Manufacturing Power: The Organizational Revival

of the National Association of Manufacturers, 1941–1945," *Business History Review* 78 (summer 1998): 279–317.

86. "Summary of War Labor Board Action in Cases Involving Rights and Responsibilities of Management," n.d., box 19, Industrial Relations Division, acc. 1412, NAM Records.

87. Falk, quoted in Berkowitz, "Growth of the U.S. Social Welfare System," 236.

88. Bartholomew H. Sparrow, *From the Outside In: World War II and the American State* (Princeton: Princeton University Press, 1996), chap. 2; Ira Katznelson, Kim Geiger, and Daniel Kryder, "Limiting Liberalism: The Southern Veto in Congress, 1933–1950," *Political Science Quarterly* 108 (1993): 283–306.

89. Arthur J. Altmeyer, "The Need for Social Security in the Postwar World," address delivered at the fifteenth annual meeting of the Controllers' Institute of America, New York, 16 Sept. 1946, reprinted in *Social Security Bulletin* 9 (Nov. 1946): 4.

90. Greater New York CIO Political Action Committee, *Insure Your Future* and *The Man and the Record*, both 1944, file 15, CIO-PAC, box 2, Saul Mills Papers.

Chapter 6
Managing Security

1. See, e.g., Lawrence Root, *Fringe Benefits: Social Insurance in the Steel Industry* (Beverly Hills, Calif.: Sage, 1982), chap. 2; Robert Zieger, *American Workers, American Unions*, 2d ed. (Baltimore: Johns Hopkins University Press, 1994); and Beth Stevens, "Blurring the Boundaries: How the Federal Government Has Influenced Welfare Benefits in the Private Sector," in *The Politics of Social Policy in the United States*, ed. Margaret Weir, Ann Shola Orloff, and Theda Skocpol (Princeton: Princeton University Press, 1988), 123–48.

2. Robert D. Eilers and Robert M. Crowe, eds., *Group Insurance Handbook* (Homewood, Ill.: Richard D. Irwin, 1965), 65–66.

3. "What the Factory Worker Thinks about Free Enterprise," enclosure in C. M. Chester to Walter S. Carpenter, 11 Feb. 1942, file 1.2, box 827, Walter S. Carpenter Papers, ser. 2, pt. 2, acc. 542, Dupont Collection, HML.

4. The quotation is from William Haber, "Pensions and Collective Bargaining," in *The Law and Labor Management Relations*, file 1, box 249, Cohen Papers. See also NAM, "Suggested Resolution on Greater Security through Employee Benefit Programs for Consideration of Resolutions Committee," 14 Oct. 1948, box 105, acc. 1411, NAM Records; Thomas Parkinson, "Opening of the Equitable Garden of Security at the New York World's Fair," supplement to Equitable Agency items, 29 May 1939, file 7, box 20C, Thomas Parkinson Papers, acc. 1984-050, Historical Collection, RG 4, ELAS Archives.

5. Thomas Parkinson, "Are Life Insurance Companies Pikers?" address at the Bond Club, reprinted in *Underwriter Review*, 23 May 1943, file 2, box 21A, Parkinson Papers.

6. *Spectator*, 24 Jan. 1935, 15, and 31 Oct. 1935, 16; Williamson to Corson, Falk, Cohen, and Stern, 12 Oct. 1940, file 050.111, box 23, SSB Records; "The

Social Security Approach," *National Underwriter*, 26 Mar. 1943, 10; quotation from ibid., 20 Nov. 1942, 27.

7. N. E. Horelick to Sales and Service Staff of the Group Department, 19 Sept. 1939, and William J. Graham to Group Patrons, 27 Oct. 1939, both in file 4, box 35A, Group Insurance Research Division, acc. 1984-050, RG 4, ELAS Archives; William J. Graham, "Incidental Notes on a Group Annuity Retirement Plan to Supplement the Federal Old Age Benefits of the Social Security Act," 1935, file 1, box 18D, Graham Papers; idem, "Social Security," radio address, 17 Dec. 1936, file 2, ibid.

8. *Spectator*, Oct. 1942, 78; *National Underwriter*, 9, 2 Apr. 1943; M. Albert Linton, "Current Thinking on Social Security—Public and Private," *Spectator*, May 1944; idem, "Life Insurance in Review," ibid., May 1949; "Group Trends," ibid., Oct 1943, 64; *National Underwriter*, 6 May, 7, 14, 22 Aug. 1942; Graham to Sterling Morton, 16 Oct. 1935, file 18, closed files, Sterling Pierson Files, ELAS Archives; Derthick, *Policymaking for Social Security*, 136–42.

9. *Spectator*, Apr. 1943, 64; *National Underwriter*, 22 May 1942, 4. Health and accident insurers also fought the proposed Railroad Retirement Bill in 1946 because it would include life and health insurance benefits. Insurers feared that this provision would set a precedent in social insurance legislation that employees in other sectors might build upon (ibid., 19 July 1946, 2).

10. *National Underwriter*, 4 Dec. 1942, 12.

11. "Hospitalization Insurance Forms and Rates Discussed," ibid., 10 Aug. 1934, 6; "Hospital Coverage Forms Suggested," ibid., 31 Aug. 1934, 5; "Hospital Cover Reviewed: G. W. Fitzhugh of the Metropolitan Life Describes Experiments in That Field," ibid., 9 Nov. 1934, 3; "Vice President Graham Presented the Following Memorandum Dated August 6, 1934," file 9, box 34B, Group Insurance, acc. 1984-050, RG 4, ELAS Archives; E. E. Cammack to Members of the Group Association, 19 Apr. 1939, box: Correspondence and Office Files, Ray D. Murphy Files, acc. 84-14, RG 2, ibid.; Louis I. Dublin, *A Family of Thirty Million: The Story of the Metropolitan Life Insurance Company* (New York: MLIC, 1943), 194–97.

12. "Group Hospitalization Insurance, History of Premium Rates," 30 Apr. 1934–1 Mar. 1939, file 7, box: Correspondence and Office Files, Murphy Files, acc. 84-14, RG 2.

13. R. T. Cann to F. B. Ridgeway, 28 Sept. 1935; Cann to Philip H. Roe, 28 Nov. 1934; Company to Roe, 28 Nov. 1934; and "Memo: To The Committee, Re: L.U. 2055—U.T.W. of A.," n.d., all in file 15, box 18, Harrington Papers. Memorandum to Harrington, 29 Mar. 1935, file 5, box 20, ibid.; Roe to Cann, 28 Sept. 1935, and Cann to Roe, 10 Oct. 1935, box 22, ibid.

14. DuPont indicated to Equitable that employees had been demanding health benefits. Interestingly, DuPont insisted that "'spouse' be substituted for 'wife' to include the husband where the wife is employed by them" (Mervyn Davis to Joseph Boldt, 22 Nov. 1935). See also M. F. Lipton to Boldt, 24 Oct., 29 Oct. 1935; Herman Steeg to Davis, 8 Nov. 1935; Steeg, memorandum to file, 8 Nov. 1935; Steeg et al. to Graham, 27 Nov. 1935; Graham to President, 19 Dec. 1935; Davis, memorandum to file, 17 Dec. 1935; memorandum for the Insurance Committee, 18 Dec. 1935; and W. G. Schelker to Graham, 20 Dec. 1935,

all in file 9, box 34B, Group Insurance Research Division, acc. 1984-050, ELAS Archives. It was also in 1935 that DuPont first offered wage roll employees paid vacations, a benefit long enjoyed by salary employees, in order to promote "employe morale and sound industrial relations." DuPont's manual instructed employees that "a vacation is not a reward for service already rendered" and that a "vacation is never earned in the sense that wages are earned, . . . it involves no contractual obligation, but is a purely voluntary reward" (*Dupont, Service Manual: Vacation Plan for Wage Roll Employees,* Mar. 1935, box 27, Harrington Papers; see esp. items 105, 202, 203).

15. Dublin, *Family of Thirty Million,* 197; "Hospitalization Experience," list attached to memorandum, Graham to President, 19 Dec. 1935, file 9, box 34B, Group Insurance Research Division, acc. 1984-050, ELAS Archives; Okonite Company to Equitable Life, 15 Jan. 1939, ELAS Archives; Piper Aircraft Corp. to Peter Bush, 17 Apr. 1939, ibid.

16. *National Underwriter,* 24 Apr. 1942, 1; T.J.V. Cullen, "Labor Migration," *Spectator,* Dec. 1942, 8–13; *National Underwriter,* 24 July, 21 Aug. 1942.

17. "Wage Ceiling Fear Boosting Sale of Pension Trusts," *National Underwriter,* n.d.; ibid., 21 Aug., 11 Sept. 1942.

18. *National Underwriter,* 19 Mar. 1943, 1. The sale of group policies also received a boost from the Revenue Act of 1942, which stipulated that employers could only receive tax-exempt status on benefit fund monies if they offered the plan to 70% of the workforce. This rule was not included in the tax bill because insurance companies pushed for it, however. Rather, the impetus came from within the Treasury Department (Christopher Howard, *The Hidden Welfare State: Tax Expenditures and Social Policy in the United States* [Princeton: Princeton University Press, 1997], chap. 6).

19. *National Underwriter,* 19 Mar. 1943, 2; 16 July 1943, 6.

20. "$12.00 Every Thursday," *Economic Security Bulletin* (NAM) 5, no. 3 (Mar. 1941), HML.

21. "Keeping Up with the Social Planners," *National Underwriter,* 1 Jan. 1943, 10.

22. *National Underwriter,* 5 Nov. 1943; Eilers and Crowe, *Group Insurance Handbook,* 66; *Spectator,* Sept. 1946.

23. *National Underwriter,* 13 Aug. 1943.

24. Ibid., 3 Apr. 1942, 27.

25. *Spectator,* Aug. 1942, 16, 18; Lizabeth Cohen, *Making a New Deal: Industrial Workers in Chicago, 1919–1939* (New York: Cambridge University Press, 1990).

26. In 1945 thirty-eight UAW locals belonged to Blue Cross service plans. The UAW workers themselves paid for these policies; even where they worked out a paycheck deduction system with employers, union members, not employers, paid the premiums. Hotel workers, printers, pressmen, and chain restaurant workers in New York all subscribed to Blue Cross by the end of the war, as did the United Furniture Workers (Walter Reuther to UAW International Executive Board, 16 Jan. 1945, file 2, box 15, ser. 3, acc. 52, UAW Secretary-Treasurer's Office/Emil Mazey, WPR; "Negotiation Committee Report," National Ford Department, UAW-CIO, to All Ford Locals, 7 July 1948, file 2, box

97, UAW President's Office: Walter P. Reuther Collection, ibid.; Hubert Person to *American Federationist,* 21 Dec. 1942, file: Hospitalization and Health, box 3, ser. 8E, Thorne Papers; Joshua B. Freeman, *Working-Class New York* (New York: New Press, 2000), 127; Raymond Munts, *Bargaining for Health: Labor Unions, Health Insurance, and Medical Care* (Madison: University of Wisconsin Press, 1967), chap. 2; U.S. Department of Labor, Bureau of Labor Statistics, *Health Benefit Plans Established through Collective Bargaining,* Bulletin 841 (Washington, D.C.: Government Printing Office, 1945); Helen Baker and Dorothy Dahl, *Group Health Insurance and Sickness Benefit Plans in Collective Bargaining* (Industrial Relations Section, Princeton: Princeton University, 1945), 11–17 and app. B; Robert William Dvorsky, "The Development of Negotiated Health Insurance and Sickness Benefit Plans of the Steel, Automobile, and Electrical Equipment Industries" (Ph.D. diss, University of Pittsburgh, 1956), 91.

27. Harry Becker to Reuther, "Notes on the Social Security Department," 27 Feb. 1948, file 6, box 160, UAW President's Office: Walter P. Reuther Collection, WPR; Gerald Markowitz and David Rosner, "Seeking Common Ground: A History of Labor and Blue Cross," in *Between Public and Private: A Half Century of Blue Cross and Blue Shield in New York,* special issue of *Journal of Health Politics, Policy, and Law* 16, no. 4 (1991): 704; Florence Thorne to Martin Segal, 21 June 1946, file: Health Insurance Plan, box 15, ser. 8A, Thorne Papers.

28. Alan Derickson, "Health Security for All? Social Unionism and Universal Health Insurance, 1935–1958," *Journal of American History* 80 (Mar. 1994): 1345. For organized labor's continued efforts on behalf of national, public health insurance, see ibid., 1333–56.

29. Munts, *Bargaining for Health,* 25 and chap. 10; Alan Derickson, "The United Steelworkers of America and Health Insurance, 1937–1962," in *American Labor in the Era of the World War II,* ed. Sally M. Miller and Daniel A. Cornford (Westport, Conn.: Praeger, 1995), 74–75; William Glaser, *Health Insurance in Practice: International Variations in Financing, Benefits, and Problems* (San Francisco: Jossey-Bass, 1991), 21; *National Underwriter,* 26 Mar. 1948; National Ford Negotiating Committee, *Ford UAW-CIO Workers Security Program, Part II: Health Security Program,* July 1949, file 5, box 60, UAW SSD.

30. U.S. Congress, Senate, Subcommittee on Education and Labor, *Hearings: Wartime Health and Education, S. Res. 74,* 78th Cong., 2d sess., testimony of George F. Addes, 1–2 Mar. 1944, pt. 6, 1995.

31. National Ford Negotiating Committee, *Ford UAW-CIO Workers Security Program, Part II,* IV-7. Harry Becker was one of the principal architects of this UAW program. It reflected all of the ideas Becker had picked up in his associations with I. S. Falk, the Children's Bureau and EMIC, and the GHA; Nelson Cruikshank, "Labor Looks at the Problem of Health Services," address to President's Commission on Health Insurance Needs of the Nation, 7–8 Oct. 1952, file: Pres. Commission, box 11, Cruikshank Papers. For the USWA version of this ideal model plan, see Derickson, "United Steelworkers of America and Health Insurance," 75; and Munts, *Bargaining for Health,* 64–66.

32. In general, unions in California remained frustrated that Henry Kaiser would not give them a voice in administration. See Rickey Hendricks, *A Model for National Health Insurance: The History of Kaiser Permanente* (New Brunswick,

N.J.: Rutgers University Press, 1993), 70–75, 92–93, 116; Dvorsky, "Development of Negotiated Health Insurance," 103–4, 140–42; Joseph Garbarino, *Health Plans and Collective Bargaining* (Berkeley and Los Angeles: University of California Press, 1960); Health Insurance Plan of Greater New York, Annual Report of the Acting General Manager to the Membership Meeting, 19 May 1949, 2–4, file 6, box 5, Saul Mills Papers; Freeman, *Working-Class New York*, chaps. 1 and 8.

33. Addes testimony, Senate Subcommittee of the Committee on Education and Labor, *Hearings: Wartime Health and Education*, 1945.

34. Paul Starr, "Transformation in Defeat: The Changing Objectives of National Health Insurance 1915–1980," in *Compulsory Health Insurance: The Continuing American Debate*, ed. Ronald L. Numbers (Westport, Conn.: Greenwood Press, 1982); Monte Poen, *Harry S. Truman versus the Medical Lobby: The Genesis of Medicare* (Columbia: University of Missouri Press, 1979), 64; Edward D. Berkowitz, *Mr. Social Security: The Life of Wilbur J. Cohen* (Lawrence: University Press of Kansas, 1995); Starr, *The Social Transformation of American Medicine: The Rise of a Sovereign Profession and the Making of a Vast Industry* (New York: Basic Books, 1982), 280–81.

35. *Eastern Underwriter*, 17 May 1940.

36. U.S. Congress, Senate, Committee on Labor and Public Welfare, *Health Insurance Plans in the United States*, 82d Cong., 1st sess., 1951, S. Rept. 359; Joseph Swire to Gordon Parker, 28 Sept. 1955, file 13, box 2107, Swire Files Correspondence, Secretary-Treasurer's Office, RG 1, IUE Records. The quotation is from Deborah A. Stone, "The Struggle for the Soul of Health Insurance," in *The Politics of Health Care Reform: Lessons from the Past, Prospects for the Future*, ed. James A. Morone and Gary S. Belkin (Durham, N.C.: Duke University Press, 1994), 33.

37. David Fitzmaurice to Swire, 14 Oct. 1953, file 6, box 2210, Swire Files Research, Secretary-Treasurer's Office, RG 1, IUE Records.

38. U.S. Congress, House, Committee on Interstate and Foreign Commerce, *Hearings: Health Inquiry (Voluntary Health Plans)*, 83d Cong., 2d sess., testimony of Nelson Cruikshank, 15 Jan. 1954, pt. 6: 1776 (hereafter *Health Inquiry*).

39. "U.S. Medicine in Transition," *Fortune*, Dec. 1944, 163. Indeed, the article declared that "the Michigan Plan seems definitely to be a delicate plant; the UAW workers are dissatisfied with the narrowness of its scope and will probably organize a broader plan of their own, somewhat along the lines of Kaiser's." The article also gave high praise to Kaiser Permanente.

40. *National Underwriter*, 4 Oct. 1946; "Dangerous Trends Seen in A&H Group Competition," ibid., 13 Feb. 1948, 2.

41. Ibid., 9 Jan. 1948, 6; *Journal of American Insurance*, May 1947, 5; "Dangerous Trends Seen in A&H Group Competition," 2.

42. Howell John Harris, *The Right to Manage: Industrial Relations Policies of American Business in the 1940s* (Madison: University of Wisconsin Press, 1982); Sanford Jacoby, *Modern Manors: Welfare Capitalism since the New Deal* (Princeton: Princeton University Press, 1997); Andrew Workman, "Manufacturing Power: The Organizational Revival of the National Association of Manufacturers, 1941–1945," *Business History Review* 72 (summer 1998): 297–317; Nelson Lich-

tenstein, *The Most Dangerous Man in Detroit: Walter Reuther and the Fate of American Labor* (New York: Basic Books, 1995), chap. 13; idem, "Taft-Hartley: A Slave-Labor Law?" *Catholic University Law Review* 47 (spring 1998); David L. Stebenne, *Arthur J. Goldberg: New Deal Liberal* (New York: Oxford University Press, 1996), chap. 3.

43. *Businessweek*, 13 May 1950.

44. NAM, *Industry's View on the Lewis Coal Royalty*, Mar. 1945, box 3, acc. 1412, NAM Records.

45. Ivana Krajcinovic, *From Company Doctor to Managed Care: The United Mine Workers' Noble Experiment* (Ithaca: ILR Press, Cornell University Press, 1997), 33–37; Lichtenstein, "Taft-Hartley."

46. Walter Chamblin, address at a meeting of the National Industrial Council Speech, box 226, 100-yy, acc. 1411, NAM Records; NAM, "Suggested Resolution on Employee Benefit Programs," 30 Nov. 1948, box 105, ibid.; *Businessweek*, 13 May 1950; NAM, *Employee Benefit Programs* (New York: NAM, Industrial Relations Department, 1947), HML; R. T. Compton to National Industrial Council, 15 Feb. 1949, box 226, 100-yy, acc. 1411, NAM Records; Derthick, *Policymaking for Social Security*, 245. Bills on federalizing unemployment compensation included S. 1274, sponsored by Democratic Senators Harley Kilgore, James Murray, Robert Wagner, Joseph Guffey, and Claude Pepper, and H.R. 3891, introduced by Democratic Congressman Aime Forand.

47. *American Economic Security: The Business Journal of Social Security* 111, no. 6 (Aug.–Sept. 1946): 1; U.S. Congress, Senate, Committee on Education and Labor, *A Bill to Provide for a National Health Insurance Program: Hearings before the Committee on Education and Labor*, 79th Cong., 2d sess., May–June 1946, testimony of Andrew Court, pt. 4: 2339.

48. NAM, minutes of the NAM Labor-Management Relations Committee, 20 Mar. 1947, New York, box 3, Industrial Relations Division, acc. 1412, NAM Records.

49. Industrial Relations Division, NAM, *Employee Benefit Plans in Collective Bargaining*, 7 June 1946, box 1, ibid.

50. Harry A. Millis and Emily Clark Brown, *From the Wagner Act to Taft-Hartley: A Study of National Labor Policy and Labor Relations* (Chicago: University of Chicago Press, 1950), 561–68. Robert Taft and Joseph Ball are quoted from "Supplemental Views," *Taft Report*, and *Congressional Record*, 80th Cong., 1st sess., 1947, 93, pt. 4:4805, in Millis and Brown, *From the Wagner Act to Taft-Hartley*, 564–65; Jacob Perlman to Wilbur Cohen, "Growth and Characteristics of Union-Management Health and Welfare Plans," 15 June 1948, file 2, box 46, Cohen Papers. Perlman found that even after the passage of the Taft-Hartley Act, "several industry spokesmen asked that the National Labor Relations Act be amended [again] to make it clear that employers are not required to bargain about pension plans and other benefits of a 'social security nature'" (ibid., 26).

51. The number of persons covered by group surgical insurance increased from 5,537,000 to 11,103,000 (Senate Committee, *Health Insurance Plans*, 26).

52. *Outstanding American Companies Insuring Their Employees through Equitable*

(New York: Group Department, ELAS, 1946), file 5, box 2A, Insurance Affairs Group Operations, acc. 82-45, RG 4, ELAS Archives; Dvorsky, "Development of Negotiated Health Insurance"; Derickson, "United Steelworkers of American and Health Insurance," 74. Sanford Jacoby shows how nonunion companies were willing to spend extraordinary amounts of money on welfare benefits to stave off unionism, often more than they would have had to spend had they negotiated with a union (see Jacoby, *Modern Manors*, chaps. 2–5).

53. Dvorsky, "Development of Negotiated Health Insurance," 32; *National Underwriter*, 29 Apr. 1949.

54. NAM, minutes of the NAM Labor-Management Relations Committee, 20 Mar. 1947, 4; "Summary of War Labor Board Decisions Affecting Management Functions," 1945, box 3, acc. 1412, NAM Records.

55. *National Underwriter*, 27 Aug. 1943, 3; *Spectator*, Sept. 1943, 64; NICB, *Company Group Insurance Plans*, Studies in Personnel Policy, 112 (New York, 1951), 48.

56. Minutes of the NAM Labor-Management Relations Committee, 6 Mar. 1947, New York, 5, box 3, Industrial Relations Division, acc. 1412, NAM Records; Leo Wolman, "The Conditions of Labor Peace," address delivered at the general meeting of the American Iron and Steel Institute, 23 May 1946, box 19, ibid.; NAM, "Preliminary Outline: Major Issues Involved in Financing of Health and Welfare Programs by Assessments on Product," 3 May 1946, box 2, ibid.

57. "Claims Expense Limitation: A Vital Feature of Equitable Group Insurance," n.d., box 3, Insurance Affairs Group Operations, acc. 1984-050, RG 4, ELAS Archives; MLIC, *Tailored to Fit: A Group Insurance Plan Designed for the Employees of Your Company* (New York, 1953), box 19 06 04, Group Insurance, Subject Files, MLIC Archives; ibid., *Employee Security Founded on Group Insurance Safeguards Employee Morale and Loyalty* (New York, 1952), ibid.

58. Edwin J. Faulkner, *Health Insurance* (New York: McGraw-Hill, 1960), 155.

59. Testimony of Charles Hill, 13 Oct. 1953, *Health Inquiry*, pt. 5: 1236.

60. Testimony of George Barrett, 14 Oct. 1953, ibid., 1265.

61. Colin Gordon, *New Deals: Business, Labor, and Politics in America, 1920–1935* (New York: Cambridge University Press, 1994), 289–90 and chap. 8; Nelson Lichtenstein, "From Corporatism to Collective Bargaining: Organized Labor and the Eclipse of Social Democracy in the Postwar Era," in *The Rise and Fall of the New Deal Order, 1930–1980*, ed. Steven Fraser and Gary Gerstle (Princeton: Princeton University Press, 1989), 140–45; Derickson, "Health Security for All?"

62. "Group Insurers Fail to Cultivate Labor Properly," *National Underwriter*, 15 Apr. 1949, 1; *National Underwriter*, 23 Apr. 1948.

63. James Baron, Frank R. Dobbin, and P. Devereaux Jennings, "War and Peace: The Evolution of Modern Personnel Administration in U.S. Industry," *American Journal of Sociology* 92 (Sept. 1986): 350–83; Sanford M. Jacoby, *Employing Bureaucracy: Managers, Unions, and the Transformation of Work in American Industry, 1900–1945* (New York: Columbia University Press, 1985), chap. 8; Jacoby, *Modern Manors*. The reports of Metropolitan's PSB from the late 1940s and early 1950s include *Employee Contact through the Bulletin Board, Outline for Organiz-*

ing and Operating an Employee Publication, Information Manuals for Employees, Functions of a Personnel Director, Employee Service Clubs, and *The Information Rack in the Communications Program* (Vertical Files, MLIC Archives).

64. David McDonald to All District Directors and Staff Representatives, 2 Mar. 1951, box A4-94, Philip Murray Papers, coll. 5, Catholic University Archives, Washington, D.C.

65. *Health Inquiry,* 12 Jan. 1954, pt. 6: 1675.

66. Joseph Swire reported to James Carey that Mr. Fitzhugh, a Metropolitan executive, had stated this point in congressional hearings on health and welfare funds (Swire to Carey, 24 Nov. 1954, file: Swire, box 2015B, President's Office—Staff Memoranda, RG 1, IUE Records). See also Munts, *Bargaining for Health,* 84; and "Negotiation Committee Report," National Ford Department, UAW-CIO, to All Ford Locals, 7 July 1948.

67. Swire to Jim Parker, 11 Mar. 1958, file 13, box 2107, Swire Files Correspondence, Secretary-Treasurer's Office, RG 1, IUE Records; Swire to Gordon Parker, 28 Sept. 1955.

68. Dvorsky, "Development of Negotiated Health Insurance," 118; ELAS, Group Insurance Department, *Fifty Representative Examples of Equitable Low Cost in Group Life Insurance: "Our Cost is Your Cost"* (New York, n.d.), Policyholder Files—Sales Ads, box 3, Insurance Affairs Group Operations, acc. 82-45, ELAS Archives; "Memorandum to Dave Lasser: Statement for Carey for Atlanta Conference," 27 Feb. 1957, file 16, box 2109, Swire Files Correspondence, Secretary-Treasurer's Office, RG 1, IUE Records.

69. Swire to Carey, "Cost Factors in GE's Insurance and Pension Programs," 1 Mar. 1955, file 30, box 2108, Swire Files Correspondence, Secretary-Treasurer's Office, RG 1, IUE Records; "Memorandum to Dave Lasser"; Swire to Jim Parker, 11 Mar. 1958.

70. Westinghouse Electric Corporation, "Social Insurance Plan for Employees," 1 Nov. 1950, file 44, box 6, Westinghouse Conference Board Negotiations, RG 1, IUE Records; notes on Westinghouse negotiations, n.d., ibid.; Office Employes International Union to George Meany, 30 Mar. 1955, file: Health and Welfare, box 11, Cruikshank Papers.

71. *Blueprinting a Health and Group Insurance Plan* (New York: Trade Union Agency, 1946), file 6, box 5, Saul Mills Papers.

72. Lane Kirkland, "Service versus Indemnity Plans," paper presented at the Health and Welfare Plan Conference, California State Federation of Labor, Santa Barbara, Calif., 22 July 1957, file: California, box 24, Cruikshank Papers; *Eastern Underwriter,* 17 May 1940.

73. Munts, *Bargaining for Health,* 136–37; Starr, *Social Transformation of American Medicine,* 330.

74. Kirkland, "Service versus Indemnity Plans." In 1955 Blue Cross covered 50 million persons for hospital benefits and 39 million for surgical, so the Blues did continue to be a very considerable competitor of the commercial companies.

75. *New York Times,* 2 Aug. 1946. Eight life insurance companies participated in this loan: Metropolitan, Equitable, Aetna, John Hancock, Mutual Life of New York, New York Life, Prudential, and Northwestern Mutual. On corporate debt after the war, see Raymond W. Goldsmith, *Financial Intermediaries in the*

American Economy since 1900, National Bureau of Economic Research Studies in Capital Formation (Princeton: Princeton University Press, 1958), 183, 217, 234; and Herman E. Kroos and Martin Blyn, *A History of Financial Intermediaries*, Books in Finance Series (New York: Random House, 1971), 214–15.

76. There are several reasons why insurance companies moved to the forefront of corporate lending at this time. The first has to do with the shift in the balance of power among lending institutions that occurred in the wake of New Deal banking legislation. Although the Glass-Steagall Act, which separated investment banking and securities underwriting from commercial banking and deposits, was passed in 1933, its effects did not become manifest until the 1940s, when American corporations were finally able to start making major capital improvements again. The Glass-Steagall Act undercut the strength of the investment banking firms because they no longer controlled significant amounts of capital; they became functionaries who wrote the securities for other deal makers. Commercial banks and life insurance companies, the institutions that had the capital, became deal makers—commercial banks for short-term loans, life companies for long-term loans. This transformation was complete by the end of World War II. Prior to this period direct placement financing had been relatively unimportant, but as borrowers began to feel the effects of New Deal banking and securities legislation, it grew in importance (see Kroos and Blyn, *History of Financial Intermediaries*, 195–99, 234, 183–97; and Beth Mintz and Michael Schwartz, *The Power Structure of American Business* [Chicago: University of Chicago Press, 1985], 67–69, 160).

77. "Discounts Old Fears of Direct Placement," *News of Insurance Companies*, 15 June 1955, file 3, box 18D, Graham Papers. That "uniquely close relationship" achieved through investment applied to the nation's top corporations. In the period 1946–48 Equitable, which had $4.5 billion in assets, purchased $100 million in long-term debentures from Gulf Oil. It lent $90 million to the R. J. Reynolds Tobacco Company and $15 million to the Borden Company, both longtime group policyholders; $75 million to the American Tobacco Company; and $40 million to TWA. In the steel industry alone, Equitable held millions of dollars in corporate bonds from the Armco Steel Corporation, the Bethlehem Steel Corporation, Jones and Laughlin Steel, Pittsburgh Steel, Inland Steel, and Republic Steel. Together Metropolitan and Equitable financed the $75 million expansion program of Republic Steel, which continued to have Metropolitan group hospital and surgical plans even after the USWA began bargaining and asking for Blue Cross. Prudential had million-dollar loans with IBM, AT&T, and Union Carbide (see *Eastern Underwriter*, 26 Nov. 1948, 3, 17; *New York Times*, 31 Dec. 1946, 25; *Schedule of Securities Owned by ELAS*, 31 Dec. 1948 and 31 Dec. 1949, file 1, box acc. 1984-050, Historical Collection, Secretary's Department, RG 4, ELAS Archives; *New York Times*, 5 Apr. 1951, 43.

78. IUE to GE, 5 Apr. 1955, reprinted in Dvorsky, "Development of Negotiated Health Insurance," 157–58; Swire to Carey, 24 Nov. 1954; "Excerpt from the Fourth Interim Report of the Special Commission on Health and Welfare Trust Funds in the Commonwealth of Massachusetts," 25 Mar. 1957, box 2015B, President's Office, RG 1, IUE Records; Swire to Irving Abramson, 8 Mar. 1955, file 6, box 2104, Swire Files Correspondence, Secretary-Treasurer's Office, ibid.

79. *Central Manufacturing District Magazine* 31, no. 12 (Dec. 1947), box 45B, acc. 1984-050, Historical Collection, RG 4, ELAS Archives; *New York Times,* 24 Sept. 1948, 44; *New Republic,* 7 Apr. 1949, 10–11; *National Underwriter,* 10 Dec. 1948; Mintz and Schwartz, *Power Structure of American Business,* 156–75.

80. Leroy A. Lincoln to Jul B. Baumann, 3 Oct. 1947, reprinted in full in *Spectator,* Nov. 1947, 8.

81. W. J. Graham, "The Contribution of Group Insurance to American Family Solidarity," *Weekly Underwriter,* 10 May 1947, 53, file 1, box 18D, Graham Papers. For coverage statistics, see Eilers and Crowe, *Group Insurance Handbook,* 66.

82. "Group Insurance at a Glance," ELAS, Group Department, Aug. 1946, file 5, box 2A, Insurance Affairs Group Operations, RG 4, ELAS Archives.

83. William Graham, "Social Security," radio address, 17 Dec. 1936. Note the use of the 1920s term *American plan.*

84. U.S. Department of Labor, *Maternity Protection of Employed Women,* Bulletin of the Women's Bureau No. 240 (Washington, D.C., 1952); idem, *Maternity Provisions for Employed Women,* Bulletin of the Women's Bureau No. 272 (Washington, D.C., 1960); Charlotte F. Muller, *Health Care and Gender* (New York: Russell Sage Foundation, 1990), chap. 4; Alice Kessler-Harris, *Out to Work: A History of Wage-Earning Women in the United States* (New York: Oxford University Press, 1982), 301–3; Marcia Bayne-Smith, ed., *Race, Gender, and Health,* Sage Series on Race and Ethnic Relations, 15 (Thousand Oaks, Calif.: Sage Publications, 1996). Martha May discusses the patriarchal goals of welfare capitalism and the family wage in "The Historical Problem of the Family Wage: The Ford Motor Company and the Five Dollar Day," *Feminist Studies* 8 (summer 1982).

85. E. Richard Weinerman, M.D., "The San Francisco Labor Council Survey: Labor Plans for Health, Summary of Findings and Recommendations," June 1952, Labor Health and Welfare Series, Committee for the Nation's Health, box 5, Cruikshank Papers.

86. Cruikshank, "Labor Looks at the Problem of Health Services."

87. David Lasser to Swire, 27 Nov. 1957, file 16, box 2109, Swire Files Correspondence, Secretary-Treasurer's Office, RG 1, IUE Records.

88. Senate Committee, *Health Insurance Plans,* 2; *Health Inquiry,* Oct. 1953, pt. 5: 1181.

89. George Baehr, M.D., "Group Health Plans—Organized Labor's Stake in Voluntary Health Insurance," reprinted in *Connecticut Federationist,* 1954, box 5, Cruikshank Papers; *National Underwriter,* 3 May 1946; *Spectator,* July 1947, 12; *National Underwriter,* 4 June 1948, 3; National Ford Negotiating Committee, *Ford UAW-CIO Workers Security Program, Part II,* IV-1.

90. *CIO News,* 26 Jan. 1948, George Meany Memorial Archives, Silver Spring, Md.; *Insurance Field,* 28 Nov. 1947, box 19 06 04, Group Insurance, Subject Files, MLIC Archives.

91. Dvorsky, "Development of Negotiated Health Insurance," 120–22.

92. *National Underwriter,* 17 Dec., 23 Apr., 25 June 1948; *W. W. Cross & Co v. National Labor Relations Board* (United Steelworkers of America, CIO, et al.), U.S. Court of Appeals, First Circuit, 174 F. 2d 875; *Inland Steel Co v. National Labor Relations Board* (United Steelworkers of America, CIO, et al.), United States Court of Appeals, Seventh Circuit, 170 F. 2d 247.

93. Presidential Steel Fact Finding Board, "Findings and Recommendations: General Summary," Sept. 1949, box 202, acc. 1411, NAM Records.

94. "UAW-CIO 1949 Demands for Workers Security: Employer-Financed Programs Providing Security to All Workers by Assuring—Old Age and Incapacity Retirement Income, Income during Periods of Disability, Hospital Care for Worker and Family, Medical Care for Worker and Family, Rehabilitation Services, Death Benefits. Contract Clauses Providing That Employer Payments Be Deposited in Trust Funds Which Can Be Used Only for Workers Security Benefits. Contract Clauses Providing for the Establishment of a Board of Trustees on Which the Union Has *Equal Voice* With Management in Administering the Workers Security Trust Funds" (cover pages to parts 1 and 2, National Ford Negotiating Committee, *Ford UAW-CIO Workers Security Program*).

95. For details of the Treaty of Detroit settlement, see Munts, *Bargaining for Health*, 68–69. Even the UAW's Health Institute was discontinued in 1955.

96. Not all of the 51 million with commercial insurance were enrolled through group policies, however. Individual and family policies accounted for about 40% of the business in the early 1950s, 35% by 1955; group insurance covered 66% (Eilers and Crowe, *Group Insurance Handbook*, 66; testimony of Edmund Whitaker, 13 Oct. 1953, *Health Inquiry*, pt. 5:1199–1207).

97. Starr, *Social Transformation of American Medicine*, 306–10; "The Work of the Health Insurance Council in Group Insurance," 16 Apr. 1959, file: Policyholder Files, box 3, Insurance Affairs Group Operations, acc. 82-45, RG 4, ELAS Archives. The Blue Shield programs at first offered prepayment terms, accepting premium fees as full payment, to anyone below a specified income level. But most participants soon found that medical societies set the income ceiling so low that most workers did not qualify for it and thus were enrolled on a cash-indemnity, fee-for-service basis (National Ford Negotiating Committee, *Ford UAW-CIO Workers Security Program, Part II*, IV-6; UAW, "Resolution: Hospital and Surgical Plans," 20 Sept. 1958, file: Blue Cross Blue Shield, 1955–59, box 8, ser. 2, UAW SSD).

98. Dvorsky, "Development of Negotiated Health Insurance," 122–44, 149; National Ford Negotiating Committee, *Ford UAW-CIO Workers Security Program, Part II*; David C. Jacobs, "The UAW and the Committee for National Health Insurance: The Contours of Social Unionism," *Advances in Industrial and Labor Relations* 4 (1987): 122; "U.S. Steel Supplementary Insurance Agreement," 12 July 1951, box A4-94, Murray Papers, coll. 5; "Bethlehem Insurance Agreement Dated 12 Jan. 1950, as Amended Aug. 3, 1951," ibid.; "U.S. Steel Company Insurance Agreement and memo, Joint Committee on Insurance. And Pensions to Employees," 24 July 1951, ibid.

99. Ken Bannon to All Representatives Servicing Ford Plants and Ford Local Unions, 27 Jan. 1956 and 7 Sept. 1955, file: Blue Cross Blue Shield, 1955–59, box 8, ser. 2, UAW SSD; "Chronological History of the Efforts to Develop a Service Type Program in the Chattanooga, TN Blue Shield Plan," 7 Nov. 1963, ibid.; Derickson, "United Steelworkers of America and Health Insurance"; Stebenne, *Arthur J. Goldberg*, 68; Dvorsky, "Development of Negotiated Health Insurance," 55–56.

100. U.S. Department of Labor, Bureau of Labor Statistics, *Health and Insur-*

ance Plans under Collective Bargaining: Hospital Benefits, Bulletin 1274 (Washington, D.C., 1959); idem, *Health and Insurance Plans under Collective Bargaining: Surgical and Medical Benefits,* Bulletin 1280 (Washington, D.C., 1959); idem, *Health and Insurance Plans under Collective Bargaining: Major Medical Expense Benefits,* Bulletin 1293 (Washington, D.C., 1960).

101. Thomas J. Sugrue, "The Structures of Urban Poverty: The Reorganization of Space and Work in Three Periods of American History," in *The Underclass Debate,* ed. Michael B. Katz (Princeton: Princeton University Press, 1993), 106–10; Michael K. Brown, *Race, Money, and the American Welfare State* (Ithaca: Cornell University Press, 1999), 164, 178–92; Health Insurance Association of America, *Source Book of Health Insurance Data,* volumes for 1959 to 1980–81 (Washington D.C.: Health Insurance Institute, 1959–81).

102. Munts, *Bargaining for Health,* 71, 102–3; negotiator's handwritten notes, file: Blue Cross Blue Shield, 1960–63, box 8, UAW SSD.

103. Arthur J. Altmeyer, "Conference on Union Health and Welfare Funds," NICB, 23 Jan. 1947, 23, in Perlman to Cohen, "Growth and Characteristics of Union-Management Health and Welfare Plans," 23; Wilbur Cohen, "The Place of Industrial Pensions in a Total Social Security Program and in the National Economy," address at conference titled "Wartime and Long Range Issues in Collective Bargaining for Pensions," University of Illinois, 16–18 Feb. 1951, file 2, box 249, Cohen Papers; "Summary of Discussion of Union-Management Welfare Plans and Their Relationship to Social Security," Cohen's statement, 2, 10 Nov. 1949, file 6, box 248, ibid. Perpetually, SSA staff and representatives would call for expanding social insurance to include new types of benefits and at the same time insist on the legitimacy and viability of supplementation. See also the statement of Ida Merriam in ibid.

104. Ronald W. Schatz, *The Electrical Workers: A History of Labor at General Electric and Westinghouse, 1923–1960* (Urbana: University of Illinois Press, 1983), 170–74.

105. See, e.g., *IUE-NEWS,* 6, 20 Feb., 3 July 1950.

106. *IUE-NEWS,* 3 July 1950; Dvorsky, "Development of Negotiated Health Insurance," 150–57; Swire to Abramson, 8 Mar. 1955.

107. "Meany Charges Misuse of Welfare Funds," *New York Herald Tribune,* 12 June 1957.

108. Westinghouse Electric Corporation, "Social Insurance Plan for Employees"; notes on Westinghouse negotiations; Benjamin Sigal to Carey, 29 May 1950, memorandum, file 44, box 6, Westinghouse Conference Board Negotiations, RG 1, IUE Records; Dvorsky, "Development of Negotiated Health Insurance," 176–88. The only electrical workers who received benefits equivalent to those of the UAW were electrical workers employed at GM (ibid.). See also Swire to Charles Spencer, 5 Dec. 1956, file 24, box 2107, Swire Files Correspondence, Secretary-Treasurer's Office, RG 1, IUE Records; Swire to Jim Parker, 11 Mar. 1958; Swire to Bill Brady, 7 Nov. 1957, file 8, box 2104, Swire Files Correspondence, Secretary-Treasurer's Office, RG 1, IUE Records; and Swire to Lasser, 27 Feb. 1957, file 16, box 2109, ibid.

109. IUE to GE, 5 Apr. 1955; Swire to Carey, 24 Nov. 1954; "Excerpt from the Fourth Interim Report"; Swire to Abramson, 8 Mar. 1955.

110. Schatz, *Electrical Workers*, 170.

111. *Home Office*, Dec. 1955, 9, file 1, box 19 06 04, Group Insurance, Subject Files, MLIC Archives.

112. "*GE* Extra *Benefits—IUE* Extra *Assessments*," *GE Employee Relations News Letter*, 16 May 1955, box 22, Industrial Relations Division, acc. 1412, NAM Records.

113. Westinghouse Electric Corporation, "Social Insurance Plan for Employees"; notes on Westinghouse negotiations; Sigal to Carey, 29 May 1950; Dvorsky, "Development of Negotiated Health Insurance," 176–88.

114. Swire to Charles Spencer, 5 Dec. 1956, file 24, box 2107, Swire Files Correspondence, Secretary-Treasurer's Office, RG 1, IUE Records; Swire to Brady, 7 Nov. 1957; Swire to Harry Block, 26 Sept. 1957, file 8, box 2104, Swire Files Correspondence, Secretary-Treasurer's Office, RG 1, IUE Records. Swire wrote Brady that "the number of people who benefit from major medical is a comparatively small proportion . . . and that the premiums are a good deal higher than the claims."

115. Herman Miles Somers and Anne Ramsay Somers, *Doctors, Patients, and Health Insurance: The Organization and Financing of Medical Care* (Washington, D.C.: Brookings Institution, 1961), 375–76.

116. "What the Labor Health Plan Offers You and Your Family," box 5, Cruikshank Papers; "Summary of Legislation Relating to Health and Welfare Funds," 9 Sept. 1954, ibid.; "Minutes of the Meeting of the AFL-CIO Committee on Social Security," 26 Nov. 1957, 3, box 8, ibid.; Executive Council Report, 17 Aug. 1959, ibid. Congressman Charles Wolverton introduced such a bill, H.R. 7700, in the House in 1954, and Senator Hubert Humphrey introduced a bill, S. 2009, in the Senate in 1959.

117. On Kaiser's success, see the testimonies of Henry Kaiser, Dr. Sidney Garfield, and Arthur Weisman and their supporting evidence, Jan. 1954, *Health Inquiry*, pt. 6:1341–1450. On the ways in which Blue Cross used public relations campaigns to convince the public that rising prices were a necessary, even natural, part of modern medical practice, see David J. Rothman, "The Public Presentation of Blue Cross, 1935–1965," in *Between Public and Private: A Half Century of Blue Cross and Blue Shield in New York*, special issue of *Journal of Health Politics, Policy, and Law* 16, no. 4 (1991): 671–94.

118. Leonard Woodcock, "A Look at the Future of Direct Service Medical Care Plans," speech to the annual meeting of the Association of Labor Health Administrators, Atlantic City, N.J., 14 Nov. 1956, file: ALHA, box 17, Cruikshank Papers; AFL-CIO Committee on Social Security, "Report of the Subcommittee on Ways and Means of Meeting the Restrictive Practices of Organized Medicine as They Affect the Policies of the AFL-CIO" (Washington, D.C., 16 May 1957), ibid.; *Newsletter of the Association of Labor Health Administrators*, no. 6 (summer 1957); Ted Ellsworth, "Relations with Doctors and Hospitals," 28 Mar. 1957, file: ALHA, box 17, Cruikshank Papers; Baehr, "Group Health Plans"; Starr, *Social Transformation of American Medicine*, 306–10; William Green to Officers of National and International Unions, State Federations, and Central Labor Unions, 16 Jan. 1947, file: AMA, box 9, Cruikshank Papers.

119. Margaret Klem, "Recent State Legislation Concerning Prepayment

Medical Care," *Social Security Bulletin* 10 (Jan. 1947): 10–16; American Labor Health Association, *The Labor Health Venture and The Law* (New York, n.d.), 7–9, file: ALHA, box 9, Cruikshank Papers.

120. Morton Miller, "Major Medical Expense Insurance and Health Care Plans of the Equitable," July 1956, and various speeches at the Group Major Medical School Conference, 25–27 June 1956, both in Policyholder Files—Speeches, box 3, Insurance Affairs Group Operations, acc. 82-45, RG 4, ELAS Archives.

121. "Claims Expense Limitation"; Ray McCullough, "Comprehensive Major Medical Expense—Its Problems and Prospects," address at the Group Representatives Club of Atlanta, 6 Oct. 1958, box 3, Insurance Affairs Group Operations, acc. 82-45, RG 4, ELAS Archives; A. C. Campbell, to All Group Representatives, 1951, box 19 06 04, Group Insurance, Subject Files, MLIC.

122. Eilers and Crowe, *Group Insurance Handbook*, 65; Somers and Somers, *Doctors, Patients, and Health Insurance*, 383.

123. Jerome Pollack, "Major Medical Expense Insurance: An Evaluation," speech to American Public Health Association, Atlantic City, N.J., 15 Nov. 1956, file: ALHA, box 17, Cruikshank Papers.

124. Walter Reuther, "Statement on Michigan Blue Cross Rate Increase," 28 Dec. 1955, and Leonard Woodcock et al. to All Michigan Local Union Presidents, 12 Nov. 1954, both in file: Blue Cross Blue Shield Rate Increases, 1955, box 6, UAW SSD; testimony of Cruikshank, 15 Jan. 1954, 1673; Somers and Somers, *Doctors, Patients, and Health Insurance*, 383–86. Labor representatives from the AFL and the CIO hated major medical (see the 19 Jan. 1954 testimonies of I. Walter Abel and David McDonald of the USWA, Joseph Childs of the United Rubber Workers, John Edelman, Textile Workers Union, officials of the International Association of Machinists, and Jerry Voorhis of the Health Insurance Federation of America, all of whom denounce deductibles and coinsurance, in *Health Inquiry*, pt. 6:1954; Swire to Charles Spencer, 5 Dec. 1956; Swire to Brady, 7 Nov. 1957; Anne Ramsay Somers, *Health Plan Administration: A Guide to the Management of Negotiated Hospital, Surgical, and Medical Care Benefits* [New York: Foundation on Employee Health, Medical Care, and Welfare in association with Martin E. Segal & Co., 1961], 13; and Department of Labor, Bureau of Labor Statistics, *Health Insurance Plans under Collective Bargaining: Major Medical Expense Benefits*, 6–7, 3–4).

125. McCullough, "Comprehensive Major Medical Expense"; Somers and Somers, *Doctors, Patients, and Health Insurance*, 386.

126. Department of Labor, Bureau of Labor Statistics, *Health and Insurance Plans under Collective Bargaining: Major Medical Expense Benefits*, 4.

127. Health Insurance Association of America, *Source Book of Health Insurance Data*, volumes for 1959 to 1980–81 (New York: Health Insurance Institute, 1959, 1963, 1965, 1967, 1972–73, 1980–81). On the idea of decommodification and welfare state regimes, see Gosta Esping-Andersen, *The Three Worlds of Welfare Capitalism* (Princeton: Princeton University Press, 1990), 21–23.

128. Teresa Ghilarducci, *Labor's Capital: The Economics and Politics of Private Pensions* (Cambridge, Mass.: MIT Press, 1992), 23–24, 29–30; Steven A. Sass,

The Promise of Private Pensions: The First Hundred Years (Cambridge: Harvard University Press, 1997), 130.

129. Ghilarducci, *Labor's Capital*, 30–36, 46.

130. Steelworker's wife to Philip Murray, 10 Nov. 1951, box A4-94, Murray Papers, coll. 5; see the file U.S.W.A. Pensions and Insurance for letters from workers complaining about deductions of Social Security from company pension allowances. See also Executive Committee to Employee Relations Department and Treasurer's Department, "Pension and Retirement Plan," 2 Oct. 1953, 12, and DuPont News Release, 1 Dec. 1953, box 43, acc. 1410, NAM Records; and Swire to Carey, "Suggested GE Pension Program for 1954," 1 Dec. 1953, file: Swire, box 2015B, President's Office, RG 1, IUE Records.

131. Swire to Dean Laurence J. Ackerman, 14 May 1956, file 6, box 2104, RG 1, IUE Records; Swire to Oscar Berchtold, 26 Oct. 1956, ibid., file 9.

132. "A Program for Employment Security for Westinghouse Employees Presented to the Westinghouse Electric Corporation by the IUE-Westinghouse Negotiating Committee," Pittsburgh, Pa., 4 Aug. 1960, box 233, Westinghouse Conference Board, RG 2, IUE Records. The union's solutions to job flight and automation was to press for further private, employment-based security plans, specifically firm-based supplemental unemployment benefits.

133. Ghilarducci, *Labor's Capital*, 23, 26–29, 36, 55–56, 78; Leo Jandrean to Swire, 27 Aug. 1957, file 12, box 2106, Swire Files Correspondence, Secretary-Treasurer's Office, RG 1, IUE Records; Sass, *Promise of Private Pensions*, 137–41; Jacoby, *Modern Manors*, chaps. 4 and 6.

134. David Witwer, "Westbrook Pegler and the Anti-Union Movement" (paper presented at the annual meeting of the Organization of American Historians, Los Angeles, Apr. 2001); Rick Perlstein, *Before the Storm: Barry Goldwater and the Unmaking of the American Consensus* (New York: Hill & Wang, 2001), chap. 2.

135. U.S. Department of Labor, *Legislative History of the Welfare and Pension Plans Disclosure Act of 1958, as Amended by Public Law 87-420 of 1962* (Washington, D.C.: Government Printing Office, 1962); William J. Isaacson, "Employee Welfare and Pension Plans: Regulation and Protection of Employee Rights," *Columbia Law Review* 59, no. 1 (1959): 104.

136. U.S. Congress, Senate, Committee on Labor and Public Welfare, *Welfare and Pension Plans Investigation: Final Report Submitted to the Committee on Labor and Public Welfare by Its Subcommittee on Welfare and Pension Funds Pursuant to S. Res. 40 as Extended by S. Res. 200 and S. Res. 232*, 84th Cong., 2d sess., 16 Apr. 1956, 2, 54, 136. The subcommittee included another labor liberal, Senator James Murray of Montana. The committee itself was staffed by Democratic liberals, including Herbert Lehman of New York, Pat McNamara of Michigan, Murray, and John F. Kennedy of Massachusetts.

137. Department of Labor, *Legislative History*, 14, 45–49; Senate Committee on Labor and Public Welfare, *Welfare and Pension Plans Investigation*, 7; Isaacson, "Employee Welfare and Pension Plans," 103–4.

138. Senate Committee on Labor and Public Welfare, *Welfare and Pension Plans Investigation*, 7, 158–59.

139. Ibid.

140. Ibid., 3, 6.

141. Ibid., 54.

142. Ibid., 3.

143. *Congressional Record* 85th Cong., 2d sess., 1958, 104, pt. 6:6303.

144. There are several files on this subject in boxes 11, 5, 6, 7, Cruikshank Papers. AFL and then AFL-CIO officials actually offered an even more conservative proposal. They wanted disclosure to be under the jurisdiction of the Bureau of Internal Revenue rather than under the secretary of labor. They feared that if the forms were submitted to the secretary of labor, irregular practices in pension and welfare funds would always be construed as "labor corruption" problems.

145. Stebenne, *Arthur J. Goldberg,* 160–63; Lichtenstein, *Most Dangerous Man in Detroit,* 348–49.

146. Reuel Schiller, "From Group Rights to Individual Liberties: Post-War Labor Law, Liberalism, and the Waning of Union Strength," *Berkeley Journal of Employment and Labor Law* 20, no. 1 (1999): 6, 8–9.

147. Senate Committee on Labor and Public Welfare, *Welfare and Pension Plans Investigation,* 8.

148. Stebenne, *Arthur J. Goldberg,* 160–63, 441.

149. Department of Labor, *Legislative History,* 91–95; Isaacson, "Employee Welfare and Pension Plans," 124.

150. Department of Labor, *Legislative History,* 100, 99, 157; U.S. Senate, *Hearing to Amend the Welfare and Pension Plan Disclosure Act,* 87th Cong., 1st sess., testimony of James Carey, 31 July 1961, 155–69; Welfare and Pension Fund Disclosure Act with Amendments, in Department of Labor, *Legislative History,* xxi.

151. On the 1958 Social Security amendments, see Julian E. Zelizer, *Taxing America: Wilbur D. Mills, Congress, and the State, 1945–1975* (New York: Cambridge University Press, 1998), 124–30. On the Landrum-Griffin Act and the substitution of individual rights for group rights, see Schiller, "From Group Rights to Individual Liberties."

152. USWA, Insurance, Pension, and Unemployment Benefits Department, *Special Study on the Medical Care Program for Steelworkers and Their Families,* report prepared for the USWA tenth constitutional convention, Atlantic City, Sept. 30 (Pittsburgh: USWA, 1960), i, 13.

153. Ibid., 7, 96–97, 10, 3.

154. Ibid., 98, 3, 6.

155. Garbarino, *Health Plans and Collective Bargaining,* 17–19; USWA, Insurance, Pension, and Unemployment Benefits Department, *Special Study,* 7.

156. USWA, Insurance, Pension, and Unemployment Benefits Department, *Special Study,* 10.

Epilogue
The Limits of Private Security

Epigraph: NAM, "Suggested Resolution on Greater Security through Employee Benefit Programs for Consideration of Resolutions Committee," 14 Oct. 1948, box 105, acc. 1411, NAM Records.

1. Steven A. Sass, *The Promise of Private Pensions: The First Hundred Years* (Cambridge: Harvard University Press, 1997), 169; Joseph White, *Competing Solutions: American Health Care Proposals and International Experience* (Washington, D.C.: Brookings Institution, 1995), 40–41; Anne Ramsay Somers, *Health Plan Administration: A Guide to the Management of Negotiated Hospital, Surgical, and Medical Care Benefits* (New York: Foundation on Employee Health, Medical Care, and Welfare in association with Martin E. Segal & Co., 1961); Herman Miles Somers and Anne Ramsay Somers, *Doctors, Patients, and Health Insurance: The Organization and Financing of Medical Care* (Washington, D.C.: Brookings Institution, 1961), chaps. 12 and 13; U.S. Congress, House, Committee on Ways and Means, *Overview of Entitlement Programs: 1994 Greenbook*, 103d Cong., 2d sess., 15 July 1994, 945.

2. Sass, *Promise of Private Pensions*, 194.

3. Theodore R. Marmor, *The Politics of Medicare*, 2d ed. (New York: Aldine De Gruyter, 2000), 97–98.

4. Marie Gottschalk, *The Shadow Welfare State: Labor, Business, and the Politics of Health Care in the United States* (Ithaca: ILR Press, Cornell University Press, 2000), 53–57.

5. Lawrence Brown, *Politics and Health Care Organization: HMOs as Federal Policy* (Washington, D.C.: Brookings Institution, 1983).

6. Teresa Ghilarducci, *Labor's Capital: The Economics and Politics of Private Pensions* (Cambridge, Mass.: MIT Press, 1992).

7. Marmor, *Politics of Medicare*, 154, chaps. 8–9; White, *Competing Solutions*, 37–38; *EBRI Health Benefits Databook* (Washington, D.C.: EBRI, 1999), 67–68; *New York Times*, 11 August 2002, 18.

8. GE Workers United, "GE Pension Fund Story: Workers Pay, GE Benefits," 18 March 2002, *http: www.geworkersunited.org news index.*

9. Ghilarducci, *Labor's Capital*, 68–69, 1; Kristine Witkowski, Charita Castro, and Xue Song, *The Gender Gap in Pension Coverage: What Does the Future Hold?* (Washington, D.C.: Institute for Women's Policy Research, 2002); Donald Bartlett and James B. Steele, *America: Who Stole the Dream?* (Kansas City, Mo.: Andrews & McNeel, 1996), 139. According to Bartlett and Steel, the median annual pension benefit for 2.2 million women is $3,000, or about $60 a week; for men it is $7,800, or $150 a week.

10. Kim Moody, *An Injury to All: The Decline of American Unionism* (New York: Verso, 1988), chap. 6; Sass, *Promise of Private Pensions*, 228, 233; *New York Times*, 20 Jan. 2002, sec. 3, p. 7; Bartlett and Steele, *America: Who Stole the Dream?*

11. *New York Times*, 5 Apr. 2002, A1; "Firms Are Replacing Traditional Pensions," *Philadelphia Inquirer*, 30 June 1996, E1, E5; "Retirement's Worried Face," *New York Times*, 30 July 1995, Money and Business section, 3, 1.

12. Ghilarducci, *Labor's Capital*, 158–59; Nancy S. Jecker, "Can an Employer-based Health Insurance System Be Just?" *Journal of Health Politics, Policy, and Law* 18, no. 3 (1993): 660; White, *Competing Solutions*, 40. On pension trusts, this tax expenditure represents taxes not paid by corporations and shareholders. Retirees still pay income tax on pensions received.

13. White, *Competing Solutions*, 5, 40–43; *New York Times*, 24 Nov. 1997, 1; "Insurance as a Job Benefit Shows Signs of Overwork," ibid., 1 May 1991, 1;

House Committee on Ways and Means, *Overview of Entitlement Programs,* 496; William Glaser, *Health Insurance in Practice: International Variations in Financing, Benefits, and Problems* (San Francisco: Jossey-Bass, 1991), 40–42; *New York Times,* 26 Sept. 1998, 1; ibid., 19 Jan. 1999, A1, B6. In 1998, 41.2% of year-round, part-time workers received employment-based health insurance coverage (*EBRI Health Benefits Data Book,* table 5.5 [p. 63]).

14. Jecker, "Can an Employer-based Health Insurance System Be Just?" 662, 665; Stephen H. Long, "Public versus Employment-related Health Insurance: Experience and Implications for Black and Non-black Americans," *Milbank Quarterly* 65, suppl. 1 (1987): 203; Charlotte F. Muller, *Health Care and Gender* (New York: Russell Sage Foundation, 1990), chap. 4; *New York Times,* 4 Oct. 2000, A1, A24; Alan Monheit et al., "Access to Health Insurance and Health Care for an Aging Workforce" (paper presented at the annual meeting of the National Academy of Social Insurance, Washington, D.C., Jan. 2000), 4–7; *EBRI Health Benefits Databook,* table 5.4; Marcia Bayne-Smith, ed., *Race, Gender, and Health,* Sage Series on Race and Ethnic Relations, 15 (Thousand Oaks, Calif.: Sage Publications, 1996), 9; Health Insurance Association of America, *Source Book of Health Insurance Data, 1990* (Washington, D.C., 1990).

15. Karen Pollitz, "Extending Health Insurance Coverage for Older Workers and Early Retirees: How Well Have Public Policies Worked?" (paper presented at the annual meeting of the National Academy of Social Insurance, Washington, D.C., Jan. 2000), 6–7; *New York Times,* 17 Mar. 1998, 1. New York and Vermont, however, passed laws requiring community rating, under which neither age nor health status of workers may cause a small group's premium to vary. Three states—Hawaii, Michigan, and Pennsylvania—offer community-rated coverage through particular carriers (Pollitz, "Extending Health Insurance Coverage," 8–9).

16. Health Insurance Association of America, *Source Book of Health Insurance Data, 1990,* 3–4.

17. CIGNA purchased Equicor, Equitable's health insurance business, and United Healthcare purchased MetraHealth, Metropolitan's health insurance (see *Wall Street Journal,* 30 Mar., 12 Oct. 1990; *New York Times,* 9 Nov. 1994, D21; ibid., 8 Sept. 1994, D13; ibid., 2 Sept. 1994, D4; *Wall Street Journal,* 27 June 1995, A2; and John Rousmaniere, *The Life and Times of The Equitable* [New York: Equitable Companies, 1995], chaps. 20, 21). When life insurance companies converted to mutuals in the second decade of the twentieth century, mutualization was seen as a great Progressive Era experiment. As Olivier Zunz has written, "Transformation of the corporate structure through mutualization brought the company closer to the goals of the fraternal organizations" and to the broader impulses of social reform (Zunz, *Making America Corporate, 1870–1920* [Chicago: University of Chicago Press, 1990], 96–97).

18. Brown, *Politics and Health Care Organization,* 268.

19. CCMC, *Medical Care for the American People: The Final Report of the Committee on the Costs of Medical Care* (Chicago: University of Chicago Press, 1932), 47–48.

20. *New York Times,* 1 Dec. 1994, 1.

21. Theda Skocpol, *Boomerang: Clinton's Health Security Effort and the Turn*

against Government in U.S. Politics (New York: W. W. Norton & Co., 1996), 107–20.

22. Cathie Jo Martin, *Stuck in Neutral: Business and the Politics of Human Capital Investment Policy* (Princeton: Princeton University Press, 2000), chaps. 3, 5. Debates over health benefits often dichotomize the insurance picture too simply: workers in larger firms get health and pension benefits, those in small firms do not. Yet ever-growing numbers of Americans work for large, low-wage companies such as J. C. Penney, General Mills, the Marriot Corporation, Merry Maids, and Manpower, Inc. Wal-Mart is the largest private employer in the nation.

23. Skocpol, *Boomerang*, 118–19; White, *Competing Solutions*, 6–8, 24–26.

24. Joshua Micah Marshall, "Privatization, Inc.," *American Prospect*, 30 July 2001, 8; *New York Times*, 18 June 2001, A14; *Financial Times*, 19, 22 May 2001.

25. William F. Buckley Jr., *Up From Liberalism* (New York: McDowell, Obolensky, 1959), 187; Ronald Reagan, "Televised Nationwide Address on Behalf of Barry Goldwater," 2 Oct. 1964, in Reagan, *Speaking My Mind: Selected Speeches* (New York: Simon & Schuster, 1989). "Those who would trade our freedom for security have embarked on this downward [totalitarian] course," said Reagan (26).

Index

POLITICS AND SOCIETY IN TWENTIETH-CENTURY AMERICA

Civil Defense Begins at Home: Militarization Meets Everyday Life in the Fifties by Laura McEnaney

Cold War Civil Rights: Race and the Image of American Democracy by Mary L. Dudziak

Divided We Stand: American Workers and the Struggle for Black Equality by Bruce Nelson

Poverty Knowledge: Social Science, Social Policy, and the Poor in Twentieth-Century U.S. History by Alice O'Connor

Suburban Warriors: The Origins of the New American Right by Lisa McGirr

The Politics of Whiteness: Race, Workers, and Culture in the Modern South by Michelle Brattain

State of the Union: A Century of American Labor by Nelson Lichtenstein

Changing the World: American Progressives in War and Revolution by Alan Dawley

Dead on Arrival: The Politics of Healthcare in Twentieth-Century America by Colin Gordon

For All These Rights: Business, Labor, and the Shaping of America's Public-Private Welfare State by Jennifer Klein